In the 1980s and 1990s, Alice King was one of the UK's best-known wine writers, with columns in the *Daily Mail* and *Marie Claire*, and she was a regular on TV and radio. She became Tesco's face of wine and is the author of a dozen bestselling wine books, including *The Hamlyn Atlas of Wine*. Now no longer drinking and sober for three years, Alice has written columns about her recovery in *The Times* and *You* magazine and has turned her finely tuned palate to tea, coffee and soft drinks tasting. She lives in Berkshire with her three sons.

High Sobriety

Confessions of a Drinker

Alice King

For Jaci –
Best enjoyed with a
glass of rose lemonade in a
Georgian champagne saucer!
Alice King April 20/8.

An Orion paperback

First published in Great Britain in 2008
by Orion
This paperback edition published in 2009
by Orion Books Ltd,
Orion House, 5 Upper St Martin's Lane,
London WC2H 9EA

An Hachette UK company

1 3 5 7 9 10 8 6 4 2

Inside illustrations by Eva Byrne

A CIP catalogue record for this book is available
from the British Library.

ISBN 978-0-7528-8451-6

Printed and bound in the UK by CPI Mackays,
Chatham, ME5 8TD

The Orion Publishing Group's policy is to use papers
that are natural, renewable and recyclable products and
made from wood grown in sustainable forests. The logging
and manufacturing processes are expected to conform to
the environmental regulations of the country of origin.

Every effort has been made to fulfil requirements with regard
to reproducing copyright material. The author and publisher will
be glad to rectify any omissions at the earliest opportunity.

www.orionbooks.co.uk

CONTENTS

For my mother

AUTHOR'S NOTE

This is my story. Some names have been changed to protect the innocent, and the not so innocent. I've called my sons Numbers One, Two and Three for their privacy. This is not how I think of them! My experience of AA is my experience and my experience alone and does not necessarily reflect AA's opinions.

THE SERENITY PRAYER

God grant me the serenity
To accept the things I cannot change;
Courage to change the things I can;
And wisdom to know the difference.

FOREWORD

When I was asked to write this, I wasn't sure quite what to say. One thing is for sure, I am proud of my mummy.

When I found out she was writing a book about alcohol and recovery, I thought it was a good idea, as it may help other people to understand what alcoholism does to you and all those around you. I know, because I was there when many of these events happened. It was bizarre when she came home some evenings, seemingly dizzy and floppy, loping around, slightly slurring from time to time – I wasn't quite sure why.

Sometimes she used to be, well, let's say 'unreliable', to put it mildly, at picking us up from our nursery. This was because we had to wait for her to find a driver (guess why *she* wasn't doing it) to come and collect us. Now, she is not as embarrassing to us in front of our friends' parents (notice the *as*!) at school. Today, she actually talks to them, instead of hanging around by the wall, trying not to fall over in her spiky red high heels, looking for her three kids.

That was a few years ago. Now, it seems like a miracle how she has changed her life. I am delighted to have our real mummy back; she spends much more time with us, her children. Now when we go out, and we do lots of the time, it's as far away from a pub as possible! She even went surfing with us – we were amazed when we saw her in the water!

I thought it was really cool when she started writing her

column 'Sobering Up' for *The Times* – it made me feel very proud. Her recovery has not only made a big difference in our lives, we can see a huge improvement in her well-being and confidence. I'm very happy for her. Through watching Mummy recover, I can see she can still have fun without a drink; she will always love to taste, though, so today we blend all kinds of lush non-alcoholic cocktails.

In recovery, Mummy has become a much nicer, kinder and generous person!

Number Two son (age twelve)

PART ONE

*The Froth
of Daydreams*

First Taste

My first taste of champagne was at my christening, a golden drop from the tip of my mother's little finger. My second, frothier still, came via her milk. That was me – always up for seconds.

As far back as I can remember, I loved champagne. Those dancing bubbles are the froth of daydreams. In reality we weren't affluent enough to drink it on a regular basis, though my father conjured it up for every christening – and there were nine of us.

My father was a wine shipper. While my classmates would write lovingly of their pets, bringing photographs and bits of fluff for school projects, I was soaking the labels off wine bottles and teaching my friends how to differentiate between a Bordeaux and Burgundy bottle from its shape. I was clinking bottles in a bag on the school bus as young as seven. At Christmas, when the other children would take the teachers boxes of chocolates or flowers, I would take wine. This was in the 1960s, long before the advent of super-market wine. Wine was a luxury. That was me all over, from the very beginning – wanting to do something to be noticed, something bigger, better, more unusual. I always wanted to prove something. I don't know what.

I knew I was loved as a child, but I felt that somehow I was different, that I didn't fit in. The sixth child of nine, I felt too big to be one of the little ones and too small to be one of the big ones. In a tantrum, I once asked my mother, 'Why am I always the odd one out? Everyone else has someone to play with – what about me? I bet you didn't really want me, did you?'

She told me, 'Alice, when your father and I got married, we decided to start off with half a dozen children and see how it went from there. You were the last of the original six planned, so you are really special.'

But somehow I could never feel it.

At home, we jostled for position around a huge dining table. We often had friends over, so twenty or more for a meal was not unusual. My mother was (and still is) an extraordinary woman, not least in her capacity to turn out wholesome, delicious food from very little. We had to wait until our guests had a plateful before we started in case she had miscalculated.

Daddy was a stickler for table manners, but mealtimes were fun – instant cabaret with a full cast. Ever-taller stories were swapped and we competed to have the last laugh. Exaggeration was born out of the competition to be noticed. Towards the end of a meal, we became quiet, desperate to think up excuses as to why we didn't have to wash up – no mean feat for such a sizeable army.

There was an air of excitement when my parents had people round for dinner, often business associates of my father. Once, I pointed out to my father's boss that Daddy had a bigger car than he had. Ours was a Ford Zephyr, green with shiny chrome bumpers and a bench seat. He had a brand-new Jag. He just smiled at me.

We'd set the table with a crisp white damask tablecloth and starched napkins. I'd polish the silver candlesticks. We always had green candles, and to this day the smell of hot candle wax conjures up a feeling of anticipation. I'd pick flowers from the garden. Sweet peas were my favourite, with their intoxicating, heady aroma and vibrant colours. The house would be full of exotic scents – the rich, sweet smell of reduced red wine and garlic mingled with herbs. Sometimes I'd be the waitress. I would swell with pride, feeling wanted and important.

My mother would look so glamorous, every so often in a new homemade dress, with her cleavage on show, her hair newly set and lipstick on. I yearned to be part of this sophisticated, secret adult world. I would listen to the grown-ups from the kitchen – their conversation, the merriment, the laughter.

I loved the ritual surrounding wine. I'd watch with wonder as my father carefully opened a bottle, sniffed the cork and decanted the claret over a candle. 'Look, Daddy!' I'd exclaim. 'You've got sentiment in your wine!'

I counted the number of different-shaped glasses at every place setting. My favourites were the fine German wine glasses, made of the thinnest glass and engraved with stars. They made the most exquisite ringing if you tapped them gently with a spoon. Daddy could make them sing. We'd watch entranced as he ran his finger round the top of a glass, and listen to the beautiful note.

My first taste memory is of a wine served in one such glass. I can still picture the tall, green bottle and the indecipherable Gothic script on the label. My reward for polishing the candlesticks was the little black cat attached to the bottleneck on a loop of stretchy gold thread. I treasured my prize, but I was even more excited when my father gave me a tiny taste of Schwartz Katz, a German Riesling, in one of those singing, starry glasses. None of my siblings was around and I felt special, chosen and different.

I can recall the heady rush and the warming sensation as this oily nectar trickled down my throat. Daddy asked me to describe it. 'Pineapples, butterscotch sauce and lemons,' I pronounced. He was impressed, I could tell.

And I was smitten. One taste instantly transported me, as

if on a flying carpet, to a faraway fantasy world of princesses, castles, jewels and attendants – all a far cry from the banality of living with eight brothers and sisters.

CHAPTER TWO

Too Big, Too Small

I was eight years old and on my first trip to France. Mummy had bought all nine of us matching red, white and blue striped towelling jumpers from Bonds in Norwich. I was on the deck of the ferry with a sister or two, duly uniformed, when two other siblings – a couple of the boys – went by.

Two old ladies walked past. 'Look! There's another one!' said one to her friend.

'No . . . we've seen that one before. But *she*'s a different one, I think,' the other replied, looking me up and down. They thought we were from a children's home.

We were staying near the village of Montfort l'Amory, north of Paris, invited there by Pascal, a French boy who had been to stay with us to learn English. He was related to one of the Little Sisters of the Assumption, the local order of nuns, who used to come and look after us when Mummy had another baby.

Pascal was tall, with dark hair and olive skin. He had a different smell about him to that of my brothers – musty, leathery, bookish somehow, like an old library. He had a kind, melancholic smile and was very quiet. I used to chat to him while he was mending my bike. He didn't interrupt me, like my brothers did. It never occurred to me that he couldn't understand me.

He had already been to our house two summer holidays running when his mother had invited us to stay at his family's summer château. We were amazed when we drew up outside. It was enormous – red brick with sixteen huge windows, all with shutters. The older boys slept there, while the little ones, our parents and I stayed in a cottage in the grounds. On our first night I found it hard to sleep. Over-excited yet tired, I wanted it to be morning. I kept complaining about the strange, damp, hay-like smell of the bed.

'It's probably just horsehair,' Mummy said. 'Now go to sleep – we've driven hundreds of miles today and we're all exhausted.'

'This pillow is hard and lumpy,' I said.

'It's not a pillow, it's a bolster, and if it's uncomfortable, throw it on the floor,' she replied wearily.

Next morning we made our first expedition into the village boulangerie. I went with my eldest (and favourite) brother in my new holiday dress – orange nylon with a kipper tie. On our way down to the village, I was amazed at how everyone we passed said '*Bonjour*', even an old man on a bicycle.

'Why do they say hello when they don't even know us?' I asked my brother.

'Because they're French,' he replied.

We arrived at the boulangerie, drawn by the scent of freshly baked bread. People walked past me clutching what looked like polished sticks of wood. We waited in the queue. I held on to my brother's hand, baffled by the incomprehensible babble around me.

'*Vingt-deux croissants, s'il vous plaît*,' my brother said. Twenty-two croissants, please.

'*Vingt-deux? Vraiment?*' asked the baker, looking incredulous. Twenty-two? Are you sure?

My brother nodded and handed over the funny-looking money. He bought me a packet of fruit-flavoured chewing gum with the change. It was French and exciting and utterly, utterly wonderful.

We returned to the cottage, where everyone was sitting

expectantly round the table. Hands grabbed at the bags and then there was silence. Within seconds all twenty-two croissants were gone, leaving a trail of flakes across the kitchen table and floor.

After breakfast Daddy announced he was taking my elder siblings exploring. 'Can I come with you?' I asked.

'No,' he said. 'You're too little, it's a long walk, and you'll get too tired. Once we've explored, we'll take you another day, when we can go part of the way in the car.'

'It's not fair!' I wailed, but he was gone. I tried to appeal to Mummy: 'It's not fair!'

'Alice,' she said, 'life is not fair. And the sooner you learn that, the better. Go and play with your other brothers and sisters. Look, they're playing football. Join in.'

'But—'

'That's enough! Now go!' She pointed to the door.

I stalked out, slamming the door behind me. I'll show them, I thought. I *will* go – I'll go somewhere and then they'll be sorry. I walked out of the gate and stomped off down the road. I wished I were one of twins – then there would always be someone on hand of my own age. Indignant tears trickled down my face. I could taste the saltiness. An old man passed by on his bike. He had gnarled, wrinkled skin, like tree bark. '*Bonjour!*' he shouted cheerily, and waved. I put my head down and ignored him. It was *not* a good morning.

I had a one-franc piece in my pocket. I resolved to go back to the boulangerie and buy myself a packet of that wonderful chewing gum. I turned round to see if anyone was following me. No, it looked as if I was alone.

As I entered the village, I saw the old man who had greeted me earlier sitting in a café chatting with another man. Each had a steaming cup of coffee and a glass. One glass I recognised as a brandy balloon – we had some at home. It was half full with an amber liquid. The other was a long, tall glass with the word 'Ricard' on the side. It was filled with ice and a cloudy, pale-yellow liquid. What a strange lot they are, drinking before lunch, I thought.

I noticed the *boucherie* on the other side of the square and crossed over to look in the window. I couldn't work out what the furry creatures hanging there were. Their eyes stared out at me blankly. I suddenly realised they were rabbits, and shuddered. Who would eat a rabbit? My friend at school had one, called Benjamin. I must send her a postcard, I thought. 'The French eat rabbits!'

I walked back across the square, past the old men, who smiled and waved. I was momentarily disorientated, but was then relieved to see the orange awning of the boulangerie. One lonely baguette was left on the shelf, alongside a single large apricot tart, shiny with glaze. I entered, chose my chewing gum, handed over the franc and left the shop, contemplating the gum's strange synthetic taste, which was reminiscent of the orange and pineapple flavoured squash back home.

I looked around me. There were two roads leading out of the square and I hesitated, unsure which to take. Had I passed the *tabac* on my way? I walked up the road. None of the shops looked familiar. There was a boutique with a lime-green wraparound dress in the window. The mannequin had a sinister leer on its face. My chest began to feel tight. What if I couldn't find my way home? Who would know where I was? Would I end up strung up like the rabbits in the butcher's shop?

Retracing my steps to the corner of the square, I started up the other road. Beads of sweat trickled down my forehead, and the palms of my hands grew clammy. I wiped them on my kipper tie and felt my heart beating faster. Nobody knows where I am, or that I've even gone, I thought. I gulped and realised with alarm I had swallowed my gum. I hoped I wouldn't choke. I opened two more pieces and stuffed them in my mouth.

The shops had petered out and I was walking past houses now. I saw a plump woman mopping a floor one-handed while balancing a blond, chubby toddler on her hip. He looked a bit like my youngest brother. I felt a tear trickle down my cheek.

I kept walking and eventually came full circle and passed the two old men at the café again. Their glasses were empty and they were standing up to leave. By this time tears were streaming down my face, their salty flavour making the chewing gum taste sour and soapy. The old men walked towards me. I knew I shouldn't talk to strangers, but in any event I couldn't speak French. They gabbled at me. One smiled and winked.

'I'm lost!' I wailed in English. 'I can't find the right road. I'm lost!'

Frowning, they started talking to the waiter. He was dressed in tight black trousers and a white short-sleeved shirt. He had dark hair and a moustache. All three started gesticulating.

'What you name?' the waiter asked in broken English.

'Alice,' I whimpered. 'Aleeze,' I tried again, in an effort to sound French.

They were pointing at a house across the square. I shook my head. Did they think I lived there?

'You come,' said one of the two elderly men.

I followed at a distance. Where were they taking me? We stopped in front of a red-brick house with a large wooden door and the word 'Gendarmerie' carved in stone above it. They disappeared inside.

I stood outside the door, unsure of myself. It opened and two younger men came out. I realised from their uniforms and peaked caps that they were policemen. One had a gun in a leather holster. I couldn't take my eyes off it. The gendarme carrying it had deep creases in his forehead when he frowned. The gendarmes beckoned me inside. I sat on a wooden chair, looked at the bars on the window, opened my mouth and howled. They stepped back, shocked, and huddled together, talking incomprehensibly.

'Do you speak English?' I finally managed to stutter.

They shook their heads. One scrabbled around in a desk drawer and drew out a small pocket dictionary. I kept looking out through the bars on the window, hoping that every shadow was Mummy or Daddy, here to rescue me.

One of the gendarmes gave me a boiled sweet. It was red and hard and cherry-flavoured, like the cough mixture I'd had the last time I had flu. The other was writing something on a piece of paper. He handed it to me. 'We you wish help,' it said. I nodded, relieved I wasn't in trouble with them. But what were Mummy and Daddy going to say about me running away?

I was handed a tissue and I wiped my eyes. They gave me another sweet, an orange one. It tasted like Mummy's marmalade. They looked at me and smiled. How strange it was that we could both speak yet not understand each other. I was really worried now. What if I was still here when it was dark? Nobody knew where I was. Mummy probably thought I was with Daddy and vice versa.

The phone rang. There was more gabbling and waving of hands. One gendarme was smiling and pointing at me. He disappeared out through the door.

A bluebottle was buzzing, trapped at the window. I watched it crash into the window again and again. I began to count the times it flew in and out of the bars. I was up to twenty-two when the door opened. The returning gendarme handed me an enormous ice cream, complete with a chocolate flake. What a treat! I licked carefully round the chocolate, smoothing out the furrows in the ice cream and thinking how envious my brothers and sisters would be when I told them.

The door opened again and I saw the curly hair of Pascal

– closely followed by Daddy. I leapt up – holding on to my ice cream – and ran towards them, laughing. My father squeezed me so hard I thought I would burst. 'Daddy, be careful of my ice cream!'

Outside, I could see one of my younger brothers sitting in the back of the car. I ran out of the door and waved my ice cream at him.

'That's not fair!' he said. 'You run away and you get an ice cream. I want one. It's not fair!'

'Life's not fair,' I told him. 'And the sooner you learn that, the better.'

CHAPTER THREE

Lunch With the Countess

Many of our family holidays were spent in France, thanks to my father's job. One year, when I was about ten, a cognac supplier invited us to lunch. And not any old cognac supplier. This was a real countess.

The Ford Zephyr had gone by now and we had a Citroën DS. I loved our frog-eyed car, which would mysteriously rise up from the ground when the engine started – high suspension meant high drama to me.

That summer all eleven of us piled into our Citroën DS and set off for France. Occasionally we would turn from a junction and Daddy would set off on the left-hand side of the road. '*Roule à droite, Papa!*' we'd chorus from the back. Drive on the right, Daddy! I noticed that Mummy would often close her eyes when this happened.

After forty-five minutes we arrived at the château. The intricate, curly, gold gates looked like the entrance to Heaven.

'Are they real gold, do you think?' I asked.

'Yeah, sure, pure gold – eighteen carat, no less,' sniggered a brother.

I was never sure whether he was being serious or not. I guessed by the others' derisive laughter he was probably joking. But how was I to know? If I was a countess and money was no object, I'd have solid-gold gates. Why not?

The gates opened, seemingly of their own accord, and we drove up the gravelled drive. The château was a real fairy castle, Gothic with four turrets. I found myself holding my breath. A small woman, dressed all in black, opened the door.

'Doesn't look much like a countess to me,' muttered a brother.

I didn't know. Having never seen a countess before, I had no idea what one should look like.

'That's because she's a servant,' said another.

I nodded. Yes, that must be right. A maid. I had never seen a maid before either.

Another woman emerged from the door behind the servant. She was petite, bird-like. I squinted and pressed my nose against the window. My eyes were dazzled.

'Wow, look at those rocks!' said one of my sisters. 'They must be real diamonds in her earrings.'

The countess shook each of our hands in turn, even crouching down for the little ones.

'*Bonjour,*' I said. '*Je m'appelle Alice.*'

She smiled and answered. I didn't understand what she was saying, but I loved her sing-song voice. She sounded like my musical jewellery box at home.

We were shown into the salon, a huge room with faded velvet drapes and a large, dark, cracked oil painting of a girl and a dog. The girl in the picture looked the same age as me and was of similar colouring. Her blonde hair fell in perfect ringlets about her face. I felt the back of my own hair. It had been cut short – 'easier for summer' – only the week before. It had been my idea, but I had left the hairdresser's in tears, gazing forlornly at the six inches of my life strewn on the floor.

I wandered around the room and spotted a chaise longue, not unlike one we had at home. This one was smaller and more ornate, with a carved end. I noted with surprise that the gold brocade was faded and slightly threadbare. Ours at home was upholstered in brown Draylon – altogether much smarter. I spotted a delicate, button-back, padded leather chair, child-size, by the open French windows. I headed straight for it and got into a tussle with an equally determined younger brother. 'I saw it first,' I hissed at him.

'Alice,' Mummy said, 'come here.' I walked over and sat down sulkily on the tatty chaise longue. It was extraordinarily uncomfortable.

Another servant appeared, a dark-haired man, even older than Daddy, with a sunken, lined face like a walnut whip. He wore a white jacket, a black bow tie and white gloves. He was carrying an ornate silver salver with a magnum of champagne and several small, engraved champagne flutes.

I was surprised and delighted when he handed me the most exquisite glass I'd ever held, etched with a coat of arms bearing what looked like a fleur-de-lis and a crescent moon. I watched the dancing bubbles catching the sunlight. I felt like Princess Alice. I wondered if the countess drank champagne every day.

My tiny taste of fizz disappeared almost immediately. There was something thrilling about the tingle I felt throughout my whole body as the prickly bubbles hit the top of my mouth and the back of my throat – quite different from the orange Corona I was used to. I realised I was holding out my empty glass at right angles. Mummy shot me a warning look.

'Why don't you go off and explore with the boys?' she suggested. 'And help yourself to water. There's a bottle and some tumblers over there.'

Fancy being rich enough to buy water in a bottle rather than simply get it from the tap!

Reluctantly, I acted out draining my already-empty champagne flute in exaggerated fashion, helped myself to a glass of water and skipped off through the French windows on to the lawn. I felt curiously light-headed, as if sparklers were going off in my brain. I nearly missed my step as I followed the boys' shrieks. I sat down on the grass and began to make a daisy chain. Marrying a count was obviously the thing to do. I could drink champagne, have water from a bottle and drip with diamonds every day.

Daddy wandered out into the garden. 'A table!' he announced. Dinner's ready! We traipsed in through the salon into the dining room. I noticed that Mummy had relaxed. Her cheeks were glowing like two ripe peaches.

The enormous round table was dressed in crisp white damask, like we had at home for best, with two ornate silver candelabras and pale-pink candles the colour of the fox-gloves at the bottom of our garden. In the centre was a posy of roses, streaked pink and white like raspberry-ripple ice cream, with an exquisite aroma that reminded me of Fry's Turkish delight. Each place setting not only had four glasses but a bewildering array of cutlery, including something that looked like a spoon someone had jumped on and flattened. We each had individual name cards. This was truly impressive. 'Alice' was written out in swirly calligraphy with a curly flourish underneath. I altered my title in my head. 'Countess Alice' sounded more unusual, more arresting somehow, than my previous aspiration of 'Princess Alice'.

We held our breath before the starter arrived. What would we do if it was snails, or frog's legs, or even that liver pâté the French seemed so fond of? We needn't have fretted. The manservant walked in with a platter piled high with asparagus. We were familiar with this, as we had two asparagus patches in the garden at home. Every June saw us eating asparagus hot with melted butter – we used the sticks to write our names in dripping butter across our plates – or cold in salads and sandwiches. I distinctly remember eating an asparagus sandwich with Branston pickle.

This asparagus was different, though. It was white and juicy and quite the bigger, plumper brother to the pencil-thin green sticks at home. And we were all surprised that it was served cold. Was the kitchen so far away? Mummy always managed to put our food hot on the table, however many people were round. Not only was today's asparagus cold, it was served with a creamy sort of salad cream I had never tasted before, something called 'mayonnaise'. The combination was delicious.

The next course looked less familiar – '*canard*', whatever that was.

'Don't worry, Alice, it's just like chicken,' Mummy said.

'Yes, but what *is* it?' I pestered. 'Tell me!'

'It's duck. Now just eat it and stop causing a fuss.'

The meat was much darker than chicken, a red-brown colour. I waited for the potatoes, but after five minutes, when nothing had appeared, I tentatively put a tiny bit in my mouth and swallowed it quickly. It was stringy with a slightly bitter flavour. Picking up a piece of bread from the table – I thought it odd they had no side plates – I covered the remains of the meat up with it and put my knife and fork together.

The manservant was solemnly circling the table, pouring red wine from a decanter. Daddy was gesturing to him to pour us each an inch or so. I could see that this wine was not in fact red, more an orangey colour, like the colour of the bricks on our new extension at home.

'Ah, Château Montrose 1893,' murmured the countess, sounding out the years in that sing-song voice. '*Une bonne année, je crois.*' A good vintage, I believe.

I knew this was amazingly special, to be served such an old wine, but it was difficult not to giggle as, round the table, I could see my elder brothers and sisters mimicking my father's wine-tasting antics just as we did back home at Sunday lunch. I closed my eyes, composed myself, pursed my lips and took a big sniff. The smell was curiously sweet, like strawberries melted in Bourneville.

The taste gave me a stab of guilt – I had once eaten a bar

of Bourneville someone had bought for my mother. She didn't find out, but I never felt the same about plain chocolate again. I looked over at Mummy and saw her in animated conversation. She glanced across at me and smiled. I hoped she couldn't read my mind.

When I tasted the wine, the flavour exploded on my tongue. It was like a velvety, liquid jam – a mixture of black cherry, raspberry and strawberry – mingled with cinnamon and cocoa. I retrieved the bit of duck on my plate from beneath the bread and washed it down with the wine. The meat didn't taste so bitter now – it was delicious, in fact, leaving me with a tangy, sweet-sour taste in my mouth. I wanted more.

I drained my glass and looked around in triumph. Wait until I told them at school that not only had I been invited to lunch with a real-life countess, but I had drunk a seventy-eight-year-old wine! I realised that the countess was looking in my direction and speaking.

'She's asking what you think of the wine,' Daddy said.

What should I say?

'*Encore une bouteille!*' I blurted out. Another bottle!

There was total silence. Mummy's eyes had widened in horror. I held my breath.

Madame La Comtesse laughed. She raised her hand and signalled to her manservant. 'Henri, *vous avez entendu la gamine – encore une bouteille!*' she said. Henry, you heard the little one – another bottle!

CHAPTER FOUR

VODKA AND LIME

Green-gold glycerine coats the inside of my glass, making it opaque, like oil on water. My mouth puckers and my tongue curls as my brain registers the flavour in my mouth – like Rose's lime marmalade with a kick, I decide. This luscious liquid slips down my throat and I experience an instant, breath-snatching sensation in my chest.

I like it. My eyes water. I take another gulp to see if the sensation is the same. It is, only intensified, and suddenly I feel an important part of the secret adult world. I feel grown-up. Each further gulp drowns the butterflies in my stomach. My confidence soars and I feel taller.

'I see you like vodka and lime,' says my friend Gina. 'That's what I drink too.'

I nod, trying to look nonchalant, and crunch an ice cube. I don't admit that I'd no clue what to ask for at the bar and only ordered vodka and lime because I heard her doing so. I'd simply nodded when the barman had asked, 'Large one?' It didn't look that large to me: the vodka barely covered the ice.

Gina goes to gymnastics. She has a tumbling routine ending in a graceful, high back flip. She is petite, with naturally corkscrew-curled dark hair – everything I am not. Try as I might, I can't get my liquid eyeliner to flick up at the corner of my eyes like hers does. We get on well, even though, at eighteen, she is four years older than me.

I hear a shout. Another friend – Nicci. 'Hey, Al, want another drink? Same again?' I nod.

I have been badgering my mother for ages to be allowed to come to a Young Farmers' Dance. Finally she has relented, providing I come with one of my elder brothers. My major concern has been what to wear. After changing outfits several times, I settled on my new stack-heel, over-the-knee, tan leather boots – a fourteenth-birthday present – checked shirt and a string of amber beads I have slung jauntily over one shoulder. One look at Nicci fills me with dismay. She is dressed in fitted straight-leg jeans with a thin blue belt and a striped red and white linen shirt with the collar turned up. She has straight brown hair cut like a beret – short on one side, long on the other. She gets it done free every month by the trainees at Spears, the trendy hairdressing salon in Oxford. We had recently all moved from Norfolk to Chipping Norton in the Cotswolds.

Nicci, too, is older than me, by two years, and goes to school in Woodstock, making her more exotic than my classmates. She lives alone with her mother, an architect, who is often away, so her home is a welcome refuge from all the chaos at mine. Nicci, however, seems to prefer coming over to my house.

'You are so lucky to have all those brothers and sisters,' she always says.

'I doubt you would think that if you lived here,' I reply every time. 'And the washing-up is awful. You are so lucky, having a dishwasher.'

She is confident and seems to attract boys with no effort. As she hands me a drink, a tall guy with dark-blond curly hair taps her on the shoulder. 'Hey, Nicci, how are you? Want a drink?'

She throws her head back and drains her glass. Only then does she smile, apparently coyly, and reply, 'I'd love one – large whisky and lemonade, please.'

Whisky. I shudder. I cannot bear the smell or the taste. I once helped myself to my father's Glenfiddich. The sour, malt flavour made me gag and I nearly spat the mouthful straight back into the bottle.

I shift from foot to foot, uncomfortable. Nicci whispers something into the boy's ear. He turns to a smaller guy standing next to him at the bar. 'Hey, Noddy, why don't you buy Nicci's friend a drink?'

'OK. What do you want? Aren't you Edmund's sister? Alice, isn't it?'

'Yes, that's right. Thanks. I'll have a large vodka and lime, please.' I follow Nicci's example and down the drink in my hand. My eyes water. I smile and cough to cover up the tightening in my chest.

We take our drinks and stand by the dance floor. Strobe lights flicker and the disco is playing 'Le Freak' thuddingly loud. Two girls I vaguely know from school, fifth-formers, are dancing.

'That's what I'll be doing – freaking out,' I tell Nicci. 'I can't imagine dancing in front of all these people.'

'Don't worry – you'll be fine, especially after a few more of those,' she says, pointing at my glass. 'Look, you give me the money and I'll go and get two more. They mightn't serve you.'

She disappears and after a while I notice Noddy at my side. 'Do you want a cigarette?' he asks, holding out a packet of Benson & Hedges.

'No, thanks. I don't smoke.' My experiment with a packet of Piccadilly at the end of the garden with a friend had not been successful. 'But I do drink!' I laugh and empty the glass Nicci has just handed me, which seems to be the way it's done.

The two fifth-formers on the dance floor have stopped dancing and are looking at me. Being seen talking to Noddy gives me cred – he's in the band that's playing later.

'You want to be careful – we like people dancing when we're playing, not falling over,' he says. 'Don't you get a headache when you drink like that?'

'Oh, no,' I say dismissively, 'though I do need to find the loo.'

I am hot, queasy and my head feels foggy. I haven't eaten much tea – too excited – so I can't understand why I feel sick and disorientated. Nicci has disappeared, but I spy Gina.

'Hey, Gina, where's the loo?' I ask.

'Are you all right?' she asks. 'You look white. Here, come with me. You look like you're having difficulty walking.'

'Yeah, it's my new boots – they're quite high, you know.'

She raises a finely plucked eyebrow. 'I think you're a bit drunk. You want to take it steady.'

Gratefully, I open the loo door and plonk myself down on the seat. The fluorescent overhead light seems to be moving. I close my eyes and feel like I'm spinning. I open my eyes again and cling on to the toilet-roll holder, staring at the back of the door. The graffiti seems to be alive, moving. Closing one eye, I focus. 'Shaz luvs Steve.'

'You all right in there?' comes Gina's voice.

'Yes,' I reply, struggling with my tights. I open the door.

'You're just a bit tipsy,' says Gina.

'I can't be – I've only had a few drinks.'

'How many?'

'Only three or four, I think.'

'You twit. They were large ones. You're doing well to be standing. Come on, let's go dancing – the band's started playing. That'll sober you up.'

I follow her to the dance floor. I have practised my moves many times in my bedroom mirror. I look around for my drink, forgetting that I had already downed it, and pick up a glass. I've swallowed most of it when I realise it tastes completely different – flowery, almost soapy, perfumed. It must be someone else's, but it gives me a boost and after a few minutes I feel good. I can't believe I'm doing this. The two fifth-formers are watching. I wonder what they think of my dancing. I reckon I'm pretty cool, jiving and mouthing the words to the Eagles song. Noddy waves at me from the stage. More cred. I nearly slip over and just manage to steady myself on a chair.

'Someone must have spilt their drink,' I mumble to no one in particular, as I sit down and empty the glass in front of me.

My brother walks across the dance floor. 'We're going in a minute. John is going to give us a lift. Best if you come with me, then we don't have to ring home. See you outside.'

I looked around for Nicci. She's nowhere to be seen. I feel thirsty and I need some air. I stand up, stagger and grab on to my brother's arm.

'You OK? How much did you have to drink? You better not let Mummy see you falling around – she'll go mad.'

I sit in the back of the car and several of my brother's friends pile in. John has borrowed his mother's blue Morris Traveller. Leaning my head against the cold, wet window, I feel tired and ill. Maybe I'm sickening for something. I can't be drunk. Surely you had to drink more than this to be drunk? Besides, the vodka didn't taste very strong.

It is only five miles home but it seems to be taking for ever. I close my eyes and open them again as it makes me feel more giddy still. Please, God, don't let me be sick in the car, I pray silently. I swallow hard.

The car suddenly swerves to the left, then to the right. Everything shudders into slow motion. I hear a screech of brakes. The car is turning over. My face is pressed against the window, harder and harder. This isn't happening. This can't be happening. The car finally comes to a halt and I am wedged in my seat upside down. There's an eerie silence and a strange acrid smell.

My brother is at the window now. 'Hurry up! Get out of

the car before it sets alight!' He yanks open the door and pulls me out. The others in the car pile out after me.

I'm confused. 'How come you were outside?' I ask my brother.

'I was thrown out of the back doors before the car turned over.'

I feel my stomach cramp. The next thing I know I'm leaning over, vomiting in the road, acid bile rising from my stomach. Rose's lime marmalade with diced carrots. How do they get into everything? I heave again. Definitely too much lime in my drink – too much bloody lime.

A car stops and someone wraps me in a blanket. I am still retching. 'Must be the shock, poor thing,' someone says.

The police arrive, blue lights flashing. Rather like the disco, I think. I wonder if Noddy has got off with anyone. John's mother arrives, takes one look at her crumpled upside-down car and throws up. Has she been drinking vodka too?

Sometime later I open my eyes and see my mother looking at me. My head is throbbing and my throat is sore.

'How are you?' she asks.

'Awful. How did I get home? I don't remember getting home. Did I bang my head?'

She pokes around in my hair. 'I can't see anything. You were all incredibly lucky. All eight of you could have been killed. It's no wonder you feel dazed and shaky. Perhaps you blacked out.'

'Was I talking when I got home?'

'Nineteen to the dozen – mainly slurred gibberish. I held your toes to calm you down, like I used to when you were a baby. You don't remember, do you?'

'No. Must have been the shock, like you said.'

But my mind tells me something different.

When we had first moved from Norfolk to Chipping Norton, we were the source of much curiosity – a family of nine children who had moved into a former convent, Mary-croft, on the edge of town. My parents couldn't initially afford the asking price of this rambling, run-down house, but after my mother had talked to the nuns, and they had seen her traipsing in and out with all of us, I think they felt sorry for her and sold it to us at a knock-down price. No doubt it helped that we were Roman Catholics.

Much of my early summers were spent at the open-air swimming pool. Various local girls would say, 'I likes your brother' – whichever one happened to be around – and were even more impressed to discover I had five of them.

Up to this stage I wasn't that comfortable at school. I was clever enough, but somehow uneasy. We didn't have accents, on account of my mother being a speech and drama teacher, so without the broad local burr were seen to be posh. For-tunately, such potential for bullying evaporated when my three elder brothers appeared. The fact that they were all at boarding school made them more of a novelty to those at the local comprehensive, which is where I went. It is difficult to appreciate (or even acknowledge) good looks in your own brothers, but the number of comments and phone calls from giggling girls made me realise what an asset they were. I had a steady stream of girlfriends, including some, like Gina and Nicci, a good bit older than me, who were eager not only to get a look inside our house but to spend time in such hallowed male company.

We had no TV – a source of great embarrassment for me, but rarely commented on or even noticed by my friends. They marvelled at the size of our dining table and loved to be part of our chaotic, fun family meals. An old croquet set my mother had bought at an auction brought out the com-petitiveness in us all, though I was never sure whether it was the croquet that attracted my friends or the chance of get-ting close to the boys.

Life changed for me when at fifteen I was voted 'best bum

of 1976' by the boys in my year. Suddenly I had a choice of suitors. My first real boyfriend – 'Mr Boyfriend', my brothers nicknamed him – was older then me, old enough to drive. He had a silver Ford Escort. At the weekends we would go shopping in Oxford or even Cheltenham. He lavished gifts on me – expensive grey culottes for school, an emerald-chip ring and a silver puzzle ring. The kudos of going out with someone older meant respect from the rougher girls at school.

Mr Boyfriend was kind, gentle and neat. He wore Levi's with creases down the front, and expensive shirts with the collars turned up. Every month he had his spiky hair trimmed at Spears. He was interested in me, and I had his undivided attention – not something I was used to. I was intoxicated.

We often went out for meals, where I would browse confidently through the wine list, choose and order the wine. I saw nothing unusual in this, having been around wine since childhood.

In one restaurant – the Shaven Crown at Shipton-under-Wychwood – I sent the Sancerre back because it smelt mouldy. 'This wine is corked,' I told the waiter.

He looked at me, hesitated and disappeared. A few moments later he reappeared with the restaurant owner. I held my glass out defiantly. Mr Boyfriend was squirming in his chair. The owner took the glass from me, sniffed at it pretentiously, then sniffed again. 'You are absolutely right, madam,' he said. 'I'll bring you another bottle straight away.'

This recognition of my prowess delighted and amazed me. Perhaps I had a super-sensitive sense of smell. I knew there weren't many fifteen-year-olds who would recognise a corked wine. I loved this feeling of superiority, of possessing a knowledge that was out of the ordinary, an inbuilt talent that made me special. I couldn't wait to get home to tell my father.

From then on Mr Boyfriend would jokingly call me 'Madam'. That was until, unkindly, I decided he was too boring for me – too nice, too kind, too reliable. I wanted someone more exciting, more dynamic. I didn't want to play safe. I dumped him. He cried.

Yes, 'Madam' was a fine description.

CHAPTER FIVE

SMILING ANGEL

Occasionally I used to accompany my father on business trips to France, ostensibly to practise for my French A level. One particularly memorable trip was to Heidsieck Monopole's cellars in Reims, the heart of the Champagne region.

We had lunch at the Moulin de Verzenay, the company-owned windmill majestically set among the acres of vines of the Montagne de Reims. Our hostess was Lucy, an Englishwoman with pale, almost white skin. Her eyelashes were invisible under a head of auburn hair, cut in a bob. She was striking-looking – she had presence and dressed with the precision and flair of the French in a fitted pencil-line skirt, silk blouse and high-heeled court shoes. I wore a lilac linen shift dress I'd made for the trip – I was good at dress-making – teamed with maroon strappy suede sandals. I was mesmerised by Lucy's ability to flick between languages, and in awe of the easy confidence with which she talked.

Taken aback by the number of glasses at each place setting, I watched her to determine whether I was meant simply to taste the champagnes or drink them. Judging by her empty glasses, I concluded that drinking them was the answer.

Initially I was tongue-tied, hesitating to practise my faltering French, but after the first two glasses of vintage rosé I found the words flowing, able to join in with the conversation, even joke in French. I began to enjoy myself. Lucy asked me what I would like to do when I left school. 'The same as you, if you get to drink wines like this every day,' I said.

We had been served a mystery champagne with a pudding of *tarte aux pommes*. Lucy asked us to guess which vintage it was. My father had warned me this might happen but reassured me it was just for fun, not to be taken too seriously. He had also briefed me on vintage champagne, explaining that vintages were only declared in the best years; 1970, 1971 and 1973 being the top recent vintages. The only decent harvests in the 1960s were 1961, 1964 and 1966.

The sun had caught the champagne in my glass, casting a hypnotic shadow of dancing bubbles across the table. By this stage I had drunk at least four glasses and my mind was buzzing, high on adrenaline and the drama of the occasion. I mused how lucky I was to be sitting drinking wines like this on a Monday when I should have been at school. I couldn't wait to tell my friends back home. Eavesdropping on the conversation around the table, I deduced that this was a wine from the *les soixantes* – the 1960s.

'So, Alice,' said Lucy, 'which vintage do you think it is?'

I looked at the wine and tasted it again. It had a delicious bitter-sweet, hazelnut and pear flavour. What years had Daddy said they declared vintages in the 1960s? My brain was beginning to feel a bit fuzzy. The only one I could remember for sure was 1961, the year I was born. Looking Lucy in the eye, I replied, '*Soixante-et-une, je crois.*' I think it's 1961.

She looked at me and smiled. 'It is indeed. Well done. That definitely calls for another bottle,' she said, clicking her fingers at the waiter.

Daddy looked across the table and beamed at me.

I had been joking (or half joking) when I told Lucy I wanted her job, but in the strange way these things go, little more than a year later I had it, or close to it. At eighteen, on leaving school, I was escorting visitors and tourists around Heidsieck Monopole's cellars, which were hidden deep in the rock below Reims.

There are thousands of kilometres of Gallo-Roman cellars hewn out of the chalk seam that underlies the Champagne region of northern France – Heidsieck Monopole alone had twelve kilometres of tunnels. I traipsed around all of them, trying to commit the route to memory. Every passageway looked identical, with thousands upon thousands of prone champagne bottles. My predecessor had devised a system of arrows for me to follow, but the walls were so damp and crumbly that the arrows all but disappeared in a day or so. I have never had any sense of direction and I experienced a few scary moments, stuck in the dark with only a torch. Still, I wouldn't die of thirst, I reflected.

At first I was a little lonely and missed my brothers and sisters, but as I settled into the job and was able to find my way around and answer visitors' questions with growing confidence, my homesickness abated. I began to appreciate my incredible luck.

Most mornings at eight o'clock saw me in the tasting room with the chief winemaker, Monsieur Simon, tasting the fifty different wines, or *crus*, that would be blended to make that year's vintage. '*Tu goûtes comme un roi*, Alice, *comme un roi, vraiment!*' he would say. Truly, you taste like a king, Alice, like a king! Although I realised he was making a play on my surname, there was a part of my normally self-doubting brain that believed him.

I took to visiting the Gothic cathedral most days after work – or, more accurately, the bar opposite. There is something deliciously wicked about drinking in the shadow of a cathedral, both calming and naughty. I would sit writing my journal, a glass to hand, glancing up at the famous *Sourire de Reims*, the smiling angel that adorns the cathedral entrance. She is no ordinary angel. Her smile is anything but angelic –

more a mischievous grin. It is impossible to look at her face and not smile. She is raising her right hand, as if calling for another glass of champagne, I decided. 'Just the kind of guardian angel I need,' I wrote in my journal.

One afternoon a tall, blond man interrupted my writing. It was one of the Dutch tourists I had been showing around the cellars that afternoon. 'Excuse me,' he said, 'you remind me of the *Sourire de Reims*. Do you always smile like that when drinking champagne?'

'Always.'

CHAPTER SIX

Decanted

Drinking champagne for a living was a decadent way to spend my summer holidays, but all too soon it was time to return to take up my college course. Disappointing A-level results meant I didn't secure a place at university – instead I returned to the UK to study at the London College of Fashion. I was fascinated by textiles and loved to write, so I decided to pursue a career in fashion journalism.

I was not eligible for a grant, so, taking advantage of my mother's sewing machine, I set up a business making cotton sweatshirts. I would buy roll-ends of fabric for 50p from the market. Each sweatshirt took thirty minutes to make and I sold them for £5. In my usual all-or-nothing way, I worked night and day. In four months I had accumulated enough to pay my fees and live in London for a year. My mother's sewing machine was never the same again.

Having literally sweated to go to college, I worked hard at my studies, came top of the year and was earnest that I should succeed in fashion journalism. There was, however, a problem – watching fashion shows bored me. Moreover, this was 1981 and jobs were difficult to find. Two of my brothers had good degrees, were bright and personable and had found themselves jobless. Several of us on the course realised there weren't enough openings in fashion journalism or fashion PR for all of us. I went round the class asking people what else they were interested in, aside from fashion.

What were their hobbies? Together we brainstormed, calling out relevant magazines, newspapers or companies to contact for jobs depending on our interests.

Arabella, one of my fellow students, was rich, short and snooty. She looked like a character out of *Dallas* and was always impeccably made up with bouffant, Barbie-blonde hair. Her claim to fame was that she had slept with one of the actors in the TV series *Minder*. I can picture her now standing at the back of the class, hands on hips. 'So,' she said to me, 'what do *you* know anything about?'

While delivered sarcastically, this was a good question, and one that – in my concern to motivate everyone else – I hadn't considered. I thought about it. 'Um . . . I know about wine. Especially champagne,' I replied. 'And I certainly know how to drink it.'

'Well, write to a wine magazine and ask for a job,' said Arabella. It was one of those chance remarks that change your life.

I wrote to three wine magazines. 'My name is Alice King, I am nineteen, and I think you should give me a job.' Two days later I received a reply from *Decanter*. 'The world's finest wine magazine,' it said on the letterhead. They were interviewing for an editorial assistant and had already shortlisted a few people, but invited me to come in 'for a chat'.

I panicked. What would I wear? Finally I settled on a Lady Diana-style white polka-dot blouse I had made. My friend Harriet, who later went on to become fashion editor of *Harpers & Queen*, lent me a striped Daniel Hechter pencil skirt and high-heeled navy court shoes. I had recently written a piece for the college magazine on a stonemason who had retrained as a hairdresser with Vidal Sassoon and so went straight to his Avery Row salon, where he gave me a free haircut. I emerged with a sleek bob and golden highlights.

I went to the interview looking confident on the outside.

Inside, I was quivering. I wished I had taken more notice of my father when he had talked about wine, instead of imitating him to entertain my brothers and sisters.

The interview seemed to be going well until Colin Parnell, the editor-in-chief and proprietor, asked me if I had ever actually written anything about wine.

'No,' I gulped. 'Well, not yet, but I could write you a piece about the trials, tribulations and triumphs of being a guide in the champagne cellars of Reims.'

He looked at me over his glasses. 'And what would the headline be?'

My stomach hit the floor. I grabbed for my mother's favourite line: 'Champagne makes you sing!' Well, it does, doesn't it?

A week later I was offered the job of editorial assistant on a starting salary of £4,500 a year. I was ecstatic.

Years later I asked Colin why he had employed me.

'Because I rang your course tutor, who told me I would be mad not to,' he replied.

CHAPTER SEVEN

LEARNING CURVE

Taste has always been the ultimate sensation for me. I am electrified by instant oral gratification. I need only the tiniest drop to wet my tongue and my mind races back through the bottle banks of time, searching for the memories evoked and the perfect, salivating adjective.

Fate had dealt me a trump card with the *Decanter* job. I loved watching people's faces as I told them, 'I'm a wine writer.' Everyone was interested, especially men. I was precocious with my newfound passion. My inexperience didn't faze me. I was determined to taste as many wines as possible, and I simply couldn't pull the corks fast enough. I relished the prospect of such a steep learning curve and was delighted that at last I had found something I was really good at.

In my early days in the trade I marvelled at how far and accurately people could spit. My father laughed when I told him I was losing sleep over my spitting prowess. What if I were to miss the spittoon at a big trade tasting? 'Practise in the bath,' he said. 'You'll soon sharpen your aim.'

Bathtime was never the same again. I knew I was on target when I could accurately deposit a slurp of tepid bathwater on to the floor beyond the end of the bath.

Decanter's monthly tasting was an event I looked forward to as much as payday. It was part of my job to contact the wine trade for specific samples of wines. I would catalogue and number the wines, and decide on a tasting order, generally youngest to oldest, driest to sweetest. Wines were always tasted blind, meaning that their identity was kept secret to ensure tasters weren't influenced by the label.

I learnt not to fill the glasses right up – about a sixth of a glass was ideal. This allowed tasters to tilt the glass, look at the colour of the wine and swirl it round without spillage. This releases the wine's aroma, dispelling the inch or so of stale air trapped between the wine and the cork.

I noted that the majority of our tasting panel swirled the wine in an anticlockwise direction. They would take a good sniff before tasting it, swill the wine round in the mouth, then spit it out into a bucket filled with sawdust, like the lucky dip at a fair. While some tasters were relatively silent spitters, others sounded like gagging cats. Tasters made notes – C, N, P, for colour, nose and palate – and rated the wines out of a possible twenty. I collated the results, quizzed the panel and wrote a report on their findings.

At first, as I analysed the tasting results, I was surprised at the disparity that occasionally occurred. If the experts couldn't agree, what hope was there for a trainee like me? I was delighted if any of my descriptions tallied with the panel's and congratulated myself if I awarded a wine the same or similar marks.

I quickly identified the tasters who seemed to have similar palates to mine. I would pore over their notes for hours, noting the adjectives and descriptions they came up with. Some I was familiar with – 'sweaty saddles' for French Syrah, and 'cat's pee' for the textbook aroma of the Sauvignon Blanc grape. Others could be more flowery and obscure – 'wheelbarrows full of ugly fruit . . . mimosa . . . kumquats' had me re-tasting in an effort to lock these aromas and flavours into my memory. It would irritate me if I couldn't instantly conjure up a certain aroma or flavour memory. I would return to the tasting room again and again, trying to recall an elusive taste.

After a tasting of the top Rhône Syrah wine Hermitage, I puzzled all day to recall what the aroma had triggered in my brain. I knew it was an early memory but I couldn't pin it down. Finally, after smelling the wine literally hundreds of times, it came to me – it was the smell of the hard, white rubber from my pram, an old-fashioned Silver Cross. Instantly I could picture myself sitting on the little folding seat that clipped on to the pram. This became a direct trigger in my aroma memory that said, 'Hermitage', or 'Syrah', to me thereafter, a handy, failsafe marker in blind tastings.

I was tasting more than a hundred wines a week in the office. In addition I started to be invited to trade tastings. When the first formal invitation – to a Louis Latour Burgundy tasting – arrived with my name on it, a stiff white card with curly gold script, I thought I had arrived. Soon I was receiving a dozen or so invitations every week.

The trade was generous with its knowledge, and I quickly identified my tasting heroes. Fellow *Decanter* panel tasters were happy to help me, or mark my tasting card, as there would often be as many as two hundred wines at a time. Mark Savage, a Master of Wine who owned a company called Windrush Wines in Cirencester, was to become one of my tasting heroes, as was fellow Master Julian Brind, then the buyer for Waitrose. 'Always happy to help a pretty – and intelligent – blonde,' he would say. And I have never forgotten Terry Horton, the modest yet passionate Marks & Spencer buyer. On one occasion, after an arduous blind tasting of fifty or so Liebfraumilch, he silenced us all by correctly identifying his own M&S brand as well as those of rivals Sainsbury's, Tesco and Waitrose – and then picked out Blue Nun. This impressive performance made me more determined than ever that I too would become such a magician. It seemed the ultimate party trick.

I always dressed carefully for tastings. The majority were held in smart London hotels I had never been to, such as the

Dorchester, Inn on the Park and the Intercontinental. I favoured fitted skirts and striped shirts with the collars turned up, or tailored dresses. I had one favourite, a black crêpe Jean Muir I had paid £150 for – three times the amount I had ever spent on any item of clothing. I decided it was money well spent, as it helped me feel grown-up, powerful even – a proper journalist. I teamed it with a pair of Zandra Rhodes black suede court shoes with silver lacy bows. Sometimes I put my hair up, Lois Lane-style. I convinced myself that the outfit made me look older. Perhaps I could pass for late twenties, rather than late teens. At home, I would pose in the mirror with a wineglass, practising swilling water round to ensure I didn't show myself up by spilling wine on the floor at a tasting.

I was always the youngest at these tastings, sometimes by as much as ten years. Often I would be one of only a handful of women in a sea of suited, middle-aged former public schoolboys. I was taken aback when one chinless wonder commented, 'I say, aren't you lucky? I wouldn't let my secretary go to a tasting.'

Looking down my nose at him, I replied, 'I am not a secretary, I am a journalist. And what's *your* name and who do *you* work for?' I regretted it immediately, softened my voice and added, 'Perhaps you'd like to tell me how you think the wines are showing today, and how they compare with the last vintage?' but he had scuttled off.

Once or twice I found myself being introduced to my father: 'Alice, have you met Dominic King?' We would laugh and one of us would reply, 'Yes, we've met a few times, actually,' then shake hands or kiss each other French-style on both cheeks. I was determined to go this one alone, however. I wanted acceptance in the trade; I wanted to be known for my own skill as a taster and a journalist. Asked how I had developed an interest in wine, I rarely confessed to the family connection, concocting instead evasive stories around working as a student for a champagne company – which was, of course, true.

My first Sauternes tasting was memorable. I had never encountered such intensely sweet wines before. I found the concept of their production tricky to fathom – the wines were made from shrivelled grapes that had been infected with a desirable type of 'noble rot', *Botrytis cinerea*. It sounded like a nasty disease to me, but the resulting golden, honeyed wines were sensational. Adjectives flew around at the tasting – 'freesias . . . peaches . . . pears . . . caramel . . . lychee . . . citrus'. The secret of a top sweet wine is in the balance between luscious, sweet fruit and the citrus-like tang of acidity. I decided these wines were extraordinarily 'moreish', a word I was never quite sure how to spell but one that became not only part of my tasting notes but a mantra for me – I loved moreish wines, moreish people, moreish places.

On the day of the Sauternes tasting, the bosses left the office early and the rest of us set about a spot of intensive research among the leftovers, including the legendary Château d'Yquem 1967. Even then it retailed for over £50 a bottle. We calculated that this worked out at more than £1 a sip.

At six o'clock, the last drop of Château d'Yquem long gone, we divided the remainder of the spoils and left the office. I was teetering down the stairs to Blackfriars Station when I realised that, in my rush to swipe the best bottles, I had left my purse on my desk. As my Tube pass was in my coat pocket and I only had to get to my father's London flat, where I was now living, I decided not to bother returning to the office. I had already struggled to make it this far with two carrier bags of wine. As I walked through the underpass, a tramp with matted ginger hair and bloodshot green eyes asked me for the price of a cup of tea.

'I haven't got any money on me,' I mumbled, hesitating and feeling guilty. I had just been drinking a £50-a-bottle wine but had nothing for a tramp. I opened one of the bags. Which should I give him, the delicately elegant, coconutty Château Lafaurie-Peraguey, or the majestic, deep-orange, apricot and cream Château Rieussec 1976? I handed over the Rieussec.

The tramp smiled. 'God bless you,' he said.

CHAPTER EIGHT

WELL DONE, GIRLIE

After less than a year on *Decanter* I was promoted to assistant editor. There was my name – *there* – on the masthead of 'the world's finest wine magazine'. I stared and stared at it.

By way of recognition for my promotion, Colin, the editor-in-chief, sent me to a Muscadet tasting in the Loire Valley. I was the only woman among the bevy of wine merchants and restaurateurs on the trip, and the youngest there by a good fifteen years.

I was nervous. On the plane to Paris – club class, no less – we drank quarter-bottles of stylishly elegant Pol Roger champagne. I felt more relaxed after the second. You have nothing to be afraid of, I told myself. As we clambered off the coach at the vineyard, a big guy with wild, black, curly hair and mischievous, twinkling eyes introduced himself.

'What's a young lass like you doing here?' he asked.

'I'm the assistant editor of *Decanter*,' I replied. 'Like you, I'm here to taste the new Muscadets.'

He looked at me and laughed. 'OK, girlie, and I'm Black Jack – John Milroy from Milroy's of Soho. You been to one of these before?' I shook my head. 'Stick with me and you'll be fine,' he said. 'Nice legs, by the way.'

I wasn't sure how to reply to this. I followed him into a marquee, next to the winery. We were greeted with a large glass of Muscadet. Black Jack virtually downed his in one.

'Always get the leaky glass, that's me. Come on, lass, drink up. Shall I get you another?'

I looked at my glass – there must have been at least a third of a bottle in it. 'No, I'm fine. What are they doing over there?' I said, pointing towards a long table laden with bottles covered in foil.

'Ah, that's the grand tasting – blind tasting – that's what we're here for, girlie. Taste the wines and score them, rate them. All the growers taste their wines and the marks are added up to determine which grower's wine will be the co-operative's top wine – the Coupe d'Or. You have to sing for your supper. No such thing as a free lunch, girlie.'

Several tasters were already handing in their completed tasting sheets to Louis Metaireau, the film-star-handsome vigneron who headed up this unusual Muscadet cooperative. Someone was playing an accordion, and several of the winegrowers were standing around smoking. Oh, no. It was one thing blind-tasting wines at home, but in public? Now I was panicking. What if people realised I was no good?

I picked up the first of seven wines the growers had pre-selected as the best cuvées. I had only drunk Muscadet once before, in a fish restaurant. What should I be looking for?

I tasted along the line of wines, dutifully spitting them out on to the earth floor of the marquee. I felt like the new girl at school again, the odd one out. Everyone was laughing and chatting. Several of the growers were swallowing rather than spitting.

I re-tasted what I thought to be the best wine. It was crisp, dry and had an attractive, distinctive yeasty aroma and a tangy, citrus, almost pineapple-like finish. This one definitely seemed to have the most complexity. There were layers of flavour. Some of the others were all mouth-searing acidity and no fruit, leaving a nasty, astringent taste in my mouth. No, this was the one. Every time I re-tasted it I detected new flavours. I just needed to pinpoint them. I swallowed another mouthful and noted that the aftertaste lingered on – apple and pear fruit salad. I had just taken another mouthful to check on this description when I felt a tap on my back. I turned round to see Louis Metaireau. Had he seen me swallow the wine?

'Aleeze, *vous avez choisi?*' he asked. Have you chosen?

I nodded, not knowing whether to spit out my mouthful in front of him or swallow it. It would be more professional to spit it out, I thought and, turning my head to one side in an exaggerated fashion, spat to my left.

He was smiling and holding out his hand. I handed him my empty glass. He laughed, shook his head and wagged a Gallic finger – '*Non, non, tes notes,*' he said, pointing to my tasting notes. I handed them over.

Black Jack approached. 'Done the tasting? Right, come with me, girlie. Now the party really begins.'

I followed him to a table and we sat down with five or six others. There were two huge silver platters piled high with oysters. I had never tasted oysters before. I looked around to see if there was anything else to eat. Aside from baskets of bread and bowls of red-wine vinegar and chopped shallots, the rest of the table was covered with bottles and glasses – six at each place setting.

'Let's get started on the shucking,' said Black Jack. I glanced sharply at him. Had I misheard him? He carried on, oblivious. 'Hope you like oysters, girlie. I'll open you a dozen to start with, eh? They do great things, you know.'

I watched as he skilfully opened the oysters, sticking the stubby knife between the shells and prising them open. I remembered watching my father doing this when I was a little girl, which is exactly how I felt at that moment – small and out of my depth.

'Actually,' I said in what I hoped was a conspiratorial air, 'I've never eaten them before.'

Black Jack laughed, selected one, doused it with the shallot and wine vinegar and handed it to me. I looked at it with horror. Milky-white, globby-looking – I couldn't imagine putting it in my mouth.

'Down it in one,' he said. 'Don't try to chew it, just slurp it – like you would a wine.'

I closed my eyes and did exactly that – trying not to gag as the oyster slithered down my throat. I swallowed and picked up my glass, taking a large gulp of wine to drown the flavour of seawater and vinegar. The combination was . . . interesting. I was trying to work out in what way the flavour of the wine changed the taste of the oyster when I heard someone chinking on a glass.

'*Silence, silence,*' said a voice.

Louis Metaireau was welcoming us to the tasting. Every so often I would jot something down in my notebook. I wrote in shorthand because I thought it appeared more professional, and it meant that my neighbours couldn't read what I'd written. The downside was that after the event, and certainly after a few glasses, I usually couldn't read it either.

I was considering the shorthand outline for 'Muscadet' when I heard my name. I looked up, alarmed. Metaireau was holding up my tasting sheet. My heart started to race. What was he saying? His French was too fast for me. He was gabbling and smiling. I felt sick.

Black Jack slapped me on the back so hard I nearly dropped the empty glass I was cradling. 'Good for you, girlie!' he said. 'Good for you!'

'What have I done?' I whispered, terrified.

'You're the only one who placed the wines in the same order as the growers. Well done, girlie! Go on, up you get – he wants you at the front.'

The marquee had gone silent. I stood up, my stilettos sinking into the grass. I felt light-headed and queasy. Everyone started applauding as I made my way up. Metaireau shook my hand and kissed me on both cheeks. My prize –

once bottled – was a case of each of the top three wines.

Blushing, I mumbled, '*Merci*,' and returned to my table.

'Top girlie,' said Black Jack. 'Here, let's have a celebration drink. Cheers!'

Everyone at the table chinked glasses as I sat there letting all this approval wash over me. I might not have gone to university, but I could taste! It felt good. My face was glowing. I felt special, clever, recognised.

I wasn't quite sure what to do, so after a giant slug of wine I simply beamed at people. A sea of faces was talking to me, asking me what I did, how long I had been working at *Decanter*, how I had learnt to taste. I felt as if I had just won an Oscar. Meanwhile, a little voice somewhere at the back of my mind was sneering, 'It's just chance – a fluke.' For a few seconds I pondered the probability. Then I shrugged, dismissed it, reached for another oyster and re-charged my glass.

CHAPTER NINE

CUPID'S BOTTLE

As an ambitious journalist, I wanted to see my name in print as often as possible, so, in 1982, I suggested we run a series of articles on country wine merchants. *Decanter*'s August edition was dedicated to New World wines – then still a novelty in the UK – so I asked my editor, Tony Lord, which merchant I could interview who sold Australian and Californian wines.

'Go and see Naughty Niall over in Hungerford,' he said, drawing on a Silk Cut. 'He's good for a laugh.'

'Why "Naughty"?'

'You'll see.'

I dressed in a striped linen suit and pointy, tan heels. I was still living in my father's London flat, above his office in Ebury Street, and Daddy said, 'You look smart. Where are you off to today?'

'I'm going to interview a wine merchant in Berkshire,' I said. 'But I'm nervous I won't know what to say – that I'll say the wrong thing.'

'I've never seen you at a loss for words. You'll be fine.'

'But what if he asks me what I think about a wine I've never tasted, or even heard of?'

'Just be honest. No one has tasted everything. Anyway, remember you're interviewing him. If in doubt, turn the question round and ask him what he thinks. Flatter him. That's the salesman's trick – works every time.'

I stepped off the train in Newbury and looked around. Niall was meant to be meeting me. At first I couldn't see anyone waiting for me, but then a slim young man in tight red cotton trousers, a striped shirt and bow tie came bounding towards me. He had narrow, drooping eyes surrounded by laughter lines, a big nose and enormous, full lips. 'You must be Alice – I'm Niall,' he said, shaking my hand. 'I'm late because the car wouldn't start. I've had to leave it running.'

I followed him to a grubby VW estate. I flicked cigarette ash off the passenger seat, sat down and crossed my legs, trying to appear nonchalant. There was a loud crack and something exploded under my shoe. I nearly jumped out of my skin. He burst into loud, raucous laughter. 'Oh, sorry,' he said, 'that was left over from last night. I play bass in a band called Haze and we had a gig in London. We use those little fire crackers onstage.'

As we pulled away, he told me how he had got a job as a van driver for a wine merchant so he could use the firm's van to transport the band's equipment. 'Then I realised how much I loved wine, so – as they say in the ad – I bought the company.'

He talked non-stop in a public-school accent. Wines were 'amazing'; wine producers were 'amazing'; his mail shots and special offers were 'amazing'; even my suit was 'amazing'. I had the impression he thought he was amazing. Even so, I was struck by his confidence. I had never met anyone quite like him before. I didn't know what to make of him or how to respond.

In Hungerford, the town hall clock struck twelve as we walked into Niall's shop on the Georgian high street. It was crammed with hundreds of wine bottles. I noticed a rubber hand sticking out of a pot plant. A smallish chap with glasses and pockmarked skin, Niall's assistant and housemate, was sitting hunched over invoices in the back office. A whoopee cushion lurked on a nearby chair.

We went out on to a lawn at the back of the shop, where Niall handed me a glass of his house champagne and busied himself with a barbecue, cooking lunch.

'So, Niall,' I said, 'what makes you sell Californian wines in a town like this?'

'Fuck knows. Nobody much buys them.' It was the first of many unprintable remarks.

I asked him what he thought of the New World wines and began to note down his comments, which became increasingly eccentric as the afternoon wore on. I tasted all the wines he opened, conscientiously spitting them out on to the lawn, and scribbled down my own tasting notes.

At four o'clock I closed my notebook and decided I may as well indulge in a glass of champagne. At least with fizz I was on familiar ground. Niall opened a bottle of Bollinger NV. I drank the first glass quickly. The excitement of the day pushed the creamy, toasty fizz into my bloodstream. I stopped worrying about what I was going to write. I had always been able to come up with something. It began to rain, and there was a fine mist in the air.

It was Friday and that weekend feeling began to envelop me. I confessed to Niall how champagne fired me up and gave me inspiration. He listened to my stories about working in the champagne cellars. 'Amazing, amazing,' he said, as he refilled my glass.

Three glasses into the Bollinger I felt bolder but still curiously thirsty. I was mesmerised by Niall's flamboyant and exaggerated eccentricity. I felt elated. Rather than come out and ask him how old he was, I used the old wine-trade trick of asking him if he was born in a good vintage.

'Would that be claret or port?' he asked.

He's got me, I thought – I wasn't really up on port vintages. 'Either or, indeed, both,' I replied.

'Actually it was an amazing year for both – 1955,' he said. That made him twenty-seven, six years older than me.

He seemed to have achieved a lot – he had his own company, was his own boss and also a would-be pop star. He had a degree in music, played the cello and had been a Queen's chorister at age eight. He knew about wine – could taste it, buy it, sell it – and had a shop full of it. And by the looks of things, he knew how to drink it.

'I was born in possibly one of the greatest claret vintages of the century,' I said, trying to match him.

'Well, it wasn't 1928 or 1945,' he said, looking me up and down. 'So 1961, then, was it?'

'Yes. I understand it was a great vintage for champagne too. Have you ever tasted a 1961 champagne?'

'Oh, yah,' he replied. 'I think so.'

'Which house?'

He hesitated. 'Actually the best champagne I've tasted recently is Bollinger RD 1973. What do you think of that?'

I went to stand up, but my heels sank into the wet grass of the lawn and I nearly toppled over. He caught my elbow.

'Do you know,' I said, 'I don't think I've ever tasted it. Tell me about it.'

'I can do better than that,' he said. 'Let's have a glass.'

I was beginning to feel light-headed. Time to go. 'I'll need to find out about trains back to London,' I said. 'Can I use the phone?'

'Oh, don't worry about that. I'll get my housemate to check in a minute. In fact, why don't you stay for supper? I'll cook and we can drink a few really good bottles.'

I opened my mouth to decline but found myself uncharacteristically mute. My stomach lurched and I caught myself smiling coyly.

'OK. That sounds like fun. I can get a train later. Thanks for the invite.'

An hour later I was sitting in the kitchen of Niall's cottage, glass of fizz in hand. The three of us – Niall, his housemate and me – had demolished the best part of a magnum of champagne and I was watching Niall cook. Was there no end to this man's talents?

'Is there anything I can do to help?' I asked.

'Yah, chop these mushrooms.'

I set to, making sure to use the safety bridge I had been taught in school cookery classes. These knives were sharp, I thought. 'Fizzed-up wine critic bleeds to death chopping mushrooms,' ran the headline in my head. I looked at the higgledy-piggledy chopped mushrooms and laid down the knife. 'I need to call my dad,' I said. 'He'll be waiting to know if I need a lift from the station.'

'You can always stay here. We have a small spare room. Then we can have dinner at a more leisurely pace. I have some friends popping round later I'd like you to meet.'

Was this man flirting with me? 'OK,' I said.

I called my father, trying to sound more sober than I felt. 'I'm staying on for supper – I'll get a train back tomorrow.'

'Well,' came my father's voice down the line, 'if you're staying for supper, it has obviously gone well. I told you you'd be fine. So, what is he like?'

'What do you mean?'

'The wine merchant – young, old, middle-aged?'

'Oh, definitely middle-aged.'

It was midnight and Niall and I were still sitting at the dining table, alone now. His friends had been and gone, and his housemate had long retired to bed. There were empty glasses, bottles and decanters all over the table. We had eaten well – lamb chops, Jersey royals, courgettes with coriander and mushrooms sautéed in garlic. There were a few stray mushrooms left on my plate, finely chopped into regular, wafer-thin slivers.

'I didn't chop those,' I said.

'No. Yours were such weird shapes I threw them away and chopped some more.'

'Oh,' I said, feeling deflated by this put-down. 'What's that smell? It smells like something's burning.'

'Stock. I've thrown the lamb bones into the stockpot. It's the only way to make decent sauce, you know. Fancy an Armagnac?'

'Oh, I don't really drink spirits, but as I'm here, why not?'

He poured an inch or so into a large brandy balloon.

'Whoa!' I said. 'Are you trying to get me drunk? Anyway, on a more technical note, tell me about this Armagnac.'

'Amazing company, amazing aroma . . .' Off he went again, 'amazing' this, 'amazing' that, but I wasn't listening. I was watching his mouth, fascinated, trying to work out how I would describe his lips in my article. He had a caricatural mouth – his lips looked like rubber, rather like those red plastic ones from a joke shop, the kind you operate with your fingers. Yes, that was it – 'finger-puppet lips'. They were stained nearly black from the Californian wine we had been drinking, Alicante Bouschet 1975, from Angelo Papagni.

I realised he had stopped talking and was staring at me. 'What are you looking at?' he asked. He sounded faintly unsure of himself for the first time that day.

'Um . . . your lips.'

He roared with laughter. 'I sell wine to Roald Dahl,' he said. 'He's always talking about my lips. He writes to me as "Ruby Lips".'

Charlie and the Chocolate Factory popped into my head, with all those sweets. I looked at the bottles on the table. That's what Niall was like – a kid in a sweetshop. There was something magnetic about this man. I wished I had his confidence. I lived in constant fear that I was going to be found out, exposed as a fraud and not a real wine critic at all.

'I need to go to bed,' I said.

'Good idea. I'll show you your room.'

I staggered up the stairs. 'Which way?'

'Straight on.'

I opened a door and sat on an unmade double bed. He sat down beside me. 'This is large for a small spare room,' I said, recalling what he'd told me earlier.

He laughed. 'Actually, it's my room. You could always stay here.'

He leaned over and kissed me with those enormous lips – a wet, squishy kiss. I could taste the caramel residue of Armagnac.

I drew back. 'I don't sleep with people I interview.'

That laugh again. 'Best show you the spare room, then.'

The following morning we set off to walk along the canal into the town. My head was hazy, but the sun was shining and I felt curiously uplifted, as if I had left my body and was looking down at myself from above.

We chatted like old friends. He grabbed my hand as I teetered along in my high heels, laughing at the ducks and marvelling at the water lilies. Something had happened overnight. Cupid had hit me over the head with a bottle. Then it came to me – I was going to marry this man; of that I had no doubt. No matter that I had planned to make a career and get married at around thirty. I was just twenty-one, but I could have a career anyway – what could be a more perfect combination than a wine writer and a wine merchant?

Rather than let me get the train home, Niall drove me to my parents' house in Chipping Norton. 'Hi!' I said, bouncing in. 'Meet Niall.'

Ah, yes,' said my father. 'The middle-aged wine merchant.'

CHAPTER TEN

WEDDING DAZE

Six months later Niall and I bought a cottage together in a village outside Hungerford, and six months after that we were married. My father did us proud and from his bottomless cellar produced scores of bottles of Heidsieck Monopole – the Deluxe Cuvée, Diamant Bleu 1961. 'The wine has immense style and charm and all the staying power of a good marriage,' he joked in his speech.

I wore a calf-length 1920s guipure lace dress, nipped in at the waist. I had vintage Swiss lace court shoes and tiny pink roses in my hair. I look about fourteen in the photographs. Niall and I drove from the reception in a yellow open-topped 1919 Citroën. We spent our wedding night at Brown's Hotel in London, where I fell asleep over dinner – tired, happy and full of fizz. We honeymooned on the Isle of Mull. I packed two cases of champagne with my trousseau.

Back home and settling into married life, not a day passed without us sharing a good bottle or two over supper or stopping at the pub on the way home from work. I was Alice in Wonderland, with Niall as the zany March Hare for company. It was perfectly normal to talk, write, taste and drink wine all day at work, then come home and carry on. Our social life, inevitably, revolved around wine. There was only one thing to do with the hundreds of nearly full bottles left over from big tastings – invite friends round to drink them. We were the golden couple. Everyone wanted to know us.

Boozy dinner parties were the norm – we surrounded ourselves with other passionate wine-lovers and heavy drinkers, who were only too happy to help us dispose of the leftovers.

I worked hard, adored my work and began to travel extensively. I enjoyed the life of a cosseted journalist, treated to the best of everything – first-class travel, the best wines, restaurants and hotels. I worked out that if I paid attention carefully, tasting and making notes on the wines at the start of dinner, I could relax and indulge myself towards the end of the evening. I rarely had far to go to fall into bed.

Generally Niall and I kept our working lives separate, but in an effort to comprehend the intricacies of Bordeaux – his area of expertise – I joined him on a week-long tour of the leading classed-growth châteaux. His knowledge of claret was impressive and he was fast building a reputation in the *en primeur* market – the practice of buying and selling clarets at advantageous prices before the wine is bottled.

My thirst for tasting was only matched – indeed, surpassed – by Niall, whom I nicknamed Billy Whizz for the speed at which he tasted and tore around the châteaux of the Médoc. In that one week alone we sampled more than a thousand young clarets, which, to my palate, tasted simply tart, bitter and tannic. I marvelled at Niall's ability to predict how theses wines would taste when mature in ten to twenty years' time. To secure the best prices he had to put his money where his mouth was. He would order thousands of cases of wine – tens of thousands of pounds' worth – based on what his palate told him.

During that week I drank more fine vintage clarets at legendary châteaux such as Margaux, Latour, Palmer, Gruaud-Larose, La Lagune than I had drunk in my life. The Bordelais were generous hosts, especially when they could see the order books filling up.

On the last day of the trip we spent the day with Alan Johnson-Hill, the English owner of Château Méaume, an up-and-coming Bordeaux *supérieur* property I had met while writing a feature for *Decanter*. It was a hot, airless day and we sat around the swimming pool as Alan's three young daughters splashed around. I watched Alan with his wife, Sue, and noted their gentleness with each other. It made me strangely sad. Our marriage was fiery, passionate. Fireworks were commonplace in such a volatile, wine-fuelled environment. I loved Niall with an intensity I didn't understand.

Sue served Pimm's mixed with sparkling wine and packed with red fruits – raspberries, strawberries and redcurrants. I have a hazy recollection of the barbecued quail that followed, and of eating raspberries while lying drunkenly on a lilo floating in the swimming pool.

Next morning Niall and I were due on the 6 a.m. flight back to Heathrow. Hung-over, we only just made the plane. I had an 11 a.m. tasting appointment – for the fifty top white Burgundies. Kill or cure, I thought. I noticed that my left hand was shaking. How bizarre. Jet lag, maybe.

On the Tube into London, I fell asleep. I dreamt of claret rivers, suitcases overflowing with wine and a man who stood like a fountain, red wine pouring out of his eyes, nose, ears and mouth.

CHAPTER ELEVEN

LIQUID SIN

The stretch Mercedes was waiting at Bordeaux's Mérignac Airport to take Jane McQuitty and me to the Médoc first-growth claret property Château Lafite. Jane was a respected, serious journalist from *The Times*. I was twenty-two and still feeling like the kid who got lucky, though I had at least learnt to *appear* as nonchalant as my colleagues. I was like my black monogrammed Samsonite suitcase: hard on the outside, soft on the inside. Secretly I wanted to whoop with joy. People dream of drinking Lafite – I was actually going to stay there.

As we drew up at the château, Jane and I were greeted by a scruffy man in his forties. He was barefoot and wore a torn corduroy jacket. There was a huge pink rose in his lapel. I thought he was the gardener.

'*Bonjour*,' he said. 'I am Baron Eric de Rothschild. Welcome to Château Lafite.'

I giggled as I shook his hand. I had never met a baron before.

'Come join us in the salon,' he said. 'We have just finished lunch with friends and we're enjoying some of our special cognac, which we have bottled for the château.'

'Oh, I'd like to taste some,' I replied, rather too enthusiastically.

He laughed. 'I'm sure we can arrange that.'

In the salon Jane and I were served tea on a silver salver,

and the baron handed me a generous slug of cognac in a brandy balloon.

Jane declined the cognac. 'Too early in the day for me,' she said. Was that a look of disapproval she shot at me?

'I have to write something on cognac soon,' I said, taking a large slurp. It was delicious – rich, with a honeyed, caramel flavour and a taste reminiscent of . . . What was it? Marzipan? As the spirit warmed its way down my throat, my anxiety began to dissipate. I felt more confident.

To business. I had done my homework by reading up on the château and talking in depth to Niall about its recent 1982 vintage and its pricing structure.

'So, putting up the opening price of Château Lafite 1982 by seventy per cent over the 1981 price was a bold move, wasn't it?' I put to the baron.

Jane's eyebrows shot up. 'More to the point, what do you think about all the *négociants* putting a massive mark-up on the price overnight?' she asked.

There followed a heated discussion about what was a reasonable profit margin. The baron insisted that reputable wine merchants – or *négociants* – would merely apply their standard mark-up rather than reflect the market price, which was rising daily. Jane and I knew this not to be the case – as I'm sure he did – and carried on trying to point this out.

After half an hour I noticed my brandy balloon was empty, and so was Eric's. I could hear frogs croaking in the garden and the high-pitched zing of the cicadas. I reflected that I could do with a siesta – it had been a long day, and the combination of the cognac and the afternoon sun was making me sleepy. I noticed the baron swallowing a yawn.

He asked, 'Thinking of dinner, what vintages were you two born in?'

Stony-faced, Jane replied, 'In 1953.'

I added, 'I'm 1961.'

'Aha, so you know the good vintages! What years were you *really* born in?'

We repeated our birth years.

'Well, I'll look in the cellar and see what I can do. See you for dinner at seven.' Before leaving, he winked at me. 'More cognac?'

I found myself shaking my head. If I wasn't careful, I was going to be drunk before dinner even started.

Later that day I hesitated over dressing for dinner. Both the baron and his wife had been quite casual – shabby, even – during the afternoon, but I didn't want to get it wrong. Better to be too smart than too scruffy, I reasoned, putting on a navy drop-waisted angora Louis Féraud dress.

I was glad I had because when I entered the candlelit dining room, the baron was resplendent in a velvet smoking jacket and matching velvet winkle-pickers bearing the Lafite crest, and his wife, while barefoot, had on a full-length green silk dress, her dark hair dropping in ringlets around her shoulders. What a lifestyle, I thought with a stab of envy darker than the baroness's dress. The table glittered with glasses, which twinkled in the candlelight. Down its centre stood six identical decanters arranged in precise formation. Six decanters – we were in for some dinner!

'In honour of my two guests, I present the 1961 and the 1953 vintages,' the baron announced. 'Two vintages with immense class and charm, if I may say,' he added.

Lafite 1961 was already then a legendary wine, trading at more than £200 a bottle. I couldn't wait to try it. I hardly gave my food a glance, concentrating instead on the notebook on my lap. The room seemed to be enveloped in a rich, spicy glow that spread quickly to my cheeks. The wine in my glass was the colour of smoky rubies, and had such an intense aroma you hardly needed to taste it. But taste it – or rather, drink it – I did, marvelling at its richness and spicy, plum-like, fruit-cake flavour.

'Would there be much bottle variation?' I asked the baron, cheekily.

'Only one way to find out.' He smiled. 'Let's try the second decanter, and the third, and taste all three side by side. But before we do that, let's try Jane's wine, the 1953.'

This was equally stunning, though a sweeter wine, and showed more brown in its colour. It had an oaky, plain-chocolate flavour. This was a moment meant for legend – six glasses of vintage Lafite lined up in front of me, calling to be drunk.

So, was there much bottle variation? My notes became more indecipherable with each glass. Eventually I gave up trying to write. I was past caring, amazed and privileged to be drinking such incredible clarets.

It transpired that the baroness was also born in 1961, and we spent the rest of the evening reminiscing about favourite pop stars and songs. 'Did *you* lose your heart to a Starship Trooper?' I asked her.

It was long past midnight when I climbed up the winding stairs of the tower to my bedroom. Giggling to myself, I kicked off my shoes. Someone had turned the sheets down, and beside the high bed was what looked like a horse's mounting block. I climbed up, swaying, and fell on to the bed.

Drunk on Lafite, I thought. It didn't come much better than this. I felt like a princess in a fairytale. So much hedonism in one night. The ultimate liquid sin!

Speaking of sin, I couldn't wait to tell Niall about this one. He often grumbled, rightly so, that we journalists were treated more regally than the merchants who shelled out the money. He'd be as jealous as sin.

CHAPTER TWELVE

Blind Tasting

Decanter's hundredth edition and our biggest ever. It fell to me to pass the final pages. I was determined the magazine would go to the printers on schedule, so I stayed late at the typesetters every night. The edition was finally signed off on time and I caught the train home. It was Friday night. Niall picked me up at the station at seven o'clock, reminding me we had friends coming round for dinner at eight.

'I'm not going to be good for much tonight – I'm shattered,' I said. 'I didn't get much help from the typesetters and then the train was late. I'm a bit wound up, actually.'

'Don't worry,' he said. 'I've been home and prepped the food. I've even set the table. You get into a bath and I'll bring you up a drink.'

Relieved, I lay back in the bath, full to overflowing with white bubbles. I was pleased to have got such a big edition off to the printers on time. No mean feat. I took my job – and myself – very seriously.

Niall walked into the bathroom and handed me a brimful champagne flute. 'I expect you could do with this, Queenie, after the kind of week you've had,' he said, ruffling my hair. 'What do you think it is?'

I squinted at the fine bead of bubbles racing up the glass, sniffed the wine and took a gulp. Aaaah, nothing like a glass of champagne to pick you up, liven the taste buds, make you feel alert and alive again.

'It's champagne.'

'Yah,' said Niall. 'Vintage or non-vintage?'

I took another drink. 'Non-vintage.'

'Right again. Which one is it, then? Come on, Queenie, let's see how good you are at this blind-tasting lark.'

I looked at the pale-gold colour, took another large mouthful and let the delicate bubbles trickle over my tongue and down my throat. It reminded me of apple pie with a tangy kick of acidity on the finish. Cox's apples. What had I tasted before that was like this? I thought of the fizzes Niall stocked in his shop. He could be pulling a fast one, but this seemed like a good place to start. It wasn't rich enough to be Veuve Clicquot or Bollinger – more likely Taittinger or Joseph Perrier. I tasted it again. The apple flavour seemed to be more pronounced, and the finish was honeyed with a hint of honeysuckle that triggered my taste memory. That gave me the clue I needed.

'Joseph Perrier.'

'Wow! Yes, it is. Well done.'

I laughed. 'More, please!'

He disappeared with my glass. I felt better, refreshed by the fizz and glowing with a sense of achievement. Was it fluke or skill? I wondered, not for the first time.

Niall reappeared with a new flute. 'What's this, then, Queenie?'

This was clearly champagne, but much deeper in colour with very fine bubbles, much less fizzy than the first wine.

'Champagne, but vintage this time,' I said before tasting it.

'Yep, but what type and what vintage?'

I sniffed it and took a gulp. This was seriously classy stuff, with a biscuity aroma and honeycomb-like fruit on the palate. The flavour lingered in my mouth, reminding me of dried apricots. 'Bollinger RD 1973,' I pronounced. The champagne Niall had served me the day we met.

'Christ, impressive or what,' he laughed. 'Well done. You'd better get a move on – our guests will be here in fifteen minutes.'

I lay looking at the glass in my hand, resting the stem on my belly button. I was happier now, buoyed up with confidence. It couldn't be a fluke; I really must be good at blind tasting, exceptionally talented, even gifted. I must have a fantastic, super-sensitive palate! I had cracked it – the ultimate dinner-party trick.

I dressed and went down to meet our friends. We had two vintage clarets with supper, both served blind. I was, respectively, fifteen and twenty years out with my estimates. So much for being a blind-tasting star.

CHAPTER THIRTEEN

PARTY AT THE PALACE

Niall and I were the archetypal 'dinkies' – Dual Income, No Kids Yet – in the middle of Margaret Thatcher's more, more, more 1980s. With the money washing around, we bought a larger property in Hungerford, Avon House, a majestic, four-storey, nineteen-room Victorian townhouse, even though our cottage hadn't yet sold. We dressed in designer clothes, ate and drank in expensive restaurants and enjoyed ever more exotic holidays. Weekends in country-house hotels were the norm. For my twenty-fourth birthday, in 1985, we took over Hintlesham Hall in Suffolk, along with twenty friends. There were three black-tie dinners, culminating in the opening and drinking of a jeroboam – the equivalent of six bottles – of Château Canon 1955, Niall's birth year. Great wines need to be drunk with friends and there was no doubt as to the greatness of this Saint-Emilion Premier Grand Cru Classé. Few of our friends had seen a jeroboam, let alone drunk one.

We chipped off the wax and carefully extracted the giant cork. The room was enveloped in an enticing, sweet aroma so pungent it seemed to me you could see it. Rich with violets, mingled with cigar-box and chestnut flavours, this wine conjured up the taste of stolen chocolate digestives. It had the same addictive effect.

Pudding was accompanied by the top Sauternes, Château Rieussec 1970, an intensely concentrated, tangy, marmalade-like sweet wine. The evening ended with wild games of table tennis, accompanied by brandy balloons full of old Green Chartreuse.

I loved these occasions. I never knew when to stop. I couldn't understand why some people went to bed at midnight when there were still bottles on the table. Life was for partying, and with so much good wine around I liked to party until I dropped. I began to become blasé, continually seeking perfection – a better hotel, finer cooking, rarer wines.

But even I, with my growing delusions of grandeur, was not prepared for the magnificence of the party Niall and I attended in the orangery and grounds of the Palace of Versailles. It was held to celebrate champagne Piper-Heidsieck's bicentenary. As luck would have it, Niall and I were already in France. A strike by airport personnel had stranded the other British guests on the wrong side of the Channel.

We stayed in the Trianon Palace. Even the bathroom seemed the size of a ballroom. Lying in the bath, marvelling at my surroundings, I sipped my fifth, or perhaps sixth, glass of champagne of the day – I'd had lunch with a winemaker. Life was sweet. Niall and I had had a good holiday in the Dordogne with friends, and tonight's party was a suitable finale before going back to work. Not that work was so bad, I mused. After all, this party was work, wasn't it?

My hair was piled on top of my head, cascading in a shock of Marie Antoinette ringlets. Stepping out of the bath, champagne flute in hand, I slipped on the wet marble and slid a good ten feet before completely losing my balance and crashing to the floor. There was a split second in which I surveyed my nearly full glass, bubbling furiously in my hand, and wondered if I should drop it; but I held on tight and landed on my shoulder, clipping the back of my head on the porcelain sink.

'You OK in there, Queenie?' called Niall, hearing the crash.

He came in. 'Ah, well held!' he laughed. 'Glad to see you didn't drop your glass.'

'I think I bumped my head,' I lamented. 'Thirsty work, this skidding around the bathroom. You'd better pour me another glass.' I drained the flute dry.

I dressed in a fitted black velvet ball gown. It was an off-the-shoulder, Terence Nolder 1950s-style and had flashes of turquoise silk round the plunging neckline. I turned to Niall. 'Wonder who will be at this bash,' I said. 'I believe more than fifteen hundred people have been invited, including all the A-list French film stars. How do I look? Can you see where I bashed my head? Is there a dent in my hairdo?'

'You look fine,' said Niall. 'I doubt there will be anyone we know at the party, with all the Brits stranded. We'll just have to drink their fizz for them, I suppose.'

Once at Versailles, we strolled through the grounds. I tried to avoid the cracks in the cobblestones in my strappy black Gina heels. We saw the queue for the party, stretching in front of us like a giant serpent. I quickly surveyed the women's dresses, long and short, a myriad of colours and fabrics, all worn with that impeccable style French women seem born with.

'God, we're going to have to queue for hours,' said Niall.

'Maybe not,' I said, watching two men alight from a taxi. 'Look, there's the winemaker I had lunch with. Let's go and say *bonsoir*.'

We crossed the courtyard and the winemaker greeted me like an old friend, kissing me three times on the cheeks. After shaking Niall's hand, he linked arms with me and signalled to Niall to follow. It was one of my finest moments. We bypassed the queuing film stars and went right to the front. I felt like royalty. I realised, and relished, that we were the subject of much scrutiny.

As we entered the gate, dusk was falling. Dramatic blazing torches lit up the palace and its gardens. White-coated, white-gloved waiters stood in formation holding up silver salvers with magnums of Piper-Heidsieck. The champagne flutes twinkled. The sky was a curious crimson, streaked with amber, the sun hanging as if waiting for a signal to set behind the lake. As I stared, mesmerised, the fountains lit up and an orchestra struck up Handel's *Water Music*.

We moved with the crowd towards the orangery for dinner. Chefs in crisp, starched whites were lined up along either side of the room as far as the eye could see. I lost count somewhere over a hundred.

After a deliciously subtle consommé laced with gold leaf, the chefs really set to work. There was every cold delicacy you could imagine – roast quail, caviar, crayfish, crab, lobster. There were sizzling giant prawns cooked in woks with ginger and garlic, and delicious stir-fried *magret de canard*. Exotic aromas filled the air, mingling with an excited buzz in many languages as a new Fabergé egg, commissioned for the bicentenary, was unveiled.

We drank bottle after bottle of Piper-Heidsieck's new *deluxe cuvée*, the aptly named Rare 1976. This was a curious wine: crisp yet steely, like a tight-fitting glove, with a youthful and complex taste even though it was already ten years old. I took delight in explaining to those at my table why this wine was so tightly structured. 'It's on account of it not going through malolactic fermentation,' I said to the Belgian importer on my right.

'Are you sure?' questioned Niall.

The colour rose in my cheeks. 'Quite sure. The winemaker told me himself just this afternoon.'

The Belgian asked, 'Do you help your husband in his business?'

I saw red. 'No. I'm a wine journalist, the assistant editor of *Decanter* magazine. I was the one invited to this party. And *he*' – I jabbed a finger at Niall – 'came as *my* guest.' Suddenly I felt tired and deflated. I was sick of continually having to argue my case, defend myself, make myself heard. Why did men always assume I was a dumb blonde? I scowled and got up from my chair. I skulked around for a while, eventually spying Justin Llewellyn, the UK agent for Piper-Heidsieck.

'Come and join us for pudding,' he said. 'What do you think of the party? How do you think the wines are showing? Come and tell these Dutchmen about your tasting today.'

I joined the table, relishing the attention, and launched into my spiel. By the looks of things, these guys had enjoyed a liquid lunch too. They were drinking even faster than those on my table. We took it in turns to propose toasts. When it was my turn, I was at a loss, so adapted Marie-Antoinette's famous line: 'Never mind cake – let them, and us, drink champagne!' I raised my glass in the air. At that precise moment, almost as if I had given the signal, a rocket whooshed overhead, heralding the start of a stupendous firework display. I stood with the Dutchmen and we watched the *feu d'artifice*. Giant Catherine wheels spun so fast they moulded into crowns of burning fire, and oversized Roman candles poured golden lava into the lake.

The smoke from the last rockets cleared. It was a bright night and the stars shone like diamonds against black velvet. The almost-full moon passed behind a cloud. I left the Dutchmen and began walking. In the distance I could hear dance music. As I walked past a bench, I spied a bottle of Rare on the ground. My glass was empty so I picked up the bottle and discovered it was half full.

My feet were beginning to ache, so I took off my shoes and in a moment of defiance decided to take off my hold-ups. Irritatingly, the left one had kept falling down. I realised I had too much to carry, so jettisoned the stockings into a piece of topiary shaped like a hen. Or was it a cockerel? 'Cock with stockings,' I said aloud to the night. Yes, an apt name for this piece of garden art.

I had no idea which way to walk towards the hotel. There

were people milling around, but everyone seemed to be engaged in intimate conversations. I passed a couple locked in a passionate embrace. I felt totally alone. This is ridiculous, I told myself. How can you feel alone at a party with fifteen hundred people?

Changing direction, I headed towards a wooden gate. As I opened it, I had a split-second memory of an illustration from *Alice in Wonderland* in which Alice's hand was on a similar gate. I opened it and stepped through into a small, cobbled courtyard. Sitting on a bench was a dishevelled man with blond hair, his bow tie undone. He was about my age. Without a word he held an empty glass out towards me. I filled it, topped up mine and sat down beside him.

'*Santé,*' he said.

'I'm lost,' I responded.

'Are you alone?' he asked.

I nodded.

'We are all alone. And many of us are lost,' he said, and drained his glass.

CHAPTER FOURTEEN

WINE AND DANDY

I open my eyes. My left leg dangles out of a single bed. I gaze at it, my eyes gradually focusing on the pearly-pink nail varnish. Where am I? I try to sit up. My head feels like an unsecured suitcase on a roof rack. I lower myself gingerly back down. I can taste something strong, alcoholic and vaguely coffee-flavoured. Tia Maria. I smell the sweet, yeasty aroma of fresh bread.

On the floor next to the bed lies my Daniel Hechter navy gabardine dress, one arm bent up at an unnatural-looking angle. My black lace La Perla bra points skywards as if still nursing its owner. I can't see my knickers anywhere. My eyes dart around this strange room. Everywhere there are piles of children's comics – *Dandy*, *Beano*, *Eagle*, *Whizzer* and *Chips*, all neatly piled and tied with string. From my pillow, Desperate Dan's prickly chin stares at me. I look down and read the word '*Dandy*' on the duvet cover. I appear to be lying under a giant copy of the comic. I do not feel fine and dandy. Where am I? Is this a child's bedroom?

A cold shadow of fear passes over my heart. My chest contracts, and sweat breaks out on my forehead. My head pounds. I breathe out quickly, several times, and lever myself out of the bed. I quickly retrieve my dress from the floor. I find my lacy black knickers. As I am buttoning up my dress and looking around for my shoes, there is a knock at the door.

'I've baked fresh bread and made coffee. Would you like some?' asks a deep voice – an actor's voice, gravelly and cultured.

What the hell? I search my memory of the previous evening. There are gaps, but scenes begin to flicker through my mind, like stills from a film . . . I'd flown back from Portugal following a press trip – Taylor's port – and had gone straight to a Hermitage tasting in London hosted by Liz and Mike Berry, owners of fine-wine specialist La Vigneronne. Nice people – unassuming, knowledgeable and quietly good fun. I knew Liz, a Master of Wine, from my early days at *Decanter*, where she was a regular tasting-panel member. After the Hermitage tasting they had invited me back to their Kensington flat for supper. Liz had cooked pheasant. We had finished off the best bottles from the tasting as well as guzzling a few others.

What exactly had we drunk? I had already been tipsy when leaving the plane from Portugal, so the evening was a little fuzzy. A magnum of rich, creamy, biscuity Krug Grande Cuvée while she was cooking. Then what? The Chave Hermitage 1978, followed by Jaboulet's Hermitage. I couldn't remember the vintage. Was it 1982?

Somewhere along the line, Mike and I had shared a Montecristo No. 4 cigar and had done a spot of Armagnac tasting. Well, Armagnac drinking. They had invited me to stay, but I'd already arranged a bed at a friend's mews house near Baker Street. I vaguely remembered a cab, the driver opening the door for me. I hadn't been able to get the key to turn in the lock of my friend's house. The cabbie had also tried and failed. I'd thrown stones up at the bedroom window. Nothing. Eventually I had given up and taken the same cab back to the Berrys'.

Once back at Liz and Mike's house, I had thought that if I went round the back of their apartment and climbed over the fence, I would be able to knock on their bedroom window.

This had seemed perfectly logical to me. Unfortunately, the fence was too high. I could only just see over it in my high heels. I had asked the cabbie to give me a leg-up. He had told me not to be silly, snarling something about it being four in the morning and him needing to get to bed. 'Well, that's what I'm trying to do!' I snapped, throwing his £30 fare at him.

Then . . . Then what? Wandering around the streets, trying to find my way back to the front door. All the houses in the crescent looked the same. When I found their house again, I had rung the bell for ages, but there had been no reply. I had tried all the bells of the flats above theirs. Then the light on the entryphone had lit up and a male voice had said, 'Yes?'

'I'm Alice King.'

'Ye-e-e-s?' rising in inflection, questioning.

'I've been having dinner with your neighbours – Liz and Mike Berry. And, um, I can't get into my friend's where I was going to stay so I need to try and get back into Liz and Mike's. They'd invited me to stay, you see, but they must be asleep now. Perhaps if I knock on their inside door they will hear me. Could you let me in? Please?'

Moments later the door opened. A man with tousled red hair stood there in a short, brown towelling dressing gown. The hairs on his legs were ginger, interspersed with freckles. We shook hands. I stepped inside and rang the Berrys' internal bell. No answer.

'Come up to mine and you can try ringing them,' the man suggested.

There were four or so flights of stairs to his flat. I traipsed up behind him, able to see the bottom curve of his buttocks. It was a *very* short dressing gown.

Brown velvet drapes tied with gold organza bows lent a bohemian, theatrical feel to his apartment. Twisted gold candles burned in a crystal candelabra. Louis Armstrong sang in the background. I tried telephoning the Berrys, but the phone just rang and rang.

'What are you going to do?' he'd asked.

'I don't know,' I'd replied. 'I live miles away, and the first train back isn't for a few hours yet.'

'Well, come and sit down and we'll work something out,' he said. 'Would you like a drink of tea or coffee?'

'That's kind. I must admit I wouldn't mind a real drink. It's been a long day. Are you here on your own?'

'Yes. My wife has left me. She thinks I'm gay. She's trying to divorce me. Now, let me see what I've got . . . Whisky, gin, Tia Maria?'

I relaxed. If his wife thinks he's gay, he probably is, I thought. I'm safe.

'Tia Maria would be good,' I said. 'I went there once – to Jamaica, I mean – to the Blue Mountain coffee plantations where they make Tia Maria. I'm a wine writer. That's how I know Liz and Mike.'

He worked in the theatre, something to do with sound. He had been working late on a new show and had not been home long.

In a lull in the conversation he stood up and said, 'Why don't you stay here? Then you can rouse Liz and Mike in the morning – well, in a few hours. It's five thirty now. Don't worry. I've got a spare room.'

'Good idea,' I said. 'That's really kind of you.'

I followed him to this little room. 'I've got the second biggest collection of cartoon comics in Europe,' he said.

'Wow,' seemed the only response. I'd gone to bed.

And woken up not realising how I had ended up here, not at first.

I walked into the kitchen. The nine o'clock news was just starting on Radio 4. The man, whose name I still didn't know, was standing at the wooden kitchen table with a bread knife in his hand, still in his short dressing gown. The table was set with white and gold china plates. I stood sheepishly in my bare feet and he handed me a white damask napkin.

'Sit down,' he said. 'Freshly baked bread with honey for the lady. Coffee?'

Sober now, my imagination went into overdrive. What had I been thinking, going into a stranger's flat? Scenes from *Silence of the Lambs* flashed in front of me as he reached over to pick up the bread board, knife still in hand. Am I mad? I thought. No one in the world knows where I am. Anything could have happened to me. He could have raped me, killed me – no one would have been any the wiser. I stuffed the bread into my mouth and drank the coffee so quickly I scalded my tongue. I couldn't taste anything for three weeks.

'Thanks, thanks, thanks so much. I've got to dash – I'm going to be late for a tasting,' I said, spotting my shoes neatly paired by the front door.

He kissed me on both cheeks. 'Come again!' he called, as I scurried out of the flat and down the stairs.

My head was swimming. The coffee threatened to come back up. I hailed a cab back to the Baker Street mews. The key opened the door straight away and I realised that I must have been trying to get into the wrong house.

I vowed I would never drink so much again.

PART TWO

Fall From Grace

CHAPTER FIFTEEN

PANIC IN PARADISE

Nothing beats the thrill of your first book, of seeing your name on the cover. 'Drink what you want, when you want, where you want – it's called being winewise!' rang the opening line of mine. I followed my own advice.

Winewise was published in 1987, when I was just twenty-six, and generated huge publicity, with newspaper and magazine reviews, plus radio and TV interviews and appearances. It was all heady stuff, and on the surface I was coping but underneath I was terrified. I would throw up from nerves before going in front of the television cameras, rewarding myself with a large drink or six when I returned home exhausted from a live studio appearance on *Good Morning, Britain* at the Pebble Mill studios in Birmingham.

All this publicity resulted in a telephone call from the *Daily Mail*. The newspaper invited me to become their wine correspondent and write a weekly wine column. I believed that the way forward in the UK wine trade would be via the supermarkets and the mass market. The *Mail* was the first tabloid to promote wine on a regular basis. I was thrilled and flattered to be billed as 'Britain's youngest nationally read wine writer . . . the brightest writer on wining and dining'. I reasoned it was down to luck – I was in the right place at the right time.

As soon as my column appeared in the *Mail*, the phone started ringing off the hook. *Marie Claire, Living, Best, House*

Beautiful, *FHM* – all wanted regular columns. I had gone free-lance in 1985, retaining my connection with *Decanter* as a contributing editor, and now, less than two years later, I seemed to be flavour of the month. Each week I was asked to more tastings and lunches than it was possible to find time for and was increasingly invited on more exotic press trips – to California, Australia, the Caribbean, even India, where, yes, they do make wine. I was abroad about 50 per cent of the time.

Several magazines ran profiles on my lifestyle. Sometimes they interviewed Niall and me together. *Company* inter-viewed us for a feature on modern marriage.

'Doesn't he mind you being away all the time?' the inter-viewer asked.

'I don't know. I never thought to ask him,' I replied honestly.

'What about the competition between you?'

'He's more knowledgeable about Bordeaux than I am, whereas I know more about the rest of the world's wine, I think.'

Asked for my recipe for a successful marriage, I answered, 'To love, honour and laugh.'

Increasingly, though, I wasn't laughing. There were rows at home. I didn't really understand why this was happening, though I consoled myself that the making-up was fun. I had stopped phoning home so frequently from press trips, as it always seemed to end in one of us slamming down the phone. I became guarded about the fun I had while away.

I would wake up most mornings with my heart racing, in addition to the usual hangover. Wine was the only thing that seemed to calm my nerves, especially when I was scared or felt out of my depth, which was much of the time. The alcohol and my insecurities combined to produce a terrify-ing, drowning, suffocating feeling.

I decided I needed a holiday. I borrowed a villa from Don

Hewitson, a friend in the trade, in the tiny village of La Croix Valmer on the French Riviera with friends Jenny and Bill, my hairdresser, Julie, and her partner, Mark. Niall would join us later. The routine was bloody Marys at ten, followed by half a lobster and a carafe or three of the local rosé in the supermarket café or lunch with a Cahors red. Sometimes we would have more wine in a beach café during the afternoon or a siesta. In the evenings came dinner with, naturally, more wine, followed by cognac, Armagnac or the French eau de vie made from pears, Poire William.

En route to Nice Airport with Jenny and Bill to pick up Niall, I suffered some sort of panic attack. A pain struck me in the sternum, my heart raced, and I became breathless. White dots danced before my eyes. As I gasped for breath, doubled over, by the side of the *autoroute*, I wondered what was happening to me. Was it a heart attack?

I recovered sufficiently to carry on and we met Niall at the airport. He seemed jovial and quite merry, fresh from a cognac tasting in London. When we had a moment alone, I told him I hadn't been sleeping well. Because our cottage hadn't sold before we'd bought Avon House, we'd borrowed money from my parents and I was concerned about paying it back.

'It'll sell, eventually,' he said. 'Anyway, it's only money.'

'Yes, but it's my parents' money, and it's worrying me.'

His merriment evaporated. 'Oh, get over it. You're always worried these days – I don't know why.'

I opened my mouth to explain, but didn't bother. He wasn't listening.

Back at the villa, we settled ourselves on the balcony with drinks. We were all topless, men and women alike. Julie started cutting Niall's hair. It was a sybaritic scene, but I was wondering what was happening to my life.

Julie finished cutting Niall's hair. 'Where's my T-shirt?' she said. 'I'm feeling a bit exposed now.'

'I know what you mean,' I said. 'I always feel like that when I'm on telly. It's weird how my mind goes totally blank when they say, "On air." There's a split second when I'm asked a question and all I can see is black in front of my eyes. It's difficult to explain, it's like—'

'It's like it's time for a beer,' interjected Niall. 'Come on, Bill, Mark, let's go to the café.'

'Why do you always interrupt me?' I asked.

'Because you're always talking about yourself,' he snapped, storming off and slamming the villa door behind him.

My lips quivered. I felt my heart beating fast, as it had before the panic attack. Tears dripped down my face into my glass. I took a gulp. The taste of my tears soured the wine. I nearly gagged, but emptied the glass anyway.

'More supplies?' asked Jenny, trying to cheer me up.

'Oh, I think so,' said Julie. 'What shall we drink to?'

'Fun, prosperity and happiness,' suggested Jenny.

I sniffed into my empty glass. 'Happiness. I've forgotten what that is. Why is Niall always so stroppy with me these days? Is it me? Do I always talk about myself?'

Nobody answered. The only sound was the sing-song buzzing of the cicadas.

'Has it ever occurred to you that Niall might be jealous?' said Jenny, refilling my glass.

'Jealous? Of what?' I replied, my voice rising incredulously.

'Your success, the publicity surrounding your book.'

'I thought he was proud of me,' I replied.

'Oh, underneath I think he is. Anyway, let's not waste time talking about him. Get showered, you two. Let's go to that bouillabaisse restaurant in Gassin. Do you know the Marseille myth behind bouillabaisse? Venus, goddess of love, is said to have first served it to her husband, Vulcan, to lull him to sleep while she cheated on him with Mars.'

'Mars,' I said, 'the god of war! Sounds appropriate to me.'

CHAPTER SIXTEEN

CONCORDE

It is a grey November day and the last envelope I open in a pile of post is sent from Heaven. How would my partner and I like to take part in a supersonic wine tasting on Concorde on its way to Barbados? This has to be the Holy Grail of free-bies. I have always wanted to fly on Concorde, and what a rare treat to be invited on a press trip with one's other half. The jaunt is the idea of Peter Nixon, the then British Airways wine buyer. The West Indies in December seems like the per-fect destination.

Niall and I arrive at Heathrow, hung-over from a standard Friday night in Just William's, our local bar. I look around at my colleagues. Many of the good and the great of the wine-writing world are here. Michael Broadbent, the doyen of Christie's wine department, looks dapper alongside his wife. Fellow freelance journalist Roger Voss has come alone: his wife is too pregnant to fly. 'You should have brought a friend,' I say. 'I had hundreds of people clamouring to come with me – several of my brothers and sisters for starters.' Joanna Simon is here with her art critic husband, Robin. She has been in the game about the same time as me, only she seems much more grown-up. I feel childlike beside her, though we both write for national newspapers and have each had books published. She is pencil-thin and has long, beautifully coiffed straight hair.

We go to the first-class lounge and it is Krug all round. I cannot keep the grin from my face as we mount the steps to the plane. I glance at the other fliers and wonder if they assume we are proper paying passengers. Concorde is quite cramped, compared with flying first class, but it seems pretty good to me as we relax in our plush cream leather seats. Anyway, with three hours and fifty minutes' journey time, who cares about leg room?

Niall and I are laughing. Many of my colleagues are casually reading their newspapers, behaving as if they fly Concorde every day of the week. Over the years I have learnt to contain my excitement, but that always leaves me flat and wanting more, so I tend to drink instead – must be nerves – and today the champagne is flowing. No need to wait for take-off before quaffing a few glasses when you fly Concorde. This Mumm Prestige Cuvée Réné Lalou is superb, a hazelnut in every sip.

We roll down the runway at 175 miles per hour, and as Concorde takes off, the ascent is so steep I feel as if I am on a fairground ride, pinned to the back of my seat. Adrenaline mixed with champagne – fizz to give me whizz – and all before breakfast.

'Ladies and gentlemen, the speed of sound,' announces the pilot. As we pass through the sound barrier, it feels like a car changing gear. My ears experience a supersonic pop. 'Ladies and gentlemen, twice the speed of sound.'

There is lobster on my plate and I have a glass of Leflaive's Puligny Montrachet 1983. I want to get up and dance around the plane, but everyone else is studiously eating or drinking or looking out of the window as if this is no big deal. I am too excited to eat the fillet steak that follows, but not too excited for the velvet-like claret, les Forts de Latour 1982.

So, do the wines actually taste different in the sky? Who cares? However, surprising as it sounds, they do. They taste more mature, especially the clarets. The pressure and restricted oxygen add about ten years to a wine. It softens out the hard tannins that distinguished the wines earlier that morning when we tasted them on the ground. I had thought that if I were paying over £3,000 to fly, I would expect wines with more age. Thank goodness I could detect a difference, otherwise, I wondered – as happened many times in my career – what I could write to justify this incredible freebie?

'Wouldn't it be fun to join the Mile-High Club?' I whisper to Niall. Whenever I suppress my excitement it seems to come out in another way. Once I have a few drinks, I feel reckless, wanting to do something to shock. Niall laughs, but seems more interested in his claret as he chats to Michael Broadbent across the aisle. Typical, talking shop. I feel as if I am his guest rather than the other way round.

'I'll do a reccie,' I reply, wandering off down the plane, bottle in hand. There are only two loos, both at the back. What would Michael Broadbent think if I disappeared into the loo with my husband? I sit down with the claret bottle, pour another glass and stare out of the window. Now I am just as po-faced as my colleagues.

We stay on in Barbados for a week. British Airways pick up the tab for the weekend, and then we spend more on hotels, food and drink in five days than we have ever spent on a holiday, flights included.

On the Saturday morning, lying on the beach at Glitter Bay, Concorde comes across the sky. 'Look! Niall, Alice, there's your plane!' screeches the American on the sun lounger next to me. We have achieved quasi celebrity status on the beach, both for travelling by Concorde and for our capacity for drinking rum cocktails and Red Stripe at the beach bar.

Homeward bound, boarding Concorde for the second time in seven days, we are sun-kissed and laughing. On the outward journey, I had tried to look the part of the wine writer in a linen dress, subtle make-up and styled hair, but now I've gone native and am dressed Caribbean-style in T-shirt and striped shorts, with no make-up and my wind-blown, matted hair not brushed for a week.

Once on board, glass of Krug in hand, I am passed a copy of the *Daily Mail*. I am flicking through it to see the article I phoned through earlier in the week when I overhear the woman sitting behind me.

'Seasoned jet-setters will know there is only one possible setting for this supersonic wine tasting – Concorde,' she says, reading out loud from my piece.

I experience a moment of pure joy. It's rare in a writer's life to see anyone reading your work, let alone be a secret audience when it's being read aloud.

'"Seasoned jet-setters" – that's us, darling!' she chortles to her partner.

It has made her day, and hearing my words repeated makes mine. I am cock-a-hoop. All writers secretly wonder if anyone ever reads their words.

But there is more to come.

Niall asks one of the cabin crew if they have any of the Puligny we had enjoyed on the way out. 'Actually, today we are serving a Chablis from Laroche,' says the hostess. She returns with a glass and another copy of the *Daily Mail*. 'You may like to know there is a very interesting article about our wines in today's *Daily Mail*.'

'I know. My wife here wrote it,' he replies, like the cat that got the cream.

The hostess glances at me, then back at him and laughs, unsure whether to take him seriously.

'I'm not always this scruffy,' I tell her. 'The wines are amazing, don't you think?'

'Oh, I thought he was joking,' she laughs. 'You look about fourteen.'

I smile as she fills up my glass. Recognition from her, the people sitting behind us and Niall. It really does hit the spot. Better than the Mile-High Club.

CHAPTER SEVENTEEN

BABIES AND BOTTLES

In 1992 I discovered I was pregnant while in Sydney, on the last day of a three-week tour of Australian vineyards with a hundred members of the wine trade. We'd made the headlines by drinking the plane dry en route. It was this trip that opened the floodgates for Aussie wine into Britain.

Every vineyard we visited was anxious to outdo the previous one. Jacob's Creek, at huge expense, filled up its eponymous creek with water and took us up in a hot-air balloon to see it. Another producer transported us to lunch in a seaplane. Wolf Blass took us 'yabbie' – cray – fishing. The tastings, parties and beach barbies became ever wilder and more raucous. I tasted and tasted, clocking up over three thousand wines in the three weeks. It was a surprise at the end of it all when the blue line appeared on my pregnancy test – I certainly wouldn't have partied so hard had I known. I had always planned on having children, I just hadn't quite decided when. But after we had got over the initial shock, Niall and I were delighted.

I had an easy pregnancy, not sick once, which was fortunate as I was tasting most days and filming a BBC series with Delia Smith. I also spent weeks in France researching my latest book, *A Bootful of Wine*, written to coincide with the change in the duty-free laws that allowed consumers to bring up to ninety litres of wine into the UK. *GMTV* gave me a weekly slot, the camera angled so as not to show my swelling tummy.

Giving birth was a monumental shock. I had a difficult twenty-eight-hour labour. When my son was finally born naturally, with no drugs or pain relief, everyone in the delivery suite cheered. After I had cuddled him for a few moments, the midwife took him away to 'give him more oxygen'. One of my sisters – a midwife by training – and Niall were there. A bottle of champagne was popped, but I was too weak, exhausted and shocked to drink it.

An hour later, when I had been helped into and out of a bath, I was sitting in a wheelchair when the paediatrician came flying through the swing doors. She was wearing a Spider Man jumper. 'Your baby has just clinically died,' she said. 'We've successfully resuscitated him, but you'd better come and see him now. He might not make the night.'

I had an out-of-body experience. I floated up out of the wheelchair and saw the scene – in black and white, bizarrely – from the ceiling. Niall burst into tears. I saw the woman in the wheelchair comfort him: 'Don't worry, he'll be fine – you'll see.'

At times like this the brain needs no drugs. Survival took over and my mind went into denial, refusing to accept that this situation had anything to do with me. Things like this did not happen to me. These people were not talking to me. They couldn't be. I had never even been in a hospital before.

A day or so later my firstborn spat out his ventilator and began to breathe on his own, giving the first sign of the determined, independent boy he was to become. A real fighter.

Still weak from the effects of the birth, I threw myself into work, determined to prove I could and would be a high-flying, do-it-all mother. At eleven weeks old, my son went part-time to Norland Nursery, conveniently just down the road. For months I would express my milk into bottles for him before hurtling off to London for the allure of other, more potent bottles. Each month for a year I had to take him back to the hospital. They would never tell me what they were checking for, saying such checks were routine for any baby that had been in a special-care unit.

Normally Niall and I went together to the hospital, but unusually I was alone at our son's first-year check. The same Spider Man consultant, in a white coat this time, said, 'I'm glad to report there was no brain damage.' I was so shocked by this that on the way home I had to stop the car and weep. I realised that since the birth I had been holding my breath. Now I could heave a huge sigh of relief – it was safe to love this beautiful child.

That night Niall and I had a special dinner party to celebrate the fact that we had all survived the year. It had been a tough one.

Niall's wine company was having problems. At trade tastings I would overhear members of the trade speculating about his business. I could only stand by and listen and try to be as supportive of him as possible. Once or twice angry suppliers knocked on our door demanding money. I reacted by pouring myself another glass of wine.

Drunken rows between the two of us became the norm. I found myself drinking more, and my tolerance for alcohol became unpredictable. I would be drunk when I didn't think I should be.

Around this time, in 1993, I started writing a twice-yearly supermarket wine guide, *Check It Out*, which involved tasting 2,000 wines and deciding on the top 500 for under £5 a bottle. Pregnant again (my second child was conceived on my first-born's first birthday), I restricted my intake to two glasses a day and things calmed down at home. When I was pregnant, Niall became softer, less competitive and more supportive of my work. Or was it simply that I became gentler, less strident and more cooperative?

My second son was born in early August 1994. Expecting another drawn-out labour, I was almost caught short – I had to cross my legs to stop myself giving birth in the car on the A34! As soon as I put a foot inside Oxford's John Radcliffe Hospital, the midwife took one look at my face and showed me directly to a delivery suite. Reminding her I had planned a water birth, she eyeballed me and enunciated in schoolteacher fashion, 'No time to turn the taps on, dear. No time!' I didn't believe her and was amazed when my second son arrived ten minutes later to the strains of Johann Pachelbel's 'Canon in D Major'. We had barely turned the tape player on. I was even more surprised by my son's shock of red hair, a throwback to the Irish side of my father's family. I didn't dare tempt fate by taking champagne with us to the hospital and so enjoyed the more standard fare – a cup of tea and a slice of toast and Marmite. Four hours later I was bemused to be back at home in my own bed, wetting the baby's head with Krug. Born on a Sunday, this child was indeed 'bonny and blithe'– a joyous bundle, full of gaiety.

I took a few days off, but was soon back at my desk. With a book launch looming, I decided to stop breastfeeding my second son at three months – I couldn't face the thought of leaking breasts at the launch party – and he joined his brother at Norland Nursery.

Soon after the birth of our second son, Niall's company stuttered to a stop. He wouldn't let me accompany him to the fateful meeting, where he faced customers who claimed they had paid in advance for *en primeur* clarets. His toosuccessful PR hype and huge press coverage meant he attracted a high amount of critical publicity across the national and local press. It seemed that customers feared they wouldn't receive their wine. I wasn't involved, but I think there had been an offer of some sort whereby customers could have wine allocated to them by paying an additional amount to the company. Not surprisingly, this created a hostile atmosphere both among customers and the trade. As a result, it was embarrassing for me at trade tastings, but I couldn't avoid them – one of us had to generate some income. Now the major breadwinner, the pressure was on me to earn even more money. My drinking stepped up a notch.

Disillusioned with the wine trade, Niall stayed at home trying to think up some money-making venture. He spent endless hours at the computer. I suggested selling the house to reduce our immediate overheads – we didn't actually need all those rooms, surely – but he was adamant that we shouldn't. He had lost his company and wanted to hold on to his castle. He wouldn't discuss his feelings on finding himself unemployed. I urged him to talk to someone about how he felt – anyone, a professional or a friend – but he refused.

One night, returning home late from London, I found him in front of the Wurlitzer jukebox I had bought him one birthday. His head was in his hands, a glass by his side and 'Don't Give Up' by Peter Gabriel and Kate Bush was blaring out. There were tears streaming down his face.

I took hold of his hand and reassured him: 'It'll be OK, darling. We'll work something out. I'll earn some more money. It will be all right, I promise you.' I picked up his glass and drank it down in one gulp.

CHAPTER EIGHTEEN

'GREAT WITH' WINES

Matching food and wine was a great love of mine and something I was instinctively good at. When I had people round for dinner, I loved to try out combinations, fascinated at how the flavour of the food could alter the wine and vice versa.

A favourite trick was to give guests a glass of a lusciously sweet, sticky dessert wine such as the Rhône beauty Muscat de Beaumes-de-Venise. Sweet wines evoke strange reactions in people. If they have just started to become interested in wine and are moving away from the usual safe medium dries, they turn their noses up at all sweet wines, regarding them as a bit naff. Often I would have to cajole friends to taste a sweet wine at all. Many would politely agree that, yes, it was indeed sweet. Next I would ask them to take a mouthful of an intensely sweet pudding such as chocolate mousse and then re-taste the wine. Amazement all round – the sweetness of the chocolate would cancel out the sweetness of the wine, leaving a delightful, almost bitter-sweet, rich, yet tangy wine that complemented the mousse.

Successful food and wine matching, especially involving trickier foods like asparagus, eggs or anything spicy, is not an intellectual exercise. It requires a hands-on approach. It was music to my professional ears therefore when Tesco asked me to help them with their 'Great With' wines. I can't take the credit for this brilliant and simple concept. That must go to Bibendum's Dan Jargo. His argument was that few people had confidence matching food and wine, so why not do the job for them? The first four wines were labelled simply 'Great With Chicken', 'Great With Steak', 'Great With Fish' and 'Great With Pasta'. Supermarkets were beginning to cross-merchandise and put bottles next to the appropriate foods, making life a good deal simpler for their customers.

It was a fantastic marketing idea, but I was not so impressed with the taste of their chosen wines. Tesco wanted me to write tasting notes for the bottles' back labels and add my endorsement and signature. Already a consultant, I expressed my disappointment at the wines' lacklustre flavour and suggested I take part in the blending and selection process.

They agreed and, as a result, one rainy day I made the long journey from Hungerford to their offices in Cheshunt, Hertfordshire. I went by train because the M25 is best avoided, and besides, I always anticipated drinking at some stage in the day.

Tesco wanted me to find a wine they could label 'Great With Chinese'. When I arrived, the tasting table was piled high with Chinese food – sweet and sour chicken, Singapore noodles, beef in black bean sauce, chicken and cashew nuts, prawn chow mein and the like. We had around twenty or so white wines to try from producers the world over.

Ideally we needed a wine that could deal with the aromatic flavours of Chinese food as well as the chilli used in many dishes. Gewürztraminer from Alsace would be a natural partner, an over-the-top grape that smells and tastes like tropical fruit salad, but the idea behind the 'Great With' wines was to keep them good value, as we planned to retail them at £3.99. This meant Alsace Gewürztraminer was out of reach.

Eventually we narrowed the choice down to a handful of wines, including a sample of another aromatic grape, Muscat. This, together with a crisp, gooseberry-like Sauvignon Blanc seemed the favourites. Both were from the Val d'Orbieu winery in the south of France. Back and forth we went between the food and the wine. I had to drink, not spit, since it's tricky to spit out food. Dan Jargo was happy to settle on either and seemed anxious to conclude the tasting, but I felt that as my name was to appear on the label, the wine needed to be good, something classy that people would taste and remember.

'It needs to be "Great With" – not just "OK With",' I said. 'How about we try blending these two grapes, so we get the floral flavour of the Muscat and acidity of the Sauvignon?'

'Nobody blends those two grapes together,' Dan protested.

'Well, why don't we try? Who says we can't blend the two? Perhaps this will be something new.'

He tipped the two samples into one glass and we tasted it, along with another mouthful of sweet and sour sauce. Anne-Marie Bostock, then head of Tesco's wine team, had now joined us.

Just occasionally in life, I know when to shut up. I didn't say a word.

'This blend is by far and away the best combination,' said Anne-Marie.

Job done. I was delighted and shot a triumphant look at Dan, who scowled, but had to agree.

On the journey home, I reflected that it felt good to have been involved in the creation of something new, to be valued for my expertise, credited for my skill. On reaching Hungerford, I toyed with the idea of going home and telling Niall about my day. Then I pictured him absorbed in his computer.

The lights of Just William's loomed in front of me. I thought I'd pop in for a quick drink and tell Sarah, the landlady, my news. I would be welcomed, visible and – with a captive audience – listened to as well.

*

A month or two later it was Chinese New Year, and friends Jenny and Bill were hosting a Chinese banquet. Jenny, laid-back and generous to a fault, was an inspired cook, while Bill, a white-haired scientist with a mischievous twinkle in his eye, was the perfect host. There were a dozen or so guests, including some people I didn't know. As was my way, I took along several sample bottles from my tasting room – mainly spicy, full-bodied Rhône and Aussie reds, the perfect foil for more robust dishes such as chilli beef and spare ribs.

I thought I'd have a bit of fun so I also took two empty decanters and some bottles of my newly blended 'Great With Chinese' wine. I wondered what the guests would make of the blend, but I wanted them to taste it blind. I knew some would be sniffy about drinking super-market wine, their growing knowledge having made wine snobs of them.

Next to me at dinner was a man I'd never met before who supplied sauces for supermarkets. He'd been to a lunch party beforehand and was already the worse for wear. It was entertaining – and novel – to see someone ahead of me in the drinking stakes. But his attitude and snooty accent annoyed me. I asked him as sweetly as I could what kind of wines he particularly liked.

'The one in the glass in front of me,' he joked, draining his glass and reaching for the bottle of Pol Roger down the table. 'Seriously, though, I only drink wine from reputable merchants – none of your supermarket crap for me.'

'Don't you sell your sauces to supermarkets?'

'Yes, but that doesn't mean I'd drink their wines.'

I went into the kitchen, poured my 'Great With Chinese' wine into the classy, salmon-pink 1920s decanters I had brought along with me and returned to the table with them.

'What's this, then?' he asked.

'That's for me to know and you to guess.'

Turning to the other diners, I announced, 'This is a mystery wine. I'm interested in what you think it is, if you like it, if you feel it complements the food and how much you think it costs.'

Sound of slurping all round.

'I think it's French, maybe from Alsace, and at least ten or fifteen pounds a bottle,' ventured the sauce seller. I smiled encouragingly. 'I can always recognise pedigree in a wine,' he added.

Others round the table offered, 'Australian?' 'German?' 'Spanish?' The rate at which they emptied the decanters suggested they liked it.

Everyone guessed it to be at least £10 a bottle. 'Alice only brings us decent wines,' said Bill, 'she's that kind of gal.'

I went back into the kitchen, grabbed the empty bottles and strode back into the dining room.

'Here – a present for you,' I said to the sauce seller. 'This is the wine. It's three ninety-nine and you can buy it at Tesco. I blended it. Not bad for supermarket crap, eh?'

It works every time. Serve something in a stylish decanter and people think they are drinking an expensive wine. Or could it be that this was a genuinely skilfully blended wine?

'Come on, Bill, what did you really think of the wine?' I asked. 'I know I can rely on an honest answer from you.'

Picking up his glass, Bill swirled it, sniffed it ostentatiously and slurped heartily in a wicked parody of wine tasters like me.

'It's *grrrreat* for getting pissed on,' he pronounced.

CHAPTER NINETEEN

Whirly Pool

It was unbearably hot. Number Two son was in his pram in the garden without a nappy. He was asleep and smiling, helpless but happy. I frowned as I looked down at him. I was helpless and deeply unhappy. My head was throbbing. Perhaps it had been a mistake to down that pint of Stowford Press cider in Just William's at lunchtime. But I had finished my writing for the day and had felt I deserved a break. Anything to escape from the house – and the atmosphere following yet another row last night. Ever since the demise of Niall's company, screaming arguments had become the norm. He wouldn't stop criticising me.

'You can't even put a nappy on properly,' he'd sneered the night before. He wouldn't listen when I tried to explain I had put it on loosely because it was so hot.

'Anyone would think you'd given birth to those boys, the way you carry on!' I'd screeched at him.

Now, a butterfly alighted on the hood of the pram. For a second it flittered around the baby's nose, dusting him with its wings as if kissing him. My second son didn't wake. He just wrinkled his nose and sighed contentedly. The butterfly fluttered off. I wished I could escape so easily. I rubbed my eyes under my Ray-Bans. I felt trapped. The more work I did, and the more money I earned, the more irritable Niall seemed to become.

It wasn't as if I spent the money on myself. Once the

mortgage and the household bills and the – alarmingly high – credit cards were paid, there was little left. We were arguing all the time. The latest cardinal sin had been to put the dishwasher on at night. What was wrong with that?

'Are you completely stupid?' Niall had spat at me. 'It's a fire risk.'

'Don't be ridiculous. Why don't you just bugger off?' I'd responded.

Such was the nature of our exchanges.

The door opened and Niall came into the garden. I tensed. Not more confrontation, please. But he ruffled my hair and smiled. 'Queenie, you haven't forgotten, have you? We're meeting Venice and Steve for a picnic. We're going to have supper in the whirly pool. We'll take the wine in the pram.'

The honeyed, caramel-like aroma of Armagnac hung on his breath. His friendly tone surprised me. Was I supposed to have forgotten last night's row?

The doorbell rang and the babysitter arrived. I lifted the baby out of the pram and handed him to her. 'I expect he'll be ready for his tea now. There's some rhubarb crumble I made last night he can have. Then maybe you can give him a cool bath. It's so hot we're going to sit in the river – it's the only way to cool down.'

Niall began to pack the bottles into the pram crossways, cork to punt. The mattress cover was still warm and wet from the baby's sweat. I stood, hand on hip, counting – two bottles of Ruinart champagne, two bottles of Wairau Rivers Sauvignon Blanc, two bottles of Dujac Morey-Saint-Denis 1978, one bottle of golden-orange Château Rieussec 1976 and a half-bottle of Hine Early Landed cognac.

'Do you think that will be enough?' he asked.

'I thought we were taking the pink fizz.'

'All gone – anyway, this Ruinart is much better,' he replied.

'No, the whole idea was the rosé was to go with the salmon. I think I've got some bottles in my office. Oeil de Pedrix – you know, that very pale, eye-of-the-partridge rosé champagne – will be best.'

I found two bottles in my office wine rack and placed them on top of the Ruinart. Better to have too much than too little.

Opening the front door, we manoeuvred the pram down the steps on to the pavement, bottles clanking. I pushed the pram down the hill towards the marsh. Niall walked in front clutching a candelabra.

As we passed the doctor's surgery, the local midwife came out. 'Ah, taking the baby for a stroll?' she said, peering into the pram.

Niall roared with laughter. 'No, he's at home, asleep. Just going for dinner with friends in the whirly pool.'

'Well, it's a different use for a pram,' she said, shaking her head and smiling.

We walked through the churchyard, the church spire looking like a cardboard cut-out against the cloudless sky. Crossing the swing bridge over the canal, I stopped to catch my breath, sweat trickling down my face. I looked across the fields and saw the river in the distance. A train passed along the Great Western line. This could be a tapestry scene – the quintessential English day. Life wasn't so bad, I told myself. Even Niall seemed in good humour. We arrived at the stile.

'We'll have to lift the pram over,' I said. 'I'll go round the other side and you pass me the bottles. It will be easier then – not so heavy.'

'No, I'll manage,' said Niall, attempting to lift up the pram. 'Christ, you're right, it is heavy. You'll have to help.'

'Just take some bottles out – it's quite simple.'

He glared at me. He was opening his mouth to reply when a man appeared on the bridge with two Dalmatians. 'Need a hand?' He peered into the pram and raised his eyebrows.

Was that a disapproving look? 'Looks like some picnic you're going on. It might be easier if we take these bottles out, don't you think?'

'No!' insisted Niall. 'We can manage it like this.'

After much huffing and puffing, with the pram finally manoeuvred over the stile, bottles intact, we set off again. There were hundreds of yellow flag irises and tiny speckled marsh orchids, but I didn't stop to examine them. I was walking ahead waving the candelabra, thirsty after the trek and definitely in need of a drink.

A white plastic table and chairs stood in the river. The whirly pool was a local beauty spot where the River Kennet gathered in a dip, swirling and bubbling to form a large, natural jacuzzi on its way to the Thames. All the local children used to swim in it during summer. Venice and Steve were already there with Venice's friend Carrie. I grabbed one of the bottles of Ruinart and opened it as I walked along. The fizz spurted out into the river. Venice held out glasses and I filled them up. I kicked off my shoes and sat dangling my legs in the river. My glass was empty within seconds. The fizz was deliciously cold, as cold as the river that came up to my shins. I felt exhilarated.

'You see, champagne *is* the elixir of life,' I said to Venice.

Carrie started doing headstands on the riverbank. 'Ooh, I'm not sure I have any knickers on,' she simpered – not that it mattered, as she couldn't manage to get her legs to stay up.

Buoyed up with fizz, I couldn't resist the challenge. 'Make a triangle with your head and hands, like this,' I told her, as I executed a perfect headstand. I taught her how to cartwheel right-handed, left-handed and finally one-handed, and we cartwheeled along the riverbank until we were giddy. I felt like a child again.

I stopped in midair when I heard a champagne cork pop. 'Come on, back to the serious business. If we're not careful, there'll be nothing left!'

We sat with our feet in the clear water, eating salmon trout with new potatoes, cold asparagus and mayonnaise.

The local mayor passed by with her dog, stopping to accept a glass of Sauvignon Blanc. 'What a good idea,' she said. 'It's wonderful to see people enjoying the marsh.'

Pudding was raspberries served in a bowl made of ice with flowers and rosemary frozen inside it.

'This Ree— Reu— Rieussec is fantastic,' I told Venice. 'Well, *you* try saying that after a few glasses. Look at its glorious colour.' I held my glass up to the sinking summer sun. 'I know – let's float the raspberry bowl, Ophelia-style, down the river!'

I jumped up, knocking an empty bottle into the water, and dropped the bowl into the deepest part of the whirly pool. It caught in the current and bobbed up and down for a few seconds, making a dramatic swirling motion as it was swept away.

'It's out of control! An escaped ex-raspberry bowl being swished this way and that by the current. It's no idea where it's going and we can't do anything to stop it drowning,' I giggled.

'It's not the only thing out of control,' said Steve to no one in particular.

CHAPTER TWENTY

BIRTH OF A MAGNUM

April 1997 and I am lying in the bath, a flute of Krug Grande Cuvée in one hand and my brand-new baby – my third son – cradled in the other. It has always been a dream of mine to give birth at home in my own bed, and now I've achieved it. I am overcome with gratitude and can't stop gazing at him. Just ten minutes old, this baby looks like a fragile bird, with hungry, pouting, thick lips like his father's. The baby is thirsty, gently sucking on my left nipple.

Never has champagne tasted so good. After months of indigestion, when I couldn't even enjoy fizz, the Krug in my glass is the ultimate reward. I am high on adrenaline and can't wait to share my good news with my friends. Catherine, my midwife, pops her head round the bathroom door to check I'm OK.

'My only problem is an empty glass,' I joke. 'Such a shame you are teetotal – this really is delicious. Is there any left, or has the thirsty father drunk it all?'

Niall arrives and drains the remains of the bottle into my glass. 'Sheets in the washing machine,' he says. 'How efficient is that, Queenie?' He ruffles my hair.

'Amazing. I must ring Sarah and cancel our table at Just William's tonight.'

'I'll do it.'

'No, I want to do it – I want to tell her about the baby. Here, you take him.'

He prises the baby from my nipple and our new son looks puzzled as Niall gently wraps him in a soft, fluffy, white towel, complete with hood and little rabbit ears.

I stand up, glass in hand, feeling wobbly. Catherine appears with a huge bath towel, which she wraps round me. When I was a little girl, my mother would cloak us in our towels as if we were royalty. I used to love admiring my 'train' in the mirror. I dry myself, peering at my stretched stomach in the mirror. I hastily cover it up with an old, orange-striped poplin Paul Smith shirt. I climb into bed, lying back on the crisp, laundered sheets, and pick up the phone.

'Mum, it's Alice.'

'And how is Ally Pally?'

'I'm good. And I've got another son. It was fantastic – everything I dreamt about. He's beautiful.'

'Oh, how marvellous, you clever girl. I told Dad to put some champagne in the fridge when you didn't answer the phone earlier.'

'Oh, don't worry, I've already had a glass or two of Krug.'

Next I ring the pub.

'Sarah, it's Alice. I'm afraid I'll have to cancel our table for dinner.'

'That's a shame. I was looking forward to seeing you.'

'Oh, and Sarah,' I add with mock nonchalance, 'I have another son. Come and see him – he's beautiful.'

'That's amazing! It's Al,' I hear her say away from the phone, addressing the bar at large. 'She's had another son.' I hear a boozy cheer from the regulars.

Niall comes in with the baby, hands him to me, lies down on the bed and closes his eyes. 'I'm shattered!' he says.

I wrinkle my nose and snort derisively. *He*'s shattered?

The doorbell sounds. 'Get that. It might be Sarah.'

'What, already?'

A few moments later Sarah comes bounding up the stairs

waving a bottle of Krug. 'I had it ready in the fridge. Well done, you. I can't believe it – we were only chatting a few hours ago. You look fantastic.'

'Thanks. I've had a glass or two already. This giving-birth lark is thirsty work, isn't it, Niall?'

'You look exhausted, Niall,' says Sarah, laughing.

He makes no reply.

'Let's open the Krug!' I say.

'What, now?' replies Sarah.

'Churlish not to wet the baby's head, don't you think?'

We fill our glasses and clink them together.

'So how heavy was he?' asks Sarah.

'Good point. I don't know. We haven't weighed him yet, have we, Catherine? Can we do that now?'

The midwife sets up the scales. The baby seems to be asleep, though his mouth is firmly clamped round my nipple. I gently stick my little finger in his mouth and lever him off. He looks peaceful in his white smocked nightie. I recall with pride the A I got for my needlework O level.

'Six pounds, fifteen ounces,' announces the midwife.

'Ah, the smallest of my three.' A thought occurs to me. 'Catherine, leave the scales out. Niall, get that magnum of Mumm Cordon Rouge, can you, please? It's standing beside my desk in my office.' Catherine raises her eyebrows. 'Don't worry, I'm not planning to drink it. Well, not right now. I just want to weigh it. I'm writing a piece for the *Daily Express* about what wines to take to a friend who's just had a baby.'

Niall returns, clutching the magnum. 'Seven pounds exactly,' pronounces Catherine. 'Almost the same weight as the baby.'

We gaze at the magnum. Sarah, who has no children – just Great Danes – gasps, 'Christ! Glad I stuck to my dogs.'

We drain our glasses.

Another thought occurs to me. 'Catherine, can you measure the diameter of the magnum?'

She reaches into her bag and pulls out a tape measure. 'Almost ten centimetres.'

Sarah looks at me quizzically.

'That's the exact same measurement the cervix has to dilate to before you can start pushing,' I explain to her. 'Every woman who has ever given birth will be familiar with that magic number.'

'Yes, and it's the number that brings tears to the eyes of the men looking on,' puts in Niall.

There's a knock on the bedroom door. The doctor pops his head round. 'The front door was open, so I let—' He stops in mid-sentence and stares. I am in bed holding the baby and an empty champagne glass, while the midwife stands by the magnum still on the scales.

CHAPTER TWENTY-ONE

'ONLY ANOTHER TASTING'

The clock said 8.03 a.m. It was winter 1997 and I was trying to get the boys out of the house. I had Number Three son in my arms and Number One son, aged five, in front of me. 'Where's your brother?' I asked him impatiently. 'I'm in a real hurry this morning. We need to get going. You look upstairs. Perhaps he's hiding.'

I found Number Two son in the tasting room. There were some fifty bottles on the tasting table, all Australian reds. He turned as he heard me open the door. He had a deep-crimson moustache and a glass in his hand. He promptly put down the glass, knocking over another. Red wine splattered over the wall and down his dungarees.

'Grab that cloth over there and come here so I can wipe that wine off you. What were you doing?' I snapped.

'Tasting, just tasting,' he answered in his sing-song three-year-old voice.

'Get in the car and hurry up. I've got a long drive this morning,' I replied crossly, though it was difficult to remain cross with him for long – he was such a funny child with his spiky red hair and mischievous grin.

He skipped out of the door in front of me, laughing, and into the garden. I thought about finding him some clean dungarees but decided there was no time. When I reached the end of the garden, Number One son was nowhere in sight. I heard him shouting from the house. 'Mummy! You've locked me in!'

It started to rain as I fastened my two younger sons into their car seats and hurtled back down the garden to retrieve their older brother.

'Did you forget me?' he asked. 'I was looking for my brother. You told me to.'

'Of course I didn't forget you,' I said, guiltily. 'I thought you were in the garden. It's just that I'm in a hurry. I've got an important tasting.'

It looked as though it was going to be one of those days. I had thrown up earlier, but I put that down to nerves. I was throwing up with nerves a lot in the mornings these days. And to make matters worse, I had a headache. A friend, Jenny, had come round for supper the night before and we had ended up having a bit of a Calvados tasting, under the guise of writing about it. When I'd come down in the morning, there were five or six bottles of the stuff on the breakfast table among the cornflakes. I hadn't realised I'd had so many different types. I had no recollection of what any of them tasted like, let alone which was the best. The least-full bottle was probably the technical answer, I reasoned, as I plonked them in the pantry out of the way.

I still felt groggy and hoped I was all right to drive, though looking at the traffic, I wasn't going anywhere fast this morning. There were roadworks and the traffic was backed up almost to my house. If it was like this here, what would the M25 be like? I decided to drive across the common to the boys' nursery school.

Driving in through the gates, I was already thinking about the champagne tasting I had to do for a hundred of Tesco's wine sales staff that day. How long should I spend talking about each champagne? Would they be the right temperature? Had the tasting sheets been printed? Did they have enough clean glasses, properly polished? A hundred people, six glasses each – 600 glasses. I hoped there would be someone on hand to help.

'Mummy,' said Number One son, 'I've got French today. I can't do French.'

'Nonsense,' I said. 'You can do anything you like in this world.'

'You can't. I can think of at least two things you can't do.'

'Like what?'

'You can't kill God and you can't drill through to the centre of the Earth because it would be so hot the drill would melt.' Perfectly mimicking my voice, he added, 'Well, what do you say to that?'

Here I was, panicking about a champagne tasting and I had a child genius in my car! 'Good call,' I said.

The boys clambered out of the car and I took them to their respective classrooms. I was about to leave Number Two when I realised he still had red wine around his mouth. Hastily I licked my finger and rubbed it off. I had to scrub hard and he whinged. A few other parents gave me looks. What was their problem? I had to stop myself asking one what she was looking at. Some mother was having an interminable chat with one of the Norland nannies. I waited, impatient, looking at my watch. It was eight thirty-three. I needed to get a move on.

'Look, I'm in a real rush,' I told the nanny. 'Don't worry if you think he smells of wine – he does. Just as we were leaving he knocked over a glass of wine in my tasting room and I didn't have time to change him. There are some spares in his bag. Their father will pick them up later.'

I didn't wait for a reply. I simply climbed back into my car and took off down the drive. Thank heavens for nursery school, I thought. The boys were old hands here now. I could remember the first time I had left Number One son here. I was still weak from his difficult birth and frankly terrified of him. Other first-time mums had been crying, but I had felt relieved, looking forward to resuming my normal life. Work certainly seemed the easier, less frightening option to motherhood. I didn't think I had the imagination to be a full-time mother. Besides, with Niall not working since the company went down, we needed the money.

Number One son had started at nursery part-time, but as my work had increased, I had soon upped it to five days. Although we had had an au pair for a while, when Numbers Two and Three sons came along they had joined him – you could rely on Norland to provide consistent care. The extra plus was that with a team of nannies, the boys didn't form an attachment to one person. The downside was that it cost a fortune – £90 a day for three of them – though I reasoned it was money well spent.

The tasting had gone smoothly, I reflected, driving home. Once I'd got going it wasn't nearly as frightening as I'd feared. I had selected six different fizzes and they had all had shown well, neatly demonstrating the differences in taste.

As well as teaching the wine sellers how to taste champagne, I had given them a thumbnail sketch of each variety and described the types of food and occasion each would complement. Everything had gone well. The glasses had been clean and polished. I'd even had a round of applause. They had been responsive, lively and questioning, and had laughed in all the right places.

I smiled, thinking of the one difficult question I'd been asked. There's one clever clogs in every audience and over the years I had learnt how to deal with them.

'Do you think wine number three has undergone a malolactic fermentation?' he had asked.

'Good question,' I replied, groaning inside. I knew all about malolactic fermentation from my days in the champagne cellars in Reims, but hadn't done my homework on this particular wine. Why hadn't I looked up the technical information last night rather than getting smashed on Calvados? 'Off the top of my head, I'm not sure. But since you are so knowledgeable about the subject, perhaps *you* would like to tell us if you think it has.'

The questioner blushed and shrugged his shoulders.

'Tasting it alongside number four,' I went on, 'it appears an altogether softer, less tart wine, so, yes, my guess is that it probably has. Tell you what, leave me your email and I'll talk to the grower and find out,' I concluded, turning to the next person with a question.

'If you had to choose just one of these wines, which one would it be and why?'

This was a familiar question and I gave it the standard joking reply – 'Whichever one is in my glass' – before going on to select a wine. Then I turned the question on the questioner: 'What really interests me is what *your* favourite is. You're the important person here – you have to sell these wines.' Flattery – it worked every time.

Over lunch many of the staff had said how much they'd enjoyed the tasting, and how much easier it was to be enthusiastic and helpful in their recommendations to shoppers when they'd tasted the wines and knew something about them. Audiences were always far more vocal after a tasting than before. While I had conscientiously spat out my wines, I noted many of the spittoons in the room were empty.

The main thing was that the cheque-signing head office team had seemed impressed. I could tell it had gone well when one of the buyers started to discuss which wines we should feature in our next tasting.

Now, I stopped at traffic lights. A woman with short, spiky hair pulled up to my right in a black Mercedes estate. She smiled and I smiled back.

I used to have my hair like that when I was eighteen, I remembered. It wouldn't suit me now. God, those were the days – footloose and fancy-free, no kids, no mortgage, no husband. I watched her tapping her steering wheel in time to the music on the radio. She had a wedding ring on. I bet *her* husband was kind and thoughtful, I reflected.

I grimaced, thinking of the marriage-guidance counsellor Niall and I had been to see. I'd had to plead with Niall to get him there. It hadn't been a success. Both of us were hungover – we probably still smelt of booze. The counsellor had asked us each to make two lists, one detailing our partner's assets and one our own. My list of Niall's assets was twice the length of those I attributed to myself. His was the reverse: his list of his own assets ran over the page; the list he wrote of mine did not reach half a page. That said it all, I fumed. I could be generous enough to see his assets without believing I had many of my own. Why hadn't the counsellor commented on this?

There was another curious thing. Neither Niall nor I had said anything about drinking. It was as if we had an unspoken agreement not to mention it. It wasn't discussed at all.

On the M25, the traffic was at a standstill and the rain was falling ever heavier. At this rate, the boys would be in bed before I got home. I liked to put them to bed, to be able to check they were happy, find out how their day had been. Each night they pleaded for one of my Hungry Giraffe stories – I had invented two brothers, Horatio and Horace, giraffes who were always hungry, who helped people and were invariably repaid in food. I could do with Horatio and Horace's help right now, I thought, as I stared despairingly at the stationary traffic. That was it – I'd tell the boys a story of how the Hungry Giraffes lifted me, crane-like, car and all, off the motorway and neatly home in time for bedtime stories. The boys would always dream up the giraffes' rewards, describing in detail their feasts, often falling asleep as they conjured up ever more exotic and fantastical ice-cream creations.

Home at last, I opened the back door. I could hear Niall

in his office, coughing, but there was no sound of the boys.

'Hi, there,' I said to Niall. 'Good day?'

He didn't look up and carried on at his computer keyboard. 'Yeah, fine. I put the boys to bed.'

'I'll go up and see them, then.'

'No, don't, they'll be asleep. I put them to bed about an hour ago.'

'OK.' I felt deflated. 'Aren't you going to ask me how my day was? How the tasting went?'

He looked up for a second and turned back to his keyboard. 'I expect it was fine. It's was only a tasting, wasn't it? Nothing complicated.'

'Nothing complicated that I'm paid a lot of money for,' I replied, half under my breath. I added more loudly, 'What's that awful smell? I could smell it halfway down the garden. More stock?'

He laughed and took a swig from the glass of red wine beside his desk. 'Yeah, just boiling up the carcass and giblets of the pheasant I had for lunch.'

'Well, it smells to me as if it's burning. Perhaps you better check the bones haven't flown out of the pan.'

He took another gulp of wine and walked past me out of the door. I heard his footsteps on the stairs to the basement kitchen. I picked up the large Riedel glass beside his desk and took a sniff – a good red Burgundy. I took a big gulp. Why did he always open such good wines when I wasn't here? I finished the glass in two more mouthfuls and looked around for the bottle. God, I was tired. I'd been up since 6 a.m. and driven 200 miles. It might have been 'only a tasting' but they always left me shattered, so tired sometimes I could hardly speak.

I could hear pots and pans being banged around in the kitchen. I picked up my handbag and quietly opened the front door. Just William's was ten houses down the road. I walked quickly down the street, and as I pushed open the doors, I could hear the murmur of people, smell rosemary and roast lamb. I realised how hungry I was. I had only played around with my food at lunchtime.

'Hi, Al, how are you? You look smart, all in Armani. What have you been up to? What can I get you?' said Sarah.

'I've been doing a tasting for Tesco – lots of fizz. What I'd really like is a glass of Pinot Noir. I'm gagging.'

'The Edna Valley, then? How many glasses? Is Niall coming?'

'Dunno, didn't ask him. As ever he's tap-tap-tapping on his computer. Actually, I didn't even tell him I'd gone out. Don't suppose he'll notice for a while anyway.'

The Pinot Noir was delicious, one of California's finest, and great value for money. If only I could source a wine with this intensity of flavour that Tesco could retail for about £5.99, but there was nowhere in the world that could produce this richness of fruit at that price.

I looked around the restaurant. It seemed full of laughing couples with seemingly happy lives. Sarah turned to talk to another customer and I felt that familiar feeling of being in a crowd yet alone.

'Penny for them,' said a guy I didn't know, sitting at the bar. 'You look really sad. You OK?'

'Yep, I'm fine. I was just thinking about this wine, actually. It's delicious. You should try it. Sarah, can I have another glass, please?'

It was midnight when I left the pub. The guy at the bar and I had eaten dinner together and shared a second bottle of the Edna Valley, followed by two half-bottles of a luscious, marmalade-like Orange Muscat from Brown Brothers with our crème caramels. I'd talked about my day and he'd chatted about his. He was some kind of engineer overseeing some project. Pretty boring stuff, actually, but he'd seemed very interested in wine – his hobby, he'd said.

Climbing up the steps to the front door, I had to hold tightly on to the iron railings for support. So, so tired. I tried the door handle. It was locked. Typical! How did Niall know whether I had a key?

I felt inside my handbag and grabbed what I thought to be the key. It was Number Three son's silver rattle. I emptied the contents of the bag on to the top step and sat down. I knew my house key was in there somewhere.

A car drove by and tooted its horn. I raised my hand to wave, still holding the rattle, laughing, shaking it. It had a dainty musical tinkle, like Tinkerbell.

I realised with a start that my eyes were closing. God, so tired. Ah, there was the key, stuck inside Number One son's favourite book, Dr Seuss's *Cat in the Hat*. As if on cue, one of our two cats, Lafite – we had christened them Lafite and Latour after the clarets – arrived to investigate.

Another car drove by, blinding me with its headlights. Drunken yobs, I thought. I opened the front door. The hall was in darkness. I felt my way to the stairs, the cat padding along behind me. I was desperate to use the loo and sat down gratefully on the wooden seat, kicking off my high heels, letting my trousers and knickers slide down around my ankles. I could see the moon through the window.

The bathroom started to spin. Losing my balance, I grabbed for the bath to steady myself, knocking my wrist hard. Ouch! That really hurt! The room kept spinning. I felt sick. Stepping out of my trousers, I gingerly opened the bedroom door. Loud snoring greeted me. I climbed into bed.

I awoke to hear the town hall clock striking 4 a.m. My wrist was throbbing – I had broken it, though I didn't know that yet – and I was beside myself with pain, rocking backwards and forwards just as I had during childbirth. Niall snored on. I looked down at my swollen, misshapen wrist.

Only one thing for that kind of pain. Vodka, neat.

CHAPTER TWENTY-TWO

Light-bulb Moment

The door slammed. I stood alone in the music room. The jukebox stood slyly winking at me, one eye blue, the other red. I pressed 111. The machine clunked, the disc was selected, and the crackling sound of a kitsch Hollywood version of 'Ave Maria' came on. I savoured the berry-like taste of the Mad Fish Pinot Noir in my mouth. And then started to cry. 'Ave Maria' always made me cry. I'd told anyone who would listen that I wanted it to be played at my funeral, and right now I felt as if I would rather be dead than face the inevitable. I knew the time had come for surrender. I couldn't go on like this. Something had to change.

I looked down at my dress, an old Moschino favourite – my *Alice in Wonderland* dress, I liked to call it – soft crêpe patterned in roses, big red satin hearts, nipped into the waist, a full skirt cut on the cross, all lined with crimson chiffon. I caught sight of myself in the mirror. By some trick of the light I could see only one half of the middle heart – it was cut in two. How apt.

I was exhausted. A furry, creeping hangover did not help. The second bottle of the St Hallett's Old Block Shiraz the night before had been a mistake, I knew that now, but at the time it had been impossible to resist its spicy, plain-chocolate depths. I always felt as if it gave me strength. That was what I needed now, strength. I felt sick to the pit of my stomach. I realised I had only one course of action.

I had just told Niall that I was exhausted, that I needed a holiday, maybe just a few days away, alone.

'What have you ever done that makes you think you could possibly be exhausted?' he'd sneered.

I'd opened my mouth to reply but then closed it. What I wanted to say remained unsaid: 'Only had three children in five years, been a loyal wife, believed in you and stuck by you when your company failed and the wine trade told me to leave you, earned the odd hundred grand a year to keep us going, loved you with a vengeance.' I stood glaring at him.

And that was it. A cartoon light bulb popped into my head inside a thought bubble. It flashed and in that instant I gave up. I knew I had to leave him, that I could stand no more rows. I was beginning to doubt my every move, my every sentence. I had to get away, otherwise I was going to become madder than the Mad Fish wine in my glass.

I pressed 216 and turned up the jukebox. 'D-I-V-O-R-C-E,' sang Tammy Wynette. I wasn't going to take her earlier advice and 'stand by my man' any longer.

Decision made, I felt strangely elated, but the enormity of the decision I had been wrestling with for months made me extremely thirsty. There was only one thing to do. I went straight to my local and got drunk on dry Blackthorn cider to try to dull the pain and disappointment I felt within.

I knew that the way ahead wasn't going to be easy. The next challenge was to make the proposition attractive to Niall, to make him think that splitting up was his idea. I decided to present it as a marketing plan: neither of us was any good at saving money, we didn't like working in the same house or having an au pair living with us, so why not invest in a separate house that one of us could use as an office? We went away for a few days and I put it to him over a drunken dinner. He fell for it, and by the time we returned and set about looking for properties, he was convinced it was his brilliant idea. Although it was never discussed, I felt sure it would end up being me who moved out.

Until the famous champagne party.

CHAPTER TWENTY-THREE

Fabulous Fizz Party

Avon House was the ultimate party house. Opening the front door, you could be forgiven for thinking you were in a wine shop as wine racks flowed from floor to ceiling in the arched twenty-foot hall. Books spilled out of wooden claret boxes, and flowers drank deep in ice buckets that doubled up as wastepaper bins and spittoons. Off the hallway was my tasting room. This was originally the main sitting room of the house and it retained the original plasterwork-ceiling frieze of moulded vines.

A bay window let in north light – the perfect light in which to assess a wine's colour. The boys delighted in telling their teachers about 'Mummy's spitting room' and laughed, shaking their little heads, when asked, 'Don't you mean sitting room?'

To the far end of the hall was the music room, resplendent with grand piano, the Wurlitzer jukebox and glass doors opening on to a designer, wild yet cultivated garden. Alongside the music room was a long, narrow utility room. This housed all the usual suspects, such as a washing machine and tumble-dryer, but also a wine-bar-sized bottle fridge and ever more wine racks.

Leaning against the back wall of the four-storey house was a much-loved sculpture called *Storm Music*. Originally the trunk of a poplar tree that had crashed to the ground during the hurricane of 1987, I liked to imagine it protected me from the storms without, if not within, for many years. The end was carved to resemble the scrolled end of a cello, and I'd bought it after a solo liquid lunch in Bath as an impulsive birthday present for Niall, once a keen cellist. The sculptor's name was John Jokeas, and given its price tag of £2,000, there were those among my friends who commented that the 'joke' was definitely on me.

A half-basement below the level of the garden housed the kitchen and playroom, which were best in wintertime, when a roaring fire added warmth and colour to this otherwise chilly floor.

The best views of surrounding marshland, the River Kennet, the Avon Canal and St Lawrence's Church were from my office, which was located one flight up from the hall and directly above the spitting room. Here, on this middle floor, was my adored bathroom, which was painted sunshine yellow. It housed an original roll-top bath, which took gallons of comforting steamy water, and tiles adorned with cheery frogs on lily pads kick-started my day.

A few feet away, you stepped into the fabulous main bedroom. Two large windows flooded this room with light and glorious sunshine, which on fine days danced on the bed. Dramatic stripped vertical beams gave the illusion of a room divider where once stud walls had split this stunning space into two rooms. When the boys had been born, these were adorned with over a hundred cards from well-wishers.

The children's rooms were at the top of the house, along with another bathroom. Here, stencilled gold stars encouraged dreaming, and on the same floor, a narrow galley kitchen in the eves was a reminder that in a previous life the house had been converted into flats.

It was an easy house to get lost in. Anyone could do anything in Avon House and no one would be any the wiser.

*

A small hand clasped mine. 'Mummy,' the voice whispered in my ear, tickling my cheek like a breathy feather, 'one of the champagne bottles has exploded – the stopper has flown out.'

I turned over in bed to see Number Two son standing there, strawberry-blond hair sticking straight up like a squirrel's tail. He was looking at me with mock alarm.

'Don't worry, darling. I'll get up in a minute and sort it out. What time is it?'

It was 6 a.m. He slipped into bed beside me. He was soft and warm. 'Mummy, what time does the party start? Can I help blow up the balloons?'

'Oh, yes, the party . . . Of course you can. But it's not until tonight. Don't worry. We have plenty of time.' I looked down at him, his face spattered with freckles – God's kisses, my father use to call mine whenever I complained I didn't like them.

I had an unusually deep bond with my second son. We were almost telepathic and often went to say the same thing at the same time. We frequently knew instinctively what each other was feeling and didn't really need to talk, though we chatted endlessly.

I thought back to when I was about the same age, three or four. I could remember looking down at my red sandals and then into my mother's eyes, pleading with her, 'Promise me you love me the best?'

'I love you all, all nine of you, but in different ways, so I don't love anyone in the same way as I love you,' was her reply.

I lay for a minute, blinking. Had I come to bed late? I couldn't remember coming to bed at all. I remembered talking to someone on the phone, finishing a half-bottle of Roederer Riche demi-sec champagne and then looking for another one. After that it was a blank. What was happening to my memory? More often than not, I couldn't remember going to bed.

Best not to think of that. Guilt made me feel sick, and once I started being sick in the mornings – a regular occurrence – I couldn't stop. Besides, I needed to be on form for tasting. I couldn't afford to throw up. Just fifty more champagnes to taste, I thought to myself, lying there in the half-light. That would bring the week's total up to 300 and mark the end of the major tasting research for my latest book, *Fabulous Fizz*. The call from Anne Ryland of publishers Ryland Peters and Small asking if I would like to write a book about champagne was like asking if the Pope is a Catholic.

I might as well get up and taste them now, I thought. I never regarded tasting champagne as work, however bad my hangover. It was always a pleasure, especially since I'd left the best ones, the vintages and deluxe cuvées, until last.

I could smell the overpowering scent of white lilies long before I reached my tasting room. I had bought them for Niall as a fifteenth-anniversary present. I couldn't think of anything else – what do you buy a husband when you know it's to be the last anniversary you will have together? He had arranged them in a spectacular display with stippled pink foxgloves from the garden. I looked at them, standing up straight and defiant on top of the piano, seemingly mocking me.

Later, the tasting finished, I surveyed the last glasses on the table. The three best wines stood there, bubbling in the sparkling light, calling to me. I knew it was early in the day but what the hell, I'd done my work and it was my wedding anniversary. The least I deserved was a glass of fizz for surviving fifteen years, I told myself, settling down on the squidgy sofa with a glass of Taittinger Comtes de Champagnes Blanc de Blanc 1989 – elegant, rich and creamy. I felt curiously elated. Champagne had that effect on me. I knew I was doing the right thing leaving Niall. Just don't think about it, I told myself sternly. To drown out the chattering committee in my head, I swiftly drained my glass.

The door opened and Number One son stood there, bleary-eyed. 'Can I have some cornflakes? And then can we start blowing up the balloons? I bags the gold ones!'

Both baths in the house were filled with gold and purple balloons and bottles of champagne left over from the tasting. There were bottles of champagne everywhere, in fact – 300 of them, in three fridges and in a big cast-iron bath outside in the garden. Having a party to dispose of them seemed an obvious solution. It would have been sacrilege to tip them down the sink. I looked out from the bedroom over the candlelit garden and sipped a glass of Schramsberg Napa Valley Rosé Cuvée de Pinot 1994 – a sensational wine with a curious hint of raspberries, peaches and cinnamon. I pulled my slinky Umani Ronchi black dress over my head. Number Two son was sitting on the end of the bed. 'Mummy,' he said, sounding shocked, 'you haven't got any underwear on.'

'No,' I laughed. 'You can't with this dress – it would show.' I pushed up my breasts, which were held in place by a thin piece of silver chain, which joined up the dropped deep-cowl neck of the dress. Not bad for having fed three children, I thought. Now, which shoes? Number Two son chose a pair of gold and silver strappy Charles Jourdan sandals. The heels were so high it was tricky to stand in them. I teetered around in front of the mirror, careful not to let the narrow heels disappear between the cracks in the floorboards.

'Do I look OK?' I asked. He nodded his head.

The doorbell clanged and I set off downstairs to let in the first of the guests. The house was strangely quiet, as if awaiting some momentous occasion. When I opened the door, I noticed that the sky was a strange shade of translucent grey. There were smudgy rain clouds in the distance.

I greeted our guests. 'Help yourself to a bottle – they're all over the house and the garden. Glasses in the tasting room. Enjoy. And I shall expect a full report later on all the bottles you've tasted.'

'What style!' said Bruce, a dentist friend. 'Normally you get given a glass – here, it's a bottle.'

Next to arrive were two men from our local Chinese take-away van, bearing woks and prawn crackers and ingredients to cook Singapore noodles for a hundred. More people came streaming in through the door. The jukebox started pounding. Every few seconds or so I'd hear the pop of another champagne cork. Some of the guests I barely knew. I assumed Niall had invited them. A dozen or so handed me happy-anniversary cards that I promptly abandoned, unopened, in the hall.

One of my younger brothers, Francis, disappeared upstairs to the top kitchen in search of the best bottle I'd stashed in the fridge. I caught him on the stairs armed with Perrier-Jouët Belle Epoque 1990 in its distinctive art nouveau painted bottle.

'Ah . . . definite aroma of violets,' joked Francis.

'My tasting notes exactly. But to be sure, I'd better sample it again.' I held out my glass.

The doorbell clanged again. I adjusted my dress, yanking up my boobs. I opened the door to Maria José, one of my Spanish friends whose family produced Viña Tondonia Rioja. Her arms were full of crimson peonies, which she thrust into my hands.

'Come upstairs with me,' I told her. 'I've hidden the best wines in the top fridge, reserved for family and favourite winemakers.'

'I can't wait to taste them!'

'Oh, there's no serious tasting going on here – everyone is simply drinking.'

At the top of the house, I peeped into the boys' room. The two younger boys were there, but there was no sign of their elder brother. Roxanne, the nanny, was reading a book.

'Fancy a glass of fizz, Roxanne?' I asked, pouring out three glasses. 'This is Iron Horse 1996, one of California's finest.'

'What shall we toast?' asked Maria. 'Ah, look – it's called Wedding Cuvée, that's appropriate – isn't it your wedding anniversary?'

I looked away. 'No. Let's toast the success of my book,' I replied.

We raised our glasses and I downed the spicy, red-berry-like fizz in two neat gulps. For some reason I was left with a nasty taste in my mouth.

'Drink up and I'll find you another one, Maria. Let's try this – Veuve Clicquot's top cuvée, La Grande Dame 1990. This has to be one of the most complex fizzes I've tasted. Grab a glass of this, come down to my office and I'll show you some of the photographs for my book. It's so exciting – ten books and finally one that's going to look amazing. Peter Cassidy – the photographer – has done a fantastic job. When I saw the photos, I actually cried with joy. And I don't do that very often these days.'

On the top step, I almost lost my footing, my left heel catching on the edge of the carpet rod. As I stumbled, I kept hold of my glass, but the contents cascaded down the banisters to the ground floor. Somebody looked up and squealed.

'The best champagne and it's gone over their heads,' I shouted down the stairs, pleased with my private joke. This whole party was that – a supposedly happy occasion, champagne flowing. A sham, I thought. If only they knew. Not that any of them would truly care.

'You OK?' asked Maria. 'You look really sad.'

'I'm fine,' I lied. 'Look at this cover picture.'

I heard a kerfuffle outside and looked down from my office window into the street. Two people were having difficulty leaving, climbing into a car and straight out of the other side. Bill, my scientist friend, was wandering down the middle of the road, bottle in hand, kicking his legs up and bawling 'New York, New York' along with the jukebox. He was out of time with the music.

A strange, detached feeling washed over me once again, as if I wasn't really there – as if I were simply an observer, watching this madness going on around me.

On my desk stood more abandoned bottles. 'Pelorus 1993 – now, you need to try this one, Maria. It's a really rich, unusual, biscuity wine from New Zealand. Look, we're in luck – there's enough left for two glasses.'

Maria José was laughing. 'How do you do it? I mean, drink so fast and stay standing, especially in those shoes?'

'Years of practice. Come on, come downstairs and have some noodles and meet some other people. Niall's around somewhere – though I've not really seen him all night.'

The ground floor was buzzing. There were people everywhere – sitting on the stairs, draped around the banisters, dancing in front of the jukebox. Someone was playing the piano, and someone else lay underneath, bottle in hand, twitching in time to the music. I picked my way across the dance floor to the pulse of 'Le Freak' and picked up a few empty bottles. Through the garden door I could see the evening primroses, now open, a strangely fluorescent yellow in the candlelight. There were bodies and bottles strewn around. I stopped to chat to a group of people sitting on the *Storm Music* sculpture.

'Hey, Al, have you tried this one? It's from Lorigan, I mean Oregon, Willamette Valley. I'm having difficulties saying that,' said Tim, Niall's brother. We were drinking partners and soul mates who shared some unspoken link that led us on several occasions to telephone each other at exactly the same time.

'Of course I've tasted it, you twit, that's why we're having the party, because I've tasted them all. But, well, I had better taste it again, just to refresh my memory. Ah, yes, this is the one that tastes like liquorice fizz. It would be good with the Singapore noodles. Have you had any?'

'Two platefuls. Hey, Al, some of your friends are outrageous – especially that Scottish girl in the green dress with her tits all on show, the one with the stud in her nose. Music teacher. She keeps offering blokes mouth-organ lessons.'

'What do you mean, mouth-organ lessons?'

'Come on, use your imagination – you're the writer. Anyway, no one, to my knowledge, has been stupid enough to take her up on it. Mind you, I don't know where she is now.'

'Come on, let's dance. Hey, Maria José, it's Madness – "One Step Beyond". I love this record!'

Some hours later I was doing my Leaning Tower of Pisa impersonation, beginning to feel weary and woozy. Not that I felt that drunk. I had taken it easy because I didn't want any scenes with Niall. I hadn't seen him all night. He seemed to be keeping out of my way. The fizz was beginning to wear off and I felt flat. Although many of the guests had left, there was a hard core of a dozen or so dancers and various bodies floating around.

'Can't find any more fizz,' moaned Bruce.

'Try the basement fridge. Or right down the garden.'

He lurched off.

I climbed the stairs up to my office, stepping over two or three people on the way. My office door was closed and the room was in darkness. I sat down at my desk and swivelled round on my chair. Looking at the window, I could see light over the church – the sun was coming up. I had been up for twenty-four hours. I needed to go to bed.

I stood up, lifted my dress over my head and opened the door. Looking straight ahead, high heels still on, I took the two steps across the hall to the bedroom. As I was about to close the door, I noticed someone sitting on the stairs.

'Sorry,' I said, 'I didn't realise anyone was there. Hope you didn't see my stretch marks.'

'I wasn't looking at your stretch marks,' came a man's slurred voice as I collapsed on to an empty bed.

CHAPTER TWENTY-FOUR

THE MORNING AFTER

The next day I was woken at eleven by snoring. I poked Niall and tried to wake him. He was out for the count.

Pulling on a short denim skirt and a spotted silk T-shirt, I opened my bedroom door. Empty champagne bottles lay around like scattered skittles. Glasses, streamers, deflated balloons and cigarette ends littered the stairs. A bowl of forgotten noodles perched precariously on the banister.

'Good party,' said Roxanne.

'Was it? I'm not sure. God, look at all this mess. What time did the boys wake up?'

'We came down about seven thirty. I made them pancakes for breakfast.'

Roxanne and I made our way down the two flights of stairs to the kitchen, the champagne battlefield becoming more treacherous with every step. Number Three son pulled at my leg. I bent down to pick him up and almost toppled over.

'You OK there?' asked Roxanne.

'Just thirsty. I could do with a can of Coke.' About to open the fridge, I spied a half-full bottle of Bollinger left on the high chair. What a waste. There were no clean champagne flutes in sight so I poured myself a tumbler. It was lukewarm and barely fizzy, but one gulp cleared the fuzziness in my head. I laughed – an alcoholic Alka-Seltzer.

Bleary-eyed guests carrying empty bottles were emerging from rooms all over the house. I saw one guy I didn't recognise at all. Where had he come from? No matter. It was time to go to the pub for brunch – the clearing-up could wait until later.

Wandering down the road, I bumped into an old friend, Wendy. People often mistook us for sisters. We settled in the pub garden, me with my customary Sunday bloody Mary in hand, to discuss last night.

'What an amazing party!' she said. 'I've never, ever seen so much fizz or so many people drinking so fast. It was a full moon – perhaps that's what drove people into such a frenzy. We didn't leave until seven. We met the paperboy!'

'You lasted longer than me,' I said. 'I went to bed about four thirty. Were there many people left at seven, then? Was Niall still up? He was fast asleep this morning. I couldn't wake him.'

Wendy looked at me and hesitated. 'I don't know how to say this . . .'

'What?'

'Well, he was still up. . .'

'There's no surprise!'

'He was in the hall when we left with that Scottish girl – the mouth-organ woman – and . . .' She stopped, blushing, her eyes wide.

'And what?'

'She was giving him a blow job. Right there in the hall, just outside his office.'

I choked on my bloody Mary. '*What*? Are you sure?'

'Alice, I couldn't miss it. I had to walk past them to the front door.'

I emptied my glass and stared in disbelief. I locked away my anger and outrage and began to laugh manically in shock. 'Ye-e-esss! There *is* a God! I've got Niall now! I told him we were splitting up and now I'll get to stay in the house. Bloody hell! Well, I'm blowed – if you'll forgive the pun. This definitely calls for another drink. Large one!'

The following morning, Monday, Niall and I overslept. We still hadn't spoken about what had happened. Our youngest son was in bed with us. I was suddenly awakened by a knock at the bedroom door. My eyes felt as if they had been massaged with grit. It was difficult to focus. It was Number Three son's nanny. She started gabbling and I had to concentrate to keep up.

'Good morning. So you survived the party, then? Wow, some party – we had a ball. Thank you so much. You sure know some wacky characters. Who was the lady with the diamond stud in her nose, the one in the green dress with her boobs spilling out – she seemed to be having a good time?'

'Well, she certainly gave me a good time,' said Niall. 'She gave me a blow job in the hall,' he continued, smirking across at me.

The nanny's eyes widened and she looked at me uncertainly. I shrugged my shoulders. I heard myself laugh, a high-pitched squeal as if I'd inhaled helium. There was a second or two of silence. The baby stirred, nuzzling his head into my breast. I could feel my heart beating fast.

'There are two bottles of milk made up for him in the drinks fridge,' I told her, handing her the baby.

I escaped to my office and busied myself with a VAT return. Nothing like numbers to concentrate the mind – a fire door against troublesome thoughts. Come lunchtime, Niall poked his head round the door. He was dressed in a double-breasted Yves St Laurent suit, his standard hangover outfit. 'I'd like to take you out to lunch to apologise for embarrassing you,' he said, looking boyish.

'You didn't embarrass me, you embarrassed yourself,' I said, raising my eyebrows and looking down my nose at him.

'I'm not sure I want to have lunch with you.'

But I knew we needed to discuss what had happened away from the kids so we went anyway, taking a taxi to a pub in the next village – in fact the first pub Niall ever took me to. He ordered a bottle of Barratt Hills Australian Pinot Noir. I ordered potted shrimps and played around with them. The tiny shrimps looked helplessly trapped, drowned in the yellow clarified butter. I knew how they felt.

After ten minutes of silence I asked, 'Why did you do it? How could you? Do you think that was acceptable behaviour, you who insisted on putting "fifteenth wedding anniversary" on the party invitations, even though I asked you not to? It was luck, not judgement, the children didn't catch you at it. They came downstairs minutes later.'

He took a large gulp of his wine. 'Just get over it,' he sneered. 'I don't really see what your problem is. We're splitting up anyway, so what's the big deal? Typical of you to make such a drama.'

I'll give you typical, I thought. I stood up, picked up my glass of wine and poured it over his head. Grabbing my handbag, I marched out of the pub and across the road to the train station. Waste of a decent glassful, I thought, as I stalked on to the London train.

Two days later I caught the train home – sober. I had been retching almost continuously, literally sick to my stomach. I felt like a fish that had been gutted but left alive, twitching on the riverbank for passers-by to gloat over. I'd had my mobile phone on voicemail, avoiding the humiliation of admitting to more friends and acquaintances that, yes, the gossip was true.

How would I hold my head up in Hungerford again? If someone had chopped off my hand the word 'hurt' would have appeared in blood, running through my wrist like letters through a stick of rock.

CHAPTER TWENTY-FIVE

LADY BY THE LAKE

A week after the party Niall and I were invited to lunch at our old friends Debbie and Steve's. We were putting on a brave face for our children while we tried to sort out the details of the separation. Debbie was petite, self-effacing and vivacious, and Steve was super-bright with a penchant for dressing up like Freddie Mercury at fancy-dress parties. We had all known each other for years, as Niall's mother had looked after their sons. Debbie and Steve had seen Niall and me at our best and worst, and we enjoyed many a good bottle with them at home and on holidays in Ireland and Spain. I envied their relationship – passionate yet tender, just how ours had been in the very early days.

On this Sunday we ate outside, lunching on barbecued chicken, tomato, basil and onion salad with balsamic vinegar and potato salad dressed with black pepper and chives from the garden. Sludgy summer pudding followed with whitecurrants and blackcurrants. We were drinking Beaumes-de-Venise.

'It's amazing how the wine seems to taste of raspberries,' said Debbie.

'Yes,' I agreed. 'Niall, do you remember we used to drink gallons of this the first summer we met? We would barbecue trout and eat it with salad and Stilton. I was so impressed – we always had champagne to start, and the odd bottle of red and white in between, and would finish with bowls of raspberries and huge glasses of this in bed. I'd never tasted Beaumes-de-Venise before I met you.'

He looked at me glassy-eyed. A chalk-blue butterfly landed on the table. 'Look, a chalk-blue,' he said.

Was that all he could say?

There was an awkward silence.

Steve stepped in. 'Niall, come and see my new car.'

Glasses in hand, they walked over to the gleaming green 7-Series BMW. I looked up as I heard Niall's familiar laugh. 'Love the registration,' he chortled. 'BJB – that's me, Blow-Job Boy! I presume you've heard how the party ended.'

A look of horror crossed Debbie's face. 'God, how can you bear it?' she hissed at me. 'How can you even speak to him? Come on, let's make some Pimm's and take it down the garden.' I followed her into the kitchen.

'I don't like to think about it,' I told her. 'It hurts so much. But I'm trying to tell myself that it's all worked out in my favour, as now I'll get to stay in Avon House. I'll have to pay him off, but I think it's settled. He appears quite chuffed that the whole town seems to know. He seems to have told everyone. Sad, isn't it? Fifteen years of marriage, only to end like this, in public humiliation.'

Debbie was furiously chopping apples. 'You have all those rooms and he chose to do it in the hall. Almost as if he wanted to be seen. It must have been a shock for those leaving, drunk or not.'

'Well, I was going to leave him anyway. This just served to sharpen my resolve.'

I suggested we strengthen the Pimm's with a slug of vodka. I found a bottle of Stolichnaya and poured about a third of the bottle into the jug. Adding ice cubes with raspberries frozen inside them, I realised I had overfilled it.

'We'll have to sample it – just to make room, you understand.'

I poured out two tumblers. We each took a drink and

Debbie screwed up her face. 'Wow, that certainly packs a punch. It's made my eyes water.'

'I could do with packing a punch right now. OK, all we need now is the borage.'

'We'll go down by the lake. You grab the glasses and we'll pick it on the way.'

Steve and Niall had disappeared. The air was warm as we walked down to the lake, the setting sun a deep, deep red.

I felt numb inside. Since the party I couldn't seem to stop drinking. I felt drunk after just one or two, but then I felt worse, not better. My tolerance to alcohol seemed to be low. My tolerance to everything seemed to be low. I felt as if I was operating outside my body, that all this was happening to a stranger.

'What a beautiful sky,' said Debbie. 'How would you describe that shade?'

'Blood red. Angry red.'

We settled down at a white plastic table by the lake. I added the borage flowers to the Pimm's and poured out two more glasses. I thought back to all the Sundays Niall and I had spent together in the early days. We had been young then, in love. What had happened? Where had all the feeling gone?

'What shall we drink to?' asked Debbie.

'Freedom.'

I took a big mouthful and closed my eyes. How was I going to tell my parents I was leaving Niall? How would I tell the children? I couldn't bear the thought of their crumpled little faces. Was I right to give up? I had never given up on anything in my life. But this wasn't a life. It wasn't good for the children. It wasn't good for me.

When I opened my eyes, Debbie's chair was empty. I closed my eyes again and dozed.

A shadow crossed in front of me. I opened my eyes again to see a woman walk past. She was taller than me, with dark-blonde hair cut in a bob. She was dressed in an olive-green raincoat, belted, with the collar turned up. I shivered and the hairs on my arms stood up. Was I seeing things? I closed my eyes once more and then half opened them. The same thing happened – the same woman. But as soon as I blinked, she was gone. I turned round and looked back to the house. No one in sight. What was going on? Was it the Pimm's? Was I that drunk? I topped up my glass and sat there glugging it.

Debbie returned with a bowl of pistachios. 'You OK? You're as white as a sheet.'

'I can't believe my own eyes. I know we've been drinking all afternoon but I've just had the strangest experience. A woman with dark-blonde bobbed hair, dressed in an olive-green raincoat just walked past me. Twice.'

Debbie stared at me. 'That's Anne,' she said quietly.

'What do you mean, Anne? Anne who? Where is she?'

'My friend Anne. Her husband murdered her when she tried to leave him. We often used to sit here and drink Pimm's. She loved Pimm's. We were sitting here the night before he stabbed her. Did she say anything to you?'

'No, nothing. She didn't even look at me. I must have dozed off and when I woke up she was here. She disap-peared. I closed my eyes and when I opened them she did it again. This is weird!'

We sat in silence, the sun sinking lower, the sky like a blood-stained shroud.

I blinked. There were tears in my eyes. 'It's a sign,' I said. 'I think she appeared to tell me to have the strength to leave Niall. Only this afternoon I was wondering if I would have the courage. It's a sign. Do you really think that was Anne? Is that what she looked like?'

'Definitely. She loved it down here. Sometimes I would find her sitting here, when she was alive, looking out over the marsh.'

'And she died doing what she believed in, trusting her heart.' I drained my glass. It was becoming difficult to keep my eyes open.

CHAPTER TWENTY-SIX

Even Old Wines Die

There is nothing quite as seductive as the taste of the Pinot Noir grape. It's difficult to grow but a delight to drink. A bit like a man – hard to train but, hopefully, worth the wait. I was drinking Pinot Noir the night before Niall moved out.

After seemingly endless delays – the lease on his rented house wasn't right, the removal men were busy, the phone lines couldn't be changed in time, he had important meetings to attend – the removal van was scheduled to arrive one rainy midwinter Saturday morning.

I had spent the evening before in the pub, propping up the bar, drinking copious amounts of Edna Valley. I have no recollection of how much I drank or who I bored with my story. I do remember coming to on the hard, lumpy futon in the spare room, where I had been sleeping alone ever since the week after the champagne party. I found myself holding my breath. Would he really move out today, or would there be more excuses?

I got up, tiptoed down the stairs and peeped into the boys' room. They were all fast asleep. Number Three son was wedged sideways in his cot. No matter how many times I turned him over, he would flip back and lie on his front, knees tucked under him, nappy-clad bottom stuck in the air. I covered him up with his ABC duvet and stood looking at him for a while.

Outside the bedroom, I paused on the landing. Little over

a year ago I had crossed this landing from my office to my bedroom, just minutes before giving birth to him. Today, I could hear Niall's snoring from behind a firmly shut bedroom door.

I was halfway down the stairs when I sensed someone behind me. I turned to see Number Two son's pixie-like face grinning at me, his strawberry-blond hair static and sticking up at right angles as if he had back-combed it.

'You're up early, Mummy.'

'Yes. Lots to do. Daddy is moving to his new house today.'

'Oh. I'm hungry. Do we have any Sugar Puffs?'

'Look in the pantry,' I replied.

'I can't get in there, it's full of boxes. Is Daddy taking all the food?'

'Of course not.'

'Why does Daddy call the pantry a larder?' he asked innocently.

'I don't know. Look, here are the Sugar Puffs.'

We cleared a space on the kitchen table. He aimed the Sugar Puffs packet at his favourite Aladdin bowl, scattering cereal across the table. He stopped with the milk bottle in midair.

'Which house will my bowl be in?' he asked.

'You can keep it here if you like. I'm sure we can buy you another one for Daddy's house.'

'I doubt we'll find one the same. They're very rare, you know,' he replied, solemnly.

I turned away and stared at the cooker, avoiding his eyes. He took his bowl of Sugar Puffs off to eat in the playroom. On the cooker was a huge saucepan full to the brim with stock. The fat had risen to the surface and partially solidified. It looked like crazy paving. A lamb bone was just visible, surrounded by grey scum.

My stomach turned. Niall and his foul stockpots. But now there'd be no more mornings of having to come down to this. No more questions from guests as they came into the house: 'What *is* that smell?'

I picked up the pan and tipped the contents down the sink, watching the slimy liquid slither down the plughole. I knew this was sacrilege. Niall had sulked for weeks when our cleaning lady had mistakenly thrown away his precious stock. I washed the saucepan and fished the nasty debris from the sink, feeling queasy. I was drying the pan when I heard his familiar cough behind me. Guiltily, I placed it on the back of the cooker and busied myself clearing up the scattered Sugar Puffs. He went straight to the cooker.

'Where the hell has my stock gone?'

'Down the sink,' I replied. 'I thought you'd need the pan.'

'You stupid cunt! I was going to take it with me!'

I winced at his use of that word. I'd made the mistake of telling him that this one word was the worst possible insult for a woman. 'I can't see what your problem is,' he'd said. 'It's simply an Anglo-Saxon word. Look it up in the dictionary.'

A huge white van pulled up in front of the kitchen window. The cavalry had arrived. Good old Andy, the man with the van, always smiling and used to moving the great and good – and the not so good – of Berkshire. It was reassuring to see his good-humoured grin. 'What terrible weather,' he said when he came in.

I set about making tea, filling the kettle and placing it on the ring next to the empty stock pan.

Number One son peered round the door, took one look at the chaos and headed straight for the playroom, shutting the door behind him.

'Well,' said Andy, 'we may as well start down here.'

I escaped upstairs and watched from the boys' bedroom window as the packing cases were loaded into the back of the van, my vision distorted by the rain streaming down the windowpane. I turned round and caught sight of my reflection in the mirror on the far wall. I still had red horns above my mouth from last night's wine. Why had no one told me? I rubbed furiously at the corners of my mouth, smearing the stain into the grotesque shape of a clown's mouth.

Number Three son was stirring. I changed his nappy and put him back in his cot, handing him a book. He threw it back at me and bounced up and down. I lifted him up and lay down on the bed, cradling him. I wanted to close my eyes and drift off to sleep – to block out reality, go back to Pinot Noir wonderland – but, no, the chances were there'd be nothing left in the house if I did that.

My son started a loud, hungry cry. I'd have to face the kitchen again to get him some milk. I trudged down the steps with him in my arms. In the kitchen, Niall went to take him from me.

'I'm just going to give him some breakfast,' I said, shoving the baby into his high chair. The baby beamed and began banging a toy brick. I snatched a favourite cup from Niall as he went to take it. 'You're not taking that! That was a present from my mother.'

A toy brick came flying across the kitchen table, knocking the cup out of my hand on to the floor, smashing it. Niall smirked.

Andy reappeared. 'The van's virtually full,' he said. 'We'll get going.'

Number One son was standing by the door. 'Can we go with Daddy to see his new house? Please, Mummy?'

'I suppose so, if Daddy says it's OK.'

They got into the car, ready to follow the van. I closed the door before they'd left and climbed the stairs to our old bedroom, which was mine again now Niall had gone. The bed was unmade and there was a dirty shirt on the floor. A half-empty glass of red wine stood abandoned by the bed on top of a French cartoon comic, *Fluide Glaciale*. I pulled the sheet off the bed and lay down on the bare mattress, pulling the duvet over my head.

*

I opened my eyes, blinking with confusion. My cheek chafed on the bare, stained mattress. It was dark outside. It took me a minute to work out that it was five in the afternoon. I reached to switch on the light and almost knocked over the glass of red wine. I picked it up and drank it. It tasted oxidised.

I ran a bath, adding two capfuls of bubble bath, and climbed into the huge Victorian claw-footed tub. The house was silent. The door creaked and in stalked Lafite, the cat. He stretched, arched his back and lay lazily down next to the hot-water pipe, one eye half open. 'Surprised he hasn't taken you too,' I muttered.

Tired, I closed my eyes. I had expected to feel elated, but I felt flat, and strangely hollow. My eyes and throat were sore. My throat was often sore from early-morning retching.

I'll go over to my dad's, I thought. Mum's away and I can cook him supper. They lived in Devizes now, which wasn't too far to drive.

I looked at the picture over the bath – an illustration by Karen Ludlow I'd bought from the *Guardian*. It was called *This Year's Fashionable Accessory* and depicted women with babies made into handbags, headdresses and fastened like pets on leads. I thought of my three boys. Accessories to the crime of a broken home. I recalled Tina, the one girl in my class at junior school whose parents were divorced. Everyone had looked down on her. Now my house was a broken home. I gazed down at the floorboards, studying the one that was split, with the hole that all three boys loved to post things into – pennies, hairgrips, shampoo-bottle lids, bubblegum, pebbles. I had once caught Number Two son feeding tangerine segments into it.

'Bro-ken ho-mmme, bro-ken ho-mmme,' I repeated out loud. The cat looked at me. I shivered. The skin on my fingers was white and shrivelled. Time to move on. What should I wear? 'What *does* an about-to-be-single mother wear?' I asked Lafite.

It was pouring with rain as I stomped down the garden to the garage. I climbed into my MX5, switched on the headlights and the frog-eyes popped up. I jabbed a tape into the player. Kid Creole and the Coconuts came on – 'Annie, I'm Not Your Daddy'. I stopped the car at the end of the road. I couldn't see where I was going. I wiped the inside of the windscreen and realised with surprise that I had tears streaming down my face.

'This is ridiculous,' I said to the night. '*I'm* divorcing *him*!'

I unzipped the roof and folded it down. Devizes wasn't far. I already had mascara running down my face – I might as well go the whole hog. Pulling a baseball cap over my dripping hair, I screeched away, narrowly missing a car that seemed to appear from nowhere.

What was my dad going to say? He and Mum had been married for over forty years. As good Catholics, they didn't believe in divorce.

I had some fillet steak with me for supper and some boiled new potatoes I could fry. There would probably be some frozen peas in the house. My father could not cook at all; it would be good to make him a hot meal.

As I neared the Avebury roundabout I was dazzled momentarily by the lights of the Wagon and Horses. I toyed with the idea of stopping for a drink. No. I'd get something far tastier at my father's. I indicated for the Devizes exit, but at the last moment decided to carry on round the roundabout towards Avebury. As the stone circle came into sight, the full moon came out. Christ, the whole world would be mad. I slowed down as I neared the centre of Avebury. A leather-clad biker roared past, tooting his horn. I smiled and waved back. Perhaps life wasn't so bad.

Kid Creole and the Coconuts came to an abrupt stop and Classic FM automatically clicked in. Dvořák's 'Cello

Concerto' swelled from the speakers. This was the first piece Niall ever played to me, the first weekend we had spent together. I swallowed hard and swiftly switched off the radio, nearly yanking off the knob. I turned the car round and set off towards Devizes.

When I arrived, I turned into the gravel drive. Dad was standing at the door waiting for me, his beard looking whiter than I remembered it. I realised my legs were wet as I walked into the house.

'Hi,' I said, reaching over to kiss him.

'Yuck, wet, wet, wet. You're soaked. How come?'

'I drove here with the roof down. It's OK, I didn't get cold – I had the heater and the music on.'

'You nincompoop! You've got black all down your face.'

'It's only mascara,' I replied.

'Take your wet jacket off and come and sit down.'

In the kitchen, he looked at me. 'How did it go?'

'It went. He went. And the boys have gone to look at the new house. I need a drink.'

'OK, hold your horses,' he said, taking a bottle of Heidsieck Monopole champagne from the fridge. Ready on the table were two Georgian champagne glasses. 'Maybe not very appropriate, but I expect you could do with a glass of this.'

'More than just the one. Cheers. Not sure what we should drink to . . . Ooh, that's delicious. It tastes old, honeyed, like dried apricots.'

'You and your dried apricots,' he laughed. 'You'd better go and dry your hair. Do you want to go out for an Indian?'

'No, I've brought some food to cook, your favourite – fillet steak and fried potatoes. Any frozen peas?'

'I expect there are some in the freezer. I'd better find something decent to drink, then.'

'This will be the first meal I've cooked in years. You know how precious Niall was about cooking. And you know what, Dad? I can't think of anyone better to be cooking it for.' My eyes welled up again. 'Have you heard from Mum?'

'She called last night. She was in Hong Kong, calling from the Jockey Club, no less. She said the day's examining had gone well.'

I found the griddle and heated it up. A drip of water from my hair splashed on to the surface and sent a globule of fat spitting on to my hand, burning me.

'Shit, shit, shit. Sorry, Dad, it's really hot.'

'Run it under the cold tap straight away.'

'It's OK. How do you want your steak cooked?'

'*Bien cuit, madame.*'

'*D'accord.* Hey, Dad, I've got the leaky glass again. Thirsty work, cooking.'

Steak, potatoes and peas plated up, we sat down at the kitchen table.

'Here, try this,' he said, handing me a glass of red.

I studied the reddy-brown colour. What had he unearthed? No one in the family knew what he had in his seemingly bottomless cellar. Magician-like, he would produce bottles at family parties that none of us had ever seen .

'This smells amazing.'

'Might be a bit over the hill. Taste it.'

I took a taste. This was seriously old Burgundy, rich and sweet with a flavour of ripe red cherries and a hint of sweet pipe tobacco. I was transported back to my dad's study in Norwich, age five, watching him light his pipe.

'It's Echezeaux 1949, Bouchard Ainé, of course. Don't tell Mum we drank it. She'll be cross she missed out.'

'It's fantastic. What a treat. Where do you stash all these beauties?'

'That's my secret,' he replied. 'My steak is just right. *Très bien cuit, ma petite.*'

'Refreshing to know I can cook, after all.' I took a deep breath. 'Dad, I know Niall and I splitting up is really diffi-cult for you and Mum, but—'

He held his hand up. 'Hush. Drink your wine. It's fading fast. Be quiet and just drink it.'

We chinked our glasses and solemnly drained them, sitting in silence, looking at each other.

'Even old wines die, Alice,' he added gently.

My shoulders started to shake. Tears splashed down into my glass.

CHAPTER TWENTY-SEVEN

LIFE IN THE FAST LANE

Newly separated, and after that wet drive to my dad's, I rekindled my love affair with my sports car, which I'd bought years earlier. No matter that it was a two-seater and I now had three children.

As a child, I grew up in Cringleford outside Norwich and lived one door away from Colin Chapman of Lotus Cars. On Sunday mornings one of my brothers and I used to go to the Lotus test track. We often watched Graham Hill and other drivers whizzing round in the latest Lotus prototypes. More exciting still was to be allowed to sit in the passenger seat for a lap or two. Speed and terror mixed with adrenaline – I was hooked as a little girl.

It had taken over twenty years to achieve my ambition and buy a sports car of my own, which I did with the advance for *The Hamlyn Atlas of Wine*. Back in August 1989, when I'd bought it, before the boys had been born, I hadn't been able to afford a Lotus, and although I had wanted to buy a British car, the new MGs had yet to be made, so I'd settled on a bright-blue Mazda MX5. My sports car was the only new car I'd ever owned and when I brought it home I'd thought I'd arrived.

The car became a feature in our lives. As soon as he could talk, Number One son christened her 'Little Blue Car', which quickly became shortened to 'LBC'. If, when putting the boys to bed at night, I asked them what treat they would like the next day, a favourite reply was, 'A ride in LBC with the lid off, Mummy.'

Now single again, and without my children half the time as Niall and I had agreed on joint custody, early-morning drives in LBC were the perfect remedy for sleepless nights and hangovers. A quick burn-up allowed me to start the day with a smile rather than self-pity.

It was on one such day that I was invited by Gérard Basset to Hotel du Vin in Tunbridge Wells. We had been having email discussions on the possibility of me tutoring some tasting dinners. Off I zoomed.

Gérard Basset is one of my favourite Masters of Wine. He is also one of the most talented blind tasters I have ever seen in action, but modest about his astounding ability. As I arrived, I was starting to congratulate him on the success of his hotels when he stopped me in mid-sentence.

'I've long been a fan of your writing and your books,' he told me.

Flattered, I didn't know what to say. I was moved by his kindness. Why couldn't I have fallen in love with a man like this?

We sat in the sunshine and spent the morning comparing our favourite producers, wines and grape varieties. To meet someone who shared my passion but in such a gentle, un-assuming, uncompetitive way touched me. But lunch was purgatory.

'What would you like to try – anything from the list?' he asked.

Here I was, looking at one of the best lists in the country, knowing that in an hour or so I had to drive home, because I had to pick up the boys from nursery at six o'clock.

We settled for a glass of non-vintage Pol Roger White Foil, a favourite of us both. I had described this in *Fabulous Fizz* as 'liquid sex in a glass'. We concurred on this spurious tasting note. On that day, drinking it on the sunlit terrace, the earth certainly moved for me.

We followed the Pol Roger with a glass of sensational white Burgundy, Montrachet La Garenne 1995, from one of our favourite producers, Etienne Sauzet. I savoured this beauty, revelling in its rich, buttery flavour. It was nectar and I had to be reminded to eat the salmon in front of me. I was far more interested in the wine. My mind and my body craved more.

Declining another glass, repeating that I had to drive, I felt close to tears. I must have looked bereft. Gérard signalled something to the waiter. Over coffee and a Montecristo No. 4 cigar, the waiter returned with an unopened bottle of the Montrachet.

'This is for you to enjoy with a friend when you get home,' said Gérard. I tried to decline, though not too hard. I allowed myself to be persuaded.

Driving down the M4, roof down, hair flying, I speculated as to when and with whom I would drink this Montrachet. I could still taste it. The motorway was busy. I was in the outside lane, barrelling past the Reading exit, when suddenly the engine died. I pushed my foot down on the accelerator – nothing. My life flashed in front of me. I hadn't written a will. Who would look after the boys? Why hadn't I brought my other car, the battered old Mercedes estate? If I was going to crash, that was the car to be in. Was I going to pay the ultimate price for being a poser in a soft-top? That would teach me. Except it wouldn't. I'd be dead.

I tried to indicate, but all the power had gone, including the electrics. I looked in the mirror. The motorway was full behind me. I couldn't come to a halt in the fast line – that would be fatal, and not just for me.

I took a deep breath and steered the rapidly slowing car across two lanes of traffic, coasting across the cross-hatching by the exit road, and came to a halt near the grass verge. I closed my eyes and waited for the sound of a crash. None came. There must be a God! I had hit no one and no one had hit me. Miraculously, a gap had opened as I free-wheeled off the motorway.

I got out of the car. I had no idea what to do next. I looked down at myself and realised I must look pretty odd standing next to the motorway, dressed in a long, black Moschino dress slit to the thigh. I opened the boot to retrieve my cardigan and cover myself up – well, at least the top half.

A car pulled up behind me. Out stepped a good-looking man with green eyes and wavy black hair. He was wearing overalls covered in splatters of paint and had a canvas work-bag over his shoulder.

'Are you all right?' he asked.

'I've broken down and don't know what to do!'

'Well, let's push your car off the road before anyone crashes into it.'

He lent me his mobile to ring the RAC. By this time I was shaking uncontrollably from head to foot. He agreed to wait with me until the RAC arrived. Luckily, they were quick. The fanbelt had gone – I would have to wait for a tow-truck to take me home.

'Will you stay with me?' I asked, pleading with my best little-girl-lost eyes. 'Just until the recovery truck gets here?'

'OK. But I better phone the missus to say I'm going to be late,' he replied.

We climbed back into LBC, which was by now in a lay-by. He told me about his day at work, I told him about mine. It was 5 p.m. but the sun was still hot. Once I had stopped shaking, I realised I was thirsty.

'Have you got anything to drink, like water, in your bag?' I asked.

'No. I've got a mug, but that's not much use, is it?'

I opened the boot to see if there was any water in there. I spotted the Montrachet. I picked up the lukewarm bottle.

'Do you like wine?' I said. 'This is one of the best white Burgundies in the world.'

He laughed. 'You're not going to drink that now, are you?'

'Why not? I haven't got to drive any more. It's gone five o'clock and we could be waiting for some time. What's more, I'm thirsty!'

I fished my corkscrew out of my handbag. I never travel without a corkscrew.

He looked on as I swilled out his dirty tea mug with wine and filled it up.

'Cheers!' I said. 'Thanks for stopping to help me.' I took a slurp from the mug. Even at this temperature, the wine tasted sensational. 'Try this – great wines have to be shared.' I slurped down the rest of the wine and refilled the mug for him. 'I thought I was a goner,' I said, feeling light-headed. 'Hey, have you got a light?'

He nodded and I retrieved the remains of the Montecristo. We sat there in silence for a while, passing the mug of Montrachet back and forth, surrounded by a cloud of cigar smoke and listening to the noise of the traffic passing by. I wondered what Gérard would think of me now. Not quite the setting for drinking this fine wine he had in mind.

'The trouble is,' said my new friend as the tow-truck pulled up, 'I don't think my missus is going to believe that I stopped to help someone, when I get home reeking of expensive wine and cigars.'

CHAPTER TWENTY-EIGHT

PRINCESS ON THE LOOSE

One of the first things I did after the divorce was to buy a new bed. It was huge – six and a half foot square, the kind with two bases screwed together topped by a monster mattress. Such a bed required entirely new linen, of course, and I delighted in buying fine white Egyptian cotton sheets, duvet covers and square French pillows. It was cleansing to discard the washed-out, grey shrouds of my marriage.

When the boys were at home, a bed this size was perfect. They would clamber up in the morning, the eldest hauling up the youngest, and all three would fall asleep, one on either side of me and one across the bottom. The four of us had enough space to dance the fandango in our sleep.

But when the boys were with Niall, where they lived on alternate weeks, I felt hopelessly lost in it, as if its vast, virginal expanse was mocking me. After extolling the virtues of being able to sleep star-shaped, I soon found myself sleeping curled up in the foetal position, comatose and unmoving, on the right-hand side of the bed, able to slip out in the morning leaving no need to make it.

Alone in the bed on yet another evening, nothing but a bottle of Tasmanian Pinot Noir for company, I decided it was time to christen my new bed. It wasn't the sex I missed; it was cuddles I craved.

I'd been tempted to play away from home on many a drunken press trip, but I'd always managed to extricate myself at the last minute – sometimes literally – from any compromising situation.

For years I'd had a friend I knew fancied me. We had spent a lot of time together, drunk many a black velvet together, and just about managed to keep our relationship platonic. He was up for new bed-testing, accompanied by the perfect jug of black velvet. I opted for Murphy's over Guinness, as it's slightly sweeter. Generally I would blend it with a cheaper fizz like cava, though on this auspicious occasion a bottle of the full-bodied, creamy Charles Heidsieck definitely hit the spot.

Going to bed with him was an eye-opener, not least in the exciting and tender lovemaking. It made me realise how angry I'd been about the treatment I was subject to in my marriage. It was the first time for a long while I could make love without feeling anger towards the person I was in bed with. For years I had only ever made love drunk. True, I wasn't exactly sober this time, but I wasn't blind drunk either. It also felt good to be in bed with someone I knew genuinely cared for me, actually liked me.

But there was to be no happy ever after. My friend had other fish to fry. Still, having got the deed over and done with, I was keen to do more research and didn't obsess about him. I took a friend's saying – 'so many men, so little time' – a touch too literally. Having been practically a child bride, I felt I had much catching up to do.

Match-making friends were happy to try to oblige. One introduced me to the secretary of one of London's traditional gentlemen's clubs. We went out to Little Havana in London's Leicester Square. It's amazing how rum lubricates conversation and salsa dancing. Later, back at his flat, I remember laughing out loud when I saw that his several pairs of polished Church's shoes were kept in shape with old-fashioned wooden shoetrees.

I've always been untidy, so 'Shoetrees', as I christened

him, was good for me, with his prep-school, military-like air. He gently replenished some of the self-esteem that had been eroded in my marriage. In the six months we went out together, I loved having doors opened for me and being called 'gorgeous'.

Shoetrees was a good cook and loved fine wine; but – even more gratifying nourishment for my damaged ego – he was impressed by my knowledge. While fairly clued-up himself, he didn't attempt to compete. While I was with him, my propensity for compulsive, angry drinking seemed to mellow. I think it was his simple kindness that did it. I managed, just about, to remain compos mentis at his work functions – Henley, Ascot and the like. On the occasions we did have wild, drunken evenings with friends, I would be amazed that the lectures I was used to on the following morning never materialised.

When Niall remarried less than a year after the divorce, Shoetrees was there for me. He was kind and unassuming with the children. A semblance of calm returned to my topsy-turvy household. He maintained, however, a fairly distant, hands-off approach – novel for all-or-nothing me.

After I had a foolish, brief, drunken diversion with one of his friends, he declared his undying love for me. But in my heart of hearts, I knew he wasn't right. I was bored, missing the drama to which I was accustomed. After a tasting trip to Australia I came home, arranged to meet him, spent the afternoon drinking and met up with him on full drunken, fighting form. He saw red and that was the end of Shoetrees.

On my own again, I started going to the pub more often and drinking even more. I would go out 'for a glass' and stagger home several bottles later, bleary-eyed. One Saturday I went down to a local hotel on the pretext of watching the rugby. In truth, I was lonely and depressed. I looked around – smug, smiling couples everywhere. I frowned into my glass of Chilean Merlot. What was wrong with me? Why was I the ugly ducking sitting by myself in the Three Swans? Things would be so much better in my life if I had a man. Wouldn't they?

'You don't remember me, do you?' said a voice next to me at the bar. I had noticed him drink two pints of Stella in the ten minutes or so it had taken me to finish my large glass of red. 'I rescued your son's kite out of a tree on the common last summer, then fell out of the tree and broke my ankle.'

I turned to look at him. Younger than me, suntanned skin, dark, spiky hair and speckled green eyes. 'Best buy you a pint to thank you for your trouble, then,' I said.

We drank the afternoon away, returning to my garden at around eight. He was impressed by the grandeur of Avon House – most people were – and even more impressed when he spied the hundreds of bottles of wine racked up in the hall and the tasting room. We sat in the garden watching the evening primroses unravel, marvelling as they cast a fluorescent light in the dusk. I'm convinced they have strange properties.

I had never had a toy boy before. As we finished a magnum of champagne, going to bed with him seemed as natural as opening the next bottle.

He lasted five months, long enough to help me move house and make a dent in the wine cellar. He was great with the kids, often picking them up from nursery while I propped up the bar in the pub. I think that – for a while – I fell in love with him. But after kissing him so much, he seemed to turn back into a frog. Back to the lily pond he went.

Lying in my huge bed, alone again with nothing but a bottle of fizz for company, it came to me – I would have to kiss a lot of frogs before I found a prince. He was not to be the last.

CHAPTER TWENTY-NINE

NAIL BOMB

I had only popped into the supermarket for tampons, rushing for a train on my way to London. Then I saw them. For a second I froze like a rabbit in headlights. It was the boys – *my* boys, *my* children – with their new stepmother.

She was holding my youngest in her arms. In her *arms*. The other two boys were laughing and joking with their new stepbrother and sister, lobbing a monster pack of Walkers crisps into the trolley, as I rounded the end of the aisle.

I stood there in my black leather Versace minidress and knee-length black satin boots, my Lil-lets in my hand. They stopped dead.

'I'm off to a party in London,' I mumbled. 'I'm in a rush for the train. See you at the weekend, boys.' I turned and marched towards the cash desk.

'Ooh, Mummy, love the bows on the back of your boots – especially the yellow ones!' shouted Number Two son.

I carried on walking, took out a crumpled fiver from my purse, paid for my tampons and left without turning round. I marched towards the station, blinking back the tears that threatened to cascade down my face and put paid to the sparkly make-up on my cheeks.

I felt robbed, raped of my rights. I felt my stomach contract in the familiar spasm. At the station, the large glass of white wine I'd had an hour earlier came up, the acidity burning my throat as I vomited over the platform. My breath was smoke-like in the crisp winter air. A man in a pinstriped suit looked away, embarrassed. How could I go to a party feeling like this?

I boarded the train. As it moved off, I heard an approaching rattle of bottles. I looked up and saw a steward pushing a drinks trolley. I vaguely recognised her. She smiled at me. 'My, you're looking fine,' she said in her sing-song Jamaican accent. 'Any teas, coffees, drinks for the party girl today?'

'Ah, the cavalry. A large gin and tonic, please. I've just had a bit of a shock.'

'Ice and a slice?'

I unscrewed the Gordon's miniature and poured it into the plastic cup. Mother's ruin. 'Better leave me another one,' I said, fishing a tenner out of my bag.

'More tonic?'

'No, thanks, no need. I need it strong. I need a direct line to my heart.'

I gulped it back, the bitter juniper flavour coating my raw throat. I felt my stomach contract again but swallowed hard, crunching on a piece of ice. I gazed at the flocked seat facing me. The word 'bitch' was scrawled in felt pen on the plastic headrest. It swam, magnified in the tears in my eyes.

The train trundled on, jerking to left and right. Black and white movie stills flashed through my head. Their new stepmother – younger than me, a vague acquaintance, a striking Indian girl with long hair. Bumping into her in the pub. Commiserating with her about her toy-boy husband, who had run off with a younger American model. Laughing about our newfound singledom and getting drunk together. Returning to Avon House and drinking bottle after bottle of wine. Dancing to Tammy Wynette's 'D-I-V-O-R-C-E'. Lying on the floor together, weeping in front of the jukebox. Me handing out tissues, jokingly telling her to watch out – as a single local women, Niall was bound to come sniffing around. Me confiding the financial nitty-gritty of the divorce. Another storyboard memory – returning from holiday in Spain, picking up the boys from the nursery, Number Two son asking, 'Mummy, why was Daddy in bed with that Indian lady?'

I put my gin and tonic down, realising that I was crushing the empty plastic cup.

It was the ultimate betrayal. All right, I had wanted the divorce. But in my book there were certain places you didn't go – and that included bedding friends' ex-husbands. Up until that moment, though, I'd never actually considered her role as a stepmother, cuddling *my* babies.

Nothing can prepare you for the sight of an uninvited woman playing mother to your children. It is beyond jealousy. It punctures the soul with the intensity of a nail bomb. It makes your womb ache, your heart ache and reaches parts of your psyche that have no name or recognised form. It taps into the primeval urge that makes childbirth bearable and openly laughs at it, making a maternal mockery of its role. Logic plays no part – it is a feeling that all is not right with the universe, that someone has spilled the quantum soup.

I felt the rage rising in me as I neared London. I knew only one way to quell it. I left Paddington, exited into Spring Street and headed straight for the Jingle Boy, one of the Davy's chain of wine bars. I ordered a glass of champagne – Laurent Perrier Brut NV – and drank it in two gulps. The dry, apple-like fizz rasped the back of my throat.

'Leaky glass again. I guess I better have another one – and one of those Cohiba cigars,' I said to the barman.

'You celebrating something?'

'Nope, commiserating.'

I finished my glass and headed downstairs to the loo. I looked in the mirror and saw black smudges around my eyes where my eyeliner had run. I looked like a panda that had been in a train crash. Best repair my face. Shame I can't do the same for my heart, I thought, as I applied kohl.

Another two glasses later I realised I was running late and took a taxi to Jermyn Street. Bob was there, sitting waiting for me. I had met him at a Tondonia Rioja tasting shortly before Niall and I had split up. I had been amazed that he should find me interesting, attractive even. We were mates rather than lovers. He had just split up with his wife. We would compare notes and suggest coping strategies to each other. I would cry on his shoulder and we'd drink good wines together, both relieved that we shared many seemingly irrational emotions. It was gratifying to find I was not alone with those.

The evening's dinner and party was an attempt by Bordeaux producers to convince the wine press that affordable claret had a place in the market. But the wines on our table were mean, ungenerous, tart and austere.

'I don't want to drink this crap, do you?' I said to Bob. He had been attempting to shush me ever since I'd arrived. Fortunately, as I was late, we had been put on a separate table for two, so I didn't have to make small talk with colleagues. One walked past me and waved, heavily pregnant with her first child. Bet she wouldn't have to go through the gut-wrenching feeling of seeing another woman with her children, I thought bitterly.

'Come on, let's go. I don't want any pudding anyway, do you?' I said.

We took a taxi to his appartment in Farringdon, a stunning loft conversion in an old silk factory with twenty-foot windows. I would often stay there, regularly turning up the worse for wear, raging, late at night. But once inside Bob's flat, I felt calmer. He was kind to me, never shouted, and would always find me a bottle of something decent that I'd drink until I passed out. He would put me to bed or cover me up with a blanket. I could never explain to him how this unconditional tenderness stirred something inside me that made me cry late into the night.

'I'll get a bottle of the 1978 – perhaps that'll make you feel a bit better,' he said.

I gulped it back, the flavour of soft cherries and sweet vanilla ice cream mixing with the salt from my tears, numbing my throat and my thoughts.

'They are my boys, *my* boys. MY BOYS, goddammit!' were the last words I remember saying.

It was still dark when I left to catch the train home at seven the next morning. The air was cold. As I hailed a taxi, I noticed once again that my breath made vapour trails in the air. I was surprised I could breathe at all, surprised that life was still, somehow, simply carrying on around me.

Sitting on the train, my head throbbing, I opened my notebook and wrote:

> *So there I was in Somerfield*
> *With a box of giant Lil-lets in hand*
> *When I came across my little boys –*
> *Who the hell had that planned?*
>
> *Has it ever occurred to her*
> *What that might do to my heart?*
> *Having to witness another woman*
> *Playing my own special part?*
>
> *It was tearing at my heartstrings*
> *I couldn't bear the sight*
> *Of my three stolen sons.*
> *I wanted to down bag and fight.*
>
> *Instead I focused on the party*
> *And I looked straight ahead,*
> *I talked and drank and laughed*
> *And wept later in my bed.*

CHAPTER THIRTY

Pick Me Up

It was 4.30 a.m. and I had only the Groucho Club night receptionist for company. London was dead – no late-night partygoers, no cars, just the rain in the empty streets. I thought of my bed with its crisp, clean sheets and knew it was time to go home. I'd been here for days, setting out to go home at least once but only getting as far as a pub in Paddington.

The only way to get from Soho to Hungerford at this time was to take a taxi. The Groucho's taxi company, Dallas Cars, was used to me. I was loading my bags into the car when a man came walking down Dean Street.

'It's crap,' he said. 'Central London and nowhere to get a drink.'

'Yes,' I agreed. 'I guess a hotel would be the best place now. Even the Groucho bar closed two hours ago.'

'So where are you going?' he asked.

'Home. I've been here for days. It's always the same. I come for a day and end up staying for three. I've had enough of London.'

'Perhaps I should come with you.'

'Well, you can if you want, but it's seventy-five miles away.'

He climbed into the taxi. We sped away. In the streetlight I glanced across at him. He was beautiful with grey-green eyes. What is it about men with green eyes? I felt disorientated. Normally, Dallas Cars sent a Mercedes. Tonight they had sent a people carrier. It felt very empty. I glanced behind at the empty row of seats and wondered where everybody else was. My boys could fit in there easily. I supposed they were asleep at their father's now.

Best not to think about that. Too painful.

I was sitting directly behind the driver on the middle row of seats. My Soho hitchhiker was sitting at the other end, leaving a polite gap in between. I studied the velour back of the seat in front of me. It was difficult to focus after all that vanilla-flavoured vodka earlier. Whose idea had that been? Gingerly, I reached out my hand and stroked the fabric against the pile, creating a darker shade of grey.

I looked across at my passenger. 'You are delicious,' I said.

'Don't say that, it frightens me.'

I closed my eyes and went to sleep. It was daylight before we reached home.

As I opened the front door I could see the jukebox winking at me. I must have left it on.

'Is that really a Wurlitzer?' my companion asked. They were the first words he had spoken in over an hour.

'Yes. I bought it years ago.'

'Do you have to put money in?'

'No,' I replied, laughing. 'Not unless you have an old two-bob bit.'

He studied the records and pressed 101. Glenn Miller's 'In the Mood' filled the room, the richness of the sound permeating my skin.

'My mother learnt to dance to this,' I said. 'Would you care to dance?'

As we danced, we were dazzled by dawn sunlight reflecting off a copper-sheeted picture. The strobe effect made me dizzy, giddy with excitement. The music stopped and he followed me into the hall and down the steps to the brick-floored kitchen.

'Can I have a cup of tea?' he asked.

'Of course.' I made lapsang souchong and served it in my favourite green dragon Coalport china cups. He drank his quickly. I drank quickly too, burning my mouth, watching him. That would put paid to tasting for a while, I thought. But, then, I didn't have any tasting to do. I hadn't written anything for months. Where had all the work gone?

He was looking around the kitchen. 'Can we drink that?' he asked.

'What? Give me a clue – there are hundreds of bottles in here.'

'That bottle of champagne, there on top of the apothecary's chest.'

'Impressive. You're the first person I've met who knows what that piece of furniture is. I've been looking for an excuse to open that bottle of Veuve Clicquot La Grande Dame 1985 for some time. And you've just provided it.' I put the bottle in the freezer. 'Madame Clicquot would turn in her grave. She was an It-girl, you know, way ahead of her time.' I suddenly realised I didn't know his name. 'What's your name, Soho Hitchhiker?'

'Sean,' he replied.

'You look like a James to me.'

I climbed two floors up to my office, leaving him reading Kafka's *A Hunger Artist*. I was hungry myself, come to think about it. I couldn't remember the last time I'd eaten. There were twenty-seven messages on the answering machine. I felt my stomach tighten. It was bound to be trouble. I was always in trouble. Best not listen to them. Tomorrow would do . . . except it *was* tomorrow.

There was a miniature bottle of Kummel on top of a huge pile of unopened post on my desk. I unscrewed the top and the smooth, sweet aroma of caraway filled the room. Such a dinky bottle. I drank, feeling the spirit hit the back of my throat. My chest felt less tight and my heart rate seemed to slow as I swallowed.

I went back downstairs, took the champagne out of the freezer and opened it. 'Such a tone on that gentle hiss,' I said. 'Bit like the sound men make when they come, don't you think? This champagne is definitely as good as sex.'

He laughed. He was staring at me intently. He stuck out his tongue and started panting like a dog. 'Well, are you going to pour it or just hold the bottle?' he said. 'I'm very thirsty.'

I poured it out into Georgian champagne saucers. The tiny bubbles danced as they shot up the hollow stems. Looking down into my glass, I noticed the bubbles swirling together into a furious whirlpool. The perfect pick-me-up – especially with a Kummel chaser.

'These are fantastic glasses,' he said, as we clinked them together.

'Yes – apparently modelled on Marie Antoinette's left breast.'

'Well, she must have had small boobs,' he replied, laughing.

I sat down on my favourite cane chair draped with a real antique leopard skin.

'That leopard skin, is it real?'

'So many questions!' I laughed. 'I'm not sure I know what's real any more. Drink your champagne. This is seriously special stuff.'

'Can we drink it in bed?'

'Which of the spare beds do you want to drink it in?' I asked, looking at him with an amused grin.

'I'd rather drink it in yours, preferably with you in it as well.'

I laughed. 'Fair enough. Follow me.'

I led him up the stairs. I took off my clothes and dropped them as we climbed. I was wearing new yellow Lejaby lingerie I'd had to buy in London because I'd not taken enough underwear with me.

We climbed into bed. He leaned on one arm and gazed at me. He had sandy-coloured stubble poking through a sprinkling of freckles on the side of his face. His nose was slightly turned up.

'What exactly do you do?' I asked him.

'I pick up women like you in the middle of the night,' he said, refilling my glass.

When I awoke, he was gone. A champagne cork was placed dead centre in the middle of the pillow.

CHAPTER THIRTY-ONE

SUNDAY, BLOODY SUNDAY

My arrangement with Niall to have the children one week on, one week off suited me at first. In my head, I told myself it was like going on a press trip. I reasoned this would mean I wouldn't miss them too much. After all, travel was a normal part of my life. I was often away. But the reality hit me a few months in. A press trip revolves around being entertained and meeting interesting new people. Weekends home alone sat heavy on my heart.

To begin with, I convinced myself that I was a single thirty-eight-year-old with the world at my feet every other weekend. 'Fill your diary,' advised friends who longed for such freedom. But the novelty soon wore off and I grew to dread 'bloody Sundays', as my state of mind deteriorated and I failed to invite people to stay or organise places to be. I lacked the confidence to produce the elaborate meals I'd once presented as a matter of course. More than half of me – my boys – was absent every other weekend, and it hurt deep down in a place I didn't know how to reach.

Sunday soon became the day I would go to my local pub and pontificate about the components of the perfect bloody Mary (having had them for breakfast) to anyone who would listen. Inevitably this led to a session, usually followed by a few bottles of wine back at the house. I always shared them around – I didn't drink alone, did I? Other waifs and strays became my Sunday playmates. Sometimes we would cobble together some sort of Sunday lunch. Every script involved the wine flowing freely.

As my new Sunday pattern emerged, visiting friends and family was out of the question. One drink and I couldn't drive anyway. By late afternoon I would be ensconced in a mantra of 'Poor me, poor me – pour me another.' One Sunday I phoned the Samaritans. They listened patiently to my drunken ramblings.

How had it come to this? This hadn't been the life plan.

Monday morning. Dim flashbacks were playing in my head. I had been on the phone. Talking to . . . Who had it been? Ah, yes, the police. Oh, my God. The *police*? Judging by the empty bottle of Absolut by my bed, I hadn't been sober. What had happened? Why had I been talking to the police?

Memories started crowding back. I had dropped the boys off at their father's – the 'other house'. It had been full of large brown cardboard boxes. When I asked what they were, he told me they were to do with his new line of business.

I heard disquieting hints around town and asked a couple of mates to browse on his website. I wanted to know, even though I didn't want to face the reality. A glance at his website, Eros UK, left me feeling uneasy and queasy. And I am no prude. 'Eros Bodyglide lubricant – probably the longest-lasting condom-safe lube' was one product. OK, I thought, I can handle this. Rather a waste of Niall's fine brain, but, hey, nothing to do with me.

I continued looking down through the product range and an involuntary shudder went through me. Dildos, condoms, fetish toys, escorts, bondage tape, hair remover, plugs . . . Plugs? Oh, yes, of course.

All absolutely fine for consenting adults, the logical side of my brain said. But my drunk, illogical brain went into overdrive at the thought of all these things lurking in brown cardboard boxes in a house with children. It was just before

Christmas, when children are inquisitive. I had grotesque visions of my boys sneaking around opening vibrating boxes, confronted with giant dildos.

This new business was not one operated in private either. Ever the publicist, Niall was shouting it from the rooftops. It seemed the mothers in the school playground knew more about it than I did.

'I hope you don't think Niall's business is anything to do with me,' I told a neighbour of his.

'Oh, I use the bondage tape on my cat,' she laughed. 'It's a bit of fun, you know.'

I couldn't see the funny side. I ranted to some of the other mothers, who asked me what my problem was. Wasn't he simply selling a commodity?

I challenged them: 'How would you feel, honestly, if the father of your children ran such a business?' That shut them up.

I made sure Niall was aware of my distaste at his new line of work. 'It's none of your business,' he told me. 'Would you rather I sold illegal arms?'

Actually, I think I would have preferred that.

I knew he would never deliberately expose our children to this stuff, but reason can go out of the window when emotions kick in. It was after a session of beating myself up about my inability to change things for my children that I tried ringing Niall's mother – perhaps she could make him see sense.

'Do you know what your son is selling?' I slurred down the phone. 'Sex aids. And they are all in his house where the children might find them!'

'Don't be silly, ducky,' she replied. 'I've lots of croissants and prawn cocktails I could bring over,' she added, rather surreally.

I put the receiver down on the table and walked into the kitchen to open another bottle of wine. When I returned and picked up the receiver, she was still talking. I had watched with horror many times when Niall had hung up on her, but now I did the same.

Crying into my glass, I decided to phone the police. I drunkenly explained my concerns to whoever answered the phone. I tried to enunciate carefully, knowing I had poured the best part of two bottles of wine down my neck. They listened politely for some time, finally advising, 'Get yourself a good lawyer, love.'

I've no idea what happened, but the next time I saw the children they told me a door had been fitted and all 'Daddy's workboxes' had been locked up.

CHAPTER THIRTY-TWO

DOWNSIZING

In 2001 I had to sell Avon House. An income-tax demand for £46,000 was one thing; no income to pay it with was another. Where had all the work gone?

Ever since Tesco had declined to renew my consultancy contract, my income had nose-dived. All right, I had got horribly drunk at one corporate dinner. Embarrassing. Not a good plan. Actually, I couldn't really remember much about it, so didn't know how bad I'd been. Or perhaps it was simply that I had completed the job they wanted me to do – to help them become the biggest wine retailer in the UK. Maybe it was nothing to do with my behaviour at all. They hadn't replaced me with anyone, had they?

I could have remortgaged the house, but the thought of even higher monthly payments frightened me. I had already increased the existing mortgage to give Niall half the collateral in the house. That's what happened to you if you were a wife and mother who worked, I thought bitterly – you have to pay your partner off. I should have been the kind of wife who draped herself feebly across the chaise lounge, saying, 'Peel me a grape, darling.'

With the bills piling up, I'd taken in lodgers. I came back from one weekend away to find they had thrown a party. The kitchen had been half-heartedly cleaned up, but the bin was overflowing with squashed Carlsberg cans and soggy cigarette ends. It smelt just like the pub. There was another, worse, sewer-like smell hanging in the air. I followed my nose into the downstairs bathroom and looked around. I noticed a half-full bottle of Zinfandel Blush stood abandoned on the floor beside the shower. Christ, couldn't they drink something decent? Still, at least it wasn't one of my bottles.

Where was that smell coming from? I opened the glass shower door and the stench hit me. The shower tray was full of grey, sludgy water coated in scum. A long, black, fusewire-like pubic hair was stranded on the soap. I didn't like to look any closer to see what else was floating around. I slammed the shower door so hard it came off its hinges. The sewer must be blocked. The contents were coming up through the plughole. It had happened before – they had probably blocked the system throwing condoms down the loo.

That was the moment I decided I couldn't do this any more. I didn't need this huge house. It was falling apart and soaking up money. I decided there and then to sell it. If I was lucky, I might be able to buy something outright and have no mortgage.

I felt relieved to be moving out of Avon House at first, but something in me changed. The fight went out of me. It had been my house of dreams, where my third son was born, my daily reminder that I had achieved something in life and bought the largest house in the street. I felt as if I was leaving part of my soul there.

Even so, financially, I had no option. I sold Avon House and used the money to pay off the mortgage, my credit-card debts and the taxman. I had about enough left to buy a two- or three-bedroom house, but I hadn't found anywhere to buy yet. I put in offers on two places, but they fell through. I wasn't quite sure what to do next. As a stopgap, I went to live with my parents in Devizes.

'There is only one condition,' my mother said. 'I don't want you coming in rolling drunk.'

I looked at her coldly. 'Of course not.'

I would wait until she had gone to bed to creep in through the garden gate from the local pub.

In the end, I moved back to Hungerford and rented a tiny house – the Doll's House, I called it. I went from owning the biggest house in the street to renting the smallest. I stopped looking at houses to buy. They were all too expensive. And, anyway, if I took out a mortgage, how was I going to pay it?

My capital seemed to be disappearing fast and I was soon down to the end of it, with barely enough to put down a deposit on a house, let alone buy one outright. Where had all the money gone? I hadn't been that extravagant, had I? Well, all right, I had stayed up in London a few times, holing up in the Groucho, sometimes catching cabs home. Well, quite often, actually. But surely that was safer than risking the last train with all the drunks.

The boys always needed new things – clothes, books, bikes. It was 2003 now and they were getting so big. On the weeks they lived with me in the Doll's House, all three would be sardined into one little bedroom. I must have been crazy not to realise they would grow, need more space. I hadn't thought about that when I'd made my decision to sell Avon House. Still, no point thinking about that – it made my stomach feel tight.

Indeed, my stomach was hurting and my back ached continuously. I thought that perhaps I'd picked up some kind of bug somewhere, some sort of parasite. Every time I went to the loo, bright-green or yellow liquid poured out of me. Mum asked me if I thought it was to do with my drinking. She seemed hypersensitive about my drinking – what was wrong with her?

'Don't be stupid!' I snapped. I didn't drink *that* much. I'd always had a weak stomach.

To prove her wrong, I didn't have a drink for a whole day and a half. The condition continued unabated. So that proved it was nothing to do with the drinking, didn't it?

Not that I felt any better this morning. The sheets were covered in blood. Surely it wasn't normal to be having periods as heavy as this? Only one thing for it, one thing that could take away the dull ache in my back – neat vodka, straight from the freezer. A quick slug of Stolichnaya – buffalo-grass flavour was a favourite – seemed far more effective than painkillers. I prided myself on not taking drugs. They didn't agree with me.

I had to find a job. Perhaps it would make me feel better, less lethargic, less depressed. I leafed dispiritedly through the *Guardian*'s *Media Appointments* supplement. What kind of job could I apply for? It wasn't as if you saw many ads for wine writers. Or burned-out forty-two-year-old wine writers, more like, I thought.

I would have to rewrite my CV. Where was my laptop? I hadn't seen it for days. Maybe it was in the car. I looked out of the window. The car wasn't there. Oh, yes. I'd left it in the pub car park down the road last night. I'd only popped in for a quick one. But we had started playing spoof, and each time someone lost they had to buy a round. That would account for all the change that had fallen out of my jeans this morning.

The rain lashed against the Doll's House windows. I started counting the drops as I had done as a little girl. God, this was depressing. Stuck at home in the rain. I felt a tear trickle down my face, stopping on the top of my lip. I looked in the mirror. I looked pale and washed-out. There were the remains of a bruise on my cheekbone, gone yellow. God knows what I had bumped into. I couldn't remember doing it. I looked at my watch. Only ten thirty.

I walked into the tiny kitchen. Cocoa Pops were strewn like rabbit droppings all over the black and white tiled floor. The sink was full of dirty dishes.

What was that? An open bottle of unfamiliar-looking red

wine on the draining board. I hadn't bought it. Someone must have brought it round, but when? I didn't remember anyone coming over last night. I looked around to check how many dirty wineglasses there were, to give me a clue, but there was so much washing-up in the sink it was impossible to tell.

I opened the cupboard to look for a glass. It was empty. Goddammit, there is nothing in this house, I thought, slamming the cupboard door. I picked up the bottle and swigged at it. Ugh. God, this stuff was rough. Vin de Pays de l'Aude? More like Vin de Pays de Load of Rubbish. I found a plastic Bambi mug and sloshed the rest of the wine into it.

I could apply for a job tomorrow. There had been another job ad I had cut out, something for a PR company. Had I missed the closing date? I couldn't see the cutting anywhere. Well, I wasn't going to stay here all day and drink Vin de Pays de Load of Rubbish, I thought, taking another swig. It tasted even worse this time. The tannin made my tongue curl. I know, I thought. I'll finish this and then go down to the pub. Do the crossword. My friends Spike and Terry had been painstakingly patient in trying to teach me to do the cryptic one. Yes, that was a good idea, a good plan for the day. Finish this, get out of the house, have a bit of air. I'd definitely apply for that job tomorrow, once I found my laptop.

My black suede beaded Anna Trzebinski skirt was at the foot of the stairs. Strange place for it, I thought. Now, where were my black high-heeled Rodier ankle boots? They looked best with it.

I bent down to look under the sofa for the boots and felt the blood rush to my head. Whoa! I felt faint. I ought to have something to eat, really. I'd already been sick this morning. I was sick every morning. Weak stomach.

I put on my black trilby, grabbed my gold Moschino umbrella, left the house and walked down the road, the beads on my skirt jangling, past Avon House. Cardboard boxes were stacked in the window of my old office. There was a white plastic garden table in the bay window of my tasting room. It looked like a squat.

I arrived at the Three Swans just as the town hall clock struck 11 a.m., sat myself down at the bar and ordered a vodka and tonic.

Alice in bloody Wonderland, I thought.

CHAPTER THIRTY-THREE

Blow Job

Congealed claret-coloured blood is sticking to my inner thighs. A globule breaks free and trickles from my crotch to my calf. Browner, Chianti-like spots of it are spattered across the floor.

It's all coming back. I can barely breathe. Pictures flash through my head. Realisation dawns and bile surges from my stomach to my throat. My left hand is shaking. I stand up on trembling legs and hammer on the cell door.

I had dropped the boys at their father's. There was the usual acerbic exchange and I had driven off at speed, raging. I stopped at the Italian restaurant at the bottom of town. I asked if I could leave my car in the car park overnight – I prided myself on not drinking and driving – and ordered a bottle of Montepulciano.

Smiling couples were all around me. Why was I sitting here at the bar by myself? They were all judging me, I thought. I downed my fifth glass and glared at a woman who kept looking at me. Huh – one day you might be on your own, sweetie. I was tempted to stick my tongue out at her.

I couldn't face eating here. I ordered a takeaway pizza – American Hot, extra chillies. I was waiting for it when an acquaintance came in. I cringed to think about the drunken fling I'd had with him, and the humiliation I'd felt when he'd put the few belongings I had at his house – a few pairs of knickers, a bottle of Absolut citron vodka and two bottles of Wairau Rivers Sauvignon Blanc – into a black bin liner and left it outside his door to be picked up.

He came across to the bar and ordered another bottle of Montepulciano. Well, that was the least he could do, I thought angrily as I drank it down. I snarled at him. The bin-bag episode was unkind, I told him. He was an 'uneducated waste of space'. He left.

I picked up my pizza, asked for a cork for the bottle, stuffed it my handbag and zigzagged to the door. Outside, the cold air hit me.

I thought of my dark, empty cottage. Perhaps I should go after him. He wasn't that bad really, was he? I unlocked my car on the passenger side and put the pizza box on the seat. I clambered across to the driver's seat, snagging the gear-stick on the way. Not far to go. I would be fine. I started the car and began pulling out of the car park. At the exit, I hesitated – should I turn left and go after him or turn right and go home? Perhaps I should toss a coin.

Suddenly, flashing blue lights were heading for me. A policeman knocked on my window. I couldn't find the switch to open it. He was mouthing something at me. Broken blood vessels criss-crossed his nose like angry threadworms and he had the beginnings of a sty under his left eye. Pig sty, I thought.

I located the electric-window switch, pressed it. Whoops, wrong window – that was the passenger side. This one.

'You're causing an obstruction, madam. Have you been drinking?'

'I am on private property,' I retorted. 'I hadn't decided which way to go. And, anyway' – pointing at the bottle in my handbag – 'I was taking the rest of the wine home to drink.'

'You are half on the road. Get out of the vehicle.'

'Hold your horses. I was just going to reverse. I've asked if I can leave my car here, anyway.'

A policewoman appeared from somewhere. Or was it the woman who had been staring at me in the restaurant earlier? She looked similar.

Suddenly – how did that happen? – I was in the back of a panda car, moving fast in the dark. We arrived at a police station, where two officers were standing behind a counter. Both had big, protruding beer bellies.

One of them removed the bottle of Montepulciano from my handbag, raised an eyebrow. The other tipped my handbag upside down. Out cascaded a litter of old tissues, train tickets, half-unwrapped tampons, sticky sweets, an old notebook, hairgrips and Threshers receipts. My purse was bulging with £50 notes. I began to mouth an old childhood game: 'I packed my bag and in it I put. . .' One of the policemen looked up. I realised I was talking out loud. He narrowed his eyes and appeared to wrinkle his nose. Was he trying to insinuate I smelt?

'Is this your bag?' he asked.

I considered a sarcastic reply but left it at a sulky nod. His colleague began laboriously listing the bag's contents in childlike writing.

'Take off your jewellery and your shoes.'

'My shoes?'

'Yes, your shoes.'

The list of my handbag's contents was handed to me to check and sign. It seemed interminably long. I'd better read this carefully in case they'd planted something on me, I thought. I started reading through it, slowly.

'Just sign it and get on with it.'

'I'm reading it,' I replied sulkily.

He snatched the list back and scrawled, 'Defendant refuses to sign.'

I was led to a room and asked to blow into a contraption

attached to a computer. My heart was beating fast and I began hyperventilating. At forty-two, this was my only brush with the law since getting lost in France aged eight. The French police were much kinder.

'Blow harder, it's not registering,' the officer barked.

My mind worked. Perhaps if I blew faintly, I would be OK. One of the policemen smiled encouragingly. I smiled back. Maybe they would realise it was all a silly mistake and let me off. He looked a bit like my dad. I blew twice more.

'You're not trying hard enough. Don't worry – we'll do you for failure to provide. You'll get eighteen months, anyway.'

They took me to a cell. I lay down on a sort of ledge. I looked around for a blanket, but the cell was bare. It was cold and I began to shiver. I could hear angry, drunken male voices from another cell. Then I passed out.

Nobody is coming. Blood is now running down both my legs. I look around for my handbag. It's not here of course. Oh, God. What time is it? I knock on the door of the cell again and again until my knuckles ache.

Finally, somebody comes. A young male officer.

'I need a tampon,' I say, pointing at the congealed blood on my ankles. He closes the door and returns minutes later, handing me a mini tampon, the kind I had for my first periods at twelve.

'I've had three children!' I snort, looking at it incredulously.

'Well, that's all we've got,' he replied, taking me to a lavatory with no door. On the way back to the cell, I persuade him to give me a pencil and a piece of paper. I promise not to write on the walls. With nothing else to do, I can at least try to write something, but no words come. I feel numb. I cannot believe I'm here. I'm sure this is a dream, that I will soon wake up from another drunken nightmare.

An hour later the blood is gushing down my legs again. I feel faint and scared, alone and shaky. I knock on the door over and over.

I hear jeering, singing: 'The more fuss you make, the longer it will take!'

I write this down on my piece of paper. I think of words that rhyme with '-ake' – fake, lake, wine lake, sake – yes, sake, for God's *sake* open the door and give me another tampon. Eventually the door is opened. It's the same young officer. He hands me two tampons and again accompanies me to the doorless lavatory.

I ask him what will happen. They are waiting for the duty officer, he says. I give him the name of my lawyer. I had given it to the two officers the night before but they'd claimed they couldn't find his number. This policeman finds the number straight away.

I speak to my lawyer. He says he doesn't deal with drink-driving but knows someone who does. He'll try to get in touch, otherwise there'll be a duty solicitor. 'You'll be fine,' he assures me.

I'm taken back to my cell. A woman comes in. She's about my age, with dark-blonde hair, and carries a clipboard. 'I am here to talk to anyone who thinks they have a problem with alcohol,' she says.

'What a relief,' I answer. 'I haven't got a problem with alcohol, but I've been in here for hours and would really like someone to talk to. I don't suppose you have any giant tampons on you, do you?'

She shakes her head. 'Well,' she says, 'if you haven't got an alcohol problem, I better go and speak to some of the others.'

'Yes. From the sound of things last night, some of the other people in here were really drunk. They may have a problem.'

She stares at me.

'I don't normally drink and drive,' I add. 'I'd had an argument. I was just unlucky, you know.'

'Do you ever drive in the morning after a session?' she asked.

'Of course I do – I have to take the kids to school. But I don't drink first thing in the morning.'

'You'd be surprised – you may well be over the limit in the mornings.'

Then it hits me. I am bound to lose my licence. How will I get the children to school? What will I tell Mum and Dad? Niall would be cock-a-hoop. How could I organise it so he didn't know? There must be a way – perhaps I can say I've developed epilepsy. Mind you, gossip is bound to get around. Maybe he will help out and take the children to school.

I sit in the cell for another hour or so. My shakes get worse. I still can't take it all in. I am brought a breakfast of soggy, microwaved hash browns and baked beans. Next, I am charged, fingerprinted, swabbed in the mouth for DNA, photographed. The flash almost blinds me. The police mugshot of Hugh Grant pops into my head, the one that was wired around the world after his debacle with a lady of the night. Blow job of a different kind.

This amuses me and I laugh as I am released from the police station and head straight for Café Rouge. I order a large glass of red. And another. My shaking stops. I am on my fourth when a friend arrives to pick me up.

I was a contrite girl in court, in my navy crêpe Armani trousersuit. I'd always associated it with the pinnacle of my success and done several deals in it. But as I stood n the dock, shame seeped into my soul. One inner voice told me I was bad, weak and reckless. Another whispered, 'You were just unlucky. How many times have you knowingly drunk and driven in your life? Less than a handful of times in twenty years. You're just unlucky.'

I received a year's ban to be reduced to nine months if I agreed to attend a drink-awareness course on Saturday mornings. There were fourteen of us on the 'naughty course', as I came to call it. We would carry on our research in the pub afterwards.

CHAPTER THIRTY-FOUR

Death of a King

My father died.

Mum said he'd been sitting in the garden while she was planting peas when she heard a thud. And that was it. A massive heart attack and . . . gone. She had been just about to make him a coffee, once she'd finished planting the peas.

I stood at the lectern in the church, looking down at my high-heeled pink and red suede boots, laced from ankle to toe. Dad loved them and used to call them my Moulin Rouge boots. 'You ought to be doing the cancan in those,' he had smiled.

I hadn't planned to wear them for the funeral, but in my hung-over rush to get to my mother's house, shouting at the boys to make sure they wore their best shirts, I had forgotten about my own clothes. Hence my unlikely mishmash of short, zip-up black Paul Costello dress, thick black tights and my outrageous Moulin Rouge boots. At least they had black laces.

I looked across at my dad's naval medals glinting in the sunlight on top of the pine coffin. How could he be dead? He who gave me beard rubs, who used to call me 'my Alice fair' and sing me to sleep with Irish lullabies; he who was always there for me and loved me unconditionally, even when I grew into a woman. He made me feel special. When he talked to me, it was always as if I was the only person in the world.

I took a deep breath and looked out over the congregation. The church was full. I focused on Number Two son's angelic face. I must get his hair cut, I thought.

I swallowed hard. Suddenly my throat felt dry. I had resisted the idea of slipping out of Mum's back gate to the local for a large vodka and tonic. Dad wouldn't have approved. He was always uncomfortable with any of us drinking spirits.

'A reading from the Prophet Isaiah,' I began. 'On this morning, the Lord of Hosts will prepare for all peoples a banquet of rich food and wine.' I paused and many of the congregation smiled. Dad loved good food and his passion for wine was matched only by my own. Our shared interest gave us a special bond. I knew he was proud of me and my books. 'The Lord will wipe away the tears from every cheek,' I went on. At this line I faltered. I will not cry, I told myself. I gulped and it echoed around the church like a desperate, strangled sob. My left hand started to shake. Somehow I managed the next few lines. The reading over, I teetered back to my pew and sat down. Number Two son squeezed my hand.

Pictures flashed up in my head. Daddy building me a sandcastle and giving me the flag to stick in the turret. Me running down a hill in the Brecon Beacons so fast that as he caught me we both fell over and tumbled further down the hill, crying with laughter. His beaming face beside me as I took him for his first drive in my new sports car, my beloved LBC.

Mum climbed to the lectern to give the eulogy. She is a magnificent speaker. Not for nothing did she teach speech and drama. I never knew my father had learnt to fly with the US Air Force. She spoke of how he studied hard to learn about wine and to speak French. The wine came more easily to him than the language, she observed wryly. I could hear him answering the phone at home in his appalling French: '*Ici Monsieur King de Londres.*' On one occasion, in spontaneous unison, all nine children had mimicked him.

'He was flamboyant, self-willed, outspoken, stubborn, irascible, quick to anger but always quick to beg forgiveness. Dominic King. A lovely man, a good man – we like to think a great man. God rest his soul.' Mum stepped down. There was a silence, then several people began to clap. Clapping in church!

We followed the coffin out into the churchyard as children from a neighbouring school ran out to play. As their squeals and laughter sounded in the background, the grandchildren threw handfuls of spring blossom and rose petals over the coffin.

I cadged a lift back to the house with an old friend of Dad's. I hadn't yet admitted to anyone I'd lost my licence. I needed to be back first to open the champagne. Dad had been quite insistent about that – had left instructions that we were to have a champagne party. Magnums, naturally.

I opened the door. The house was silent. I expected my father to walk round the corner, ask me where I'd been. Magnums of champagne on ice were floating in his naval rum barrel. Mum had bought it for him at an auction, delighted to have tracked down such a memento from the aircraft carrier he served on during the war. I read the polished brass plaque: 'The King, God bless him.' And he was my king, both in name and nature. I feel strangely comforted standing by his barrel.

I pulled out a magnum and tore off the gold foil. I could hear his voice, telling me at ten years old, 'Hold the cork and twist the bottle, not the cork – that's the trick.'

The cork popped and I poured out a glass with such haste that the bubbles fizzed furiously over the top. Tutting to myself – Dad would never have approved of that – I picked up the glass and drained the contents in two gulps, the bubbles pricking my dry throat. I poured the other twenty-three glasses with more care. I repeated the exercise with the second magnum, savouring this glass a little longer – three gulps rather than two.

The guests started to arrive. Since Dad's death all us children had been referring to this wake as 'the reception'. We had only ever organised weddings before. But the atmosphere was more in celebration than sorrow – Dad would have approved of that.

A friend came to sit beside me. 'So, how are you, Alice?'

I snort. 'Well, I'm not drunk, am I? Bet that surprised you, didn't it?'

She touched my arm. 'How are you really? On the inside?'

I paused before answering. 'Hollow, empty, numb. But OK hollow, OK empty, OK numb. I feel at peace with Dad. There was no unfinished business between us. And I haven't cried.'

'What is that pile of handkerchiefs doing over there?' my friend asked, pointing to the dresser.

I turned my head and looked at the stack of Dad's neatly ironed and folded hankies. Mum, walking past and overhearing, stopped and answered, 'There's one for each of the children to take home.'

Tears sprang from my eyes.

CHAPTER THIRTY-FIVE

COWBOY HAT

I opened the courtyard door and stepped gleefully out into the night rain. It was a light summer shower, just enough to coat the hydrangea leaves glistening in the moonlight. After three weeks in dusty, dry Arizona, where the daily temperature was 120 degrees Fahrenheit and there had been no rain for over a hundred days, rain was a novelty about which I had fantasised.

I did a little rain dance, clicking the heels of my new cowboy boots and laughing as I watched the beaded tassels on them bounce up and down. And that was not the only thing that was bouncing.

How ridiculous would I look if anyone could see me now? I thought – a forty-something woman naked but for her stretch marks, new suede cowboy boots and black cowboy hat, dancing in the rain around a pot of hydrangeas.

It was almost a full moon. Would that account for my madness? Was it jet lag and rain deprivation? Or had the number of salt-encrusted margaritas done their worst – or best – and destroyed whatever brain cells I had left?

I looked up at the sky. A single large raindrop landed on my eyelashes and in the split second before I blinked the mighty planet Mars magnified in size. There had to be some intergalactic significance that Mars was the closest to Earth it had been for millions of years. It must be some sort of sign. But a sign of what? I wondered, as I twirled faster in the rain. I could see why it was called the Red Planet, with its fiery, golden-crimson, almost artificial brightness. And if the god of war was named after it, perhaps it was time I went to war with some of my demons.

I knew I was drinking too much. In the weeks since my father's death, life had become surreal. Drinking was the only way to blot out the ache that took my breath away. The stronger the drink, the better. I had rocked myself to sleep for many nights, composing imaginary conversations with him. I was grateful that he had died before he found out about me losing my driving licence. I wondered what he would have thought about my demeaning night in the cells.

A few friends had dropped round on their way back from the pub that evening on the off-chance of a late drink. They always knew they were in luck when they saw the light on through the dimpled glass of the red door of the Doll's House. They had left as soon as the bottle of golden tequila was empty. I was alone again, an empty bottle for company. I had picked up a last glass of tequila that had somehow been forgotten, stripped to my cowboy boots and hat and come dancing in the rain.

'Captain of My Heart' was belting out of the jukebox. I went back inside, pirouetting on my stack heels to turn up the volume when the phone rang. In an exaggerated Arizona drawl I answered, 'Well, howdy!'

A surprised-sounding, slightly northern English accent replied, 'Good evening. You sound like you're having fun. What are you up to?'

Laughing, I thought how apt it was that this was a call from the god of war himself, a bloke I had met in the pub who loved to row with people, mostly in good spirit. 'Mr Confrontational Man' I had christened him. After years of such arguments during my marriage, I felt strangely comfortable with him.

'Dancing naked in the rain sporting my new cowboy

boots and a cowboy hat, drooling over Mars,' I answered, unable to keep the giggle out of my voice. There was a momentary silence.

'What, with nothing else on?'

I looked down. 'Nothing – except my stretch marks.'

'Well, why don't you come down here? I'd love to see your new boots.'

I hesitated. I was about to cite jet lag as an excuse when he added, 'I've got a bottle of Appleton golden rum. Come as you are.'

'See you in ten,' I replied, putting down the receiver. Reaching for my old pale-grey cashmere coat, I briefly considered going up the twisting stairs to put some clothes on. But those stairs were notoriously slippery. Best not to test my agility with new, rain-soaked leather soles.

The silk lining of my coat felt cool and curiously welcoming on my naked skin. I grabbed a large brown carrier bag marked 'Sedona Boots' and stepped out into the night. The puddles glistened in the streetlight as I clip-clopped along.

The town hall clock struck 1 a.m. Staring up at it, I recited, 'The clock struck one, the mouse ran down, hickory, dickory dock.' I smiled as I walked down the high street, passing a solitary late-night pub-goer. 'Hiya!' I waved. He looked the worse for wear and I chuckled into my collar, feeling decidedly wicked that he couldn't see the real naked me, concealed under my coat.

I stomped in every puddle on the way. By the time I arrived my coat was covered in teardrop-shaped splashes. I hammered on the door, calling, 'Howdy there, cowboy-boot delivery!'

He opened the door, handing me a tumbler full of golden rum. I took a gulp and my eyes watered as the fiery, caramel-like spirit hit the back of my throat. I opened my coat quickly, to prove I had brought my stretch marks with me, and closed it.

'I like the hat,' he said. 'And the boots aren't bad either.'

'Here, try yours on,' I said, handing him the carrier bag. 'Hope they fit. Black, size ten.'

He pulled them on and marched around the flat, a vision in black cowboy boots and a short towelling dressing gown, beaming like a schoolboy.

'So, how was Arizona?' he asked.

'My dad learnt to fly there during the w—'

Damn, damn, damn. Tears in my drink again.

CHAPTER THIRTY-SIX

LIVER TESTS

I had to pass a liver function test before I could reapply for my driving licence, which meant I had to give up drinking. I was not too daunted by that. I'd stopped drinking several times in the past – every year during the month of January and each time I wrote a wine book because I had to work at such a rate I couldn't afford a hangover. This always resulted in me writing quickly so I could get back on the sauce.

I realised, though, it had been a long time since I had stopped for more than a day. I was also shocked to realise I hadn't written a book for years. Where had the time gone? I calculated that I'd probably need to stop drinking for about three months. I put the drink down after a particularly heavy farewell weekend. I had flu symptoms for a week, with sweating and high temperatures, but strangely no runny nose. Could this be to do with drinking? It didn't seem like withdrawal to me – besides, I wasn't shaking, I smugly told friends.

The boys remarked on my bad temper. I was furious when I overhead Number One son telling his brothers, 'She's so stressy now she isn't drinking.'

I went to see a homeopath about my liver. 'Surely I can beat the system if you give me something to restore and speed up my liver's rejuvenation,' I said.

She told me I needed to look at my drinking long term.

'You don't understand,' I insisted. 'All I need is to get my driving licence back.'

Over some weeks, and despite not drinking, my liver functions tests were erratic. What was the point in stopping if the tests kept fluctuating?

I found myself tetchy and withdrawn, barely talking to anyone except to rant about my liver. My anger at the system grew. 'There are probably thousands of people walking about with odd liver function tests, but because they haven't lost their licences, they're OK to drive,' I whinged endlessly in the pub over my ginger ale. Ginger ale! My friends told me to stop ranting.

Angrily, I decided to go along for my official medical anyway, despite the fact that my tests still weren't normal. As soon as the blood test was over, I celebrated in the pub, relieved I didn't have to face a Christmas without booze. I couldn't understand it – I seemed to be getting helplessly drunk on very little, so drunk I couldn't remember anything after the third glass. 'It just shows you what happens if you don't keep practising,' I joked.

After a six-week wait for the results, my doctor called me in to see her. It was two o'clock in the afternoon and I'd already guzzled two large glasses of wine.

I had failed the medical.

I took the news very badly. I left the surgery in high dudgeon and moaned about it in the pub. I was angry at people I knew who drank more than me without apparent ill effect.

My doctor had suggested I go to see a liver specialist. I asked my sister Juliana to come with me.

'I'm pleased to report we can't see any evidence of cirrhosis on your scan,' the consultant told me.

My sister looked relieved.

'Look,' I said to him, 'I just need to know how long you think I will have to stop drinking to get my driving licence back. It's as simple as that. How long?'

'I'm afraid it's *not* as simple as that. Your driving licence is really neither here nor there. It's your health I am interested in. Livers are funny things. They can be fine one minute and then suddenly deteriorate. We need to look at your drinking. How much do you think you're drinking?'

It was if I hadn't heard his question. I shouted, 'And how am I supposed to get my children to school if my driving licence is "neither here nor there"? How long do I have to give up for – six months, seven, what? Just tell me!'

My sister was looking embarrassed.

'I cannot give you an exact answer,' came the specialist's cold reply.

I continued my rant outside in the car park. 'Calls himself a consultant! Why didn't he just answer my question? How bloody long do I need to stop drinking for? It's not rocket science, surely!'

CHAPTER THIRTY-SEVEN

STING IN THE TALE

I came to. Sweat was running down my body like rain down a windscreen. My heart was beating so fast it felt as if Duracell bunnies on speed were banging their drums in my chest. I ran my tongue around my mouth and realised I hadn't cleaned my teeth the night before. My throat was sore and it was difficult to swallow. The roof of my mouth felt like one of those insect strips that catch their prey in that gloopy syrup. Bile was rising in my stomach.

I could smell red wine. An upended glass was lying beside the bed, the wine soaked into the carpet like a child's drawing of a long, red tongue. I knew without looking at the clock that it would be 4.35 a.m. It was the same time every morning, and it was too early – too much of the day stretching ahead. I kept forgetting to ask my mother what time I had been born. Maybe that's why I always woke up so early.

This sweating was getting ridiculous. I moved my foot around, searching for a dry spot – the sheets and the duvet were as wet as if they had just been taken out of the washing machine. Perhaps I was having an early menopause, I thought. Or I was sickening for something – though come to think of it, these night sweats had been going on for a long time.

I tried closing my eyes, conjuring up my favourite visualisation of Dunn's Falls, the spectacular waterfall in Jamaica I'd seen on a press trip once. Maybe that would send me back to sleep. But I felt as if I'd been standing in the water-fall. I blinked my eyes open as a globule of sweat dripped off my forehead. Sighing, I raised my head slowly. I got out of bed, side-stepping the glass, and went into the kitchen.

There was broken glass on the floor. My favourite red stilettos were lying jack-knifed on their sides inside the front door. I put them on. I glanced at my bloodshot eyes in the hall mirror. They were a similar colour to my shoes.

I looked around for an idea of what had happened the night before, where I had been. The bin often provided clues. Ah, yes – takeaway cartons still coated with the remains of salt and chilli prawns and noodles, lying slimy and worm-like, gleaming in their protective monosodium glutamate. A visit to the Chinese takeaway van, then. How had I staggered there? Who had seen me? What time had it been?

The fear kicked in. My chest felt constricted. I made a dash for the sink and retched into it, again and again, watch-ing the yellow bile swirl down the plughole, taking with it a single helpless noodle.

Crossing to the freezer, I noticed it was 4.50 a.m. Bending down to pick up a discarded Rowntree's ice-lolly wrapper, I almost toppled over on my stilettos as the blood rushed to my head. I opened the freezer, retrieved the bottle of Absolut from the bottom drawer and held it up to the light. It was difficult to see through the frosted glass, but it looked as if there was about an inch or so in the bottom. Who had drunk all that? I had only bought it the day before. Who had been round the night before? There were no glasses on the table. I peered into the dishwasher – no, none there either.

The broken glass crunched underfoot. Looking down, I saw it was one of the boys' *Lion King* glasses. Opening the cupboard to find the dustpan, I was surprised to find six more Absolut empties lined up like bottles in a shooting range. I must tell my loyal cleaner, Stef, to throw them out. I'm sure this cupboard had been empty a few days ago.

Looking at the bottles, I felt a hot flush of shame. Discarded different wine bottles were easy to explain – they were for work, weren't they? – but six identical vodka bottles? Looking at the one in my shaking hand, I reasoned I may as well finish it, and poured it into a child's *Aladdin* glass on the table. One small one wouldn't do any harm. Perhaps it would help me go back to sleep. I noted how the oily vodka coated the sides of the glass. It was halfway to my lips when someone patted me on the back. Jumping, I turned to see Number Two son sleepily rubbing his eyes and smiling.

'Hee! Thought I'd surprise you, Mummy!'

'Well, don't!' I snapped. 'I nearly jumped out of my skin. Keep out of the way while I sweep this glass up. Anyway, what are you doing out of bed? It's only five o'clock.' I realised I was still clutching the Absolut bottle and placed it in the cupboard next to the other six, quickly slamming the door.

'I couldn't sleep,' he said. 'And I'm thirsty. I need water.'

I ran the tap and handed him a glass of water. 'Yes, I'm thirsty too,' I added more gently, as we drained our glasses together.

'You know what, Mummy?' he added. 'That's my glass you've got there.'

We walked out into the garden, where he climbed into the hammock and promptly fell asleep. I stood looking at him. Nothing seemed to rattle him. Despite the quicksand nature of his homelife, he retained his own pixie-like smile and his sense of humour. I gazed at the sprinkling of freckles across his nose and marvelled at how his hair glinted in the early-morning sunlight, like spun gold. He had an inner peace that I envied. Where had that come from?

The snowball tree was laden with flowers, and there were petals all over the lawn. It was going to be a scorcher. The birdsong seemed inordinately shrill. I went back to bed.

I awoke three hours later and started the familiar process

of piecing together the flashbacks from the night before. I recalled going to the Three Swans while waiting for the Chinese. I didn't think I'd been in the pub for long. Well, just a few drinks. I prided myself on only drinking single vodkas even though the house doubles were the same price. There was no way I'd drink that cheap stuff, anyway – Smirnoff was so much better. I vaguely recalled talking to a guy with blond dreadlocks who was drinking the cheap crap, which was why I'd started talking to him, explaining how much less pure it was and how deadly the resulting hangovers were. I remembered elaborating at some length about how Smirnoff Black Label was filtered through char-coal, which gave it a more creamy flavour, and was why those who knew about vodka drank it neat. Yes, that was it. Perhaps he had come back later for a drink. That explained it. *He* must have drunk the vodka.

My heart started racing. I couldn't remember him leaving. Where was my handbag – and all my credit cards?

Number Three son popped his head round the door. 'Mummy, I'm hungry. Can we have some croissants?'

'OK, I'll do you a deal. You find my handbag and I'll go and buy some croissants from Somerfield.'

'It's in the pantry,' he laughed. 'That's a funny place to put it!'

He returned with my leopard-skin bag over his shoulder. I checked my purse – all my credit cards seemed to be there, plus one crisp, red £50 note. I preferred fifties. I thought I'd had two – though it was possible I'd spent one in the Three Swans. Yes, that's right – I remembered handing one to the bad-tempered barmaid. I couldn't see the change anywhere.

Pulling on my Wrangler jeans and an old striped navy T-shirt, I looked around for some shoes. It was too far to stagger in my stilettos. My Reeboks were around somewhere. As I peered under the bed for them, I felt faint, light-headed.

The air was so close it felt like a storm was brewing. My skin was hot and clammy.

I looked in the mirror. My hair was unkempt, matted and curly, so I pulled on a linen hat. Rubbing the sleep dust from my eyes, I noticed my eyelashes were like hairy spider's legs, clogged with the remains of last night's mascara. More mascara was smeared under my eyes. I had a red horn of wine over the right side of my top lip. I rubbed it furiously. I hoped I hadn't walked round like that all yesterday – the last time I remembered drinking red wine was the glass, or two, I'd had at lunchtime. I put on my brown Ray-Bans.

'Can I come with you to the supermarket, Mummy?' asked Number Three son.

'No, you stay here and I'll be quick.'

'You always say that and then you're gone for ages!' he whinged.

'OK, OK, come with me, but hurry up.'

Once in Somerfield, he disappeared to find the croissants. 'I've just got to get a few other things,' I said to his retreating back. The store was air-conditioned and I felt cold and shivery.

May as well get another bottle of vodka while I'm here, I thought – it would save coming back later. I looked up and down the empty aisle and reached for the bottle. Why was the Absolut always on the top shelf? And why did they have security tags? Surely people didn't steal vodka?

On my way to the checkout, I looked at the bottle lying alone in the basket and hastily rounded the corner to add some Fairy Liquid, then covered the vodka up with some dishcloths. With three little boys around there was always a mess to clear up.

Why does everyone do their shopping at eight thirty in the morning? I thought, waiting impatiently at the checkout. I realised my left hand was shaking so, after wiping the sweat from my brow, I pushed it deep into my pocket.

Why did I always bump into people I knew? Number Two son's gymnastics teacher stood in the next queue.

Number Three son appeared beside me and put the croissants on the conveyor belt. The spotty youth on the cash desk seemed to be taking for ever. He rang a bell and held up the Absolut in his hand. Feeling my face colour, I watched the supervisor come to the checkout and, in slow motion, nod like a bloody nodding dog. I made a mental note to pick cashiers over eighteen who didn't need authorisation to sell alcohol for my next early-morning vodka run.

'We're having a party later,' I mumbled to him, hastily putting the bottle into a carrier bag.

'Are we?' asked Number Three son, too loudly. 'Who's coming?'

'Well, actually, we're going to one in the village,' I replied, already out of the shop and striding down the road so fast he had to run to keep up.

Once home, I disappeared into the pantry, opened the new bottle and filled my glass. After a few quick slugs I felt better. My anxiety lessened and I began to breathe more easily.

'That's still my glass, Mummy,' pointed out Number Two son, as he grabbed his croissant and danced out into the garden, humming.

By noon the heat was unbearable and my two younger sons were fighting.

'Let's go out for lunch,' I suggested.

'Only if you promise we don't have to stay too long,' negotiated Number One son, who had had his head stuck inside *The Lion, the Witch and the Wardrobe* all morning, barely speaking to anyone.

We trundled across the road to be greeted warmly in the Plume. 'Warm enough for you?' asked the barmaid.

'I'm boiling – and so-o-o thirsty!' I said, ordering three Cokes for the boys.

'What'll it be, then?' she asked.

'Oh, yes, I could do with a drink – er – a glass of white – the Sauvignon, please.'

'Large?' A conspiratorial wink.

The boys ate chicken goujons and chips. I wasn't hungry and was halfway through my second glass of wine when Number One son announced he was going home.

'Well, take the others and I'll be back soon,' I said, giving him money to buy ice creams from the teashop by the bridge. 'I know you're eleven now but still mind how you cross the road.'

After a third glass I reluctantly got up. Just as I was leaving, a friend arrived. 'Stay for another drink,' she urged. 'I haven't seen you in ages.'

'OK, just a quick one,' I replied.

'How have you been? You look a bit, um . . .' she hesitated '. . . well, frazzled.'

'Yeah, well, wouldn't you be if you had to put up with three fighting boys? Anyway, how was your holiday?'

I wasn't really listening as she began to tell me, sniffing my drink, then gulping it down when I realised it was two o'clock. 'Christ, I'd better be going – we've got to go to a party with the great and good.'

'Monsieur Le Chauffeur' – a friend who had borrowed my car since I'd lost my licence – was waiting outside the house. The arrangement suited him as he'd written off his own car and this way didn't need to stump up for a new one yet. It suited me as I had a way of getting the boys to school.

He looked hot. His sandy hair was sticking to his forehead, and there were imprints on his nose from his glasses. A lithe and fit dreamer, he had a passion for dancing – and the women he met at his nightly dance classes around the country. I was always envious I wasn't one of them.

'Ready in a minute,' I shouted.

'*D'accord*, Madame Le Roi,' came the weary reply.

Five minutes later the boys trooped out of the house, Number One still holding his book, Number Two with an armful of lilac from the garden, and Number Three clutching his football.

Halfway down the street Number Three piped up, 'Mummy, you've forgotten the vodka – you know, the bottle you bought this morning?'

'Oh, that wasn't for the party.'

'But you said it was. Why did you tell the boy at the supermarket it was for the party?' he persisted.

There was a silence in the car. Number Two son kicked him on the shin.

'So, where exactly is the party?' asked Monsieur Le Chauffeur.

'That big house to the left – the one with the wooden blinds, almost next to the butcher's.'

He dropped us off. The front door was open and we walked through the house to the garden. I couldn't help feeling envious. The hostess was moving to Bristol – to an even bigger and better house, I thought sulkily – and this was a farewell party. We each had a child in the same class, but our friendship had never been the same after a drunken weekend we'd spent together a few years ago with our husbands in Wales. I wasn't really sure what had happened, who had said or done what, but there had been an uncomfortable silence between us for a while.

Going into the garden, the boys ran off to be with their friends. Looking around for someone I knew, I saw a group of women sitting at a wooden table. They all looked the same – all blonde-haired, carefully made-up and in a seeming uniform of crisp, pressed white trousers or skirts and preppy shirts.

Scanning the length of the garden for some more lively

company, I was about to walk past when I noticed they were drinking rosé. I felt sure they had all stopped talking when I'd arrived. Christ, have I got my dress tucked into my knickers, or my boobs hanging out? I checked down at the flowery dress I had hastily changed into. Nope, all looked in order.

I sat at an empty seat. Wasn't anyone going to offer me a glass of wine?

'Is this a spare glass?' I asked, enunciating slowly. 'Mind if I have a glass of wine? I am so thirsty.' Someone passed the bottle down the table and I filled my glass. 'Cheers!' I said to the hostess. 'Happy moving.'

I looked around the table. I vaguely knew some of the women's faces from the school playground, not that I went there much. No doubt they had heard lots of bad press about me from the ex. I felt isolated.

'That's an unusual dress. Did you make it yourself?' asked the woman next to me. I looked down my nose at her own outfit, noting that her neatly ironed shirt looked as if it came from Primark.

'No, I didn't – actually, it's Moschino.'

'Oh. I thought you had crocheted it or something.'

'I think the technical term is "tatted",' I retorted. I noticed with alarm that my glass was already empty. 'Is there any more wine down that end of the table?'

Five minutes later the bottle in front of me was empty. I got up. What a boring bunch of women – Stepford wives! All perfect, with perfect lives, perfect husbands, perfect children. Which was all they were talking about. As I had no idea whose children were whose, it was difficult to concentrate. And, frankly, I wasn't interested. I wondered why I'd bothered coming. I could have stayed in the pub. No one seemed to be paying me any attention. I stood up.

I wandered out of the front door and on to the village high street. Number One son followed me. 'OK if I go up to my friend's, Mummy?'

'Which one?'

'You know, the one whose mum is an artist,' he replied.

'Good idea. I'll come with you – it's well dull here,' I announced, just as some other guests were arriving. My son cast me an embarrassed sideways glance.

We walked in silence together up the hill. He was still clutching his book.

I went into a garden following a sign that said, 'Open Studio'. The garden shimmered in the afternoon sun. Suddenly I felt really weary and almost tearful. I vaguely knew this woman, though I couldn't remember her name. Our sons played tennis together. She was one of the few mothers who spoke to me in the school playground.

'Hi,' she said. 'It's great to see you.'

'Were you not invited to the great and good party down the road, then?' I asked.

'No, seems not. Would you like a glass of wine?'

'Oh, yes – I'm really thirsty,' I replied, glancing around the studio. I wanted some new paintings, having banished several that reminded me of my ex to the garage.

'Hope you don't mind that it's nothing special – I know you're a bit of a connoisseur,' she apologised, handing me a large glass of white.

'Oh, don't worry, I'm just really thirsty.' The wine was cool and refreshing. Far nicer to be here among interesting, arty, creative people.

I wandered around, looking at the pictures. 'I really like the calligraphy one,' I said, stumbling over the word. 'Difficult word to say at this time of the afternoon, isn't it?'

It was a framed poem, 'Harlem' by Langston Hughes. Screwing up my eyes, I could just make out the first line: 'What happens to a dream deferred?' What had happened to all my dreams? They were more disintegrated than deferred.

'I'd like that one,' I said grandly. 'I haven't got my cheque-book with me, but I'll drop a cheque round tomorrow.'

'Are you sure? It's a hundred and fifty pounds.'

'Yes, yes. Look, I know it's a bit cheeky, but can I have another glass of wine? It's so hot.'

'It'll have to be red,' she replied.

'Oh, that's fine.'

'We're just about to eat. Would you like some spaghetti bolognaise with us?'

'Yes, please, I'm really hungry. And thirsty,' I added, laughing. 'Look, I think I've got the leaky glass again.'

I sat down with my hostess and her husband and devoured two plates of spaghetti without saying much, concentrating on trying to get the wayward pasta into my mouth. I tucked the paper napkin into the top of my dress to catch the splashes of sauce. I felt safe with these people. They didn't seem to be judging me.

'It's really nice to be here,' I said. 'I didn't feel very comfortable down the road – you know, all those people. And they seem so . . . well . . . up themselves, really.'

She just nodded.

Her husband disappeared to get another bottle. 'It's only bog-standard Rioja from Tesco,' he said when he returned.

'Don't worry, I probably chose it – I used to work for them, you know.' Was he looking at me strangely? Or was it the thick glasses he had on? I felt the familiar paranoia at the pit of my stomach and smiled weakly at him. 'Thanks,' I mumbled. 'As I said, you're really kind.'

My glass was empty again. How did this keep happening? I looked at my watch. Nearly six o'clock.

'Best get back to the party,' I said. 'Thanks for the food, and the wine. I'll see you tomorrow with a cheque. Love the picture.'

I walked back down the hill with Number One son and spotted my car. I tried to focus on it as Monsieur Le Chauffeur waved. I felt a bit woozy. Sweat was dripping down my face.

'You OK, Mummy?' asked Number One son.

'Yeah. It's just the heat,' I replied, steadying myself on a wall. I walked through the open front door of the party house and was about to go out to the garden when the hostess pounced on me.

'Where the hell do you think you've been?' she snarled. 'Your youngest son has been stung by a wasp and has been crying his eyes out. What kind of mother are you?'

My youngest son walked by. He looked fine, though his face was bit smeary.

'Well, he's not crying now, is he?' I said.

'That's because it happened about two hours ago and we've been looking for you ever since. We've called Niall to pick them up.'

I sighed and looked around for Number Two son. It seemed the same women were still sitting at the same table, their lipstick as perfect as ever. They were staring at me. Stuck-up cows. I bet *they*'re drunk by now. 'Tipsy', as they would probably put it.

I spotted Number Two son and managed to get all the boys in the car.

'Where did you go Mummy?' asked Number Three son. 'Four of my friends and me got stung and you weren't there. Look at my sting.'

I was examining it, leaning over him and trying to get his seat belt done up, when a taxi pulled up close by. Oh, Christ, I thought, here comes their father. The last thing I needed after this was a confrontation with him. I ducked down, hoping he wouldn't see me.

'Monsieur Le Chauffeur, home, and fast!'

'How was the party?' he asked.

'Oh, typical Stepford wives. Load of fuss about a wasp sting.'

CHAPTER THIRTY-EIGHT

Vampire Lips

It was January 2005, and I'd just been to see my therapist. I started seeing her five years earlier shortly after the divorce, to try to work through my feelings. I'd only had one large glass of Fetzer rosé. I had gone to the pub after my appointment to kill an hour while I waited for the train back to Hungerford. She had talked about responsibility – about me taking responsibility for my own life, about not operating from a place of blame, about taking a look at myself and not blaming everything and everyone else for my perceived misfortunes – for the mess I seemed to be in.

And it *was* a mess, of that there was no longer any doubt. I couldn't hide from that any longer, not even in a glass. I had fooled myself for long enough. What had I become?

After seeing my therapist, I had been standing at the bar in my leopard-skin coat and my pink trilby, just about to start on my second glass of rosé, when I had felt hot, my legs went weak, the pub went fuzzy . . . and the world went out.

I had come to on the floor with the publican looking at me in shocked concern. I had been able to taste blood in my mouth. Apparently, I had gone down like a felled tree.

I had told the paramedics I was fine. I was more embarrassed than anything else. I wasn't even drunk – not on one glass of rosé, surely? I had taken a taxi home and gone straight to my bedroom.

Now look at the state of me. I peer into my bedroom mirror.

My face is ashen, greyish-white, almost translucent. I rub some rouge into my cheekbones. They are prominent now. When I was eighteen, I used to use expensive green gunk, Ultima 2 from Revlon, to take the high colour out of my face. Now I am trying to put it back in.

My eyes are bloodshot, the mascara smudged. I've been crying. The man who arrived to fix my computer shortly after I returned home told me, 'Don't worry about the bill. I can see you've had a nasty fall.' I was so touched by his kindness it seemed to flick a switch in my soul and I burst into tears.

Not much I can do about the chip on my front tooth. My tongue searches it out every few seconds. There is something perversely comforting about this jagged edge. I've always been proud of my perfect teeth. Now they're not perfect any more. Still, if I keep my mouth shut and don't smile, this tiny chip won't show. I don't feel like smiling anyway. I comb my fringe straight to cover the scrape on my forehead. In this twilight, the graze looks like tiny red ants marching from my hairline to my eyebrow.

I tip the contents of my handbag on the floor. God, what a mess. I pick up a lipstick. Squinting, I look at the tiny gold print on the end – it makes me feel dizzy, sick. I must have banged my head when I fell. Elizabeth Arden's 'Captivate'. It's a deep-brown, dried-blood colour. How apt. That'll do to cover the bruise on my lip. With any luck, no one will notice in the pub's dingy light.

My left hand is shaking. It's never been the same since the time I broke my wrist falling off the loo, drunk. Perhaps I banged it again when I fell today. I stare at the hand and will it to stop shaking. It takes no notice. I transfer the lipstick to my right hand. If I paint my pinched, narrow lips a bit fuller, perhaps the bruise won't show. Someone once said I had a perfect Cupid's bow. Huh. What had Cupid ever done for me?

Five o'clock. I'd better get a move on, the pub is open and it's Friday. Or is it Thursday? I'm not sure. If I don't know what day it is, I must have bruised my brain. Actually, I feel faint again. When did I last eat something?

I start to shape my lips. I hate my face. I hate my lips. I hate my eyes. I hate me.

'I hate you,' I say to my reflection. 'I hate you, do you know that?'

My frown makes my head hurt. I've never been any good at putting lipstick on. They say you're supposed to use a brush, but that takes ages. I know what I'll do – I'll drink red wine, something really deep in colour like an Aussie Shiraz, and then the bruising won't show.

Angrily, I wipe the lipstick off the top of my lip with my thumb. It stings. 'Captivate'– what a name for a lipstick. Who could I captivate like this?

Cap-ti-vate. Rhymes with 'hate'. 'Hate, hate, Cap-ti-vate,' I say to my reflection. My voice is beginning to rise. There is a hysterical edge to it. I seem to hear it coming from a long way off, like a police siren in the distance.

'Blame, blame, that old game. Blame, blame, that old game,' I say, as soundbites of my therapist's words whirr around my head.

Using my little finger, I gingerly rub lipstick over my lower lip. My lips are numb. I have the strangest detached feeling, as if they belong to someone else.

I really am becoming hysterical now. I yell at myself in the mirror, 'I'm sick and tired of this!'

My mouth – black lipstick on the bottom lip, black bruising on the top – twists itself to form words with these lips that are not my lips. 'Responsibility,' it tells me. 'It's your responsibility.'

My eyes stare. Picking up my kohl pencil, I pull down my left eye. The pink of my eye is angry red. I rest my forehead against the cold glass of the mirror. Gilt bunches of grapes around the top of the frame mock me.

It's true. I am responsible for my life. No one else. I can't keep doing this to myself. I can't keep drinking.

No wonder I keep passing out.

No wonder I'm covered in bruises.

No wonder I'm alone.

No wonder I can't drive.

No wonder I've no money.

No wonder I've no work.

No wonder I no longer own a house.

No wonder I don't see my family.

No wonder the phone never rings.

No wonder my friends have given up on me.

No wonder my own children are scared of me.

No wonder I look such a mess.

No wonder I hate myself.

It is the drink: I have to stop drinking.

I drop the kohl pencil and watch it fall to the floor in slow motion. I walk across the room, fall face down on to my bed. The lipstick leaves a sinister vampire's smile on my pillow. I curl into the foetal position and rock.

'Sick and tired,' I whisper. 'Sick and tired. Sick and tired. Sick and tired of *being* sick and tired.'

PART THREE

One Day at a Time

CHAPTER THIRTY-NINE

Shadow Angel

I knew what was happening. I'd had it before. Withdrawal.

I awoke at 4 a.m., fully clothed. The ghastly vampire's smile was still there in lipstick on my pillow. A full moon stared rudely straight through my bedroom window, bathing me with madness. I felt odd, disconnected.

I was hot. Sweat poured down my face. My fringe was wet, plastered to my forehead. A river of perspiration ran between my breasts. I wrestled off my cowboy boots. My skin was itching. I took off my trousers. I could feel a bumpy rash, like nettle rash, all over my thighs. I traced it round to my now-protruding hip bones, scratching. My arms were itching too and had the same uneven texture, like woodchip wallpaper.

I knew what to do. Vodka would fix this.

The screensaver on my mobile phone suddenly lit up, casting a shadow-shape through the lampshade beside my bed. The outline of an angel, wings raised in salutation, was projected on to the wall. The light faded and the angel disappeared. My heart thudding, I froze for a few seconds. Was I hallucinating?

I pressed my mobile's keypad and the angel appeared again. Oh, God. She must be my guardian angel – the Sourire de Reims, my smiling angel from all those years ago.

It's a sign. I can do this. I can sit it out.

*

The next few nights followed a similar jittery, restless pattern. I found I could conjure up the shadow angel at any time, and did. The boys were intrigued. I told them she was my guardian angel, that we all had one. On the second day my left hand started to shake. It was always worse at night and I slept fitfully, clutching a tennis ball.

Daylight brought new hope. I tried to keep myself occupied and – never one to watch TV – began picking up books around the house. Short stories and poems were all I could manage, my concentration span short. Nothing much happened. I stayed at home, out of the pub. I fed the children. I felt like a child myself, living in good-girl limbo.

Whenever I had stopped drinking in the past I would feel as if I was flat-lining, then eventually I would reward myself with the rollercoaster drama of drinking again. But not this time. Not a single sip of wine for me. I had the same conversation with the committee in my head time and time again. Only total abstinence would ensure the reissue of my driving licence. *That* would be my reward, I told myself repeatedly, to be able to be a proper mother and drive my children around, take them to football, cricket, swimming, ballet – invite their friends round to tea and be able to drive them home.

I asked Number Two son when his homework was due in. 'Why do you want to know all of a sudden?' he asked, surprised. 'You've never asked before.'

Lunchtimes and 6 p.m., drink-trigger times, were the worst. I took to pacing around the garden, then decided to take my morning bath at lunchtime and take the boys to feed the ducks on the canal at 5 p.m.

When I told them to get their coats on, they sighed. 'Are we going to the pub?' I shook my head. As we traipsed down to the canal, they darted knowing looks at each other. I sensed they were holding their breath as we walked past the three pubs en route. I was doing the same. I crossed the road, so we took the zigzag route to where we fed the ducks. 'I will, I will,

I *will* get my driving licence back' became my silent mantra.

I felt relieved and bereft at the same time, but once past the first week, it was a joy to fall asleep rather than pass out. Waking up in the morning being able to remember going to bed was a novelty.

I told myself that this self-imposed abstinence would not be for ever – six months, say, or however long it took for my liver function tests to return to normal. A nagging voice in my head said, 'What if they don't? What will you do then?' I ignored it.

I began to eat again, taking delight in my food, though a meal without a glass or six of wine was purgatory. Water didn't do it for me.

Time moved on and I stopped counting the days and started counting the weeks. It was extraordinary how quickly I felt physically better. I decided not to tell any of my family I had stopped drinking. They'd heard it all before.

By week four I felt more connected, slightly less shell-shocked. I started to think about making a concerted effort to find some work. I reckoned I had enough capital from the sale of Avon House to survive about another year, tops.

Then I received a phone call from Meridian Television. I had done a few local news items for them in the past, mainly publicising wine tastings I was holding or commenting on award-winning wines in the news. When the call came in, I held my breath, wondering how I could explain that I wasn't drinking at the moment.

Fortunately, the job didn't involve drinking alcohol. Was I up for doing a piece to camera involving a water tasting? Did I think I could tell the difference between bottled and tap water? This was to link in with a report from *Which?* on the cost of bottled water. The filming could be done in a nearby coffee shop.

I couldn't believe my luck. Was my smiling angel orchestrating this? I wondered.

CHAPTER FORTY

TEMPTATION

Week five without a drink and I was getting ready to do the water tasting. Clothes were strewn all over my bed. I hadn't realised how much weight I'd lost. Many of my TV-type dresses hung off me.

I'd felt so nervous when I woke up I'd had to run, retching, to the bathroom. It wasn't until later that I realised this was the first time I'd been sick in five weeks. Five whole weeks!

I settled on a pair of black crêpe flares and a purple cashmere jumper. Still two hours to go. I always used to get nervous appearing live on TV. Back then I had survived by obliterating the anticipated anxiety with a few drinks the night before, operating the following morning on a cocktail of the leftover alcohol in my bloodstream mixed with adrenaline. I could feel the Three Swans Hotel calling me from just fifty yards over the road. Surely one or two vodka and tonics – singles, of course – couldn't do any harm? Such a tiny amount wouldn't affect my liver function tests, would it? The voice in my head was getting louder. I was pacing around my office, flexing my fingers, when the doorbell rang. It was Sue, a friend I'd asked to come and hold my hand during the shoot. I hugged her.

'You OK?' she asked. 'You look a bit pale. What's wrong?'

'I'm scared, really scared. Why don't we just pop across to the Three Swans for a sharpener?'

'Don't be daft. You're not drinking. And you don't need one now – you've lasted all these weeks. You'll be fine,' she assured me. 'You're always really good at these kinds of things. You're looking good, too. Very slimline.'

'Oh, come on,' I protested. 'One won't do any harm.'

'Alice, you don't need it. And it won't do any good either.'

We sat in the kitchen and drank Earl Grey, trying to do *The Times* crossword – the quick one. Six across, five letters. 'V-o-d-k-a . . . There may well be some vodka in the freezer. Let's have a small one, shall we?'

'No, no, no, no and *no*!' she insisted. 'Let's go down to the coffee shop and see if we need to set anything up for the shoot.'

The filming went well. I duly tasted the waters, able easily to detect the difference between bottled and tap.

'We just need some final drop-in shots,' said the producer. 'Let's use your friend and find someone else – a man, preferably.'

'Yes, well, we're both looking for men, aren't we, Sue?' I joked.

'What about him?' she asked as a man, stocky with thinning dark-blond hair and startling blue eyes, walked into the coffee shop and smiled at me. 'Do you know him?' she asked.

'Actually, I do, vaguely. His name's Martin.'

We filmed Martin and Sue drinking a coffee and a bottle of water together, laughing and nodding in mock conversation for the camera. Satisfied, the camera crew packed up and left. Hugely relieved it was over, I sat down for a cup of coffee with a Perrier chaser.

'We ought to be celebrating with a glass of champagne,' I lamented to Sue.

'A nice strong double espresso, that's what you need. That'll do the trick,' suggested Martin.

I looked at him. 'You look really well, much better than

when I last saw you. Have you been on holiday?'

'No, I haven't,' he replied. 'But I've stopped drinking.'

'Oh? And you used to drink shedloads, didn't you?'

'Yep, my drinking was totally out of control,' he replied. 'I used to drink during good times to celebrate and bad times to drown my sorrows and cheer myself up. I used to drink if the sun was shining or if it was raining – in fact, I used to just drink all the time and my life had become totally unmanageable.'

'You weren't that bad, were you?' asked Sue.

'Yes, I was – I was worse.'

'I've stopped drinking too,' I announced proudly. 'I haven't had a drink for five weeks now.'

He switched his gaze to me. 'Yes, I'd heard you drank a lot. So why have you stopped?'

'It's a long story. Basically, I lost my driving licence – not that I was in the habit of drink-driving, you understand – and I have to have a medical to get my licence back. I've already had one medical, but due to some kind of mix-up, even after four months of not having a single drop, my liver function tests were still over the top. But I am determined to get my licence back.'

'Alice,' he said, 'surely it's not your licence you need back – it's your life.'

'Yes!' Sue interjected. 'You're right. I keep trying to tell her this isn't about getting her driving licence back, it's about her health and sorting out the damage she might have done to her body.'

'Oh,' I gabbled, 'even the liver specialist thinks there might have been a mistake in my last blood test. So, anyway, Martin, if you're so clever, how did you stop?'

'I go to AA – you know, Alcoholics Anonymous.'

'Do you? Is it like the Masons? I've always wanted to know what goes on at those meetings – you know me, the nosy journalist.'

'Have you really? I'll take you to one if you want. There's one tomorrow.'

'Um, I might have the boys,' I stuttered. 'But by all means give me a ring. God, this coffee is so strong it's making my hands shake. I bet you used to get the shakes all the time.'

CHAPTER FORTY-ONE

FIRST AA MEETING

I wasn't an alcoholic, of course, but I had reasoned that since I wasn't drinking anyway, I might as well go to Alcoholics Anonymous. You know, for support. My therapist agreed. Anyway, going to AA didn't make me an alcoholic, did it? Going to France didn't make me French.

Now we were whizzing along the country lanes in Martin's car, on our way to the meeting, and this was reality. I was nervous. I was thinking, What am I doing in a car with this man? I had no idea why I had expressed an interest in going to an AA meeting. It must have been a caffeine rush from the coffee, a moment of madness in my – let's face it – otherwise staid, self-imposed dry desert of a life.

As Martin slowed the car, I was overwhelmed by anxiety, creeping up into my chest from the pit of my stomach – that sense of being in trouble, the way I used to feel after a bout of heavy drinking. I immediately felt thirsty. A nice, calming vodka and tonic, that's what I needed – that would dissipate the feeling.

'So, what actually happens at these meetings?' I asked. 'They're not formal, are they? I'm not sure now why I'm coming. Perhaps I could wait for you in the pub. There must be one nearby.'

He laughed. 'No, this meeting is in the middle of nowhere. Don't worry, you'll be fine.'

'What if I see someone I know?'

'Then they'll be there for the same reason you are. So it's OK, really – you have no need to be scared.'

'Hey,' I protested, 'hold on a minute – don't lump me into the same category as all the other . . .' My voice tailed off as I looked at him, unsure of the terminology, thinking the word 'alkies' may be a little harsh. 'Anyway, I'm here because I am curious, not because I've got a problem. You do understand that, don't you?'

He didn't answer and just nodded knowingly, as an indulgent parent would with a child who has been caught red-handed stealing biscuits and is still denying it.

I pulled my pink trilby down over my eyes. For once I didn't want to draw attention to myself. I was dressed sombrely in a black jumper and trousers, though the trilby and the leopard-skin coat I had grabbed as we left were hardly inconspicuous, it occurred to me. We got out of the car. I followed Martin, feeling sheepish. I was thirsty. God, this coat was a mistake.

There was a knot of people standing around outside what looked like a village hall. They didn't look like alcoholics to me – more like the sort of well-dressed, sober, respectable residents you would expect in a posh village like this. Two were around the same age as me, two looked older, and one guy with black spiky hair was in his early twenties. They were laughing, joking with each other. I was introduced to them, first names only. They all shook my hand and smiled at me. I felt as if I was at a drinks party with the vital ingredient missing. A large vodka and tonic – ice and fresh lime, yes – would be perfect right now, I thought, and would give me something to do with my hands.

As if he had read my thoughts, an older man, a retired military type with sparkling blue-grey eyes and silver hair, shook my hand and kept hold of it. 'First meeting?' he asked.

I nod.

'Well done you for coming along. I can assure you you'll never regret getting sober. It will change your life.'

'Actually, I'm sober already. I've just come along to see what happens at an AA meeting.'

'Well, you're very welcome. Try to listen out for the similarities rather than the differences in people's stories,' he suggested.

Stories? I think back to *Jackanory*.

'And don't worry if you don't feel like saying anything. Take time to reflect and listen.'

A picture of my father popped up in my head. He would regularly tell us to 'take time', whether time to think or, indeed, to laugh. What would he have thought of his daughter at an AA meeting? Suddenly I felt tearful, vulnerable and unsure of myself. Somebody handed me a cup of tea. He looked familiar, but I couldn't place his face.

Inside the hall, it was light and airy, open to the rafters. Chairs were set out in a circle round a small oak arts and crafts table. Two crimson roses drank deep in a vase in its centre. On the floor were white cards with slogans, like the flash cards I was taught to read with. These slogans were 'Keep it simple', 'First things first', 'One day at a time'.

The man who had given me the cup of tea started talking. I definitely knew that face from somewhere. He introduced himself: 'My name is Joseph and I'm an alcoholic.'

My mind went into overdrive. Did that mean he still drank? Had AA taught him to drink sensibly? Did I know his face from the pub? He introduced a man sitting to his right. 'I'd like to welcome Stewart, who has come from another group to share his experience with us.'

Stewart looked self-assured. 'I'd like to welcome Alice – I can remember my first meeting, when I came in, desperate, virtually on my knees,' he said.

Obviously he drank far more than I did, then. I wasn't that bad. The military man was looking at me from the other side of the circle. Christ, perhaps he could read my mind. 'Listen for the similarities, not the differences,' he had said.

Stewart began to tell his story. After a few minutes I found myself nodding in agreement. He described the exact emotions I had wrestled with all my life. How he had felt different as a boy, the odd one out. How he was successful in his job but felt like a small child underneath who would eventually, somehow, be found out. How he had always run away from his feelings – first literally, by running away from home at age six, and then as an adult by drowning them in drink. How he had started drinking to change the way he felt and to kill his fear. How once he started drinking he couldn't stop, often setting out to have just one or two and then not remembering coming home. How his life revolved around alcohol, how he used to surround himself with people who drank at least at much as him, ignored his family and spent huge swathes of time in the pub.

As he said all this, I felt my face colour.

He told how he had been a functioning alcoholic for years without realising it – how he used to think it totally normal, cool even, to get drunk every day, revelling in telling cronies his drunken stories. How, as his drinking progressed over the years, his circle of friends had shrunk. His wife left. He had become increasingly angry and bitter, not seeing his children. He had drunk all the more on the strength of it, in a vicious circle. How he had lost his driving licence, his job, and still didn't think he had a problem. On and on he went.

It was my story. Exactly.

My face flushed and my heart beat fast. I looked around the room. Everyone was listening intently. Was there some sort of scam going on here? Had Martin filled this guy in on the details of my life? It was uncanny. It was as if Stewart had been reading my journal. Not only were there alarming similarities in his actions, but his emotions mirrored my own. The similarities scared me.

He told a story about downing a bottle of Southern Comfort before a family party. I shifted uncomfortably, having flashbacks of the last drunken Christmas I had spent with my family and how upset my mother had been.

He described how much he had loathed and detested himself and how he, too, drank to obliterate those feelings. I felt a tear trickle down my cheek. I started to sniffle and a lady next to me handed me a tissue. I felt panic-stricken, as if something or someone was holding me under water. I found myself holding my breath, staring intently at the roses on the table, studying their petals. They were exactly the same colour as those I threw over my father's coffin as it was lowered into the ground.

Stewart explained how one morning, after waking up covered in blood with no memory of how he'd got home, he'd felt so desperate he knew he had to do something. That was when he had picked up the phone and called AA.

Then the tempo of his story changed. It became upbeat, full of hope and talk of recovery. He told how his life had been transformed since he'd stopped drinking and started coming to AA. How, slowly, by not drinking – one day at a time – he had begun to regain his self-esteem. His relationship with his children had improved, he'd found a new job, and friends had started calling again. It hadn't been easy at first, getting through days such as Christmas and his birthday without a drink, but if at any time he felt desperate for one, he simply picked up the phone to another AA member or went to a meeting.

I began to feel detached from my body. I gazed ever more intently at the roses, blinking my eyes. Was I really sitting in an AA meeting? How did I get here? What was I doing here? Snapshots of my own drunken behaviour from as long as twenty years ago flashed by in my mind like a slideshow.

I looked up as Stewart concluded: 'AA has given me the

tools to live a happy and fulfilling life, where I can hold my head up high. With the help of mates in AA and my higher power, I've not had a drink for over five years now, a day at a time.'

Five *years* without a drink? That's 5 times 365 days, not including leap years. Oh, come on now. That seemed beyond the realms of reality. Why give up for that length of time? To give up for ever seemed extreme. Whatever would I do with myself? Life would be so dull, flat-lining, being a good girl. Still, I reasoned, I probably wasn't as bad as him and would be able to start drinking again after I'd got my licence back.

What did he mean by 'It's the first drink that does the damage'? Surely he didn't get drunk after just one drink?

People in the circle started 'sharing' with Stewart, one at a time. No one interrupted each other. All recounted memories his story had evoked for them. They talked about what kind of week they'd, how they'd felt, what had been going on at home, at work and in their heads. Everybody simply listened to each other; no one commented; no one offered advice.

I was amazed – especially listening to the men talking about their emotions, about how things in their everyday lives had upset them, and the actions they had taken rather than reach for a drink.

I thought back over my life, realising that every time something had happened I hadn't felt comfortable with, my knee-jerk reaction had been to have a drink. In fact, that had been my knee-jerk reaction to any event – good, bad or indifferent. Was I really like these people? Surely I couldn't be an alcoholic, could I? Anybody would drink if they had my life, wouldn't they?

My mind went back over Stewart's story, how he had kidded himself for years that he didn't have a problem, how he had come up with innumerable weird and wonderful excuses as to why he drank. Had I done that?

All the signs in Stewart had been there for others to see,

but he had been blind to them, he had said. Was I like that? Surely it was just bad luck, losing all those work contracts? And losing my licence was definitely a case of wrong place, wrong time. Wasn't it?

The room went quiet for a moment. I spoke up: 'My name is Alice and I've come along to find out what AA is all about. I was interested to hear Stewart's story. I'll just leave it there for now.' I faltered, for once in my life at a loss for words. Was this a dream? A quiet, calm voice in my head said gently, firmly, 'This is not a dream. You are here. You are here because you need to be here.'

The meeting ended, and everyone stood up and held hands. What was going to happen now, ring-a-ring-a-roses? Someone pointed to a laminated prayer on the table: 'God grant me the serenity to accept the things I cannot change, courage to change the things I can and the wisdom to know the difference.' I recited it with the others.

I was quiet in the car on the way home, going over Stewart's words. I have the ability to remember people's words verbatim, a useful trick as a journalist.

Martin was talking to me: 'What did you think? Do you think you'll go again?'

'It was . . . interesting,' I replied, cagily. 'I have to admit, I was surprised. All the people look so, well, *normal*. I was expecting a load of down-and-out drunks, you know, tramp types. They were all so friendly. Several people gave me their telephone numbers. Is that usual?'

'Yes. Lots of us call each other most days. It's a great support network, especially if you're feeling down or if you feel like picking up a drink.'

'Well, I still don't think I'm an alcoholic. I know I'm a heavy drinker, but I think I've just been a bit unlucky.' He was silent, so I babbled on: 'Still, it's somewhere to go rather than the pub while I'm not drinking, and the people did seem really friendly.'

'There is another meeting tomorrow lunchtime. Why don't you come along?' he asked.

'I'll see. I may be busy. I'll call you.'

After Martin dropped me off, I realised where I'd seen Joseph before, the one who'd given me the cup of tea. He was a friend of a friend – he'd been round to my house once for a vodka tasting. Well, more of a session, actually. Yes, that was it. He'd been drunk when he arrived and his coat had been at mine for months after. Come to think of it, I must have been quite out of it myself. I couldn't recall the end of the evening.

Was that what Stewart had meant by 'blackouts'? They should have been a telltale sign that he had a problem, he'd said. I thought memory lapses were perfectly normal after a few drinks. If that was a blackout, I had been having them almost as far back as I could remember. There was that time, just before I got married, when Niall had exploded with rage, telling me I'd stolen a bottle of wine from a party. If it hadn't been for the bottle in my bag, I wouldn't have believed him.

I felt oddly tense as I opened my front door. I had the strangest feeling of something tugging at me, as if I was being pulled along by a speedboat but couldn't stand up on my waterskis.

I looked in the mirror. 'Am I an alcoholic?' I asked my reflection. The house was resolutely silent. The moon shone in, lighting up the gilt grapes on the top of the mirror.

CHAPTER FORTY-TWO

Mad Hatter's

I felt lighter when I awoke the next morning, as if I was floating rather than drowning. I lay in bed, thinking about the meeting and what I'd heard there. I felt something I hadn't felt since . . . oh . . . since I couldn't remember when.

Hope.

I was convinced that somehow, everything would be OK if I only believed that it could be. I had seen and heard hope in the meeting, and it was contagious – I wanted what these people had. There was some magic ingredient in their lives that made their eyes shine.

I had been told, 'If you put half the effort into your recovery as you did into your drinking, you'll be OK. The advice to any newcomer is to get to as many different meetings as possible.'

Not normally one to take advice, for some reason I accepted this. I took Martin up on his offer of a lunchtime AA meeting and found myself at what was nicknamed locally the Mad Hatter's Tea Party.

I could see why they called it that. This was a much more fluid, relaxed meeting with people popping in and out depending on their lunch breaks. It was held in a small church room around a table piled high with sandwiches and homemade cakes.

Again I was amazed by the openness of the people there, how friendly everyone was. I sat spellbound as these strangers bared their souls. It was humbling, listening to them explain how they had reached their respective rock bottoms in drink – some more dramatic than others – and what had made them decide to stop drinking. I realised with a start that I had hit my own rock bottom when I had collapsed in the pub. Perhaps the bang on the head had knocked some sense into my pickled brain.

Suddenly, I no longer felt alone. I was among people who understood my compulsion to drink, better than I did, and didn't judge me.

I felt more at ease to ask questions in the relaxed atmosphere. I took a deep breath. 'My name is Alice and I might be an alcoholic,' I said. The room fell totally silent in that second. 'How do you know if you are an alcoholic?'

'No one comes here by accident,' came the reply. 'If your life has become unmanageable due to alcohol, there is a fair chance you may be an alcoholic.'

Was my life unmanageable?

Well, I got by, didn't I? Or did I?

Having had such a successful career, I now had no work and no house. I had few friends and a history of broken, messy relationships. I thought about the thousands of nights I couldn't remember going to bed, the dreadful hangovers, the shame I constantly lived with. I contemplated the deep unhappiness I felt, my overwhelming feeling of hopelessness, the hollow loneliness of my life and how time and time again I had sought solace in the bottle. I had no purpose. I had lost sight of who I was. My self-respect and self-esteem were on the floor. Were all these things really down to alcohol?

I didn't have a chance to ponder much further, as a woman, a similar age to my mother, with silvery hair and twinkling hazel eyes, started to speak. She told how drink had taken over her life, how she had often ignored her children in her never-ending quest for the next drink. Like

Stewart, she was telling a version of my story. 'I didn't realise I'd been ill, that alcoholism is a disease – a physical, mental and spiritual illness,' she said.

An illness? I thought I drank too much because I was greedy and weak-willed. Had I been ill?

She started to describe my own symptoms – constant nausea, diarrhoea, headaches, back pain and panic attacks. She thought she'd been going mad. She'd had no direction in life and loathed herself for her behaviour.

I stared at her. I took a gulp of tea. The bitter tannin hit the roof of my mouth as if saying, 'Sit up! Pay attention!'

'By finally accepting that I was an alcoholic after years of denial, and staying sober one day at a time, I have a totally different life today and a wonderful relationship with my children,' she ended.

I frowned in thought. What kind of relationship did I have with my children?

A sudden, vivid, monochrome image came into my mind. I was cradling a bundle wrapped in a shawl. But there was no baby's face peeking out – there was a bottle. In that second I realised with horror that I had been an absent mother, that alcohol had become my all-consuming baby.

It was true. I was not here by accident. I was in the right place, at the Mad Hatter's Tea Party. I was Alice, after all, who had found the bottle and taken the direction 'Drink me' too literally.

Something stirred and shifted in my heart. I felt as if something had tenderly wrapped me in a soft, pink, cashmere blanket. Feeling safe, and held by some intangible force, I accepted it – I was an alcoholic.

CHAPTER FORTY-THREE

HIGH AS A KITE

Lid down ready for the road, gleaming blue in the June sunshine, my Little Blue Car is positively smiling. I know I am. I have my driving licence back after two years, four months and one week. It has been four months since my first AA meeting.

The squat leather gearstick feels good in my hand. Can I remember how to drive? I start her up and grin at Number Three son beside me. We listen to the car's throaty purr. We're off for a picnic – 'To celebrate that you can drive again, Mummy,' he says.

To me, this is a different kind of celebration – of freedom. I have regained my life.

'Will you start drinking again now you have your licence back?' a few doubters had asked.

One day at a time, the answer is a categorical 'No.' Why would I? Today I have the option to choose life over drinking. Without alcohol I am now free to have feelings and reactions, and to be the best me I can be. Life and health is coursing through my veins again.

Racing along the country lanes, I recall one of my father's pet sayings: 'Success is failure turned inside out.' Not for the first time I thank God I *did* lose my driving licence. I shudder to think where I would be now if I hadn't.

We meet up with an old friend, Jenny, one of the few friends honest enough to mourn the demise of her favourite drinking partner. We used to have a lot of fun together in my early days of drinking, when it still *was* fun. She is also a fantastic cook, so my son and I decide to let her supply the picnic.

And what a picnic it is. In a field of yellow cowslips is a fine spread – spicy chorizo sausages, potted shrimps and raspberry meringues with little flags with the words 'King of the Road'.

I watch my son's kite cavorting wildly in the sky. Jenny hands me a glass of ginger ale. As I take my first sip, I hear a familiar sound, the pop of a champagne cork.

'It's a bloody shame that you can't enjoy a weeny glass of this Pol Roger,' she says.

I look at her flute and watch the bubbles racing furiously upwards, glinting in the sun. 'It is not that I can't,' I say. 'It's that I choose not to.'

When I was in the grip of my compulsion, I had no choice. Once I had had one glass, I had to have another, and another, and another until I was drunk. My addiction had shackled me. Now that compulsion to drink, and keep on drinking, has miraculously been lifted right out of me.

I know what Stewart meant when he said, 'It's the first drink that does the damage.' Without the first there can't be a second, a third, or any more at all. I only ever have to decline one drink – the first.

'Even if I could have one, it would just be a flute full of consequences,' I add. 'You cannot imagine the relief I feel to be free from the guilt of drinking and then throwing up, the constant covering-up for my bad behaviour. I have the freedom to choose to go wherever I like. Freedom from all that drunken mayhem. Freedom to eat these sausages without puking up.'

While my friend snoozes, glass in hand, I reflect on the seeming paradox that this newfound freedom has come about by an act of surrender – by admitting I was powerless over alcohol. The day I decided I couldn't drink was the day I started to get better. By admitting defeat, I won back my life. I am out of my alcoholic prison and – as long as I don't take that first drink, just that first one – I will remain a free woman. AA has given me my Get-Out-of-Jail-Free card. Without my now-regular meetings I wouldn't be here at all, let at alone driving.

'Look at this!' shrieks my son as his kite loops the loop. He runs along with it, whooping with joy.

I jump up and follow, running across the field, chortling, 'I'm free! I'm free!'

'You've been drinking, Mummy!' he jokes.

'No. But I'm as high as your kite!'

CHAPTER FORTY-FOUR

CRAYFISHING

My first summer of freedom rolled on in a passage of surprising days. A friend I had meet at AA invited the boys and me out for a day cruising on his narrowboat. I had heard about an alternative way to catch crabs, baiting net bags with fish fingers. I wondered if the method would work for the many freshwater crayfish in the local Kennet and Avon Canal.

We looked under the sink for the little net bags you put washing-powder tablets in. There was a nest of saved carrier bags and old dishcloths (do they breed under there?) but not a net bag in sight.

'We'll get one at Somerfield when we buy the picnic,' I said.

'We'll need three,' pointed out Number Two son.

'You can share one,' I said. 'My mum didn't buy nine of everything.'

He rolled his eyes. We ended up buying three.

Attaching string to each bag and baiting them with fish fingers, we set off in the boat along the canal, the boys laughing and trailing their baited bags in the wake, or launching them lasso-style at other boats and the bank. There was great excitement when we spied our first crayfish, trapped on the gates of a lock. Like many of the great things in life, it was just out of reach.

I lay on top of the boat watching the sunlight through the

trees. White water lilies as intricate as origami floated in the still water. I thought back twenty-three years to the first time I had been along this stretch of the canal, walking hand in hand with Niall. I was twenty-one then, blonde and beautiful and already in love as I teetered down the towpath in my stilettos after a good, long, liquid lunch.

A lot of wine had flowed under the bridge since then. Too much, for me. But here we were today, with the sun well over the metaphorical yardarm and not a drink in sight. In the old days I would by now have appeased my hangover with a bloody Mary, celebrated our departure with a glass or six of fizz and be well into the second bottle of white Burgundy.

I was brought back to the moment with a squeak and a splash. Number Two son had toppled overboard. By the time I had sat up, he was laughing, lying back in the water, floating.

'It's quite relaxing really, Mummy.' He grinned. Minutes later, after we had hauled him out, Number Three son fell in – or did he jump, so as not to be left out? Number One son, sensible elder brother that he is, threw him the lifebuoy, which caught him squarely on the nose. There wasn't too much blood.

Peace resumed, we tootled on down the canal. Four miles an hour is about the right speed. We moored up, clambered off and dropped our lines. In less than a minute, Number Three son squealed. His line was twitching. He pulled it up. Three crayfish were clinging to the net bag. Amazement all round.

Forty or so crayfish later, we selected those with the biggest claws, dropped them in boiling water and barbecued them. I made garlic mayonnaise and we feasted on these finger-licking freshwater beauties. Number One son suggested we set up a stall selling them, such was the interest from passers-by. The crayfish tasted delicious, especially the sweet meat in the claws. We washed them down with English

Cox's apple juice. The combination was sensational.

The sun began to drop in the sky, turning it crayfish orange. The boys took to the towpath and raced the boat home, where they put themselves to bed, too tired to shower at an unprecedented eight thirty.

What a perfect day. And I'd not even thought of a drink.

Next time, I mused while lying in the bath later, when I'm a bit slimmer, I'd like to lie on the boat in my leopard-print bikini.

I felt a surge of gratitude flow through me. Recovery was only ever one day at a time, I had learnt, but this had been a good day. Getting out of the bath, on an impulse, I knelt and gave thanks – to what, I'm not sure. Perhaps my smiling guardian angel, perhaps my childhood God, perhaps AA. But something, somewhere, some higher power, was keeping me sober.

CHAPTER FORTY-FIVE

NAKED AT THE BOOK CLUB

Only 8 p.m. In my newfound sobriety, the days were getting longer. No longer drunk, comatose or hung-over, I cooked the tea, helped the boys with their homework, played Scrabble with them, read a book, twiddled my thumbs. And *still* only 8 p.m. I decided I needed to get out more. The pub had obviously lost its allure. There's a limit to the pints of lime and soda a girl can drink. I decided to join the local book club.

I gazed at a table covered in bottles of wine. Someone asked me what I'd like to drink.

'Coke, please,' I mumbled, eyeing the bottle of creamy New Zealand Lindauer fizz.

'Coke?' echoed the voice, unbelievingly. 'I thought you were a bit of a wine buff.'

I opened my mouth but no words came out. I wondered blackly if the owner of the voice had ever had a bottle of New Zealand Lindauer fizz over her head. Buff that.

The hostess arrived at the table. 'Ah, there you are. Do you know the others?'

All around me playground mums nursed large glasses of wine, red, white and rosé. Inwardly, I groaned. Those Stepford wives again. I clutched my glass of Coke so hard I almost crushed it. I shifted uncomfortably from foot to foot and reconnected my handbag with my shoulder, except that my shoulders were so hunched they seemed attached to my ears. Exposed, I felt naked without my liquid armour. My brain was crying out for a drink.

A woman with blonde hair and a green jumper looked at me. In a strong Scottish accent, she said, 'I don't know you, but I know who you are.'

The words of song 145 on my jukebox popped into my head: 'Alice, who the fuck is Alice?' Invisible Woman would have suited me right then – Wonder Woman had long since departed. 'All alone with the playground witches,' whispered a voice in my head.

I made no reply and she knocked back her glass of red. I watched her swallow it in slow motion. I could virtually taste it – Wolf Blass Cabernet, a ripe, intense blackberry flavour with a hint of eucalyptus. I smiled at her. Perfect. She had red-wine horns around her mouth. I thought that was just me.

'Well, you know what playground gossip is like,' she added conspiratorially.

No, actually, I didn't. No one ever used to speak to me. God knows what she had heard about me. 'Confirm the playground gossip true and neck that bottle of fizz in five minutes flat,' urged a sly voice in my head.

The hostess saw my discomfort. 'Come and meet some of the others.'

I followed her round like a little lamb. I had to practise self-censorship, as every time I was introduced to someone my inclination was to say, 'Hi, my name's Alice and I'm an alcoholic,' like I was used to doing at meetings. That would have livened up the proceedings.

But really, I was furiously thinking, Who am I?

It's easier to work out who I'm not. I am no longer Alice the wine writer. Without that label I feel disorientated, unsure as to my status. Equally, I am no longer Alice the drunk. In the bad old days I would have arrived half cut, if I had arrived at all.

I am no longer Alice the wife, though listening to some of the book-club chat I think that can only be a positive thing. Looking on the bright side is a new experience for me. In the throes of my addiction I would opt for the negative stance in every situation. Unsurprisingly I attracted people of the same ilk, ensuring my downwards spiral into depression. Drowning my feelings with alcohol only served to accelerate the decline.

I was still unsure as to how to deal with Mrs Green Jumper, who was telling her neighbour she didn't enjoy the book we were here to discuss.

'So what didn't you like about it?' I asked gently, trying to tone down my old confrontational approach.

Her face contorted as she thought, slurping her wine. I recognised the look on her face – it was fear, the same emotion I'd felt arriving here tonight. She was worried about what I would think about her comments. It was a relief to know that fear was not exclusive to me, any more than red-wine horns.

'I can't explain,' she said. 'You're the journalist.'

'Oh, don't worry,' I replied, laughing. 'I'm nothing but an ex-drunk.'

CHAPTER FORTY-SIX

WRITING FOR THE GOOD OF MY SOUL

I suppose I should not have been suprised to meet another journalist, Pete, at an AA meeting. Us journalists are credited with being a hard-drinking bunch. Slight and eager, Pete looked more the starving Parisian poet than the archetypal florid hack.

'All my life I've written about drinking,' I complained to him. 'What am I going to write about now?'

He shrugged. 'Write about not drinking.'

I had made the capital from the sale of Avon House last four years, but it was running out fast and I was in a quandary as to how to make a living. Looking for work as a wine journalist didn't make sense if I planned to stay sober. True, you can taste wine without drinking it, but the whole lifestyle, the lunches, the dinners and the press trips would make total abstinence problematical. I had to find some other way to support the boys and myself.

Pete suggested I write a newspaper column describing the progress of my recovery. I was still less than a year sober and I was learning new things every day, whereas he'd been sober for some years.

I wasn't sure.

'I can write about wine standing on my head . . . but baring my soul and writing about my emotions? I've no idea how to do that. Anyway, if it is such a good idea, why don't you do it?'

'I'm too far away from the early days of my recovery. It's all raw for you. Give it a go,' he replied. 'What have you got to lose? Besides, you need the money.'

I sat down at my computer with butterflies in my stomach. I hadn't written for years, beyond a few poems and short stories. My confidence was at rock bottom, but it felt positive and exciting to be taxing my brain again.

I reminded myself of an old school report my mother used to quote: 'Words cannot express the verbal and written abilities which are Alice's outstanding features.' (That same report had added: 'Alice would do a lot better if only she believed in herself.')

But there it was, the blank screen. Where to start? It was one thing to write about wine, my passion for twenty-five years, quite another to write about something that had happened to me only relatively recently and that I still didn't fully understand.

I made a beginning, but I found it difficult to come to terms with the words on the screen describing my own behaviour. Had that really been me? How could I have ignored my problem for so long?

Talking about my illness in the safety and anonymity of the AA rooms among like-minded people was easy. Writing it down made it real – and much more serious. I had greater difficulty typing the words 'I am an alcoholic' than I did speaking them.

I wrote three sample columns and gave them to Pete to look over. He was gentle with me but harsh with my copy. I decided to aim for the top and a day or two later, terrified, I picked up the phone and rang an old friend at *The Times*. We arranged to have lunch.

I was nervous as I sat waiting in the vodka bar where she had suggested we meet. Gazing at the line of flavoured vodkas, I weighed up the possibility of a swift one – vanilla was a favourite. It would put me at my ease. But it was only the old 'just the one' lie in action. The irony of it: to be drunk on vodka at an appointment to try to sell a column about my recovery from alcoholism. That's the insanity of the disease. I was relieved when she walked into the bar.

I hadn't seen her for a few years, not since I'd got horrendously drunk at her fortieth-birthday party. After ten minutes or so of chat about our children, I told her I had accepted I was an alcoholic, stopped drinking and changed my life. I started to apologise for my behaviour at her party when, smiling, she interjected, 'Is this step nine?' A friend of hers was also in recovery and she was familiar with the twelve-step programme.

A conversation I had dreaded for days was over in seconds, and it had been so simple! It was a good lesson on the futility of projection and worry. I was so relieved by the geniality of her approach I nearly burst into tears. Kindness still touches me like that.

Lunch over, she took my articles away. She couldn't promise anything but would show them to other section editors at *The Times*. Securing a column was difficult, she warned.

It was one of those drab autumn days when the only certainty was more rain. I had taken the boys to see *Chicken Run*. Back home, I listened to my voicemail. Could I ring Sandra Parsons, editor of *The Times*'s T2 section? I closed the door of my office and took a deep breath.

Ten minutes later I walked out smiling.

'Boys, let's have a celebration tea. I can't believe it – it's so exciting – I'm going to write a column for *The Times*!' I exclaimed.

I rang my mother. 'It mightn't be the ideal way to see your daughter in *The Times*, Mum, I know, but I'm really chuffed – and scared.'

'I'm so proud of you,' she said. 'And your father would have been too.'

I cooked the boys their favourite tea of toad in the hole and we drank ginger ale from the hollow-stemmed Georgian champagne glasses I reserve for special occasions. The rain had stopped and winter's early dark had fallen. Number Two son called me out into the garden. 'Look, Mummy, look at the stars twinkling at us.' We chinked our glasses and stared upwards. The stars really are brighter in sobriety.

My first weekly column, 'Sobering Up', was published. The editor emailed me to say how much she liked it. Several hundred readers emailed me, many to say how they identified with my story.

I had a one-line email from Number Two son, then at boarding school: 'Mummy i am so proud of u.' I pinned it up in my office. I felt sated, contented to the core – a feeling I was unfamiliar with.

A friend and I decided to go out and celebrate. On a bright, chilly November day, eight months after my first AA meeting, I took LBC out of the garage and put the roof down. We drove to a roadside breakfast van on the A4.

Never had bacon and egg doorstep sandwiches with white bread tasted so good. We toasted the winter sun with mugs of builder's tea, the steam rising in upward spiral wisps that caught the wind.

Sue Peart, editor of the *Mail on Sunday*'s *You* magazine, had been avidly following my column. She thought my story would resonate with her readers and invited me to write a feature. I did so.

The first email arrived at 7.02 a.m. on the Sunday the article appeared: 'My name is Sally. I have read your article and just realised I am an alcoholic. I identified with so much you described – the downward spiral of my life, my loss of friends, job and self-respect. I am desperate. My life is in chaos. However hard I try, I cannot stop drinking. Am I a bad person? I think my husband might leave me and I am afraid he may take the children. I am ashamed. I don't know what to do. Please help.'

Sally's email set the tone for close on a thousand more that flooded in over the next few days. Many people were desperate in their loneliness, suicidal in their hopelessness. Others sought advice in dealing with friends or loved ones with a problem. 'I am tired of keeping secrets about my father's drinking, sick of not being able to bring friends round to the house,' said Jill. 'Where can I find help or support?'

All were pleading for advice. I realised I had touched a nerve. One in six Britons is thought to have some sort of problem with alcohol, either through their own drinking or someone else's. With the help of others in AA and Al-Anon (for relatives and friends of alcoholics), I replied to each and every email.

Many asked, 'Am I an alcoholic?'

'Only you can decide,' was my reply. 'But if you think you have a problem, you probably do. The question would simply not arise otherwise. If your life has become unmanageable because of alcohol, you are probably one of us.'

Another often-asked question was, 'How does AA work?'

This set me thinking. The short answer is, I have no idea. AA offers the support of like-minded people who don't judge, having been there themselves, and offers alcoholics a tried-and-tested methodology of changing their behaviour by following its famous and much imitated twelve-step programme. All I know for sure is that is *does* work, for me. The compulsion to drink disappeared. I don't know how that happened, exactly – and frankly, I don't give a damn!

People were concerned that they couldn't go to AA while still drinking. This is not the case. All you need is the desire to stop drinking. Action and acceptance – living in the solution and not the problem – is the key to continuing recovery.

It felt good to be able to put something back into a world I had taken so much from. Helping other people also helped to keep me sober, grounding me and serving as a reminder that I could have all my misery back, with interest, any time I chose.

No, thanks.

CHAPTER FORTY-SEVEN

ONE STEP AT A TIME

I was invited to a ball at London's Dorchester Hotel. How could I refuse? I could no longer afford designer ball gowns so I headed for TK Maxx to find something to wear. I was delighted with my £29.99 full-length black velvet dress with diamanté shoestring straps and a plunging neckline. My cleavage was possibly the only part of me that had remained constant through drunkenness to sobriety.

I preened in front of the mirror at home, seeking advice from Number Two son, my in-house fashion consultant, as to which shoes I should wear. 'Definitely the strappy black Gina ones,' he counselled, having given my suggested shiny red stilettos the thumbs down.

Number Three son pressed 307 on the jukebox – 'This will get you in the mood, Mummy.'

'Dancing in the Street', the Mick Jagger and David Bowie cover, pumped out into the room. I sang along with the words: 'It doesn't matter what you wear as long as you are there!' but stopped in mid-song.

Oh, my God! How on earth was I going to dance without a drink or six inside me? Indeed, how would I get through an entire evening with people drinking all around me? This ball would be the first big social event I'd been to in eleven months of sobriety. I'd been worrying about Christmas looming. This would be a dry run for the festive season, I told myself.

I arrived at the Dorchester. Reluctantly parting company with my favourite red velvet Yves St Laurent jacket, I felt exposed and clung on to my brocade clutch bag as if it housed the Crown Jewels. My date for the night, an old friend, smiled encouragingly, even though I was gripping his arm tight enough to stop the circulation.

A waiter came forward with a tray of champagne glasses. The glasses were whispering to me, 'Just one, just one.' I selected a glass of fizzy water and, putting on my professional head, observed the 'bead'. The bubbles were considerably larger in the water than in the fizz. I noted how much more sluggishly they rose up the glass. Anything to quieten that sneaky siren's song.

I was introduced to a group of people. Most of them would have had a sharpener or two at home before coming out, I thought wistfully. I hoped the knot in my stomach wasn't evident through my dress. I looked up to the ceiling, at a loss for words. I had been to more Krug parties at the Dorchester than I could remember – indeed, I couldn't remember several of them at all – but never before had I noticed the spectacular moulded ceiling.

We sat at our table. I was separated from my date and placed next to a charity auctioneer. He was rotund, jovial and most concerned about my empty glass. 'What, you never drink?' he asked.

I opened my mouth and it gushed out, 'I am an alcoholic. I used to be a wine writer and now I'm writing a column about sobriety for *The Times*.'

He raised his eyebrows, smiled. 'How interesting. I used to – well, still do, really – have a similar problem with food.'

I eyed his glass of claret, rich, red and mellow, its cigar-box aroma wafting up my nostrils. I looked away. Glancing around the table, I noticed how slowly people were drinking. The man opposite me had had the same glass of white wine in front of him for over half an hour. The life expectancy of drinks in front of me was measured in seconds.

The time came for the auctioneer to sing for his supper. He managed to bid the room up into paying £21,000 for the pleasure of having Albert Roux cook a dinner party in the winner's home. Two couples were bidding so Roux offered, generously, to do it twice. I could live on £21,000 for a year! Watching the auction, I forgot about my wineless glass and enjoyed the banter around the table.

Auction over, the music started. I was relieved when my date, who was itching to dance and unable to persuade me, disappeared to dance with a woman at the next table. I sat back and watched, happy for once to be a wallflower – albeit a dehydrated one. No one on the dance floor seemed drunk.

I looked away as I saw my date heading in my direction, but he pulled me on to the dance floor. My mind raced back. Had I ever danced sober in my life? No, was the quick conclusion. The last time I could vaguely remember dancing was rum-drunk in a favourite Jamaican restaurant, the Hi Lo in Oxford, with a group of guys who claimed to be Bob Marley's Wailers. 'Imagine you are a worm that has been cut in half,' one had told me, pulling me up on to the table. 'Each part of your body needs to writhe separately. Come on – wriggle!'

But right then at the Dorchester, I felt more like a worm that wanted to slither into the earth. I faltered, Bambi-like, and tried to smile, though I was conscious that my *Come Dancing* grin looked sprayed on.

The music stopped and I went to make a quick exit, but my partner grabbed me again. Sweet's 'Ballroom Blitz' started up. 'Blitz, Blitz, Ballroom Blitz!' I mouthed manically. Then I changed the words: 'Dance, dance, I *can* dance!' I continued through gritted teeth. Halfway through the song, I looked around. A few people seemed even gawkier than me – and they'd had a drink. My face relaxed into a real smile. It was a relief not to be the drunken centre of attention. I began to enjoy myself. The next record – 'Le Freak' – brought back memories of being fourteen and drunk on vodka and lime at the Young Farmers' Dance. It seemed like another century. Actually, it was.

I grabbed a surprised auctioneer and we boogied. Leaving the Dorchester with my date, literally dancing in the street back to the car, I realised that rarely was anything as bad as fear made it. I could dance sober, one foot in front of the other, one step at a time.

CHAPTER FORTY-EIGHT

First Christmas

Laden with bottles of vintage champagne, I piled the boys into the car and headed for my mother's house for the 2005 Christmas family party. The boys were excited. They loved meeting up with their eighteen cousins almost as much as they loved the presents.

For myself, I was terrified. The year before saw me arrive drunk, ignoring the family's fine wines to disappear to the pub for large vodkas and drunken rubbish-talk with the locals. I had ignored my mother and my brothers and sisters, who were all trying to come to terms with Christmas without our father, in favour of my constant comforter, the bottle. They had faced their pain. I had tried to obliterate mine.

An uncomfortable memory surfaced – my eldest sister losing her temper and shrieking, 'Stop ruining your life and your children's! Just stop!' I couldn't recall my indignant, slurred reply. Just as well.

There was a large pop from the back of the car. 'Look out!' yelled Number One son. 'Everybody duck – exploding champagne corks!' The boys jabbered on excitedly in the back.

As my anxiety had increased, so had my speed. I eased my foot off the accelerator – I had to slow down, think about my behaviour. No point trying to hide it away in the bottle banks of my mind and pretending it didn't happen. My mother had had to deal with my drunken phone calls and my selfish, spoilt-brat behaviour. My brothers and sisters had been subject to my drunken prima donna antics at family parties going back years. My behaviour had caused a rift between my eldest brother and myself, and I had missed the closeness we had shared through my teens to my early thirties.

My sister Juliana had been saint-like in her patience with me, while I had ranted and raved. She'd invited the boys and me on several family holidays. My other brothers and sisters had remained in touch, albeit at a distance, and when I had spoken to them it had always been about me, me, me. I had no clue what was going on in their lives. Counting up, I realised with a shock that there were five whose houses I had never visited.

Although I had stopped drinking, I knew it was unreasonable to expect my siblings to greet me with open arms. The tornado may have stopped blowing, but the devastation remained. Making amends to my family was going to take time.

'Are you looking forward to seeing your brothers and sisters, Mummy?' piped up Number Two son. 'You look really worried – you keep frowning.'

'Yes,' I said. 'I'm worried about my drunken behaviour last year.'

'Don't worry,' he replied. 'They'll forgive you. They're your family, after all.'

What a child – eleven going on eighty. I hoped he was right.

We arrived and marched in with the bottles. 'I come bearing gifts,' I joked to my mother.

'How wonderful,' she replied, hugging me. 'We were getting low on champagne. Weren't you tempted to drink them?'

'I was the other day. Not today,' I replied.

My siblings came out in ones and twos. They all greeted me warmly, as did their partners. I served the champagne. My left hand was shaking.

'So, which one is best?' asked one brother.

'Oh, all of these are good. I only brought the best ones. Here, try this – Billecart-Salmon Rosé 1996. Summer pudding in a glass – delicious.'

Juliana handed me a glass of pomegranate juice. 'Not quite the same, I know,' she said.

We chinked glasses.

'Thanks,' I replied. 'For everything.'

Lunch was served. Everyone sampled the champagnes, expressing appreciation. No one was in the least bit drunk. I sat and watched them enjoy the Krug Clos du Mesnil 1995, one of the most complex, multi-layered champagnes I had ever tasted, with its unusual creamy, floral flavour. It is produced in tiny quantities – unlike the forgiveness and love my family appeared to possess.

I started to apologise to my eldest sister for the previous year. 'Don't worry,' she said. 'You've been ill. You look so well now. It's just wonderful to see you getting better.'

I blinked back tears and took a gulp of pomegranate juice. It went down the wrong way and I started to choke. 'Drinking too fast again!' laughed my brother.

We started giving out the presents, youngest cousin first. It felt good watching all the happy, excited faces and I felt blessed to be part of such a large family. I no longer felt different or alone. I started to relax, grateful that they weren't judging me, glad not to be the embarrassing, intoxicated centre of attention. The children attacked their presents with glee, tearing the paper off with delighted shrieks. After two hours I retired to the kitchen for a cup of tea. Number Two son followed me in.

'What was your best present, Mummy?' he asked.

'Good question. I'm not sure.'

'What about being sober? That's like a different present, isn't it?'

I looked at him in amazement. 'Good thinking,' I replied.

'Yes . . . the gift of sobriety. You're right. What a funny boy you are!'

He winked at me and left, tossing his new juggling balls to his cousins.

I sat down and savoured the delicate aroma of my Twinings Rose Pouchong tea. What had sobriety meant to me in the last year?

I looked up the word in my mother's dictionary – 'Absence of drunkenness,' it read. I could improve on that – absence of guilt, shame, remorse, hangovers and retching. My gain was colossal. I had recovered my self-respect. I had banished the self-pity I used to drown with drink. I was more at ease in my own skin and slowly rebuilding relationships with friends and family. I was touched by my brothers' and sisters' forgiveness and continually delighted in the ever-deepening closeness of my relationship with my sons. I even had my sense of humour back. All this in less than a year.

My mother came into the kitchen. 'You know, Dad would be really proud of you,' she said.

'Mummy,' I replied, with a tear in my eye, 'thanks. Thanks for not giving up on me. I bet you wanted to kill me this time last year.'

'No,' she replied softly. 'We could see you were killing yourself.'

CHAPTER FORTY-NINE

First Anniversary

I woke up and saw it was still dark, the stars shining. An old crescent moon was sinking into the west. It was a special day – my first anniversary – a whole year without a drink.

There had been a time when I couldn't have imagined a day without a drink, let alone 365 of them. It hadn't been easy. When I first stopped drinking I didn't think I would ever enjoy myself again. I lay in bed and, as on every other day of my recovery, thanked God I didn't have a hangover. I felt grateful and pleased with myself, eager to celebrate my anniversary when the dawn came.

I got out of bed and looked in the mirror. Things have definitely changed on the outside; I look totally different for a start. My skin has returned to its natural glow and I've put some weight on. When I was drinking I was a curious colour, a sort of translucent greyish-white. Actually, I rarely looked in the mirror – I couldn't face it – such was my self-hatred. But it is what has changed on the inside that really counts.

Though there was something still niggling in the back of my mind. Did I really have cause to celebrate? When I first went to AA, they told me I'd been ill – that I had an illness, a disease, a kind of allergy that once activated, resulted in me not being able to stop drinking, and, while drunk, saying and doing things I would never have considered when sober. There was a part of my brain that didn't fully accept this explanation. 'Weak-willed, degenerate and bad' were some of the things I'd been called. Was that closer to the truth?

I went into my office and switched on the computer. I Googled 'alcoholism' and found myself at the World Health Organization's definition: 'A disease marked by loss of control over drinking, caused by a pre-existing biological abnormality, and having a predictable, progressive course.'

'A pre-existing biological abnormality'? Well, that made sense. Maybe I would still have been an alcoholic if I'd become a fashion writer. Just a better-dressed one. The American Society of Addictive Medicine talked of a 'primary, chronic disease with genetic, psychosocial and environmental factors'.

There was an email from Bill, the scientist friend to whom I had mentioned my misgivings. 'This is a simplified explanation,' he wrote. 'Alcoholism *is* an illness. Pleasure centres in the brain are stimulated by chemicals such as endorphins plus alcohol, cigarettes, drugs and many other things. This causes the brain to release chemicals which then affect the brain's pleasure centres.' It was a relief to know that it wasn't simply a matter of being greedy.

'In consequence,' he continued, 'some people just can't handle alcohol and drugs in the same way. Those suffering from alcohol abuse can often not control the need to take alcohol because of the demands of their brain – you imbibe and the brain rewards the body, saying, "Thank you." This is how habit forms on many levels and is linked to your brain's own individual pleasure centres. Brains do not forget – so it will always be waiting for you!'

I twirled round in my chair. Two well-respected bodies and one scientist defined alcoholism as a disease. So it *was* a disease – 'a primary, chronic disease' – that was not my fault, but it was my responsibility. It was up to me whether or not I activated it by taking a drink.

I smiled and realised I had even more cause to celebrate. Unlike many other killer diseases, I could keep mine at bay by simply not drinking one day at a time, no drugs or nasty treatments necessary. I could now give myself permission to party.

I decided to bake a cake. My mother had recently reminded me of when I had won the cookery prize at school, age fourteen, for a spectacular chocolate confection. I baked the cake and climbed back into bed – without the cake, that is. A strange thing to do at 5 a.m. – but healthier than drinking vodka, I told myself. I dozed off and awoke again with the sun streaming into my bedroom.

Like an excited child, I found it difficult to concentrate on work as the morning wore on, watching the clock, willing it to be four o'clock, when the boys came home. I had invited four friends to celebrate and one arrived at three thirty with a huge present. I unwrapped it to find a hand-painted *Alice in Wonderland* tea set, complete with plates saying, 'Eat me,' and a milk jug saying, 'Drink me.'

The boys got home at the same time as my other friends arrived, two of them also recovering alcoholics. I almost cried when I read the cards. 'We are so proud of you.' I read those words over and over again. Where would I be without my friends and family? Drunk, likely. Or dead.

We sat round the table for cups of Earl Grey tea and huge slices of chocolate cake.

'This is just like our Mad Hatter's AA meeting,' remarked one friend. Number Two son disappeared, to return moments later with my purple velvet top hat. He plonked it on my head.

At that moment the doorbell rang. Hat still on, I answered the door to find the milkman.

'It's my, erm, birthday,' I explained, debating for a second whether to go into detail. He handed me his bill as squeals of laughter filtered through from the kitchen.

'Sounds like you're having a right old boozy time of it,' he said, winking at me. He knew me of old.

'No – just high on life, honest!' I giggled while paying him.

I wandered into the sitting room, where my guests now were.

'Mummy, can I put the Wurlitzer on?' asked Number Three son. 'Then it will be a real party.'

The jukebox lit up and cranked into action. Number Three son was grinning and frantically pressing buttons. Andy Fairweather-Lowe blasted out: 'Wide-eyed and legless, I've gone and done it again.'

Thank God I hadn't. I laughed. Cause indeed for celebration.

CHAPTER FIFTY

Cross Words

Valentine's Day came and went. No cards. I was not without male admirers, though the men I knew were friends rather than lovers. I'd had my fingers burned early in recovery by having a brief fling with a friend in AA. The advice is not to start any new relationships in the first year of recovery. Looking back, I can see why. I had simply replaced my compulsion to drink with my need for attention and approval.

Picking men up drunk was one thing, but chatting up a man sober was much more challenging. I also had no desire to hang around the pub looking for a mate. As the months went by, I found myself spending more time with Pete, the journalist who had encouraged me to write my column for *The Times*. When I met him, I was raw, still shell-shocked and massively lacking in self-confidence. I looked up to his four years of sobriety – I couldn't imagine going that amount of time without a drink.

We started going to the theatre together. One of the most memorable plays we saw was a magnificent performance by Martin Shaw in *A Man for All Seasons* at Bath's Theatre Royal. Was that what I needed, a man for all seasons? Was I ready for a 'proper' relationship, whatever that meant? In truth, any thought of a relationship scared me. The thought of failure was too daunting.

But it was a delight to find someone with whom I could

share my love of words. Our text messages became fast and furious and increasingly flirtatious. We would spend hours bantering on the phone about books, authors and poets. I had much to catch up on, having roughly had a twenty-year literary sabbatical while drinking. As he jokingly put it – at least I took him to be joking, though just as with my brothers I was never quite sure – 'I was reading Dante while you were reading wine lists.' Touché.

We took to doing the crossword together and ended up doing it in bed, playfully squabbling over it. No champagne, just raspberries and honey.

Sober sex doesn't happen by accident. Pete and I had discussed whether we should go to bed together. Would it ruin our friendship? Well, at least for a few minutes! Making love by design rather than drunken accident made it all the more tender, special and thrilling for me. And I certainly saw stars – the glow stars on my bedroom ceiling, that is.

But as the months passed, it appeared that I wanted more from this relationship than he did. He was working full-time, so much busier than I was, and I didn't feel sated. For all-or-nothing Alice, feeling like a part-time girlfriend didn't go down well and I began to feel undervalued, unimportant.

The competitiveness and quips between us that had once been so much fun started to take on an edge and it became obvious that we weren't making each other happy. One day Pete bumped into Niall by accident and commented how alike they looked. I had never noticed any similarity, but this started me thinking. Were they alike, in looks or character? And then one day, at the end of summer, after yet another row he walked out of my life. The texts stopped.

I felt gutted, but I understood that I couldn't change him; I could only change myself. I had to accept that I wanted more of a full-time relationship, or certainly more than he appeared to be offering, and that we were not good together. We seemed to be bringing out the worst in each other rather than the best, firing up each other's insecurities instead of soothing them.

I reasoned that if I could give up the bottle, I could give him up; indeed, it appeared we had given up – and given up on – each other. But logic and emotion are two different things. It was hard. I prayed a lot. I cried and raged and talked and talked to my girlfriends. I went to lots of AA meetings.

And I didn't drink.

As time went by, I began to feel better. I realised I had been needy, perhaps stiflingly so. As much as I hated to admit it, that old adage about learning to love yourself before trying to love someone else was true. It dawned on me that much as I might like a man around, I didn't *need* a man to validate me. My heart was mending, slowly.

Anger. A dangerous place for a recovering alcoholic. We can drink on anger, and – most dangerous of all – anger over the most ridiculously trivial things.

Number Two son needed new tennis shoes. So all three boys and I drove the ten miles to our nearest shopping centre hoping to find a bargain. We chose a pair and waited twenty minutes to be served. The shop assistant went off and returned after a further fifteen minutes, saying, 'We ain't got 'em in a size four. Seven is the smallest. So I've brought those instead.'

Number One son giggled, but noticing my face contorting into a sneer, he prudently grabbed my elbow and steered me away.

Number Two son, oblivious to my smouldering rage, said, 'What about these Lacoste ones? I love the crocodile.'

'You must be joking,' I snapped. 'Have you seen the price tag? They're nearly fifty pounds!'

Number One son intervened again: 'He's a spoilt brat, Mummy, and you always give in to him. Let's go to a different shop.'

We traipsed to another store. Garish signs greeted us promising 'massive reductions on Reeboks'. We went in. I found a half-price pair in size four and triumphantly presented them to Number Two son.

'Reeboks are for girls,' he sniffed.

I was overcome with rage, threw the trainers down in a tantrum and marched off across the shop to find an assistant. We waited ten minutes to be served and, exasperated, I beckoned to the boys to leave. As we walked out, Number Two son pounced on a pair of size fours lurking by the exit.

'These fit perfectly,' he said timidly. 'And they're only ten pounds.'

Number One son was about to question the coolness of the brand, Le Coq Sportif, but sensibly kept his mouth shut. Just in time, as I was ready to explode again.

I drove home. A driver cut me up at a roundabout and I tooted my horn, raised my fist and screamed, 'Road hog!' at him.

'Mummy,' said Number Three son, who had been quiet until now, 'is that road rage?'

I spluttered and muttered, 'I'll show you road rage.'

The three nodded knowingly at each other, plugged in their earphones and turned on their iPods.

When I arrived home, I couldn't park outside my house, the way blocked by a large van. 'National Blood Service', it said on the side. 'Please give blood.'

Give blood? Draw blood, more like – I could have scratched the driver's eyes out, the way I felt. I parked down the road and stomped home, chuntering, 'God give me patience! Don't these people realise I'm trying to stay sober?'

It had been a long time since I had lost my temper, and the rush of adrenaline in me pressed the 'alcoholic' button. Suddenly I had a raging thirst. I deserved a drink after a morning like this, didn't I? A bottle of chilled rosé . . . or a nice, cool beer would do the trick. I sat there, obsessing about a drink, fighting it. My mobile went – a friend from AA.

'Hungry?' he ventured.

'No, angry,' I replied.

We went out to lunch across the road at the Three Swans. I attacked a deliciously bloody fillet steak, smothered in fiery English mustard. Nothing like a bleeding piece of meat to dissipate rage. I recounted my morning's antics.

After only a few minutes we were both giggling about it. My anger – and thirst – abated. All I'd needed was to share my feelings, get them in context. In the past, I would have acted on my seething rage and would have tried to quell it with a drink – and another and another – invariably ranting and raving about other people's appallingly selfish behaviour, totally oblivious to my own.

My bad behaviour aside, nobody died and nobody got drunk. It was close, mind.

CHAPTER FIFTY-ONE

Sober Surfing

It was autumn half-term 2006 and Numbers One and Two sons had two weeks holiday rather than the standard one. Two weeks? How would I keep two active boys busy without spending a fortune I didn't have? I was pondering my dilemma when a friend piped up, 'I have a cottage at Appledore in north Devon you can have. Take them surfing. They'll love it.' I hugged him tight.

So there I was, standing on the pebbled shore on a sunny but blustery November day, looking out to sea, watching the white horses break. The tide was a long way out and I could just see the outlines of my boys bobbing about on their boards.

It was extraordinary how proficient they had become in just a few days, both of them managing to stand up during their first lesson, learning how to turn, to catch the swell at the right moment. Each evening they returned to the cottage, sun-kissed and exhilarated, full of surfer-dude talk until they crashed out, early, utterly exhausted.

Justin, one of their surfing instructors, saw me watching. 'Aren't you going to join us?' he asked. 'It's fantastic surf out there today.'

'It hadn't occurred to me,' I replied. 'Anyway, isn't it freezing? I'm not as hardy as the boys.'

'Funnily enough, we've got a wetsuit in just your size.

Come on, surprise them. I'll find you the suit and a board and we'll get going.'

'But I've never surfed before!' I protested.

'Neither had your sons until a few days ago.'

Before I knew what was happening I was trussed up in a wetsuit and striding down the beach, board under my arm, quite the surf chick. There was no time for fear, but as we struggled across the pebbles, it occurred to me how much I had changed. When I was drinking, I wouldn't have considered surfing. I probably wouldn't even have been here to watch them; I'd have been holed up in some dark, dingy pub.

Justin showed me how to do a 'pop-up' – the intricate movement from belly-down to feet – and the interim move from belly to kneeling. 'Kneel as if you were saying your prayers, only lean forward and hold on.' Once I was in the water, I could see that prayers may well be a necessity.

He held my board while I struggled on. I was pleasantly surprised that the water in my wetsuit was not that cold. 'It's had all summer to warm up – that's why this is the best time of year to surf,' he said. As my board wobbled from side to side, he shouted over the crashing of the waves, 'You need to keep your weight centred. Surfing is all about balance!'

Quite, I thought, my mouth full of my first taste of sea-water for years. I had been searching for balance all my life. Having been self-obsessed and self-centred for so many years, I'd gone totally the other way when I'd first sobered up. Much to my friends' amazement, I became so compliant and selfless I was in danger of becoming a doormat – equally unhealthy.

I was glad of the leash round my ankle, otherwise I would have lost my board in the crashing waves, so much bigger now I was here out among them.

'Watch out for the white water – if you're not paying attention, it can catch up with you and knock you off balance,' called Justin. A wave crashed over my board as I got to my knees and I slid off, head first, into the water.

'Spectacular wipe-out!' laughed Justin. 'Keep your feet inside the rails.'

'I specialise in going off the rails,' I yelled back. 'What are the rails?'

'The edges of the board. Keep your weight centred – that's the trick.'

A wave picked me up and I beamed at the exhilaration of riding it, albeit on my knees. As I stabilised myself on the board, my sons spotted me.

'Mummy, is that really you?' bellowed Number One son, his expression incredulous. 'Mummy, on a surfboard!' he shrieks across to his brother, riding a huge wave and spectacularly surfing along the 'tube', catching the white water as it broke.

Justin did a headstand on his board while riding a wave. Number Two son, a gymnast, followed suit. I marvelled that both my boys should exhibit such remarkable balance – in all areas of their lives – given what I'd put them through.

Come to think of it, I used to be a bit of a gymnast myself, legendary for my headstands – I recalled with a shudder that drunken day by the whirly pool, when I'd showed off my aptitude. For today, I thought I'd quit while I was ahead. I felt a real sense of achievement for having taken part – on the crest of a wave!

CHAPTER FIFTY-TWO

SERENITY SANTA

It was midnight on Christmas Eve. My second sober Christmas. I crept along the corridor to see if the boys were asleep. Peering through the frosted glass on their bedroom door I heard Number Three son giggling, 'Eek, look, there's a shape at the window.'

'Sure,' replied Number One son, sarcastically, 'and I suppose it has a hooded red cloak on too.'

Good idea, I thought, and began to rummage through the airing cupboard. Somewhere there was a Father Christmas outfit that used to clothe the mannequin in the hall at Avon House. Ah, found it, behind the mislaid crumpled damask napkins that had given up waiting to be ironed. I put it on, admired my reflection in the hall mirror and took deep breaths to stifle my giggles. As I looked into the mirror, I was temporarily dazzled by the twinkling lights from my alternative Christmas tree. I was proud of it. It was quite arty for me. It was a branch, part of a fallen tree rescued from Savernake Forest. Well, stolen, actually. I had dragged it along a muddy path and bundled it into the back of the ancient Merc and triumphantly driven it home with the boot open. I had rigged it up next to the jukebox, where it twisted up at a right angle along the ceiling and divided into three spindly branches. Suspended by fishing wire from the light fixture, Number Two and I had decorated it. We had opted for the minimalist approach of white fairy lights that faded on and off, clear glass baubles and shiny deep-red apples and pears coated in sugar-like glitter.

As I stood at the door, I felt as if I was looking into an enchanted forest. The magic of reality dazzled me. All my years of striving to manufacture and inhabit a fantasy world, driven by more and more alcohol- and adrenaline-filled highs, had blinded me to the beauty of normality.

I was struck by what this bit of dead tree signified for me: a new life, split branches depicting the three paths I could take. At any time I had a choice. One was drunkenness and despair; the second involved staying sober and not changing my behaviour; and the third, the right-hand branch, saw me changing my behaviour and improving the quality of my sobriety. I knew I was on the right path.

More stifled shrieks from the bedroom reminded me there was work to be done. I made a few Santa-like appearances past their bedroom door and retreated into the kitchen to finish the last of the wrapping and the stocking stuffing.

The kitchen was heavy with the aroma of cloves and cinnamon from the mulled fruit punch I'd made earlier. I smiled as I poured myself a glass. Earlier, after the carol concert, several friends had dropped by. They had commented on feeling tipsy after a few glasses of my winter concoction and were surprised to learn there was no alcohol in it, just cranberry and blackcurrant juice, slices of clementines, an orange stuck with cloves, a cinnamon stick, a pinch of ginger and a judicious dollop of runny honey.

A few drunken revellers meandered past the kitchen window, zigzagging across the road. One, complete with festive reindeer horns, missed the pavement completely and veered into the wall. He waved as he noticed me peering through the steamed-up windowpane.

'Happy Christmas,' he hiccuped, as he ricocheted off a parked car and disappeared down the street. Everything was quiet, save the rhythmical snoring of Number One son.

I lugged the three bulging red velvet stockings into the sitting room and over to the fireplace. On top of a large handmade wooden number 11 London bus stood a bottle of ginger ale, a single hollow-stemmed Georgian champagne glass, some chocolate coins and a few jellybeans. There was also a neatly written note. Holding it up to the flickering fire, I read, 'To Santa, here is your ginger ale (as you are a recovering alcoholic) and some lovely chocolates and sweets.'

Not for the first time that evening my eyes filled with tears. What a magical note, full of childlike, matter-of-fact acceptance. I climbed into bed in my Santa outfit and fell asleep.

CHAPTER FIFTY-THREE

FORGIVENESS

I am drunk. I alight from the train at Hungerford Station and reel home, my heels echoing in the clear midnight air. Avon House is lit up – there is a party in full swing. I pick my way through the bodies and the bottles down to the basement. Niall is sitting in half-darkness in the children's playroom, a giant claret glass in his hand.

'What are you doing here?' I ask.

'I've decided to move back into the basement,' he replies.

'You can't just do that,' I protest.

'This can be my bedroom.'

I think for a few seconds and then accept it. 'We'll have to find our old red bed. It may be in the garage.'

He stands up and we embrace. In that instant, I forgive him – and myself.

He follows me up two flights of stairs to my office. Guests, including several old boyfriends, move to one side to allow us through. I open the door. Two workmen, grey with plaster dust, are re-wiring my office, gouging the walls with drills, making new channels for the cable. We stand in silence and watch them. My whole body, from my hair to my heels, reverberates with the drilling. The workmen pack up and leave, closing the door behind them.

'We made a mess of things, didn't we, Queenie?' Niall says.

'Yes, we both made mistakes, amazingly big mistakes,' I reply.

We smile at each other and chink our glasses.

I open my eyes. I feel as if I have been running up a steep hill and have now reached a plateau and slowed to a steady pace. The clock tells me it's 6.50 a.m. and the dawn is silent. It is a full five minutes until I realise I've been dreaming.

Forgiveness tastes good. It seems fitting that today I have been sober exactly two years.

CHAPTER FIFTY-FOUR

SAS

The rain was dripping down the window. I lay in bed trying not to be awake. I knew I should be writing, but I wasn't. Thoughts were spinning round my head like a manic washing machine – worries, fears, anxieties that made my heart beat faster, made me sweat, made me *thirsty*.

For the first time in months the thought of a drink came into my mind. I wanted something to take the edge off everything. I thought of the euphoria I would feel after the first drink, the numbness before I blacked out. I wanted to silence the committee meeting in my head. I didn't want to think; I didn't want to feel.

The night before, my debit card had been declined at the Co-op. For just £3.32. I had to abandon my two naan breads and *crème fraîche*, hurtle home and scrabble through old handbags for loose change. Obviously I was up to my overdraft limit. And I was two years sober! This sort of thing was not meant to happen!

I was alone in the house. Even if the boys were there, what could they do? I thought of tossing a coin as to whether I should have a drink. There was at least one bottle of champagne in the pantry. The temperature of the fizz would be just right. I could almost feel the dancing bubbles on my tongue, pricking the back of my throat.

I knew there was no problem in the world that drinking would not make worse, but the coaxing voice in my head was getting louder. The compulsion – the *need* – to drink had long gone. Only occasionally, the desire to drink came back. There is a difference. There was nothing I could do about compulsion, but desire left me with a choice. I could give in to it or not.

Reluctantly I got out of bed. This would not do, duvet-diving at 9 a.m., obsessing about a drink. I needed to take action. I thought back to the AA advice: 'Don't pick up a drink, pick up the phone.' I rang my keep-fit buddies, Sue and Sue, 'Big' and 'Little'. We called ourselves the SAS – for Sue, Alice and Sue.

'Fancy a walk?' I asked.

'Sounds good to me,' said Little Sue. 'The rain has just stopped. See you in ten. Wrap up warm – there's a hell of a wind.'

I put the phone down and dressed quickly. I realised I was hungry and headed to the pantry for cereal. Where was it? Oh, yes, on top of the wine rack. I grabbed the gluten-free Vita Pro and looked at the packet. 'Protein-rich soya, rice and corn cereal flakes with honey and cinnamon.' Sounded good. A flash of gold caught my eye. I looked down and gazed just for a second at the shiny foil. Two bottles of fizz, Jacquart and Veuve Clicquot, both vintage. I closed the pantry door quickly and opened the fridge for milk. No whispering bottles in there, thank God.

The doorbell rang and I stepped outside to join my friends. It was one of those early spring days when we had already had all four seasons – wind, hail, rain, thunder, lightning and now blue sky. It was cold and we walked fast out along the road and past the marsh.

I walked with my eyes wide open, striding ahead, pounding the road.

'Hold on a minute,' said a breathless Little Sue. 'What's eating you? You're going like the clappers. I can't keep up!'

'I'm thirsty.'

'Don't worry, I've got some water in my backpack,' she replied.

I grimaced as we stopped, caught our breath and took swigs from the plastic bottle.

'I didn't really mean thirsty for water – I meant thirsty for a *drink*.'

Little Sue looked at me, her carefully plucked eyebrows almost disappearing under her black headband. 'Alice, it's only nine in the morning! Christ, do you still think about booze? How long is it now?'

We set off up a steep hill. It was as much as I could do to keep going. I felt sick. To take my mind off the hill, I did a calculation in my head. It was two years plus a month and a bit, I reckoned. Twice 365 plus 30-something.

At the top of the hill, as my breathing slowed, I opened my mouth and replied, 'Seven hundred and sixty days.'

The two Sues whistled. We marched on, arms pushing backwards and forwards, robot-like, fists clenched, bottoms wiggling – three women on a mission.

Resting for a moment, I looked around. My SAS sisters and I had become quite knowledgeable about the magnificent array of wildlife and flowers and shrubs around us. I could now tell my columbine from my chickweed. As the spring sun broke through, a herd of deer cavorted across a field in front of us.

Setting off again, my sensitive nose began twitching, detecting the unmistakeable, pungent aroma of foxes. Wild pale-yellow primroses peeked out between the horse chestnuts just beginning to sprout their sticky buds. An early gatekeeper butterfly settled on a cobweb that glistened with dew. Suddenly I realised all thoughts of alcohol had disappeared. The desire had vanished.

At the end of our circular march, we stopped at a café and sat outside in the pale sun drinking decaf coffee. I retrieved my childhood *Observer's Book of Wild Flowers* from Little

Sue's backpack and looked up the Latin names for old man's beard (*Clematis vitalba*) and cow parsley (*Aethusa cynapium*). We planned our next day's assignment – to find some *Salix aurita*, or pussy willow.

We were all three laughing, trying to pronounce the Latin names. It was clear none of us had done Latin at school. Little Sue, who worked in my local pub and saw me at my drinking worst, chuckled, 'I'd never have believed it a few years ago if someone had told me I'd see you planning an expedition to find pussy willow. Vodka, yes. But pussy willow?'

Later, as I strode home, I felt happy, joyful, heady and high – just as I used to after that first magical taste of champagne. If I'd had a glass that morning, it would have led to a bender. Thank goodness I had picked up the phone, not a drink.

CHAPTER FIFTY-FIVE

FAULTY WIRING

The irony of it. I am off to my local bookshop to sign copies of the updated edition of *Fabulous Fizz* and I can't touch a drop. The fridge is full of the stuff, chilling for the signing. Quick. Put the kettle on.

The doorbell rings. It's my old friend, Monsieur le Chauffeur, now Monsieur le Former Chauffeur.

'I arrived early for the book signing so I thought I'd drop in for a cup of tea,' he says.

I hug him, rather too tightly. 'Thank God you did. I could hear the fizz in my fridge calling to me. I was sorely tempted to open a bottle to calm my nerves.'

We sit down with a soothing cup of Earl Grey. He picks up the *Guardian* and starts reading. Looking over the top of the paper, he says casually, 'Tell me, do you think controlled drinking ever works?'

'It didn't for me, and I tried every trick in the book – not drinking in January, not drinking while I wrote a book, not drinking during the week, not drinking at the weekend, not drinking spirits, not drinking before six o'clock, not drinking when I had the children.

'Controlled drinking to an alcoholic is an oxymoron. It doesn't work. Oh, I had delusions of control, but they were short-lived. When I returned to my drinking, I always ended up drinking more and faster every time. My brain tells me that just one glass of champagne would be fine. And it would be, if it was just one. But when did I ever have *one* glass of anything?' I realise I am ranting but can't stop.

'The "I've had enough" wiring in my brain is faulty – and, here's the rub, it always will be. I can't ever have a drink, not on high days or holidays or even book-signing days like today.'

I have his full attention now. 'Hmm. Have some more tea,' he says.

But he has opened the floodgates. Nerves make me gabble.

'I know that as long as I don't take the first drink, just the first one, I will be fine. A few AA friends who had given up for years found themselves right back where they started when they succumbed to the "just one drink" scenario. It's every alcoholic's obsession, you know, that one day we'll be able to drink like normal people.'

'Do we know any normal people?' he jokes, as I pause for breath.

'Normal people, as in non-alcoholics, don't feel the need to control their drinking. It doesn't cross their minds. Only people like me, with a drinking problem, feel the need to control it.'

Exhausted I stop and step down from my soapbox. He helps me pack the champagne into cases and we wander down the road to the shop. Almost immediately a customer approaches and buys a copy of my book. I hand her a glass of champagne and sign it to her mother for Christmas.

'What champagne will you be drinking this Christmas?' she asks.

'Well, my family love champagne, and if there is any left over from this signing, I'll probably take them some of this,' I reply, pointing to the bottles of Nicolas Feuillatte Grand Cru 1996 we had brought down.

Several more people arrive, including AA friends, who chortle at my situation. The other customers drink fizz. We indulge in flutes of ginger beer mixed with ginger ale and a squeeze of fresh lime.

Relieved it's all over, I walk home. Number Two son is standing on the doorstep. 'Did you have a good book signing, Mummy?'

'Really good, thanks. We sold fifty copies and I didn't have a drink.'

CHAPTER FIFTY-SIX

Hangover From Hell

I have the hangover from hell. It is 3 a.m. and I wake up, heart hammering, covered in sweat. My head is foggy and groggy, and my eyes feel swollen. My throat feels dry, and the mouldy-cardboard taste in my mouth makes me retch. But these days there is no permanent ice bucket by my bed – the only type of sick bucket for a wine writer.

I think back to the previous night. What on earth had I been doing? What a relief it is to be able to remember. I had spent the day with Pete at the arboretum at Westonbirt, marvelling at the magnolias, intoxicated by their milky vanilla scent, picking up stray pink petals and stroking them, soft as a baby's ear. The sun had been shining and I felt good. I hadn't clapped eyes on or heard from Pete in seven months, until I had bumped into him at an AA meeting.

As we walked through the trees, the conversation started gingerly, with me trying desperately to zip my mouth and let him talk about how he'd been. After half an hour or so we had resumed our normal banter of playfully interrupting each other, talking about the books we had read and how quickly or slowly our respective writing was going. We compared notes on our recovery, discussing the good days and the bad, and exchanged notes on who was still around in AA – those that had gone out drinking again and vanished or died.

We agreed we'd missed our banter. Hungry from the walking and the talking, we stopped at the Snooty Fox in Tetbury. I had cod with thick chips and mushy peas, washed down with lashings of Fentiman's ginger beer. We joked about how the evening would have been if we'd been drinking – the magnums of champagne and bottles of port lined up at the bar wouldn't have stood a chance. And no doubt we would have ended the evening climbing the stairs to the four-poster bed.

Instead, well fed, we'd laughed and chatted, grateful that not drinking didn't detract from our enjoyment. I decided to have a cigar, the Snooty Fox being the kind of hotel to stock decent brands. The first puff was delicious and I enjoyed blowing out the smoke and watching it swirl across the bar.

Our conversation suddenly somersaulted, touching on a hurtful incident around our parting. I decided I needed and deserved another cigar. At the bar, the hotel manager and a regular were playing spoof. 'Care to join us?' they asked.

'I love spoof,' I said. 'How many coins? I'll have to be quick – I'm here with someone.'

'Just take him his cigar,' replied the landlord.

'Can't,' I replied. 'It's mine.'

We played three games. The adrenaline surge when I won surprised me. I decided to have a third cigar and returned to Pete, boasting of my success. He stood up, ready to go, but I didn't want the evening to end and had ordered another cafetière of coffee.

'More, more, more!' he laughed.

'Yep! Two addicts together – what could be *more* normal?'

We drove home almost in silence, and he dropped me off. I thought to invite him in but decided against it. To have become lovers in the first place, when we had been such good friends, had probably been a mistake, I reluctantly told myself.

Hence this humdinger of a hangover – of the emotional, coffee and cigar variety. At this moment in time, it feels as toxic as any alcoholic combination. I gingerly get out of bed and think about the day ahead. I have to attend the funeral of a friend in AA at nine thirty, and at noon a crowd of boys will be arriving for Number Three's tenth-birthday party. I have a cake to make, games to get ready and – oh, no – dozens of balloons to blow up.

It occurs to me that I will always need to keep an eye on my addictive behaviour, to face the insatiable 'more, more, more' part of my character and learn to feel satisfied. I have to steer away from quick fixes. I resolve to give up men – and cigars – and concentrate on my writing. Well, for the time being anyway.

CHAPTER FIFTY-SEVEN

Snowdrops

I am standing in a sea of snowdrops, spread out before me like a white, shimmering mirage between the trees and the river, as far as the eye can see. I've been to see my therapist and am in a contemplative mood.

When I was drinking, I would head to the pub straight after every therapy session. The bottle of rosé never used to touch the sides. Anything to avoid having to feel, to contemplate my part in whatever we had discussed. Half cut, I was never capable of processing my feelings or resolving any of the issues we discussed.

Now I no longer have booze, therapy sessions are becoming more challenging – and a great deal more painful. I'm shocked to feel stomach-churning emotions washing over my senses daily. I used to become angry after the first few drinks, exuding an aggressive, bitter sarcasm. I now realise that the anger masked deeper emotions such as grief, loss, guilt, jealousy and rejection.

Today I feel sad. I'm starting the grieving process for the loss of my dreams of marriage and happy ever after. It is spring 2007, eight years since my divorce, and this is the first time I've let myself feel the loss.

In the early days of my marriage I was madly in love. I was amazed to have found someone with whom I could have so much fun, someone who was amusing, with whom I could laugh and cry, someone who would support me in my work, make be feel visible and valued. It's easy to forget all the positive things about a marriage when it ends in unhappiness and hatred. Ours had turned into a deluge of drunken rows, the clashes of inflated egos and debilitating competitiveness. In drink – and I was always 'in drink' – it became convenient for me endlessly to dredge up the bad times and ignore the good. Now my newly active psyche can be indiscriminate in its memory selection, especially after therapy. Sobriety has opened my eyes and given me the chance to look at the past in a more balanced fashion.

Standing among the snowdrops, I realise that my marriage was more like a viniferous conjurer's trick, an illusion, clouded by a haze of fine wine. The man I married had not lived up to my childlike – and thus unrealistic – expectations. Drinking had stunted my emotional development. Despite growing older in years, I had lacked the emotional maturity to sustain a relationship.

I'm crying and the blanket of snowdrops is blurred around the edges. The scene in front of me looks more like a lake of snowdrops floating in champagne. It occurs to me that I'm not out of the woods in terms of recovery from alcoholism. I also need to acknowledge the demise of my relationship with fine wine, especially champagne, the real love of my life. I think of my father, who taught me how to appreciate it. I know he would be proud to see me facing my drink problem. I can see his smiling face and cheeky bearded grin as he salutes me, glass raised.

I realise with a start that my foot is sinking into the muddy path. This walk was a spur-of-the-moment decision and my high-heeled lace-ups are struggling to cope. I have visions of being sucked into a bog. Death by snowdrops? I move to firmer ground.

I find a church, sit down. The old, musty smell envelops me. I feel safe, held, cherished, and no longer alone. Sun streams through the windows and dances on the carved eagle on the lectern.

And I realise that it really is OK to experience all of these feelings. As I embrace them, I feel better, stronger, more powerful, like the eagle. I don't need to run away from emotions any longer, like I'd done when a little girl in France. I know these gut-wrenching feelings will pass – indeed, in only the last few hours, my grief has begun to change shape into acceptance. Magically, I feel full of hope, content to be sitting in a sun-filled church surrounded by snowdrops.

As I'm leaving, I glance at a leaflet in the church porch. I learn that snowdrops were used by the ancient Greeks as an antidote to poisonous drugs. I know I'm in the perfect place today.

CHAPTER FIFTY-EIGHT

READING THE LEAVES

'Floral, like a summer's day,' I jotted down in my notebook. I sniffed again. What was that elusive aroma? I took another slurp and let the liquid roll around my tongue. Suddenly the memory came back. Yes, definitely roses – like Turkish delight, I decided, as I spat into the sink and watched the copper-coloured liquid disappear down the plughole.

On to the next one. Concentrate. Deeper, more orangey-brown in colour. Was that a hint of nuts? But what kind? Hazelnuts? No, not hazelnuts. Not bitter enough for walnuts. Something softer, creamier, like macadamia nuts – but not quite. I closed my eyes. Chestnuts! That was it – toasted chestnuts. As a little girl, I used to eat them with salt on.

Only six more to go. To think I used to taste a hundred wines most days. I need not have worried that my taste buds would be out of practice. Although I'd been slow to start this morning, after the first few all the adjectives came flooding back, sometimes in a strange order, admittedly, but it was reassuring to know that I'd not lost my skill. It felt good to be tasting again.

I stopped and put the kettle on. How lucky I was, I reflected, looking out of the window, that I had a talent I could still use. In sobriety my taste buds were sharper than ever. No more furry tongues, thank God.

It must have been divine intervention that had made me

wake up one morning and decide to write to a tea company offering to write their tasting notes. To my surprise, they'd agreed with alacrity. So now, instead of starting the day with vodka, I start with a cup of tea. This then, legitimately, leads to another and another – until it is time to boil the kettle again.

I couldn't have predicted this twist of fortune from the tea leaves.

CHAPTER FIFTY-NINE

THREE FOR A GIRL

I am walking through a field of clover. It's summer 2007 and the early-morning dew is soaking through my new walking shoes, which are making a satisfying squelching sound in the wet earth. To my left, the ruins of Pembrokeshire's Carew Castle rise out of the mist. I'm convinced I can see ghostly figures manning the turrets, pale faces at the windows.

I blink, and as I open my eyes again a sharp ray of sunshine peeps through the clouds and dazzles me, casting silent, hopeful new daylight across the fields. A solitary fisherman stands on the causeway, casting his line into the swirling estuary.

I climb a stile into a leafy lane, the hedges brimming with pink and white dog roses. A scent hits me. Fox? No, it's a different kind of pungency, similarly earthy but fresher, sweeter. It reminds me of something, but what? Garlic mushrooms pop into my head. That's it. It's wild garlic, growing in abundance on the banks.

Crossing another stile, I enter a newly planted field of corn. Rows of sprouting shoots stand in formation like ballerinas in green leafy costumes, swaying dain- eeze. I pause to watch a tiny spider breakfast on ke a bluebottle four times its size. The web, glis- ew, reminds me of the Spirograph patterns I s a little girl.

Two and half years ago I wouldn't have woken up bright-eyed and bushy-tailed like this. I would have come to nursing a horrendous hangover, got the daily retching over with and be planning my first drink to numb my shame-soaked thoughts.

I'm on the way to the village shop to buy a newspaper. In my drinking days I hardly read at all, aside from the occasional wine book or Sunday supplement, bloody Mary in hand on my perch in the pub. I wasn't interested in what was going on in the world around me at any level – in nature, politics or other people's lives. As far as I was concerned, I was the centre of the universe. I worked on a need-to-know basis. Unless something directly affected me or my next drink I wasn't interested.

Thank God I'm not still stumbling down that old path. My eyes are open and I'm grateful someone showed me a different way. Now I can take simple pleasures in something as banal as going for a walk and marvelling at the beauty around me. It doesn't come much more beautiful or uncontrived than this, a castle set against rolling green fields and an effortlessly natural powder-puff sky.

Taking a different route back to the holiday cottage, I cross a field of lambs. They stand in a line, defiantly baa-ing at me. I open my mouth and baa back. After a few minutes I cannot baa any more for laughing, the tears tumbling down my cheeks. I scour the field for a black sheep, but there isn't one. I'm glad I'm no longer the black sheep today.

The next field is full of Jersey cows with Maybelline-long eyelashes. They would look good in mascara. They are friskier than the lambs, hoofing it down the field after me. Fear creeps in – are they bulls? – and I quicken my pace. Glancing behind, I realise they're close. I can see the milk whites of their eyes. I am convinced one has steam puffing out of its nostrils. Fight or flight?

I recall a farm holiday in Wales as a child, and being

frightened of the cows. 'Stand your ground and look them straight in the eye, they'll soon back off,' laughed the farmer.

Taking his advice forty years later, I whirl round to face the Jerseys – and christen my new shoe in a fresh, organic cowpat. No matter. I didn't get sober to be intimidated by a bunch of cows, I tell myself, standing fast. Face the fear and do it anyway. One beast bucks and hoofs backwards. Like line dancers, the others follow suit. I heave a sigh of relief and walk backwards for the stile, pirouetting at the last minute and stumbling over it.

I sit at my desk in the cottage looking out over the garden, the castle in the background, the sweet aroma of cowpat rising from my shoes. On the lawn there are three magpies. 'One for sorrow, two for joy, three for a girl,' runs the song in my head.

I always thought I would have four children. I have my three boys – is this a sign, 'three for a girl'? Probably not. At forty-six, the chances of having a daughter are pretty slim.

Then it comes to me. The girl is me – the happy little girl in me who was lost, drowned in alcohol, little Alice who was terrified every time big, angry Alice neglected her and staggered off on yet another bender.

I feel blessed to have rediscovered me.

AFTERWORD

As I come to, lying in bed, I feel as if my shoulders are stapled to my ears. What is that feeling, tightness of breathes and pain in my chest? Ah yes, fear, terror of the unknown. Today Number Three son, now eleven, starts at a new school. But it is not this that keeps my shoulders hunched, it's the fact that I, too, will be the new girl today, starting a new project, as a consultant for a pioneering drugs and alcohol rehabilitation centre, Winthrop Hall in Kent. I think back to my early days as a twenty-year-old in *Decanter* magazine's offices. I remember feeling the same terror then, that clutching feeling in my stomach that could be soothed away in an instant by a swift glass or two of wine. I recall getting up one morning in my father's flat in London and bursting into tears, crying that I was so, so scared about doing my first interview with a wine merchant and the prospect of writing my debut story. 'What will I say?' I'd shrieked. He'd smiled kindly at me, 'Alice, you are never at a loss for words, you'll be fine, I promise.'

Instead, on this autumn morning in 2008, I take several deep breaths and pour cornflakes into two bowls. I glance across at Number Three son who seems quite at ease munching away. I find I have little appetite and gaze out of the window, spoon halfway to my mouth. By way of trying to appease the rising panic within, I start to make a gratitude list in my head, the sure-fire way I have discovered during my almost four years of sobriety to quell fear and dispel self pity and anxiety.

First, I am still sober, a miracle in itself. Second, the sun is shining. Third, I am sitting here with my Number Three son, who is smiling, humming away to himself in between crunching his cornflakes. At the height of my drinking, he rarely smiled. Joy is contagious – looking at him I feel my mouth relax into a grin. Numbers one and two sons have already gone back to school, but their cheeky faces beam out at me from a surfing photo on the fridge door. Now teenagers, sixteen and fourteen respectively, today we have a healthy relationship. In the early months of sobriety it was tough for us all adjusting to the renewal of the parent–child relationship, when for a while it had been the other way around – the two of them often acting as the parent, making sure the door was the locked, the lights turned out and so on, as I descended into yet another drunken slumber. When I look at my boys today, and think of the fun I have with them and the strength of our relationship, it shocks me to think what I could have missed if I had continued drinking.

The message light beeps on my mobile phone, interrupting my thoughts. 'Break a leg, darling', it reads, 'you'll be fine. You are an amazing woman. Don't forget that'. I stare at it, willing it to be true. It's true, it is amazing that I am still sober, but am I amazing? I find myself tilting my head and smiling again, coyly, at my phone. The message sender, my new man, must be fourth on my gratitude list. He'd been a chunky prop forward in earlier life, and I'd met him at a rugby match when I had pretty much given up on men, deciding that watching sport was far safer then the risky business of taking part in the mating game. We'd fallen into easy conversation in the pale winter sun, pausing every so often to cheer the team on. It wasn't till later, looking across the Indian restaurant table, poppadum in hand, that I realised with a start, the bright, twinkling eyes behind the spectacles were green – there is definitely something magnetic about men with green eyes. Some months later we'd discovered we had much more in common than a love of rugby – a joie de vivre I never thought would return when I first stopped drinking.

We'd started out as friends, meeting occasionally to go to the theatre together or out for a meal. He'd read my book and marvelled at how I could have so much fun without drinking. As the months went on, I realised I was becoming alarmingly fond of this man and that scared me. I wanted to make sure that I was not simply falling into old patterns, but somehow this relationship seemed different, more authentic. Neither of us felt the need to compete with each other, the driving force, I can now see looking back, in my marriage. But was I really ready to open my heart and show my vulnerability to another man? Would my sobriety cope with any potential rejection or yet more newly discovered layers of emotions?

There is no doubt about it, I am definitely more cautious in sobriety, weighing up the pros and cons of things, often questioning my motives before taking action. But for cautious, do not read boring – life has never been more full; I marvel that I had the time to drink. Today, I have a policy to live life in the moment and embrace everything I can – sometimes I have problems fitting it all in. I have no idea how the job, or the new man come to that, will pan out, but what I do know is that I am enjoying taking part. No need today to view things from a bar floor.

The last few months have seen me partying (even dancing in broad daylight!) at the Innocent smoothie village fête in London's Regent Park, joining a press trip to Brussels to highlight awareness of osteoporosis and meeting legendary James Bond girl Ursula Andress, all without any thought of a drink. I've even been surfing again with my boys in Cornwall, though coming out of the sea in my wetsuit was hardly the same picture as that iconic photo of Ursula emerging from the sea in *Dr No*!

Just yesterday, I muse, early on a Sunday morning, found me on my dentist's 45-foot yacht. Four years ago, I would have been under the duvet nursing a hangover. As the sun rose higher in the sky and *Emma Keturah* cut through the waves, I was struck by the sense of freedom that sobriety continues to deliver. I was smiling rather inanely, thinking what a motley crew we were, dentist, doctor, nurse and ex-drunk, when the doctor posed a question I am often asked: 'why do you still go to AA?'

The simple answer is that I go to make sure I stay well; I am only ever sober one day at a time and have heard enough horror stories of how others have gone out for just one drink and found themselves only weeks later, jobless, homeless and having lost all the self-respect they had gained in sobriety. If I ever feel a bit low, I always feel better after a meeting. My spirit is lifted by listening to how others adjust and deal with this deadly disease on a daily basis.

Very occasionally, I am tempted by a drink. My brain thinks, I wasn't that bad, was I? But when I see new people arriving at AA, shaking, pale and riddled with guilt, I am reminded of the severity of active addiction. I realise I can have that misery back anytime I want. I shudder to think where I would be now if people stopped going to AA after a few years' sobriety – most likely drunk or more likely dead.

Yes, much to feel grateful for today.

I am brought back to the present by Number Three son drumming his fingers on the table. 'Mummy, isn't it time to go? I am a bit scared,' he admits. I pack his bags in the car before thinking of a reply.

'Courage is fear walking,' I say to him, though as much to reassure myself.

'Well, we best get walking then,' he replies stoically as he skips to the car.

*

It is midnight, a month or so later, and I am driving home after dinner with two old friends. These days I have a stack of invitations from old and new friends alike. Flashing blue lights appear in my rear view mirror. I am within fifty yards of my house. I stop the car, feeling my heart rate increase. I get out of the car at the same time as the policeman gets out of his.

'Just a routine check, madam,' he says. 'Where have you been tonight?'

'At the Harrow in Little Bedwyn. Do you know it? The food is inspired. It's one star Michelin you know. And they have a stunning wine list.'

'Can I see your licence, madam?' he asks. I fish around in my handbag, still ever messy, and hand it to him. I notice my left hand is shaking.

'And when did have you have your last drink, madam?' he asks, raising his eyebrows.

I pause and smile. 'Fifteenth January 2005,' I reply jubilantly.

He looks at me incredulously, and, somewhat hesitantly, he says, 'And may I ask you, why did you stop?'

'I had a major problem with drinking. In fact, I had become an alcoholic.'

'What did you used to drink – was it mainly wine?' he enquires.

'Certainly, to start with. But in the end it was vodka, neat, first thing in the morning.'

He looks at me, questioningly.

'The wife and me like to drink a bottle of wine every evening with our supper. Sometimes it turns into two. I do worry a bit about drinking too much. Actually, there is quite a bit of hard drinking in the force you know. You would think we would know better, given what we have to deal with and all the drunks we see in the cells, week in, week out.'

'Yes, I have experience of your cells,' I say.

'What were you in there for?'

'Drink driving,' I reply.

'You have got a current licence I take it?' he asks as if talking to a naughty schoolgirl. 'Yes, yes,' I reassure him, 'I got it back years ago.'

'Was it hard,' he continues, 'giving up drinking?'

'Oh, I got lots of help from AA. It's a fantastic self-help group. And you would be amazed at the kind of people I meet at meetings all over the world: butchers, bakers, even the odd policeman,' I add, grinning. 'One of the most challenging things has been finding a new way of making a living. I used to be a wine writer, you see.'

'Are you the girl that wrote that book about it? Me and the wife read about it in the *Mail on Sunday*'s *You* magazine and cut out the article.'

'The very same,' I reply.

'Well, I admire you. The wife will be impressed when she hears that I've met you. Good night, madam, and good luck. I admire your courage. You'll probably never know how much difference your book will make.'

He shakes my hand – a policeman shaking my hand – what a difference a few years makes.

ACKNOWLEDGEMENTS

Many people helped in the creation of this book. Thanks to Gill Morgan of *The Times* and Sue Peart of *You* magazine, who both suggested I write it; my agent, Ben Mason, of Sheil Land Associates, who sold it; Ian Marshall of Orion, who bought it; Steve Wyatt, who knocked the copy into shape; Jenny Ford, who helped and fed me; Pam Garraway, who tamed the computer when it went wild; Chris Razey, who tirelessly encouraged me; therapists Jacqui Smith and Tove Frisvold, who kept me sane; Sue Court and Sue Arkell, who kept me fit; Amanda Searle, who photographed me; my sister Juliana, who made me laugh when I cried; and my AA friends, who kept me sober.

Other people who deserve special mention are James Barnett, Big Chris, Bo and Charles, Marie Claire Brind, Hilary, Mikey Chinner, Klem Cowan, Jeremy, Paddy Lennon, Nigel Perrin, Reading Jim, Anna Valentine and Penny Wark.

Finally, thanks to my mother, who never stopped believing in me, and my three sons, who helped me retain a sense of humour.

USEFUL CONTACTS:

AA Helpline 0845 769 7555
   www.alcoholics-anonymous.org.uk
Al-Anon Helpline 0207 403 0888
   www.al-anonuk.org.uk
www.highsobriety.co.uk

"The Domestic Diva series is always worth reading . . .
Ms. Davis just keeps getting better."   —Fresh Fiction

"Davis . . . again combines food and felonies in this tasty whodunit, which keeps the reader fascinated until the killer is iced."
                              —*Richmond Times-Dispatch*

"The quirky characters are well developed, the story line is
as crisp as a fall apple, and the twists and turns are as tight
as a corkscrew."   —AnnArbor.com

"Davis finely blends mystery and comedy, keeping *The Diva
Haunts the House* entertaining and alluring."

                                          —SeattlePI.com

"Raucous humor, affectionate characters, and delectable recipes highlight this unpredictable mystery that entertains during any season."   —Kings River Life Magazine

"Reader alert: Tasty descriptions may spark intense cupcake
cravings."   —*The Washington Post*

"[A] fun romp through the world of chocolate."
                                —Lesa's Book Critiques

"[A] delightful series . . . *The Diva Steals a Chocolate Kiss*
is full of murder, secret identities, poison, missing persons,
and chocolate treats."   —Open Book Society

"Loaded with atmosphere and charm."   —*Library Journal*

"Davis plates up another delectable whodunit, complete with
recipes. Indeed, her novels are every bit as good as Diane
Mott Davidson's Goldy Schulz mysteries."   —Shine

"A mouthwatering mix of murder, mirth, and mayhem."
                        —Mary Jane Maffini, author of
                        The Busy Woman's Guide to Murder

Berkley Prime Crime titles by Krista Davis

Domestic Diva Mysteries

THE DIVA RUNS OUT OF THYME
THE DIVA TAKES THE CAKE
THE DIVA PAINTS THE TOWN
THE DIVA COOKS A GOOSE
THE DIVA HAUNTS THE HOUSE
THE DIVA DIGS UP THE DIRT
THE DIVA FROSTS A CUPCAKE
THE DIVA WRAPS IT UP
THE DIVA STEALS A CHOCOLATE KISS
THE DIVA SERVES HIGH TEA

Paws & Claws Mysteries

MURDER, SHE BARKED
THE GHOST AND MRS. MEWER
MURDER MOST HOWL

The Diva Serves High Tea

KRISTA DAVIS

BERKLEY PRIME CRIME, NEW YORK

BERKLEY
PRIME
CRIME

An imprint of Penguin Random House LLC
375 Hudson Street, New York, New York 10014

THE DIVA SERVES HIGH TEA

A Berkley Prime Crime Book / published by arrangement with the author

ISBN: 9780425282656

PUBLISHING HISTORY
Berkley Prime Crime mass-market edition / June 2016

PRINTED IN THE UNITED STATES OF AMERICA

10 9 8 7 6 5 4 3 2 1

Cover illustration by Teresa Fasolino.
Cover design by Diana Kolsky.
Interior text design by Laura K. Corless.

Penguin
Random
House

To Sandra Harding,
with appreciation and affection.

ACKNOWLEDGMENTS

Readers often ask me if I do research for my books. Of course I do! I learn fascinating things with every book I write. As the theme of this book is tea, I did quite a bit of reading online and off about tea. It has a long history with some fascinating stories. I found *The Harney & Sons Guide to Tea* by Michael Harney, master tea blender, to be most helpful. Given to me as a gift some years ago because I am a self-confessed tea addict, it has a treasured spot on my bookshelf. I highly recommend it for anyone who would like to learn more about tea. As always, any errors are my own.

While I discussed the concept of this book with Sandra Harding, it was edited by my new editor, Julie Mianecki. I am so grateful to both of them for their help. My agent, Jessica Faust, has been my rock this past year. I honestly don't know what I would have done without her.

Thanks also go to Jody Schwoerer, who gave me the idea for a specific scene. No spoilers here, but thank you, Jody!

As always, I have to thank my mother, and my friends Betsy Strickland, Susan Erba, and Amy Wheeler for their support. They make me laugh, keep me grounded, and cheer me on.

Sophie's Friends

Natasha, a domestic diva with a local
  TV show

Mars Winston, Sophie's ex-husband, now
  Natasha's significant other

Nina Reid Norwood, Sophie's best friend

Bernie, restaurant manager and best man at
  Sophie and Mars's wedding

Francie Vanderhoosen, Sophie's neighbor

Velma Klontz, Francie's friend

Robert Johnson, Velma's widowed
  brother-in-law

Martha Carter, owner of The Parlour

Callie Evans, works at The Parlour

Alex German, is dating Sophie

Elise Donovan, Alex's old friend

Hunter Landon

CHAPTER ONE

Dear Natasha,

My new boyfriend's mother loves to garden. She keeps offering me cups of home grown comfrey tea, but I'm a little nervous about drinking tea made from some weed. Do you think her herbal teas are safe to drink?

—Uneasy in Tea Kettle Corner, Maine

Dear Uneasy,

Many herbal teas, like chamomile, have been safely consumed for centuries. However, comfrey tea is not one of them. It sounds like she wants you to find a new boyfriend.

—Natasha

At three in the morning, the world was simultaneously peaceful and a little bit spooky. No cars rumbled by on my street. No warm yellow glow shone in the windows of my neighbors' homes. Of course, it didn't help that Natasha had awakened me from a deep sleep by texting the word *Intruder!*

Who sends a message like that? I had phoned her to ask if she called 911, but she didn't answer. She didn't respond to my return text, either.

My ex-husband, Mars, who now happened to be Natasha's significant other, was out of town at a political event. I had known Natasha since we were kids in tiny Berrysville, Virginia. We competed at everything except the beauty pageants she loved so much. Familiar with her predilection for drama, I hadn't hurried over. I slid my feet into sandals and threw on a fluffy white bathrobe, attached a leash to my hound mix, Daisy, and crossed the street at a leisurely pace in the warm fall night.

Nevertheless, I shrieked when a cat streaked out of the shadows and across the sidewalk right in front of us. Daisy barked once at the inconsiderate cat.

Natasha's front door was locked. I rapped on it and called, "Natasha!" I banged the knocker, which sounded unbelievably loud in the night. No response at all. I was beginning to get worried. Why wasn't she answering the door? I tried the handle again but the door was definitely locked.

"Let's go around back," I said to Daisy.

I opened the gate to the passage that ran along the side of the house. In Old Town Alexandria, Virginia, the historic homes were situated close together, often with only a narrow service passage between buildings. Daisy led the way in the darkness.

We hurried up the stairs to the deck, where I pounded on the kitchen door. "Natasha?"

Still nothing. There were no lights on in the house, either.

Daisy pulled on her leash.

"Not now, Daisy." Why hadn't I brought the key to Natasha's house? I considered smashing a window. Should I go home and look for the key or break the glass to save time?

Daisy yelped, startling me. She tugged toward the side of the deck.

I heard a soft *whoosh*. Following Daisy's lead, I tiptoed over to the railing and looked down just in time to see a person dressed in black and wearing a hood close the sliding glass door and sneak around the side of the house.

"Hey! Stop!"

I scrambled down the stairs but he or she had already vanished. I stopped short of following him or her into the dark passage along the side of the house. That seemed incredibly stupid. The intruder could be lurking there. Besides, Natasha might be hurt and need help.

"C'mon, Daisy," I whispered. We ran to the basement door. I slid it open. Where were the light switches? "Natasha?" I yelled.

Walking cautiously, and looking around in case another intruder remained behind, I made my way to the back of the room, where stairs led to the main floor. I found a panel of light switches, flicked them all on, and the room blazed. I took a quick look to be sure no one hid behind the bar before racing upstairs, calling Natasha's name. I turned on the lights in the foyer and the stairwell. Nothing seemed out of place. "Natasha!"

I wasn't sure where to start. She had probably been asleep when the intruder came in. I rushed up the stairs, hoping Daisy, who wasn't much of a watchdog, would alert me if she smelled someone lurking in the house. At the top of the stairs, I turned right, toward Natasha and Mars's bedroom, flicking on overhead lights as I went. "Natasha!"

In the master bedroom, decorated in shades of gray from the walls to the bedding, it was clear that her bed had been slept in. But she was nowhere to be seen. "Natasha!"

Daisy pulled me toward the bathroom door. I grabbed the doorknob and twisted, but it didn't budge. It was locked tight. I knocked, which seemed somewhat silly under the circumstances. "Natasha? Are you in there? It's Sophie."

Nothing. No response. Not a sound in the house.

I jiggled the doorknob, which accomplished nothing. I

backed up a step and banged my shoulder into the door. Oww. It looked a lot easier in the movies.

The thud of the doorknocker boomed through the house. When I was dashing down the stairs, I heard, "Natasha? It's Officer Wong."

Thank heaven! I recognized Wong's voice, so I unlocked the door and threw it open.

Wong enjoyed surprising people who expected an Asian officer. Her surname was the last vestige of marrying the wrong man, but she hadn't bothered to change it. Wong wasn't much taller than my five feet. Her uniform strained against her ample curves. She was African American, and wore her hair short in the back but let a sassy curl fall over her forehead. "Sophie! I didn't expect to see *you*. Everything okay?"

"I think Natasha is locked in the bathroom upstairs. But she's not responding when I call her name."

"We had a report of an intruder."

I nodded. "Someone was in the house. I saw him leave."

"Him?"

"Or her. I don't know. Someone dressed in black."

Wong frowned. "Wait here."

"What about Natasha?"

"Stay right where you are. We don't know if there's someone else in the house."

Wong had proven herself logical and reliable in the past. I followed her instructions and waited by the front door with Daisy. I could hear her moving through the rooms on the main floor and the basement, checking them out.

Wong made her way back to the foyer. "I don't see anything unusual. How'd you get in?"

"Through the basement."

Wong started up the stairs.

I hated waiting by the door. I guessed I could be in the way if I followed her and she found someone hiding in the house. Still, I couldn't help feeling time might be of the essence. What if the intruder had hurt Natasha and locked her in the bathroom? I ran up the stairs as quietly as I could, but Daisy's paws hit the stairs like thunder.

I tried the doorknob to the bathroom again. It was still locked. Who put a key lock on a bathroom door? "Natasha! Natasha!"

Wong walked up beside me. "What part of *stay right where you are* wasn't clear to you?"

"What if she's bleeding or unconscious?" I jiggled the knob in frustration.

Wong looked around, opened the drawers of a dressing table, and withdrew something.

"What are you doing?"

"Stand aside, Sophie."

She took two hairpins, pried one open and bent the other at a slight angle. She inserted them in the lock and opened the door in a matter of seconds.

Natasha sprawled on the floor, facedown.

CHAPTER TWO

Dear Sophie,

I am engaged and have been shopping for my good china.
My fiancé grossed me out by telling me that bone china
actually has bones in it. Is that true? I think he's pulling
my leg because he wants cheaper china.

—Uncertain in Boneville, Georgia

Dear Uncertain,

I'm afraid your fiancé is correct. Bone ash is part of the
composition used to make the very fine, delicate plates
and cups that are bone china.

—Sophie

"Natasha!" I knelt beside her and gently moved her dishev-
eled hair for a better look at her face.

I could hear Wong requesting an ambulance.

I leaned close and said in her ear, "Natasha, are you okay?"
She didn't respond.

Seizing her wrist, I felt for a pulse. No problem. It was strong and steady. That was a relief!

Natasha had been a thorn in my side for so long that I was shocked to realize how overjoyed I was to feel her pulse. I tapped her cheek gently. "Natasha," I sang.

She moaned and stirred. Her legs jerked slightly.

"It's Sophie and Wong. You're going to be all right. An ambulance is on the way."

She turned her head enough to see me. One eye opened wide and in her valiant effort to sit up, she twisted and smashed me in the nose with her elbow. "Sophie, help me." She struggled to get to her feet.

Doors opened and closed in the house. I assumed Wong was searching to be sure no one was hiding.

"Maybe you should wait for the emergency medical technicians, Natasha."

"No! Are you going to help me or not?" She fingered her elbow, wincing.

I rubbed my aching nose, stood up, and held my arms out to her.

Like an awkward colt, she found her legs and struggled to stand. "They can't see me this way."

"Oh, come on. They've seen much worse. Now sit down and rest until they check you out."

"Hair brush, mirror, concealer, foundation, blush, mascara, eyeliner, and lipstick," rattled Natasha.

I studied her. Was she delusional?

"Now! Hand them to me. What are you waiting for?"

A siren wailed not too far away.

"Hurry! There's no time."

I peered at her pupils to see if they were different sizes. I'd read somewhere that was the sign of a concussion.

Wong strode into the room. "Looks like you're feeling better. What happened?"

Natasha, who I had to admit looked every bit as beautiful without any makeup, said, "I heard someone in the house. I tiptoed to the top of the stairs and saw him on the main floor. He was huge. Very tall. I ran back to the bedroom, texted Sophie and called 911. I could hear the footsteps coming upstairs. And then the phone rang. Who calls at this hour? I thought he was in the guest room. I didn't answer because he would have known I was in the house. You can't imagine how scared I was. I turned to find a weapon, just anything big and heavy to use to defend myself. I hadn't taken two steps when he slammed me over the head with something. I stumbled to the bathroom as fast as I could, locked the door, and I guess I passed out."

"Did you recognize this guy?" asked Wong.

"I never saw his face."

"Did he say anything?"

"Not a word. What do you think he wanted?"

"When the paramedics are through, you can have a look around to see if anything is missing."

The siren wailed once, very close, probably on our street. I left Natasha with Wong, picked up a pillow in the hallway and tossed it onto the guest bed, then made myself useful by running down the stairs and opening the door to let the emergency medical technicians enter. While they trekked upstairs, I walked through the main floor of the house to see if anything appeared out of place.

Natasha's house was always immaculate. A local TV star with a show on all things domestic, she was constantly changing her décor, yet I was surprised to find her formal living room awash in burnt orange. She must think that would be the next trendy color. The furniture featured clean contemporary lines, though some pieces fell into the unusual category for me, like the two chocolate-brown wingback chairs with one wing flying off higher than the other. Nevertheless, the room appeared neat and undisturbed, with very few knickknacks.

Natasha's kitchen always reminded me of a restaurant kitchen. Gray cabinets lined the walls. Her stainless steel countertops were undoubtedly practical but somewhat cold. That night, for the first time, I realized that it felt like a room built of concrete. But I wasn't there to study her decorating,

I just wanted to know if anything was missing. I opened a tall cabinet and recognized her everyday china—white in the middle with a wide graphite band—and matching mugs. There was no point in opening more cabinets because I wouldn't have known what should have been in them anyway.

I could hear people clomping down the stairs and quickly returned to the foyer with Daisy.

"Is she okay?" I asked.

"Are you Sophie?" asked a middle-aged paramedic with a bald head.

"Yes."

"Darlin', you have my sympathy. Your friend is stubborn and doesn't know what's good for her."

That wasn't news to me.

"We told her to go to the emergency room but she's having none of it. Keep an eye on her tonight and call us at the first sign of a headache or unusual behavior."

"Like what?" That covered a lot of territory that might be the norm for Natasha.

"Slurring words. Inability to speak. Numbness. We'll be back if you need us."

Wong chatted with them briefly before closing the door behind them.

"Are they gone?" Natasha peered down the stairs.

Wong groaned softly. "Yes."

"And you searched the whole house? No one is hiding?"

Wong's eyes met mine. "Natasha, what would a thief want here?"

"All our things! We have some important paintings and sculptures. My jewelry. Maybe they think we keep cash in the house."

I looked around for the important artwork. I spied a few wildly abstract paintings and bits of modern sculpture. Maybe they were worth a lot. I had no idea.

"So you think this was an ordinary burglary?" I asked Wong.

Natasha gasped. "Mars is away. Maybe the burglar knew

that and thought the house would be empty." She shuddered and rubbed her upper arms. "You don't mind staying with me the rest of the night, do you, Sophie?"

"Of course not." It had to be four in the morning. There wasn't much night left anyway.

Wong looked straight at me with a sly grin. "You and Daisy can curl up down here with the important paintings."

Natasha blanched. "Not Daisy. She sheds!"

"There's no better deterrent than a good watchdog."

Daisy wagged her tail and nuzzled Wong's hand as if she understood what Wong had said. Wong massaged Daisy's ear.

Although Natasha was beautiful without her warrior paint, she seemed younger to me, and almost helpless. "You can stay with me until Mars comes home."

"Thank you, Sophie. All I need is a room with nothing but a bed and a chair. A room that has been renovated, where no dogs or cats have ever been."

Oh sure. I had lots of rooms like that. "You can have your pick of the guest rooms." I didn't bother mentioning that none of them fit her criteria. Daisy and my cat, Mochie, had the run of the house.

I waited while Natasha walked through the rooms with Wong. It didn't take very long. "Anything missing?" I asked on their return.

Wong shook her head. "Could have been something small, or even a piece of paper that won't be noticed for a while."

"Piece of paper?" asked Natasha.

"Sure. Stock certificates or bonds. Or maybe even a file about one of Mars's clients."

As a political consultant, Mars ran in some fancy circles. I had trouble imagining that he possessed anything that would implicate a client of wrongdoing, but I guessed it could be possible.

Natasha's eyes grew large. "I bet that's it! I never thought his job was dangerous, but politicians will do anything to reveal the transgressions of their opponents and ruin their chances. Sophie, I'll pack a few things I need. Wong, do you mind waiting? I feel safer knowing you're here." Natasha ran up the stairs without waiting for an answer.

Wong grinned. "That's the nicest thing she has ever said to me."

"If someone wanted dirt on one of Mars's clients, wouldn't they have burglarized the client's house?"

"Probably. I just find it hard to believe that anyone broke in for one of these charming paintings. This one would give me nightmares. I'd have to cover it just to sleep." She studied a framed piece of dripping colors, a distorted face that resembled a skull, and, beside it, what I thought was supposed to depict a pig snout.

She had a point.

Natasha heaved a giant suitcase down the stairs. "I've been after Mars to install an elevator," she panted, "but you know how he loathes change."

Having been married to Mars, I didn't think he minded change. He probably came across that way to Natasha, though, who was on a constant hunt for the next decorating trend. In minutes, Natasha had locked the doors, and we were on our way to my house, her huge suitcase rolling along the sidewalk, making little clickity sounds.

"Don't you love fall?" asked Wong. "They say cooler weather is about to roll in. I can't wait. I've had it with the humidity."

"I was almost killed," Natasha whined. "How can you talk about the weather? I'm seeing people lurking in every shadow."

Under the streetlight, I could see the look of regret on Wong's face. "You're in good company, Natasha," I said. "No one would dare attack you in front of Wong."

Wong flashed me a grateful smile.

I unlocked my door and pointed up the stairs. "Take your pick of bedrooms."

Natasha lugged her suitcase up one step and stopped. "Are any of them haunted?"

Was she kidding? "No one has ever complained of seeing

ghosts in any of them, Natasha." Of course, Mars's mom,
my former mother-in-law, was prone to conversing with her
deceased sister in my kitchen. I didn't mention that, though.

Natasha appeared to accept my assurances and pulled
the suitcase up the stairs one step at a time.

"Do you have a few minutes for a cup of a tea?" I asked
Wong.

"Sure. I'm not done with Natasha yet anyway." Wong followed me into the kitchen.

I pulled English bone china teacups out of a cabinet and
put the kettle on, while Wong settled at my kitchen table
and made notes on a pad.

I'd found the vintage cups at a little store in Occoquan.
A blue and white band reminiscent of a trellis ran around
the top edge of the cups with trailing pink roses beneath it.

Leftover peach pie seemed just the ticket for an early
morning snack. I was cutting slices when someone
pounded on the kitchen door.

Wong jumped to her feet. "Are you expecting anyone?"

"Not at this hour. Maybe Nina saw the lights on." My
best friend and across-the-street neighbor, Nina Reid Norwood, had been known to come over in the middle of the
night.

I flicked on the outdoor lights and the first thing I saw
through the window in the door was an ax with a spear on
the end of it.

CHAPTER THREE

Dear Sophie,

When I told my British mother-in-law that I was having a high tea party for her birthday, she asked why we were having it mid-afternoon. Huh? I thought that's when the English took their tea.

—Hopelessly Clueless in High Point, North Carolina

Dear Hopelessly Clueless,

What we Americans think of as high tea is actually called afternoon tea in England. High tea is an evening meal when the servants have the day off or working folks come home and don't have time to prepare a big fancy roast with all the accompanying side dishes for dinner.

—Sophie

I gasped and jumped back. But the face peering in was very familiar.

"It's only Bernie." Wong opened the door. "Are you launching an attack on hordes of marauders?"

Bernie stepped inside, carrying a vicious weapon mounted on a long pole. "It's a halberd," he said in his delicious English accent. "My mum found it somewhere and shipped it to me. She claims it's the real thing, an ancient antique, but if you ask me, the condition is too good. I think it's just a reproduction. Until tonight, I never realized that I don't keep any weapons in my house."

"And you felt the need to bring the halberd to my house in the middle of the night because . . . ?"

Bernie looked around. "Natasha called Mars in hysterics. He thought I should check on you two and sleep over. Stand guard if you will."

Bernie had been the best man at my wedding to Mars. The two of them were dear friends who went way back. While the rest of us had gotten jobs and settled down, Bernie had traveled the world, popping in for a visit now and then. A few years back, he decided to stay in Old Town and took on the job of restaurant manager for an absentee owner. None of us had ever expected Bernie, with his perpetually tousled blond hair and the kink in his nose where it had been broken, to propel the business into one of the top restaurants in Old Town.

"The intruder is long gone," Wong said.

"So there was one. Mars thought Natasha might have been pulling some kind of stunt to drag him home."

"Tea?" I asked.

"Lovely. Have you got decaf?"

Wong snorted. "I thought you were supposed to stay awake to protect Natasha."

Bernie set the halberd in a corner, ax end down. "Where is Natasha? What happened?"

Wong filled him in while I poured boiling water over tea bags. Regular-strength English Breakfast for Wong and me, and decaf versions for Bernie and Natasha. *She* certainly didn't need to be more agitated. I set dessert plates containing slices of the pie on the table, along with forks and spoons, napkins, a crystal bowl of whipped cream, a glass creamer and sugar bowl, and a bowl of lemon wedges.

Natasha finally returned, her face made up as though she was ready for the day.

"Bernie!" She smiled at him like she did her fans. "How sweet of you to come."

Bernie was not a fan of Natasha's. The sad truth was that they tolerated each other for Mars's sake. Bernie didn't let Natasha boss him around, nor did he treat her like a star, neither of which endeared him to her.

"How do you feel?" he asked.

She rubbed the back of her hip. "Bruised. He did a number on me." She accepted a cup of tea from me and frowned at Wong. "How can you eat pie when I've been attacked? Shouldn't you be at my house dusting for fingerprints?"

I gave Wong a lot of credit. She dabbed her lips with a napkin and spoke without ire. "Have a seat, Natasha. Tell me again what he looked like."

"Honestly, have you no short term memory?" Natasha sighed with impatience. "Tall, very tall. The lights were off in the house, so I didn't see his face. I just know that he was very large and wearing a hood."

"Boots or sneakers?"

"I don't know."

"Gloves?"

Natasha stared at her. A moment passed. Two. "Sophie, you saw him. Was he wearing gloves?"

I thought back. "I didn't get a feel for his size, but then, I was looking down from above." I squeezed my eyes shut and tried hard to see him in my mind. It was useless. "I don't know about gloves." I knew what Wong was getting at, though. "You don't think you'll find fingerprints?"

"Doesn't sound like a neighborhood kid sneaking in. If I had taken the trouble to dress in black and wear a hood, I don't think I would have overlooked gloves."

Natasha appeared outraged. "You're not going to check for fingerprints?"

"Put your eyes back in your head, Natasha. I never said

that. I'm waiting for the forensic crew. They should be here anytime now. But I don't want you to get your hopes up." Wong rose. "Thanks for the pie and tea, Sophie. I don't often get a nice break like this in the middle of the night."

I walked her to the front door.

In a low voice, Wong asked, "Do you know if Natasha has any enemies? Anyone who would want to hurt her?"

"No. She aggravates a lot of people but she also has rabid fans who love her. Are you saying you don't think this was just someone looking for money or valuables? You think somebody went there intending to hurt Natasha?"

"Rabid fans, eh? I'm not saying anything, Sophie. Just gotta cover all the bases. And I've known Natasha long enough to think she could have made someone very angry. Angry enough to want to . . ."

"Do her in?" That was far worse than I thought.

"I doubt he'll be back tonight. Still, I'm glad Bernie is staying over. There's safety in numbers. Let me know if you need me, you hear?"

I nodded and watched her walk away into the night. Mochie, my sweet Ocicat with an M on his forehead, who should have had spotted fur but had the swirls of his American shorthair ancestors instead, rubbed around my ankles. I picked him up, reassured by his purring, and closed the door.

It took Natasha an hour to calm down. Not that I could blame her. An intruder in the house felt like a huge violation. I'd been through that myself. Not to mention being assaulted! I couldn't even imagine the fear and crazy thoughts swirling through her head. Bernie took my cue. We changed the subject and talked about lighter matters to take her mind off what had happened.

Eventually, Natasha went upstairs to bed, and Bernie claimed the sofa bed in the tiny family room off the kitchen, insisting he would be more likely to hear someone who was trying to get inside if he slept downstairs.

When I finally slipped into my bed again, the sky was beginning to lighten with the break of day.

~~~

When I woke, Natasha was sitting on the edge of my bed, talking at me. Sunshine streamed through my bedroom window. I rubbed my eyes and tried to focus on what Natasha was saying.

"You will be there at three o'clock this afternoon, or I will make sure that you never work in this town again."

Why was she upset? Why was she threatening me? I sat up and finally spied the phone she held to her ear. Oh thank goodness, she wasn't screaming at me. I was sorely tempted to pull the covers up over my head and hope she would go away.

"Don't you dare hang up on me!" Her voice grew so shrill that Daisy howled.

Natasha gasped and jabbed a finger at her phone. She gripped my shoulder and shook me. "Sophie! Why are you an event planner? I always thought your job was a joke. How hard can it be to plan a party? But it's a nightmare. People are simply impossible."

I had a feeling I did *not* want to know what had happened. Maybe if I didn't ask, she wouldn't drag me into her problem. "Tea," I muttered. "I need tea."

"There will be plenty of tea at the high tea auction this afternoon. I need help now! The musicians just bailed."

I knew about the Tea, Brie, and Skeleton Key event and had even purchased a ticket to attend the fund-raiser for children's literacy.

"Have you paid them?"

My landline rang before she had a chance to respond to my question.

I could hear Bernie's voice downstairs. He must have answered the phone. It was time to get up. Deciding to shower later, I threw on pedal pushers and a sleeveless green cotton shirt while Natasha fussed about inconsiderate people who made promises they couldn't deliver.

When I emerged from my bedroom, Bernie was on his way up the stairs. He held the phone out to me and made a funny face that I couldn't interpret. "It's Francie."

"Hi, Francie," I said into the phone as I walked down the stairs.

But the voice that spoke back to me wasn't Francie's. Mars said, "I need to talk to you. Can you come over right now?"

"Okay." I chose my words carefully. "Where are you?"

"At my house. Meet me in the alley at the garage."

"All right. Good talking to you . . . Francie."

The scent of cinnamon wafted to me. It was difficult to pass up whatever Bernie was fixing for breakfast, but something dire must be happening for Bernie and Mars to be acting sneaky. If there was one thing that didn't interest Natasha in the slightest, it was Daisy. I grabbed her leash, latched it to her collar, and said, "Back in a few."

Bernie shot me a worried look that I didn't like, but he handed me a mug of tea to take with me.

"Thanks. I need this," I said.

As I walked out the door, I could hear Natasha grumbling about the musicians. I crossed to the other side of the street, enjoying the humidity-free days of September. The sun shone in a vivid blue sky, and the trees were just beginning to be touched with autumnal golds. I turned left at the corner, stopped for a big gulp of tea to brace myself, and walked down to the alley that ran behind Mars and Natasha's house. Mars stood with his back to me, looking into their garage, his hands on his hips.

Daisy pulled at her leash as soon as she saw him. I let go so she could run to him.

Mars immediately squatted to her level. She waggled all over and kissed his face.

He held the end of her leash when he rose. Mars had a friendly, good ol' boy look, handsome enough to be one of his clients. His kind eyes crinkled at the edges when he laughed, and even though we had divorced, he would always be special to me.

This morning, his jaw was tight, a furrow had formed between his eyebrows, and his eyelids sagged with exhaustion.

Uh-oh. "What's wrong?" I held my breath.

CHAPTER FOUR

Dear Sophie,

I love English Breakfast tea. In fact, I love it all the time, not just for breakfast. My brothers tease me when I drink it later in the day. Why is it called breakfast tea?

—The Little Sister in Breakfast Hill, New Hampshire

Dear The Little Sister,

Breakfast tea is a blend of black teas. It's called breakfast tea because it's strong and meant to wake you up.

—Sophie

"I'm leaving Natasha."

I knew they'd had problems and Natasha *had* to be difficult to live with, but it came as a shock anyway. "Whoa." I had so many questions, but decided I would be a better friend if I simply listened and let him pour it all out.

He rubbed his face with both hands. "I was going to do it before I left town this last time, but it didn't seem right to break up with her and then take off. I thought it might be better if I was gone for a long time and told her when I came home."

"There's never a good time for that sort of thing, is there?"

"I don't mean to sound cruel, but it's a huge election year for me, and I'm going to be on the road for the next couple of months. I can't come running back here all the time to deal with her latest drama. Was there really an intruder?"

The fact that he wasn't sure he could believe Natasha told me a lot about their relationship. "I'm afraid so. I saw someone leaving your house. And Natasha really was knocked out. She managed to lock herself in the bathroom before she collapsed."

He winced. "Is she okay?"

I suppressed a smile. It was typical of Mars to be planning to leave Natasha but still worry about whether she was all right. "Seems to be. They wanted her to go to the ER last night but she refused. Mostly she's shocked and scared. And rightly so!"

"I always made fun of her for wanting to turn the bathroom into a safe room. You know, like the stars have in their mega-homes? So I humored her by swapping the normal lock on the bathroom door for an outdoor-type knob that required a key to open it. I feel terrible. Looks like she had reason to be scared." He shook his head. "I should have been here."

"Mars, what could the intruder have been after?"

He shrugged. "Cash? Jewelry? The regular stuff, I guess."

"Wong asked me if Natasha had any enemies."

Mars's eyebrows jumped up. "She thought Natasha might have been targeted? Oh man, now I really feel like a louse. You know how she is, Soph. She aggravates the dickens out of everybody but not to the extent that anyone would want to do her harm. Not that I know of, anyway."

"Could it have anything to do with your clients and the election? Secrets about one of them, maybe?"

"What kind of creeps do you think I work with?"

"C'mon, everyone has some kind of dirt they wouldn't want made public."

"Really?" He grinned. "What's your dirt?"

"I'm being serious."

"I know. I'm sorry. I'm exhausted from flying all night. And look what else I came home to." He gestured toward the garage.

Their two-car garage was packed with furniture, leaving no room for a car. I walked closer. Pie safes, desks, sideboards, velvet settees, breakfronts, and a hodgepodge of crystal, china, paintings, statuettes, pottery, and baseball cards. Most were antiques or at least vintage. "They must be for the auction," I said. "It's a huge haul, though. I'm shocked that she managed to get so many donations. It will take hours to auction off all this stuff."

"That's a relief. I was afraid she had bought it." Mars exhaled noisily. "This is such bad timing. We were all coming home for a couple of days tomorrow anyway, so there's no point in flying back tonight, but I'll be leaving again soon. She's going to hate me for taking off, but I have to work."

"If she's mad at you, maybe it will be easier to break up."

"I really dread this. Now it's going to look like I'm abandoning her in her time of need. I have a call in to Natasha's mom to see if she can come up to stay with her, and I'll get someone over here today to install an alarm system." He eyed Daisy.

I reeled her leash in so she was closer to me. "No. Daisy cannot stay with Natasha. We agreed that she won't stay with Natasha if you're not home. She'll lock Daisy in the basement."

"I know. I know. Actually, I was thinking how happy Daisy will be when she doesn't have to stay over here anymore." Mars closed his eyes. "Sometimes I wonder what I ever saw in Nat."

A lot of people had wondered that. "Where will you go?"

"I'll be bunking at Bernie's. I'm not interested in most of the furniture, and we never officially tied the knot, so it shouldn't be a big deal. We'll probably sell the house. I hope she unloads all this junk. When I opened the garage door, I thought she had lost her marbles."

If she hadn't already, she might when she learned that Mars was leaving her. It wasn't going to be pretty. "So you're planning to move out *now*? Um, she has the auction this afternoon."

He tugged at his earlobe. "You see the problem? There's always some reason I should put it off. I can't wait any longer, Soph. I'm going to wing it and hope an opportunity arises *today*. That's why I wanted you to know. And I didn't want you to think poorly of me."

He didn't have to worry about that. "Mars, no one who knows Natasha would ever blame you."

He wrapped his arms around me in a big hug. "Thanks. I can always count on you and Bernie."

"Shall I tell her that you're home?"

Mars sucked in a deep breath. "Might as well get it over with."

I turned to walk away but gazed back at him. "You might want to have a look through the house to see if anything is missing."

"Nat doesn't want anything of mine."

"Not Natasha, you dolt. The intruder!"

"I should have been home," he mumbled, looking perfectly miserable.

Talk about conflicted feelings! Poor Mars. I was willing to bet Natasha would talk him into changing his mind. Daisy and I returned to our house, where Natasha paced the kitchen floor. "It's about time. Where have you been?"

She didn't wait for an answer. "I have a ton of things to do today for the auction..Please, Sophie, can you help me with the musicians? And could you go home with me so I can dress? I'm afraid the intruder will return."

"Mars is home."

"Thank heavens. I'll sleep much better tonight."

Maybe. Or maybe not. In spite of her crabbiness, my heart bled for her a little bit. She had been clobbered by a stranger in her own home, her sanctuary. Home was where we went to feel secure, which was what made it all the scarier. And now, she would be devastated by Mars's decision to break off their relationship.

"I wish you had better lighting and mirrors in this house. It's impossible to do my makeup properly," she griped.

Bernie refreshed my mug of tea. "Thanks, Bernie." Why was she still complaining about my house? "Now that Mars is home, you can do your makeup there."

"No! He can't see me until I'm all put together."

"You look fine to me," Bernie said.

She'd been a houseguest for only a few hours, but I was ready for her to go. "Doesn't he see you at night?"

"Yes."

"You don't wear makeup when you sleep."

"When he's home I do. You don't?" She giggled. "Really, Sophie, no wonder you can't keep a man."

I ignored her criticism, slightly amused by the fact that I could say the same about her soon. I wouldn't, though. She was going to have a tough enough time dealing with it. She didn't need me rubbing salt on her wounds.

Mochie sat on Bernie's lap. Daisy watched Natasha. I leaned against the kitchen island, sipping my tea and thinking that everyone was waiting for her to depart.

Natasha frowned at me. "Well, I can't sit around here all day. Thank you for coming to help me last night. You, too, Bernie." She walked up the stairs.

I waited until she was out of earshot. "How long have you known about this?"

"A couple of months."

"I thought everything was forgiven when Natasha fixed up that fancy man cave for Mars."

Bernie blinked at me and sat back in the banquette. "That was merely a plaster."

"A plaster?"

"Aargh. That's one British expression I can't quite shake. A Band-Aid. Like when a husband sleeps with another woman and gives his wife an emerald ring to smooth things over. It takes out a little of the sting but the underlying problem is still there."

"Listen to you, being so wise."

Bernie shrugged. "My mum had a lot of husbands. We all learn from other people's pain."

I peered at the pan on the stove. "What are you cooking?"

"Pumpkin pancakes and sausages. Natasha didn't want any, so I was waiting for you. I'd better make enough for Mars. I have a feeling you and I are going to be picking up the pieces today. I'll be moving furniture—"

"Why, thank you, Bernie. You so rarely want to pitch in when I could use a hand." Natasha smiled at him from the kitchen doorway. "The antiques for the tea are in my garage. Please deliver them to Robert Johnson Antiques."

Bernie shot me a look of anguish.

I tried not to laugh. He couldn't exactly tell her that he meant he would be moving Mars's furniture.

"Sophie, won't you please call the musicians for me?"

I grabbed a pad and a pen and scribbled a message. "Dial their number."

Natasha dialed and held the phone out to me.

"Say this to them." I handed her the paper.

Fortunately, Natasha was caught by surprise. She choked, but then read aloud, with the wrong emphasis. "Hi, it's Natasha again. I wanted to apologize"—she cocked her head and glared at me, her eyes huge—"for this morning. I had an intruder in the house last night who knocked me unconscious, and I'm just not myself today."

She listened for a moment. "Yes, I should be fine. That's so nice of you. At three this afternoon, then?"

She said good-bye and hung up. "Looks like it's going to be a good day after all. *I* should have thought of that. I'll have Mars collect my suitcase later on."

Bernie and I waited, frozen in place until she shut the door behind her.

"I can't believe I stepped into that," grumbled Bernie.

"I'll pitch in. It shouldn't take too long, though I don't know how we'll move some of the bigger pieces."

"I can call a couple of my bartenders. I've helped move plenty of *them*."

Bernie was right about Mars. As we sat down to eat, Mars walked in through the kitchen door like he still owned the place. "Got enough for three? There's nothing in the fridge. I've only been gone for two weeks, and all Natasha has is wine and pickled jalapeños. Not even milk or eggs. Who lives like that?"

"How did it go?" I asked.

Mars buttered his pancake and poured maple syrup on it. "I'm not sure. I expected waterworks or slamming doors, but she was very calm. Frighteningly so, in fact. She usually makes such a fuss about things that I was slightly alarmed. She said, 'You'll miss me, Mars.' And then she headed upstairs."

Yikes! I hoped she wasn't busy burning his clothes or tossing them out the window. I leaned sideways to look out my bay window, but I couldn't see their house. "Does she know you're here? She was afraid to be in your house alone."

Mars gulped tea before saying, "She never came back down. But her mom is in transit. I didn't tell Natasha that. You know how she is about her mom."

I did know. Natasha's father abandoned them when Natasha was seven. Her mom had waitressed long hours at the local diner trying to provide for her little girl. I thought her mom was a hoot, but she was something of an embarrassment to Natasha, who tried to cultivate a sophisticated image. Her mother was a free spirit who preferred a more casual lifestyle.

I frowned at Bernie, who appeared to be as surprised as I was. Something was up with Natasha. Her reaction to Mars breaking off their relationship wasn't like her at all.

Mars devoured his pancakes as though he hadn't eaten in days. "Officer Wong called. She needs me to come in so they can exclude my fingerprints." He grinned at me. "Apparently they already have yours and Natasha's on file."

"No leads on the intruder, then?" Bernie asked.

"According to Wong, if there are no prints, in all likelihood they'll never find the perpetrator, unless someone saw something but hasn't reported it yet."

"Did you notice if anything was missing?" I bit into the last piece of my sausage.

"Not a thing."

※※

After breakfast, Bernie passed me on his way out the door and whispered, "I wouldn't do this for anyone else but you."

I blew him a kiss.

"Aw, quit cozying up to Sophie," grumbled Mars. "You're going to help, aren't you?" he asked me.

"I'll be along shortly—I hope." I closed the door behind the two of them and went straight to my tiny home office.

It wasn't quite the way I had planned my day. I checked my calendar. Luckily, unlike Natasha, event planning was my business, and I had everything well in hand for the upcoming Guild of Matrimonial Lawyers meeting that started the next day. I had planned to attend the auction and tea anyway, so the late afternoon had already been blocked off. Nothing urgent demanded my attention.

When I arrived at the alley, Bernie was backing in a truck from his restaurant, The Laughing Hound, and Mars was directing him.

Three body-building types whom I recognized as bartenders and a waiter from Bernie's restaurant hopped out and opened the back doors, ready to work.

I packed the smaller items, like clocks and porcelain, in boxes. After a few minutes of loading, Natasha appeared, dressed to kill and screaming, "No, no, no!"

CHAPTER FIVE

Dear Natasha,

I always order Earl Grey tea. It just can't be beat. But what's the bergamot that's in it?

—Tea Lover in Greycliff, Montana

Dear Tea Lover,

Bergamot is an orange that grows in Calabria, Italy. The oil from the peel of the orange is used in Earl Grey tea to give it that distinctive flavor.

—Natasha

Not even a strand of Natasha's almost-black hair was out of place. She had dressed in a cream-colored dress with a boat neck that revealed her shoulders, yet had three-quarter-length sleeves. A webbed belt accented her waist, and the fabric clung to her curves. She probably would have looked great for a photo shoot, but she clearly wasn't planning to lift a finger to move furniture.

"I'm glad I caught you. Not everything goes to the auction. Some of these items are mine."

As it turned out, most of the furniture belonged to Natasha, which came as a surprise to me.

Mars shot me looks of incredulity as Natasha walked through the garage, claiming furniture. I knew why he was amazed. Not only did they already have a fully furnished house, but Natasha loathed antiques. She much preferred sleek modern furniture.

While the guys carried a faded velvet settee off the truck, Natasha sidled over to me. I braced for the worst.

"That was close! They almost stole my furniture. Imagine if someone had bid on it before I realized that my pieces had been included in the auction."

She didn't *seem* devastated by the breakup with Mars. Her makeup was thick enough to cover a multitude of sins but her eyes weren't red from crying. She chattered on about the auction while I looked around at huge wardrobes and exquisite sideboards. "What are you going to do with all this furniture?"

Natasha turned to me and whispered. "Sophie, I've left Mars."

I staggered backward a step. I had not seen that coming at all. I was so surprised by her twist on the situation that my mouth actually hung open.

"Don't look so shocked, Sophie. He's not the right man for me."

I snapped my mouth closed. Had she been thinking about leaving Mars? Or was she twisting the situation to save face? I gazed around at the furniture. "Is that why you bought all this stuff? For your new home?"

For a very long moment she stared at me, as though my question had caught her off guard. A smile crept over her lips. "Yes. Yes, it is."

There was only one problem. "I thought you weren't a fan of antiques."

"A girl can change her mind, can't she?"

She certainly could. But this was a huge departure for

Natasha. Still, whatever had happened between her and Mars, they both seemed to be happy to move on. Maybe their split wouldn't be the big drama I had feared.

"Load that one! It's my contribution to the auction." Natasha grimaced. "Ugh. Have you ever seen anything so scary? I couldn't have that in my house."

It didn't seem so scary to me. It was an old sideboard painted cream. The guys shifted their hold on it and turned it around. The front had three carved sections. Two of them were of gorgeous fruit. Very pretty for a dining room. But the middle section featured a gargoyle face that made me shudder. Who would have carved such an evil visage on a sideboard? For once, I was in full agreement with Natasha. "What possessed you to buy it?"

She flapped her hand. "I needed something to donate to the auction. It's certainly unusual."

"In other words, you got a deal on it."

"You like old stuff. Will you buy it at the auction?"

"I'm all for supporting literacy, especially for kids, but I don't think I would like that particular piece in my home."

Natasha frowned at me as though I had alarmed her. "What if no one buys it?"

There was a pretty good chance of that happening. "Then I guess it's yours."

"Ugh. I just never have understood—"

She stopped midsentence. Aha! She still disliked antiques. Something was up with her.

Bernie latched the door on the truck, and Mars climbed inside. Just before Bernie hopped in the driver's seat he said, "See you at the antiques store, Natasha." The truck pulled out.

Natasha fluffed her hair. "That wasn't so bad." She looked at her watch. "Now I can have lunch and relax for a few hours. See you later." She started toward her house.

I spun around and grabbed her arm. "You're kidding, right? Those guys are going to dump everything in a big pile if you're not there."

"But I have a lunch date."

A date? Wow! Mars hadn't needed to agonize over leaving Natasha. She'd been planning the same thing all along. "Then you'd better cancel it."

She tilted her head and whined. "Sophie . . ."

"No way. This is not my gig. You made promises, and I am not filling in for you. Pull yourself together and get going. They'll be arriving at the store any minute. And I'd suggest wearing clothes that can get dusty."

"Sophie! When did you become so selfish? Can't you do me this teensy little favor?"

I walked away—fast! Maybe Natasha could wheedle other people into doing everything for her, but I had had enough of it. Of course, when I turned the corner in front of her house, I felt a little guilty. After all, she *had* been attacked the night before. But then I saw a curtain move in her living room window and the vague outline of a man drifted away.

I knew one thing. It was not Mars.

I spent the next few hours working on the upcoming Halloween ball at the Kennedy Center and trying to put Natasha and her tea auction out of my mind. It wasn't my responsibility to fix it, I kept telling myself.

Besides, one thousand family lawyers were about to descend on Old Town for their annual meeting and they *were* my responsibility. They had taken care of their own agenda but I had been hired for a few special events like the banquet on their closing night, and special trips around Washington, DC, to entertain their families while the lawyers attended sessions.

Just before two o'clock, I walked Daisy and came home to shower and dress for the Tea, Brie, and Skeleton Key auction and tea. The announcement had said something about Victorian apparel. I located an outrageously fancy cream-colored hat adorned with lush peonies, faux pearls, and a dramatic fluffy faux feather that I had worn for an event years ago. I pulled it out of the hatbox and sought an appropriate dress to go with it. A sleeveless dress of faint pink lace over cream picked up the colors of the hat nicely, even if it wasn't exactly right for early fall. The skirt flared to mid-calf, which seemed appropriate to me. I added dangling pearl earrings and a plain pearl necklace. I wasn't sure why, but pearls seemed both Victorian and appropriate for tea.

Shortly before three, I walked across the street and knocked on the front door of my best friend, Nina Reid Norwood.

She opened the door, ready to go in a floral dress and a glamorous hat that tilted forward over her face.

We walked along the streets of Old Town, feeling wildly overdressed. I filled her in on the developments between Natasha and Mars.

"The only part that surprises me is that it took him so long," Nina said. "No one could ever say he didn't give that relationship his best shot."

"You don't think it's peculiar that she's already dating?"

"There is nothing that Natasha values more than saving face. She would do anything to make it seem as though the split was her decision, and we should pity Mars."

We approached the tearoom, where clusters of people were gathered on the sidewalk.

The Parlour had opened during the summer. Located on King Street at the end of a block, it had taken over the space of two shops. Large windows allowed for sidewalk gazing—both in and out. The owner and brainchild behind The Parlour, Martha Carter, had decorated it like an upscale European tearoom. While there were a few small dining tables where one could sit, most of the tearoom was arranged in little parlor-type groupings. Sofas and comfy chairs clustered around coffee tables where tea and goodies were served. Antique accents imparted elegance. It was comfortable while maintaining a hint of formality. I had only been there once before so I looked forward to an afternoon of tea and pastries.

I pulled the door open and stepped into a different world. A string quartet played soothing classical music. I smiled when I saw them, pleased that they had made it.

The room was already filled with patrons, many of whom had dressed in the Victorian spirit that Natasha requested. Ladies wore hats of every imaginable color and a couple of the gentlemen wore top hats. I heard my name being called and looked around. My neighbor Francie had already snagged one of the best tables by the window.

"Over here, Sophie." With a wrinkled and age-spotted hand, Francie patted the loveseat where she sat. "I'll share my sofa. Nina, you take the chair."

Opinionated and outspoken, Francie had lived in Old Town for most of her adult life. Widowed many years before, she spent her days gardening and bird watching. She wore a high-necked lacy beige blouse with a large cameo at her throat. She hadn't bothered with a hat to cover her straw-yellow hair. "Do you girls know Velma Klontz?"

A woman in her late sixties who could have stepped out of a Victorian photograph nodded at me. "Francie has told me so much about you, Sophie. And I know Nina from the shelter."

Nina chimed in. "Velma is always saving homeless cats."

Like us, Velma wore an extravagant hat. But hers was sky blue and matched her Victorian gown. It sat on teased silver hair that had surely been sprayed in place by a beautician. Wide blue eyes regarded me with curiosity.

Francie didn't have a stitch of makeup on but Velma wore it artfully, like so many Southern women. I wasn't sure about the blue-gray eye shadow, but her foundation was thick enough to cover any blemishes.

"Velma and I met at a book club a hundred years ago," Francie said. "She's a wonderful cook, just like you."

Velma clearly enjoyed the flattery but flapped her hand modestly. "I don't cook as much anymore since my husband passed, but you can tell by looking at me that I cannot pass up good fried chicken or apple fritters, though they're not easy to find these days. Seems like all the restaurants shy away from traditional Southern food."

Francie nudged me. "What's Robert doing with Natasha?"

I looked toward the entrance where Natasha chatted with a tall man whom I put in his mid-sixties. He wore his salt-and-pepper beard short, and his silver hair neatly trimmed. I wasn't sure whether it was the rectangular wire-framed glasses that he wore or his general demeanor that gave the impression of a studious, thoughtful man. He could have easily been a professor but I knew he owned the Robert Johnson Antiques store across the street.

"Natasha is in charge of the tea and the auction," I said. "They're probably discussing how to bring the auction items over here."

"That's a relief! I can't compete with a beauty queen like Natasha." Francie surprised me. She had to be a bit older than Robert.

Velma laughed. "He was married to my sister Livy," she said, evidently for my benefit. "Trust me, Francie. I loved my sister, but she was no beauty queen." Velma gazed out the window at the antiques store. "That shop was Livy's dream. Pity that she never saw it come to fruition."

"Isn't he gorgeous?" asked Francie.

I did my best not to show my amusement. "Why Francine Vanderhoosen! I believe you have a little crush on Robert."

"Me and every woman in Old Town over the age of sixty," she grumbled. "Will you look at Patty Conklin over there, squeezed into a girdle? That thing's so tight she's popping out on both ends and doesn't need a bustle under her dress. It's a wonder she can breathe. And Beverly Hazelwonder must have had Botox this week. Her wrinkles are puffed up bigger than a soufflé."

Velma roared. "He's always had that sort of effect on women. I can't tell you how many of our friends have called to pump me for information about him. I think it's still too soon after Livy's death for him to date, but I suppose I'll always feel that way. He's a dear, so it's bound to happen sooner or later."

"If it hasn't already," murmured Nina.

I gazed around the tearoom and realized that a considerable number of the ladies taking tea were over sixty. That was probably normal for a weekday afternoon tea. They were most likely retired and had the time to enjoy a tea. I recognized a couple of other antiques dealers in the crowd. One lone gentleman wore a blazer with khakis and appeared to be working on his laptop.

My musing came to an abrupt halt when the owner of The Parlour, Martha Carter, arrived with a silver tea service and delicate teacups. As she set the tray on the table, she said, "I selected these just for you, Francie. The cups are antique. They're Royal Doulton bone china."

Velma picked up one of the cups and examined it. It was cream on the outside but alternating panels of cream and pink laced with delicate tracings of gold lined the interior. A gold band flowed around the scalloped edge and the handle was gold as well. I was almost afraid to pick one up and drink from it.

"These are stunning, Martha," Francie said. "I bet Queen Elizabeth doesn't drink from anything prettier."

I glanced around. "Do you use a different pattern for every group of diners?"

Martha smiled. "I confess to being a ravenous china collector. I just love them all. Some of our guests like to choose their own favorites, which I think adds to the fun and the ambiance. By the way, Sophie, I wanted to thank you for contributing your painting to the auction."

We had only met once before. I was surprised that she remembered me. "It was my pleasure. I bought it ages ago and never had the right place for it. I'm happy to see it go to a home where it will be displayed."

"Where's Callie?" asked Francie. "You don't usually do the serving."

Martha straightened up. She always held herself very erect. Rumor had it that Martha had lived around the world with her husband, who was some sort of big shot in the military. Although she was still very attractive, crepey eyelids gave away her age. Her eyebrows had little worry hooks in them near her long, straight nose. I had only seen her with her hair pulled back in a flawless French twist that emphasized her features. I suspected she had been very beautiful when she was younger. She gave the impression of someone who had been through a lot. Maybe it was her nose, or the way her lips pulled together in a vaguely disapproving pout, but she made me feel like I should sit up straight and behave.

Martha smiled when she said, "Seems like people are always off their stride when it comes to special events like this." She lowered her voice. "Callie was running late today. I think she might have had a date last night."

Velma appeared perplexed. "I didn't see her with anyone."

It did not escape my attention that Francie nudged Velma's foot with her own.

CHAPTER SIX

Dear Natasha,

I threw a tea party and my know-it-all neighbor said it was inappropriate to serve tea without proper tea knives. I've heard of teaspoons. Are there tea forks and tea knives?

—Uncouth in Knife River, Minnesota

Dear Uncouth,

Indeed there are such things as tea knives. The dessert fork may be used as a tea fork. Every properly equipped household should have tea knives. They are approximately seven to eight inches long and may also double as breakfast knives.

—Natasha

"Maybe she went out with Hunter," said Francie.

"Who's Hunter?" asked Nina.

"He's almost as handsome as Robert but in a different way," said Francie. "He's adorable. Sophie, I had my eye on him for you, but he's simply taken with Callie. The way he

looks at her! Oh my. I'd have made sure you met him,
Sophie, if you didn't have Alex."

"I know exactly who you're talking about. I didn't think
he would show today because of the auction but he's here."
Martha nodded toward the back and winked at Velma and
Francie. "Callie deserves a nice man in her life. But poor
Natasha! Small wonder she's not very capable today. Robert
had to set up the auction preview for her over at his shop.
Natasha is so agitated she hasn't been able to concentrate
on the auction or the tea at all. Sophie, it was kind of you to
take her in last night. Imagine almost being killed by someone in your own home!"

Almost killed? That story had grown a little bit.

"And you didn't tell me about this?" demanded Francie.
"I live right next door to you. That could have been me."

Martha excused herself and hurried off.

I filled Francie in on the events of the night, trying to
make it sound a little less disturbing. Evidently my sanitized
version didn't work because Francie declared, "As soon as
I get home, I have to look for my husband's old shotgun."

Nina's eyes widened in alarm. I knew why. All we
needed was Francie running around the neighborhood with
an old shotgun.

I patted her hand. "Don't you worry. We'll all look out for
you, Francie." Hurrying to change the subject, I said, "Martha
has created an amazing place here."

Nina whispered, "I hear she runs it like she thinks she's
still a military wife."

"Her husband might be retired from the military, but I
think some habits die hard," Velma said.

Francie sipped her tea. "I don't care how she does it. I'm
just glad she opened The Parlour."

"Do you come here often?" I asked.

"Every day. This is our regular table, so we can watch
Robert's shop across the street. Now I don't want you girls
making a big deal out of it but I have a birthday coming up
day after tomorrow, and I'd like to have a little afternoon
tea here. Would you do me the honor of coming?"

"Of course we will!"

Nina nodded eagerly. "And how old will the birthday girl be?"

"Thirty-nine." Francie said it with a straight face.

Nina nearly spewed tea. "You might as well tell us. Otherwise we'll be forced to sneak a peek at your driver's license."

"Won't do you a bit of good," said Velma. "I've looked. She marked off the date with indelible ink."

"That's probably illegal!" Nina wiped the saucer of her cup.

"That's what I told her," said Velma. "She's just lucky a cop hasn't stopped her yet."

Francie smiled smugly. "I don't want any silliness. No presents or funny hats or strippers. Just a lovely afternoon with tea and friends. Okay?"

Strippers? Nina and I exchanged grins. The two older ladies were just too cute.

Before long, a woman about Martha's age brought plates and a stunning three-tiered silver server to our table. I spied watercress sandwiches with the crusts cut off, pink petit fours, macarons, tiny toasts with caviar, miniature éclairs, little cakes filled with lemon curd, fruit tarts, and pink-iced strawberry cakes. My mouth watered at the mere sight of the assortment.

The woman chatted eagerly with Velma and Francie. They introduced her as Callie. She was so slender that her cheeks sank in, making her large eyes seem even bigger. Dark red lipstick covered thin lips. She wore her long brown hair pulled back in a loose ponytail. A shorter section in front created a high wave off her forehead that was reminiscent of the big hair popular in the eighties. I couldn't tell if she had teased it or if it was naturally curly and unruly. She wore a ruffled white apron with the name *The Parlour* embroidered on it in light blue. She bent forward and whispered, "I brought you extra macarons because I know how you love them."

"Should we make room for Robert?" asked Velma.

"I think he needs to stay up front during the auction to make sure it goes well," Callie said. "I overheard him and Martha complaining about Natasha. Apparently she was attacked last night! In her own home. Can you even imagine? We're all pitching in for her. She's not pulling her weight but who can blame her?"

Nina's eyes met mine. Natasha was lucky Martha and Robert hadn't known her very long. It was typical of Natasha to expect others to do her work. Unless she didn't feel well today. Didn't people sometimes get achy the day after a car accident? Maybe she was beginning to feel the pain.

"Did you see Hunter in the back?" Francie asked.

"I can't believe he came." Callie flushed.

"I hear you had a date last night! Was it with Hunter?" Velma seemed eager to hear details.

"I'll never tell!" Callie chuckled and swept away.

Velma and Francie turned to gaze at the man working on the laptop. He noticed them and gave a little wave.

We helped ourselves to delicious treats as the auction began. Toward the front of the tearoom, where cases displayed their yummy goodies for take-out, a gentleman at a podium welcomed everyone as a younger man walked through the room, carrying the first item to be auctioned: a two-foot-tall Chinese vase.

After he passed us, Velma turned to Francie. "Why would Callie have been evasive about a date with Hunter?"

"Maybe she doesn't tell you everything about her life," suggested Nina.

Francie selected a lavender macaron. "She had no qualms telling us how she left her husbands."

"Most odious men," added Velma.

"And she has told us tales about the bakery where she used to work."

Velma dabbed her mouth with a white napkin. "And about her deceased father, who wasn't much better than that first husband of hers. Callie has had a hard life."

Nina raised her hand and waved it.

"Did you just bid?"

Nina grinned. "It's such a rush, isn't it? I love those Staffordshire dogs."

The man carrying them brought them by our table. The two dogs were white spaniels that appeared to be in good condition. Someone across the room was bidding against Nina.

Miffed, she stood up to see who it was. When she sat down, her cheeks blazed, and she stopped bidding. Her opponent won.

"Price get too high for you?" asked Francie.

Nina swallowed hard. "No, that wasn't it."

I rose up just a bit to see what was going on and my breath caught in my throat. Alex German, the attorney whom I had been dating, was celebrating the win with a disturbingly attractive brunette. Long, sexy bangs hid half her forehead, but there was no mistaking the high cheekbones and lovely face. I plopped into my chair, wondering who she was.

"I'm sorry, Sophie." Nina reached over and placed her hand on top of mine.

"What? What happened?" demanded Francie. She held on to the arm of the sofa and stood up. When she sat down next to me, she spat, "He doesn't deserve you. And to think I liked that boy!"

Velma was next to crane her neck and stand for a better look. "Ohhh. Is that your boyfriend?" Her voice was low with disapproval. She sat down. "He's very handsome. From the adoring way she's smiling at him I don't think she's his sister, though. You've got trouble with a capital *T*, honey."

A queasy shiver rushed through me. It wasn't like we were a big item. And heaven knew our relationship had been shaky up to now anyway. I sipped Irish Breakfast tea, feeling just a little bit numb. But the tea and a calm moment brought me to my senses. Maybe she *was* his adoring sister or niece. Maybe she was a client. The wife of a friend, perhaps? I eyed the cake with the lemon curd and helped myself, certain I would feel much better if I ate it. "Maybe we shouldn't jump to conclusions. After all, I go places with Bernie and Mars, and it doesn't mean anything."

"Riiight," Nina drawled, leaving no doubt that she didn't believe that for a minute.

I was grateful when another auction item was paraded by us. This time a stunning sapphire pendant drew our admiration. I dared to bid on it, knowing I wouldn't win it for the low price where the bidding started. Suddenly, three people were vying for it and the price shot up. I was out.

"I can't believe you bid on that," Nina wolfed a mini éclair.

"I'm an opportunist. I didn't think I'd really win a sapphire set in gold for that price but it was worth a shot." While I enjoyed the heavenly sweet tart flavor of the lemon curd cake, the other three began to bid. A few minutes later, Francie won a stay in a honeymoon hotel with heart-shaped tubs in the Adirondacks.

And then they rolled in the ghastly sideboard I had seen in Natasha's garage. The laughter and joking in the room quickly subsided. The auctioneer kept talking but the room was so still that we would have heard one of the light-as-air macarons hit the floor.

Martha Carter's face drew tight as no one bid. Natasha was turning a shade of red I had never seen on her before. It was, after all, her donation that had brought the entire auction to an abrupt halt.

Even the immensely dignified Robert Johnson tugged at the knot of his tie with discomfort.

Callie looked on, wide-eyed, chewing her bottom lip nervously.

I did *not* want that horrid thing. But I did want to rescue the auction. I bid fifty dollars in the hope that someone, anyone, would bid higher.

Robert placed his hand on his chin thoughtfully and gave me slight nod of appreciation.

Callie saved me when she bid, too, and then Martha bid an amount so large that the auctioneer slammed the gavel down and declared, "*Sold!*"

We broke into applause. Martha took a red-faced bow and said to the room, "That ought to buy a few books for the kids!"

The auction returned to full swing after Martha's reminder that it was all for children's literacy. We relaxed in the comfy sofas and chairs that were a lovely change from sitting at dining tables. No wonder Francie and Velma had adopted The Parlour as their favorite haunt. I sat back, sipping tea and indulging in the little sweets and sandwiches. They were too cute not to try each of them!

By the time the gavel had banged down for the last time, Velma had won a basket containing two dozen cozy mysteries, Nina clutched a certificate for a day of pampering at a local spa, and an ornate metal garden bench of intertwined vines and flowers was to be delivered to Francie's house. I had managed to accumulate a window-mount birdfeeder for Mochie's amusement, a black feather wreath with a skull on it, and a six-foot-tall skeleton for Halloween that was hinged and could be posed.

The string quartet had begun to play again as people filtered out.

I made my way to the auction cashier but turned quickly when I saw Alex in line to pay. I wasn't ready for that confrontation. Maybe I was a chicken, but I really didn't want to break up in front of half of Old Town. We would be fodder for gossip for the next month. I could just hear them asking one another, "Were you there? Did you see poor Sophie when Alex walked out with another woman?" So I dodged him and sidled toward the pastry display to wait.

As I gazed at the marvelous creations inside the case, including horns of pastry filled with cream, I couldn't help overhearing Alex's new flame telling Martha how wonderful her new boyfriend was. *Blech.*

Her long lashes touched the bangs that emphasized her lovely facial structure. I wasn't the only one who noticed. Robert watched her rather openly.

"It's interesting dating someone I've know for so long," the new girlfriend said. "I already know all his deep dark secrets."

Martha cocked her head. "Alex doesn't seem the type to have any secrets."

"That's sweet." She cast a glance at Robert and flashed

him a smile. "But all men have secrets. It's up to us ladies to ferret them out."

I turned my back to them and examined shelving that displayed so many different patterns of china that my head spun. Like Martha, I had a small addiction to collecting china. My budget didn't go very far, but I loved picking up sets at auctions and yard sales.

"Where the devil did that knife go? I just had it in my hand." I recognized Martha's voice without looking. She enunciated precisely and spoke with great caution, as though she feared she might say the wrong thing. "I dislike disorder. While I'm glad for the business, and I'm grateful to see so many new faces here, we would have been much more organized if a certain someone had pulled her weight today."

"Give her a break, Martha. You would be upset and distracted, too, if you had been attacked." Callie spoke with a distinct Southern accent. She sounded like the people where I'd grown up.

"At least I don't have *that* to worry about." Alex's girlfriend again? "He's so protective of me. It's like he can't be away from me for even a moment. It's adorable."

Ugh. I stepped outside for a minute and took a few deep breaths. Alex and the new girl turned the other way and didn't notice me when they left.

Nina and I were offering to help Velma carry her books home when Natasha sidled up to me, her skin ashen in spite of her ample makeup.

"I need a huge favor."

She seemed so desperate. "What's wrong? I thought the auction went pretty well. Are you sick?"

Her hand fluttered like a bird. "It's not that." She gestured toward the window.

CHAPTER SEVEN

Dear Sophie,

What's the difference between English, Irish, and Scottish Breakfast teas? I'm so confused. Are they all pretty much the same?

—Tea Fan in New London, Connecticut

Dear Tea Fan,

Breakfast teas are all blends of black tea. English Breakfast tea may be preferred because it's the mildest of the three. Irish Breakfast tea has a strong Assam component, which impacts the flavor. Scottish Breakfast tea is the strongest of the three, presumably to overcome the flavor of the water at one time.

—Sophie

A woman with silver hair cut like a young boy's was waiting for traffic to clear so she could cross the street. I would have recognized Natasha's mother, Wanda, anywhere. Frankly,

I liked Wanda. I had never understood how she could be so different from her prissy daughter.

"Please, Sophie," Natasha said. "Take her home? I just can't deal with her right now. Not here. Not now! She's crossing the street! Hurry!"

Natasha towed me toward the door but it was still too crowded to make much progress. By the time we reached the front, Robert Johnson was gazing at Natasha's mother with astonished curiosity.

She cut an interesting figure in tight camouflage yoga pants, a gauzy low-cut top over what I assumed must be a squeeze-and-lift bra, and a white jean jacket. "Baby doll!" She held her arms out to Natasha. "Are you okay?"

Natasha appeared reluctant to hug her mother.

Wanda promptly destroyed Natasha's carefully coiffed hair by feeling the back of her head. "Darlin', I don't feel a knot. Did you have a doctor check you out?" Wanda drew back and examined Natasha's face. "Well, you look as beautiful as ever. And I don't think your pupils are off. Follow my fingers, baby." She snapped her fingers and moved her hand in the shape of a cross.

"You haven't said hi to Sophie," Natasha muttered.

Wanda turned to me immediately for a hug. "I'm so glad you girls are friends. Thank you for taking care of Natasha last night."

While Wanda's back was turned, Natasha made a swift attempt to get Robert out the door. He wasn't budging, though.

Wanda let go of me and smiled sweetly at her daughter. "Mama's here to take care of you now."

"I'm fine. Really."

Wanda shifted her attention to Robert and held out her right hand. "Wanda Smith. I don't believe we've met. I would have remembered *you*!"

Natasha drew in a deep breath and appeared mortified. Wanda had an eye for men, and there was no mistaking the flirtatious nature of her remarks.

"Robert Johnson. I gather you are Natasha's mother?" He shook her hand, and it looked to me as though one of them held on a moment too long. "You must have had a long trip. Won't you join me for tea?"

"Well, aren't *you* just the sweetest thing! I would like that very much. Natasha, was this all a ruse to get me up here to meet handsome Robert?"

A confused smile hovered over his lips.

"Don't be shy, sugar. It's always the straight-laced ones that are the most fun in the sack. Believe me, I know!"

"Mom! You're embarrassing me."

"Oh, Natasha. When are you going to grow up, honey? You're livin' with Mars without benefit of marriage. You're hardly in a position to go gettin' all goody-goody on me."

Robert led the way to a cozy nook with only two chairs. Natasha appeared to be frozen in place.

"Natasha? Are you okay?" I asked.

"Did you see that? This is a first. I've never had to compete with my *mother* before. He took to her like a cat to cream."

I had to admit that I never would have expected Robert, who gave the impression of being so dignified, to be attracted to wild Wanda. And then I realized what Natasha had said. "Compete? Are you dating Robert?"

"What could he possibly see in my mother?" Natasha sagged against the baked goods case. "Give them five minutes. She can't go longer than that without mentioning herbs and backcountry spells. I have nothing to worry about."

I noticed, though, that she didn't take her eyes off them. "Was your lunch date with Robert?"

"Of course."

This development was astonishing on so many levels I hardly knew where to start. "He's almost old enough to be your father."

"Sophie, age is irrelevant when two people mesh." She cocked her head and gazed at him. "Do you think my dad is as debonair as Robert?"

Not even close. I chose my words carefully. "Natasha, I was seven when your father left, and I'll admit that I don't remember him very well, but Robert doesn't begin to resemble the man I recall."

"You don't know. That was a long time ago." She inhaled like she was taking her last breath. "You have the nicest father in the world. He's like a TV sitcom father. You have no idea what it's like to not know what happened to your dad. Not know if he's dead or alive. You never had to dream about meeting your father or wonder if he was out there in the world watching you, being proud of you."

I listened with deep sorrow. No wonder she worked so hard at being perfect and wanted to make a name for herself. She was trying to please a man she had lost decades ago and couldn't find.

"You have everything," Natasha hissed. "Your mother wears sweater sets and pearls. She's not some refugee from Woodstock who never got over her hippy days. You haven't lived in fear that someone would catch your mother casting spells under the light of the moon."

I was horrified by her outburst, but she wasn't finished. "And you got Mars's beautiful house. And Mars."

I didn't know what to say. Natasha had coveted my life for a long time but I had dismissed her feelings. I hadn't realized how deep they went and how long she had seen me as the recipient of all that she didn't have. It had clearly started when we were very young. As terrible as I felt for her, I couldn't help thinking of Mars, who had been sweating their breakup when all the while, Natasha had moved her affections to Robert.

"How long have you been seeing Robert?"

"You make it sound like I did something wrong."

"Up until today you were living with Mars . . ."

She glanced at me with annoyance. "You should know better than anyone that it's wise to feather a new nest before you leave the old one."

I was so taken aback that my mouth fell open again. "Me?"

"You weren't prepared when Mars left you. You still don't have anyone. Not really. I saw Alex here today with another woman."

"What happened to you?" I asked. "You used to stand on propriety. You were the model of decorum, looking down your nose at the rest of us who weren't as perfect." I kept my voice low so others wouldn't hear. "I don't know what's going on in your head, but you're acting with as little integrity as your father."

She winced. "That's not fair. I tried, Sophie. You know I did. But Robert is more my type. He's more polished and suave than Mars. We went to the opera last week."

"I didn't know you were a fan of opera."

"Isn't everyone?"

Martha must have been listening because she piped up from behind the counter. "If only it were so. I'm delighted to know someone else who would like to see *Die Fledermaus*. Perhaps we can go together."

Natasha cheered up. "I would love that!" She turned a pleased face to me.

I let it slide. Martha would know soon enough that Natasha was an opera neophyte. Maybe it would do Natasha good to befriend Martha. After all, she seemed very sensible and had opened a hugely successful business in Old Town. She might be just the sort of friend Natasha needed.

Natasha might have planned on watching her mother and Robert all day, but I didn't intend to. I turned on my heel and navigated through the crowd. Back at the table, I hoisted a basket of books, grabbed my skeleton and wreath, and asked if Nina could carry the birdfeeder.

"Sure. What's got you in such a tizzy?"

"Let's go." I motioned to Francie and Velma. They all followed me to the door.

Once outside I let out a deep breath. Why was I so upset with her? Natasha had done so many thoughtless things over the years. This wasn't really new behavior. "You know why Natasha didn't throw a hissy fit when Mars said he was leaving her? Because she's already seeing Robert!"

Velma sputtered when she asked, "My Robert? I mean, my deceased sister's Robert?"

"Apparently so."

Francie howled with laughter. "Why, that scamp!"

"It's the best thing that could happen to Mars." Nina

shifted her grip on the birdfeeder. "No guilt, no fuss. In fact, he can use it against her. He'll have the upper hand if they argue about anything."

"And it's the best thing that could happen to you, Sophie!" Francie's eyes sparkled. "You better grab Mars before Natasha realizes her mistake and changes her mind!"

"*My* Robert and Natasha?" Velma whispered as if she found it incredulous.

"Velma! Did you really have your eye on your own brother-in-law?" asked Nina.

"It happens. I'm a little older than he is but we've known each other for a long time. He's got to be fifteen years older than Natasha. What would he want with her?"

The other three of us laughed aloud. We started for Velma's home, still giggling about it all. In spite of my own laughter, my heart broke a little for Mars. Even though he had wanted to leave Natasha, he would be crushed that she had been seeing someone else while they were still a couple.

Dried leaves crunched underfoot on the brick sidewalks as we walked. Orange pumpkins and crook-necked yellow gourds decorated stoops. Bright yellow and burgundy mums sat in baskets, and a few eager Halloween aficionados had already draped ghosts and bats on their stoops. I planned to hang my skull wreath on my front door as soon as I got home.

We passed a green front door decorated with the word *BOO*.

Velma shook her head and tried to peer into the adjoining bay window. "What is it with Halloween? Seems like everyone starts the season in September these days."

Nina shot me a bewildered glance. "Uh, Velma, most folks don't appreciate people looking in their windows."

CHAPTER EIGHT

Dear Natasha,

My grandmother very thoughtfully gave me her Franciscan Cameo Pink china. I'm just sick over breaking a plate. It was discontinued before I was born! I've been searching eBay with no luck. Any suggestions?

—Klutzy Kate in Cameo, California

Dear Klutzy Kate,

Try Replacements.com. They specialize in finding discontinued patterns and will even help you identify a pattern.

—Natasha

"It's okay, darlin', this is Callie's place. It's the tiniest little thing but she decorated it quite nicely," Velma said.

"She doesn't usually close the drapes like that, though." Francie's mouth puckered. "Can you see anything?"

Nina and I exchanged a look. What did they think they were doing?

"There's a teensy crack between the curtains. I think the kitchen light might be on, and I see boxes stacked up."

"Now you stop that!" I said. "Callie is at The Parlour, working. There's nothing to see."

"I don't think she went on a date last night," Velma said. "She would have told us about it."

"Peering in her window isn't going to help," Nina pointed out.

Poor Callie probably didn't even realize that Francie and Velma thought they had adopted her.

"Maybe we can see more from my place." Velma shuffled across the street with Francie. Nina and I followed.

Velma unlocked a cream-colored front door. A cone-shaped gray metal container held fresh sunflowers, assorted greenery, wheat stalks, orange berries on stalks, and two tiny sugar pumpkins.

"Are those real?" I asked.

"Everything except for the berries. I'm mighty proud of that arrangement."

She opened the door and hurried up the stairs, with Francie right behind her.

"Are we supposed to follow them?" asked Nina.

I shrugged, taking in Velma's cozy living room. White trim accented warm beige walls. Two windows overlooked the street. An old grandfather clock ticked quietly in the corner. A brocade sofa in shades of blue faced the fireplace, along with wingback chairs in a blue and beige pattern. An Oriental rug covered part of the gleaming hardwood floors. Oil paintings hung around the room in ornate frames. A huge collection of teapots covered the built-in shelves next to the fireplace. On the other side, mysteries fairly spilled from the shelves.

It bordered on formal, yet drew me in with comfort. I could imagine Velma there with a cup of tea, wrapped up in a throw and reading quietly.

We set the baskets of books on the floor.

"Well, I'm going up there," Nina said. "What's with them and that Callie person anyway? It's like they're obsessed."

I followed Nina up the stairs and along a hallway into a bedroom. Wallpaper covered the walls from the chair rail up to the ceiling. A print of leafy green vines crisscrossed a white background and in each resulting diamond was a lush peony in shades of pink. Tall windows that reached to the ceiling lined the wall that faced the street. Gauzy white curtains hung on them. Two plush armchairs had been turned around to face the windows. A table between them held a lamp.

Velma and Francie perched in the chairs and peered through binoculars.

"I knew we should have bought that telescope," said Velma.

Francie groaned. "It wouldn't help you see through Callie's curtains."

I cleared my throat so they would know we were there. They didn't even turn around. "Francie! What do you think you're doing?"

"Velma's windows overlook Callie's apartment and Robert's house. It's the best seat in town."

"For spying?"

"Oh, honey," Velma said without moving the binoculars, "we're not spying. We're like a neighborhood watch keeping an eye on people. I don't believe Robert is home yet. Maybe customers are keeping him busy at his store."

She must not have noticed him sitting with Natasha's mother at The Parlour. Given the current situation and what was beginning to appear to be an unhealthy obsession, I didn't think I should mention that little fact. "What should we do?" I mouthed to Nina.

She hunched her shoulders and held up her hands.

I didn't have a clue, either. Were they Peeping Toms? Could they be considered stalkers? Could they get into trouble? I would have to ask Alex—if we were still speaking.

"I guess we'll go. Velma, we'll leave your books downstairs. Is that okay?"

"Sure. Thanks for carrying them."

We left them at their post. On the way down the stairs,

Nina said, "If they can't see anything, why are they still sitting there?"

"I have no idea. They didn't just turn the chairs around, either. We would have heard them being moved. I have a feeling this has been going on for a while. I'm worried that they could get into trouble for being Peeping Toms or something." We reached the living room. "Do you think we should have a talk with them?"

"Seems a little weird to scold them."

"I know what you mean. There's something uncomfortable about correcting sweet old ladies. Besides, they're not dumb. They know better than to do that." I placed my hand on the doorknob. "On the other hand, we *have* done our fair share of tailing people."

"That was *totally* different. We were trying to uncover murderers. Like the time we waited in a parking garage to follow Natasha."

"Do you remember how boring that was? Nothing happened for the longest time. We ate our way though all the snacks we brought with us. I thought she would never appear."

"I guess they're not hurting anyone. But they sure are nosy!"

We let ourselves out, and I pulled the door shut. "One of these days that will be us spying on the neighbors because we have nothing else to do."

⁓⁓⁓

Darkness was settling on Old Town much earlier, marking the end of summer. My evening strolls with Daisy were now by streetlight. A change in the atmosphere had taken place, too. Business suits had replaced sundresses and shorts, and everyone seemed to be in a hurry to get somewhere, even at nine o'clock at night.

Daisy pounced on leaves as they skittered along the sidewalk. I was busy admiring the colonial houses dressed up for fall with wreaths and pumpkins. We slowed at Robert Johnson Antiques so I could admire the items in the show window. Robert had an eye for quality. A sparkling chandelier hung over a Hepplewhite-style sideboard. A painting of a cottage, probably in England, was propped up on an easel next to it. A collection of tempting blue and white dishes, teacups, and vases graced the top of the sideboard. No wonder Natasha couldn't resist buying at Robert's store.

Across the street, the windows at The Parlour were dim as though Martha had left a small light or two on when they closed for the day. A motion caught my eye. Nothing more than a shadow, really. My radar of suspicion rose. Dodging traffic, Daisy and I crossed the street. Trying not to be too obvious, I looked in a window. Someone was definitely inside.

"Spying?"

I jumped and whipped around. "Mars! You scared me."

"What are you doing?"

"I thought I saw someone inside The Parlour."

"Oh no!" He clapped his hands to the sides of his face like the kid in *Home Alone*. "Imagine someone being inside. It could be the cleaning crew, or a baker, or the owner!"

I pretended to slug his arm.

Mars laughed at me and knelt to pat Daisy. "Where are my two girls off to?"

"Just taking our evening walk."

"Mind if I come along?"

"We would be honored, kind sir."

We ambled for a few minutes without speaking, passing historic houses, their windows aglow in the night.

"It's nice to just stroll in Old Town," Mars said. "Lately it seems like I've always been on the run."

"Have you settled into Bernie's okay?"

"That house is huge. It's really a mansion, Sophie. I think we could go for days without seeing or hearing each other."

"No regrets yet?"

"About Natasha? I wouldn't confess this to just anyone, but I had forgotten how peaceful life can be when someone isn't pitching a fuss or having a crisis every single minute. Last night I left my shoes in Bernie's den when I went to bed."

"So?"

"It was like a miracle. They were still there in the morning. Natasha would have hidden them to clean up and teach me a lesson."

"Come on, Mars. She can't be *that* bad."

"Maybe I'm too much of a slob for someone like her."

We turned a corner and a woman flew toward us. Mars shielded me with his arm.

CHAPTER NINE

Dear Sophie,

I can finally afford to buy some really fine china but I'm confused. Do I want porcelain or bone china? What's the difference?

—Setting the Table in Tabler, Oklahoma

Dear Setting the Table,

Porcelain and bone china are both considered fine china. Each has its strengths and flaws. Bone china is thinner and more delicate but may break more easily. Porcelain is thicker, but more brittle and therefore more prone to chipping.

—Sophie

"Sophie! Thank heaven it's you." Callie breathed hard, with her mouth open. "Do you see him?"

She held on to me like I was a life raft, but she looked back in the direction she had come.

We walked her beneath the streetlamp. "Callie, this is my ex-husband, Mars."

"What's going on?" asked Mars. "Is someone bothering you?"

She bobbed her head. "Following me. I thought I was imagining things but when I turned the corner he lunged at me."

She was still grasping my arm. The sleeve of her light cotton jacket was torn. "Did he do this?"

Callie released her grip and felt the open flap. "I guess so. I just ran as fast as I could. I've never been so scared."

"Do you know who it was?" I asked.

She paused for a second, for a beat too long. "No. I don't."

Mars pulled out his cell phone and dialed. "Wong had better know about this."

"No! No police. Please."

Mars threw me a doubtful look. "Somebody broke into my house and attacked my girlfriend last night. It could be the same person. You have to report it. It might prevent this person from hurting someone else."

Callie appeared to be thinking about it. "I'd really prefer to go home. Would you walk with me? It's not far from here, just a few blocks."

"What's your name? Callie?"

"Callie Evans."

Right in front of her, Mars called 911 and reported the incident.

We waited for an officer. I found myself straining to peer into the darkness around us. "What did he look like?"

"I didn't see much," Callie said. "You know the feeling that someone is watching you? I started glancing back but didn't really see anyone. But I had the creeps, so I walked faster. And when I turned the corner, somebody grabbed me from behind, and I ran."

A young cop arrived. She asked Callie to step away with her.

While they were talking, I asked Mars, "Do you think some whacko is running around and jumping women?"

"I think you won't be walking Daisy alone at night anymore until they catch this guy."

No problem. I certainly didn't want to be his next victim.

The officer finished with Callie and promised to see her safely home. Mars and I hurried back to my house. We didn't talk much. I suspected he was keeping an eye out for the guy, just like I was.

When we entered the kitchen, Mars said, "If you don't mind, I'll bunk in the den tonight. I don't like you being alone."

The sad truth was that I welcomed his presence.

We spent the rest of the evening by the fire. Even though I saw Mars now and then, there was a lot to catch up on, especially regarding his work. Probably because of the assailant on the loose, neither of us wanted to drink liquor. We settled on hot chocolate. It seemed like old times having him around the house.

I rose at seven to a gloriously blue sky. I threw on a bathrobe and tiptoed down the stairs so I wouldn't wake Mars. The old wood of my stairs creaked as usual but if he heard it, he didn't budge. I put on the kettle for tea and fed Mochie chicken in pumpkin sauce. He ate heartily, signaling his approval.

Daisy whined at the front door and a moment later, someone banged the knocker. I had a hunch that the person who was attacking women probably didn't bother knocking, but I peered out the peephole anyway as a precaution. Natasha stood outside, looking impatient.

I swung the door open. "Good morning."

"I would like to see my mother, please." Natasha brushed by me.

She was already on the staircase when I said, "Wanda's not here."

Natasha's eyes reduced to mere slits. "I'm not that stupid. Where else would she go? Of course she's here."

I didn't bother to argue. I could hear Natasha's heels clacking on the hardwood floors upstairs as she searched the bedrooms. I poured myself a bracing mug of Newman's Own organic black tea and stirred in sugar and milk. Daisy reached a paw in my direction, not touching my leg, but letting me know she wanted a treat.

"Okay, but only one. And then we're going for a walk. As soon as Natasha leaves." I fed Daisy a cookie in the shape of a bunny.

I could hear Natasha coming down the stairs. The sounds of her heels on the floor had slowed considerably. She dragged into the kitchen and burst into tears.

"What's wrong with me, Sophie? Mars left me and now even my own mother has abandoned me."

Tempting as it was to mention that she had claimed she left Mars, not the other way around, I resisted going in that direction. There was no need to depress her even more. She was going through a rough time. I poured her a mug of tea and ushered her into the living room, away from the den where Mars slept. "You're too hard on yourself, Natasha. And you hold everyone else to the same high standard. People are flawed. We're not perfect."

She sipped the tea. "I can see why you would think that. I mean, look at you. That bathrobe is just sad." She frowned at me. "Your living room is dated, and you refuse to hear me when I tell you the portrait over the fireplace in your kitchen is tasteless. I keep offering to help you redecorate but you always turn me down."

I smiled at her mention of the painting of Mars's Aunt Faye. She had left the house to Mars and me, and I had bought him out in our divorce. Faye had loved her home, and I liked her portrait in my kitchen, even if it did slide to an awkward angle once in a while—mostly when Natasha was in the house. Mars's mother thought she could talk to her deceased sister in my kitchen and a psychic had confirmed Faye's presence, but then the psychic also got some major things wrong. Maybe it *was* just a draft that shifted the portrait.

I was a little bit insulted by what Natasha had said. Who wouldn't be? I rubbed my hand across my forehead. "Think about what you just said, Natasha. Isn't the world a better and more interesting place because we all like different things?"

"Oh, Sophie! It's just pathetic that people have no taste. I have no idea why anyone takes decorating tips from you."

I was about to spew a retort when it occurred to me that I could say the same about her. "We like different things, Natasha. There's no right or wrong."

She tilted her head and patted my arm. "You keep telling yourself that, Sophie."

I clearly hadn't convinced her.

"Have you seen Mars?" she asked. "How's he taking our breakup? He won't know how to tie his shoes without me."

I couldn't tell her he seemed to be pretty happy. Thankfully, she didn't wait for an answer.

"He never loved me, Sophie. I should have realized that much sooner. I had a long talk with Robert about him. For the first time, I'm seeing everything so clearly. Robert is quite brilliant, and he's deeply intellectual in a way that Mars will never be."

At her mention of Robert, I feared I might know where her mother had spent the night. I wasn't about to tell her and give her the opportunity to make a scene, though. "Does Robert *know* Mars?"

"I don't think so. But he pointed out to me that when someone loves you, he supports you in the things you want to do. The things that are important to you. I'm not talking about going to the theater or an art gallery. I mean the big things. Mars always pooh-poohed my business efforts. He didn't believe in my line of gardening attire, he made fun of my tools for women, and he worked against my efforts to open a chocolate shop. I can't think of one thing he ever backed me on."

I couldn't exactly tell her that all those ideas had been doomed to failure and everyone, except for her, could see that. She did have a point, though. I would want my spouse to encourage my dreams, even if they were a little bit far-fetched. After all, if people didn't dream big, there would be no fabulous inventions, or cures, or spacewalks. Mars hadn't done that for Natasha. Maybe she and Robert were right about that.

Natasha grimaced. "He was only interested in me because he wanted someone more sophisticated and worldly—"

"Excuse me? As I recall, we came from the same little town in Virginia. It's not like you grew up in Paris and attended a Swiss boarding school."

Natasha smiled at me sweetly. "Sophie, you're so naïve. It's rather endearing."

Uh-huh. Naïve Sophie thought she'd better hightail it over to Robert's place to send Wanda home before Natasha found out and their mother-daughter relationship crashed and burned for good. "Have you tried phoning your mom?"

"How stupid do you think I am? She probably has the ringer turned off. She does that when she's mad at me, which is most of the time."

"Maybe you should go home in case she calls. In the meantime, I'll check around."

We were in the foyer when Mars stumbled in, yawning.

Natasha gasped and looked from Mars to me. "You certainly didn't waste any time."

I hated to say it but I did. "It's not how it looks."

"That's the standard line, isn't it? How dare you betray me like this? And you, Mars! Have you no shame? No loyalty? We were together for years, and you're already shacking up with your ex-wife?" She turned to me and her lips pulled tight. "You won't keep him interested for long looking like *that*." She pulled the door open and left in a huff.

I locked the door behind her.

Mars groaned. "You see what I mean? Every day. Every single day there's a drama."

"Want some tea?"

"I'd better get going. I have a meeting this morning."

Just as well. "Okay. I have a quick errand to run as soon as I dress."

"With that guy still out there?"

"It's broad daylight, Mars. I'm not going to hide in my house." I ran upstairs to dress in spandex-softened jeans and a big white button-down shirt. Downstairs, I slid into a quilted vest, and dressed Daisy in her harness. We left through the alley that ran behind my backyard in case Natasha had paused somewhere on our street. Maybe it was silly of me, but I wasn't taking chances. It would be such a shame if Natasha and Wanda had a big falling out over Robert. Natasha might have a lot of fans, but she had precious few friends and needed her mom on her side.

Daisy and I walked at a good clip. I was glad I had bothered to wear the vest. The lingering warmth of summer days had made a sudden departure. A chilling breeze whispered through the streets, leaving the scent of fireplaces behind.

As we walked, I wondered why Wanda would have spent the night out when her purpose in visiting was to stay with Natasha so she wouldn't be alone. Funny that Natasha hadn't mentioned being afraid last night. Maybe installation of the alarm system had been enough to soothe her nerves.

We neared Velma's house, and I couldn't help looking at the windows. From the street, I couldn't tell if anyone was spying from them.

The black door of Robert's house bore a wreath made of acorns and topped with a burlap bow. I suspected it must have been handmade. Otherwise, Robert's door seemed very plain, except for the brass mail slot. I saw neither a bell nor a doorknocker. I rapped on the door.

There was no answer. I turned around and gazed up at Velma's windows again. She probably knew if he was home. I knocked again, louder this time. "Robert?"

Still no response. Maybe this had been a stupid idea. He probably took Wanda out for breakfast.

I turned to leave but Daisy pawed at the door and whined. I froze. She had done that once before, and when I opened the door, I had found a corpse.

"Come on, sweetie. Nobody's home." But Daisy didn't budge, even when I tugged on her leash.

"One more time, then we'll go. Okay?" I knocked again, calling, "Robert!"

I tried the doorknob. It turned easily. The door was barely open a crack when I thought I heard something. Daisy reinforced that notion by whining.

The door creaked open to a dark house.

CHAPTER TEN

Dear Natasha,

I found a beautiful tea set in an antiques shop. The salesman told me it was bone china, but I'm not sure I believe him. I'm not familiar with the mark on the back. Is there a way to know?

—Wasn't Born Yesterday in Shopville, Kentucky

Dear Wasn't Born Yesterday,

There is a very easy way to tell. Hold it up to the light. Bone china is translucent. You should be able to see the shadow of your hand behind it.

—Natasha

"Robert?" I called.

This time I definitely heard it. A strange wheezing sound that wasn't familiar to me. Daisy stayed by my side, and we entered the house with caution. I left the door open for light and to beat a hasty exit should that prove necessary.

I found a light switch and flicked it on. A chandelier

lighted a narrow hallway, made even tighter by stairs on the right. Antique paintings lined the walls on both sides, and a marble-topped console held an old-fashioned globe lamp with flowers painted on it.

We ventured along the hallway at a snail's pace until I spotted a foot.

I raced toward it.

Robert lay on the floor of his living room, his eyes open and staring at the ceiling. A table lay on its side, and an old black dial telephone had fallen to the floor, the receiver mere inches from Robert's hand.

I pulled my cell phone out of my pocket and dialed 911. "Robert?" I felt his wrist for a pulse.

One of his fingers moved, almost imperceptibly. Faint rasping came from his throat. He seemed to be having difficulty breathing.

The dispatcher answered my call, but I didn't know the house number.

"I'll be right back." I dashed outside to get his house number and relayed the information to the dispatcher. She told me to stay on the line. I left the door open and rushed back to Robert. "Wanda?" I shouted. "Wanda?"

If she was there, she didn't respond. I should probably check around. She might be in a similar state. But first I had to do what I could do for Robert.

I kneeled beside him. "Can you sit up?"

He was having so much trouble breathing that I didn't dare try to move him. "What happened? Can you speak?"

The gurgle that came from his throat scared me. "It's okay. Don't try to talk. The ambulance will be here soon. Just hold on. Can you wiggle your fingers?"

The forefinger on his left hand twitched very slightly.

"Great!" I pretended like I thought that was wonderful but in reality I feared for him.

Daisy howled and a moment later, I heard the siren. That was one good thing about Old Town—it was so small that the police and ambulances never took long to arrive.

Knowing that help was on the way, I decided I'd better

just reassure Robert and forget trying to do anything to help him breathe. I placed my hand over his, hoping he could feel it. "Did you hear that? They're on the way."

He seemed unable to move. Had he broken his spine or possibly his neck?

It appeared he was trying to say something. I leaned forward. "Do you need something? Is there anything I can do for you?" Only a weak hiss emanated from his mouth. I turned my head and brought my ear closer to his lips.

"Rosie."

That was all he said. I sat back and looked at him. Clearly he couldn't be talking about a flower. What could he be trying to say? *Rosy* like a color? Maybe the *S* sound was a result of his difficulty breathing. It could be the beginning of a longer word.

"Rosie?" I asked.

He made no effort to clarify. I patted his hand, and chattered again. "Help will be here any minute." He didn't look good, though.

Thankfully, the EMTs arrived with Wong on their heels. I jumped to my feet to get out of their way. As if she understood, Daisy stayed by my side.

I answered their questions but wasn't any help at all. I didn't know how long he had been lying there or what he had been doing or if he had any allergies. "I don't really know him."

One of them stared at me like he was wondering what I was doing in Robert's house. "Do you know his name?"

"Robert Johnson. I came over looking for someone else and found him like this. Wong, I think Natasha's mother, Wanda, might be here. I'm worried that she might be incapacitated as well."

Wong nodded. "I'll check the second and third floors."

She sprang up the stairs with surprising energy. I hoped she wouldn't find Wanda in the same sort of crisis. I didn't think it was going to work out well for Robert.

Meanwhile, I searched the main floor of the house.

There wasn't a soul in the dining room. It was beautifully furnished with an inlaid table and an antique sideboard that sparkled with crystal bowls and candlesticks. Huge portraits of people from days gone by hung on the walls. The kitchen was surprisingly modern. Outfitted with dark walnut cabinets, it was immaculate. No one had cooked in the kitchen for a while, though. No loaf of bread waited on the counter. There was no bowl of fruit, not even salt and pepper shakers. A door led to the backyard. I peered through the window as the wind kicked up leaves around a wrought-iron table and four matching chairs. A high brick privacy fence separated the tiny backyard from the neighbors. At the far end, a gate led somewhere, presumably to an alley.

Daisy and I returned to the hallway.

"Robert! Robert! What's going on?" Velma sailed down the hallway toward us.

One of the EMTs stepped into the hallway. "Ma'am, are you related to Robert Johnson?"

"He's my brother-in-law. Is he ill? Did he fall?" Velma tried to push past me.

"Maybe you could step over here and give me some information?" He led her outside.

Daisy and I followed them, pausing on the way to open three doors. One led to a stunningly gorgeous powder room with a small chandelier hanging from the ceiling, and paintings in gold frames covering the walls. One was a closet, and the final one led to a basement.

I heard footsteps behind me and waited for Wong. She shook her head. "No one upstairs at all. Have you been in the basement?"

"No. But she's not on this floor."

Wong disappeared down the stairs, but Daisy and I hurried outside to Velma.

"Why won't they tell me what's wrong with him?" Velma grabbed my arm and held on tight. "Did you see him?" Velma asked.

"Yes. He was laying on the floor."

"So he fell." She shook her forefinger at me. "It's those threadbare Oriental rugs he likes so much. I told him he'd trip on one of them. Probably broke a hip."

"I don't know, Velma. He didn't look like someone who fell. Although . . ."

"What?" she demanded.

"A table had fallen over and the phone was on the floor near him." That did suggest that he'd been trying to make a call or had stumbled against the table as he fell.

While she yammered about not being allowed to see him, I was thinking that he wouldn't have trouble breathing if he broke a hip. Maybe he had a heart attack. Would that make it hard for him to breathe?

"You know, he felt a little queasy yesterday," Velma said. "I told him he couldn't skip the auction. After all, it was bringing people into his store to see the auction items." She waved her arms in the air. "Francie! Over here!"

Francie crossed the street from Velma's front door. "What's going on?"

Velma filled her in, Oriental rugs and all.

"Was your sister's nickname Rosie?" I asked.

Velma gave me a perplexed glance. "Whatever made you think that? Her middle name was a flower, but not a Rose. We called her Livy. Short for Olivia Violet. She was the fun one in the family. It didn't matter if it was a party or only a trip to get an ice cream cone. Everything was a celebration with Livy."

"How did she die?"

"It was the craziest thing, completely unexpected. You know, you go through life thinking every day will be pretty much like the one before and then out of the blue, something totally bizarre happens—she fell. It was that simple. She fell and hit her head on a rock."

"She was gardening in her own backyard," added Francie.

"That's crazy! Who dies from a fall like that?" I said.

"Apparently it's not all that unusual," Velma said. "They had some decorative boulders and as far as I can tell, it was just her time. If she had shifted a little one way or the other, she might have lived. But she conked her head and was dead almost immediately. I don't know who was more upset, me or Robert."

We stepped aside as the EMTs rolled a gurney by us. A little crowd had gathered to see what was happening.

Velma hurried to the gurney and walked beside it. "Robert, dear. How are you feeling?"

She stopped in the middle of the road.

Francie and I exchanged a glance and walked over to her. "Velma? Are you all right?" I asked.

She spun toward me. "That's no broken hip!"

CHAPTER ELEVEN

Dear Natasha,

My husband hates green tea but I heard it helps people lose weight. He likes regular tea okay. What is the difference between green tea and black tea?

—Mrs. Tubby in Green Acres Valley, New York

Dear Mrs. Tubby,

He should drink more coffee. Forget the tea.

—Natasha

"What's wrong with him?" asked Velma.

She wasn't a slender woman but she sure could move fast. She approached one of the EMTs. "What's that on his face?"

"It's to help him breathe."

"What happened to him? Why can't he breathe?"

"Ma'am, I wish I had an answer but I don't know." He told her to which hospital they were taking Robert.

"I'll take you," offered Francie. "You're in no condition to drive."

The two of them headed for Velma's house at a respectable clip.

"You leave anything in the house?" Wong asked me.

"No."

"I'm going to secure the premises."

"You mean like a crime scene?"

Wong scowled at me. "Is there something you haven't told me? Do you have reason to think this is a crime scene?"

"No!"

"Okay, then. I'll just lock up the house."

The ambulance left, and the crowd dissipated. I waited for Wong.

She stepped outside and tried the front door to be sure it was locked.

"Wong, did you get a good look at Robert?"

"Of course."

"Have you ever seen anything like that before?"

"Sophie, I'm a cop. I've seen things you don't even want to imagine."

"Eww."

The glimmer of a smile crossed her lips. "The guy looks sick, okay? I don't know what happened to him. I checked around for meds. Sometimes that helps the EMTs figure out what's up, but I didn't find anything useful."

"So you've seen people who couldn't move before?"

"Not exactly like him. But sometimes people are afraid to move or they're in pain."

I hadn't thought of that. It didn't explain his breathing problems, though.

"Why did you think Wanda was here?" she asked.

I shrugged. "Poor guess on my part. Apparently she didn't go home to Natasha's house last night. The last time I saw her, she was having tea with Robert at The Parlour. I thought they might have hit it off."

Wong snorted. "Not a chance. Robert is as prim and

proper as Natasha. I can't see him being interested in Wanda."

"I'd have thought the same thing but I was there when they met. The immediate attraction was obvious."

"How come that doesn't happen to us?" asked Wong.

I laughed, wrapped an arm around her, and gave her a little squeeze.

"Is it true that Natasha kicked Mars out when he came home?" Wong asked.

"Wow. News gets around fast. And inaccurately. She didn't throw him out. But I'm not quite sure whose idea it was to break up. Sounds like it might have been mutual. You won't believe this but apparently Natasha has her eye on Robert!"

We walked past Callie's house. The drapes on the bay window were open.

"Something wrong?" Wong asked.

"I was just thinking how difficult it must be to have windows right on the sidewalk where everyone can peer inside."

"Well, you *better* start thinking about Mars. I have it on good authority that a couple of divorcées are sharpening their claws and making Botox appointments."

"Over Mars?" I couldn't help giggling. "He'll be very flattered, I'm sure."

"Listen to me, girl. You better quit laughing and get busy or someone will snap him up before you know it."

"Oh, Wong. Would you go after your ex-husband?"

"Not a chance! But he wasn't like Mars. He was a devil rat."

Wong's radio sputtered with an unintelligible voice. "Gotta go."

"Hey! What are you doing working in the morning? I thought you were on the night shift."

"They keep switching us. Makes me crazy. See you later, Sophie." Wong walked away briskly.

"Ready for breakfast?" I asked Daisy.

She wagged her tail.

On the way home, I detoured by the take-out window of Big Daddy's bakery. I was carrying a box of croissants—plain, chocolate, and ham—far more than I could eat by myself, when I spied Wanda at my front door. She wore a rustic red, white, and black plaid shirt and jeans so tight I wasn't sure she'd be able to sit down.

"Good morning!" I unlocked the door.

"Sweetheart, you have some real food in there, don't you? I hate to beg for breakfast but Natasha hasn't got a thing in the house to eat."

I was dying to know where she had spent the night but it seemed wrong to ask that of someone my mother's age. "I've heard that about Natasha's fridge. Where is she?"

"Sittin' in her kitchen in a snit drinking some kind of fancy coffee that's too strong for me. I hope you have plain old American coffee." Wanda shut the door behind us. "Hi, Daisy! You remember me, doncha, sweet pea?"

Daisy waggled with excitement.

"You're in luck, I just picked up some croissants. I could whip up mushroom omelets."

"Don't you go to any trouble."

"No trouble at all." I took off Daisy's halter and started coffee brewing. It occurred to me that Wanda might not be well if she had been with Robert. "How are you feeling this morning?"

"Oh, a little weary. Didn't get much sleep last night. Where are your mugs, darlin'?"

I opened a cabinet and handed her two yellow ceramic mugs. I wondered if I should mention Robert's condition. Aha! Maybe there *was* a way to find out where she spent the night. "Why is Natasha in a snit?"

"Man trouble. She shouldn't be surprised. She comes by it through me. I swear we have a defective gene that makes us repel men. Too bad she messed things up with your Mars. He's a real decent fellow. Imagine him calling me because she needed me. How many men would have done that?"

"She told you Mars left her?" I pulled eggs and mushrooms out of the fridge and heated canola oil in two skillets.

"Mars told me that. Natasha made up a big whopper lie about throwing him out because she had met someone else. I hear you're back together with Mars."

Oh dear. I thought I'd better tread carefully. "He stayed over in the den last night. Natasha simply jumped to incorrect conclusions. Did Natasha say who she's seeing?" I washed the mushrooms and wiped them with a cloth.

"Robert Johnson!" Wanda shook her head as she poured coffee into mugs. "What could she have been thinking?"

I sliced the mushroom caps. "Did you know she's still pining for her father?"

Wanda nearly choked on her coffee. "Do you remember her daddy?"

"Not very well." I tossed the mushrooms in a pan and shook it to spread them out.

"Apparently, neither does Natasha. His name was Amos. Amos Smith. And, honey child, if *he* was selling antiques today, he'd be selling old hubcaps from a barn, probably stolen. But that doesn't stop Natasha from dreaming that he went through some kind of miraculous transformation"— she waved her hands through the air—"and became a gentleman in a top hat. She keeps looking around the city for him, but if Amos is still alive and kickin', he's out in the country somewhere, not hanging with her high society friends."

I stirred the eggs in the skillets. "I guess it's her way of coping."

"If I told her once, I told her five million times that she has to get over the fact that he left us. She has to move on and forget about him. Heaven knows he's not thinking about us. If he'd given one second of thought to how it might impact her, he never would have left us in the first place."

I was itching to know why he left, but I figured it wasn't the kind of thing a polite person asks.

Wanda flicked a spoon against the tablecloth. "You girls are old enough to know that we all have our vices."

I smiled when she called us girls. We would always be young girls to her. "Alcohol?"

"Oh, Amos liked his moonshine as much as any man. I used to wish that was his vice."

She didn't say more, and I didn't dare pry. But it occurred to me that if Natasha actually found moonshine-drinking

Amos, he might embarrass her more than her mother did.
Maybe finding him was one of those wishes to be careful
about. If it came true, she might be very disappointed.

"Where were you bright and early this morning, sunshine?" Wanda asked.

I slid the omelets onto yellow plates and brought them
to the table. I took a moment to add forks, knives, salt and
pepper, and place the croissants on a plate before I joined
Wanda. I considered taking the easy road and telling her I
had been walking Daisy. But it occurred to me that if Wanda
had been with Robert the night before she might have useful
information about his condition.

"I went over to Robert's house."

Wanda almost dropped her fork. "Why, Sophie! What is
it with you girls? Are you and Natasha vying for the same
man again?"

I gulped coffee to brace myself. "Natasha might be interested in him, but I'm not. Were you with him last night?"

"Sure *sounds* like you've got a yen for Robert." Wanda
shot an exaggerated wink at me.

"He's very ill, Wanda. I'm not being nosy about your love
life. He was taken to the hospital by ambulance. If you were
with him, you might be able to shed some light on his illness." I stopped short of adding *and you might be sick, too*.

This time her fork really did clank to her plate. "Ill? What
kind of *ill*?"

"I don't know. He was having trouble breathing and
seemed stiff. Like he couldn't move."

"Sounds like he needs a dose of lobelia. That or pot, which
is excellent for clearing the airways. Do you grow either one?"
She resumed eating.

Pot? Was she kidding? "I'm, um, sorry but I don't. So
did you see him last night?"

She nodded and wiped her mouth. "Should have brought
some with me. I usually travel with medicinals but I was in
such a hurry that I didn't pack many. Robert took me out to
dinner. Sugar, it was so pretty. They served miserly portions,
but the food was arranged on the plate like art."

"And afterward?" I savored the earthy flavor of the mushrooms in the omelet.

"Just to be clear, we invited Natasha along but she stayed home and had a pout party."

"She wasn't afraid to be alone?" I asked.

"Darlin', we invited her to come! If she was afraid she should have come with us."

"Did Robert seem sick?"

"Now that I think about it, we called it quits a little earlier than I'd have liked because he felt queasy. He'd been to the restroom a few times and barely picked at his food."

Wanda broke a ham croissant in two and took a bite. She swallowed and smiled at me. "I know this is fancy food, honey, but nothing beats a real ham biscuit. Tell me, where is this hospital? I think I should pay poor Robert a visit."

I wrote down the name of the hospital for her and drew a crude map.

"Natasha says they have everything here," Wanda said. "Do you know where I could find lobelia or cannabis?"

Maybe I had been too quick to dismiss Natasha's complaints about her mom. I could honestly say that was a question my mother had never asked me. "Maybe Natasha would know?"

"If she's speakin' to me! Thank you for breakfast, sweetheart."

"Let me know how Robert is?"

She promised and walked out the kitchen door.

I checked the time. "No problem," I told Daisy. "We're still on schedule."

⁓⁓⁓

In the afternoon, I walked Daisy, showered, blew my hair dry, and dressed to get through cocktails. It was early, but if anything went wrong, I wouldn't be stuck going to my own event inappropriately dressed. My midnight-blue sheath with a V-neck looked perfect. Sleek enough for office-to-dinner wear. I added dangling blue druzy earrings that sparkled when the light hit them. My one dress-it-up-with-bling concession was a chunky link bracelet with fake pavé diamonds on every other link. If time permitted later, I would retrieve shoes with higher heels, but for now, I slid my feet into matching midnight-blue flats with a hint of glitter on the toes.

Daisy followed me down the stairs and watched with a smidgen of anxiety as I slid on a light coat and prepared to leave the house. Mochie had settled on the window seat in the kitchen. I kissed the top of Daisy's head, promised her I would be back in a few hours, and locked the kitchen door behind me. I peeked in the window of the door and watched as Daisy settled near Mochie.

A breeze blew past, making me wonder if I should have worn a warmer coat. No matter. I wouldn't be that far from home. I set off at a brisk pace on the brick sidewalk. Old Town buzzed with people and traffic. I was glad I didn't have to find a parking spot.

I walked into the hotel hosting the conference and located the meeting rooms. I was looking for my contact when I heard a familiar voice say, "You cannot take these minor incidents too lightly. Make no mistake. Divorce can trigger murder."

I slipped into the room and watched from the back. I had been right about the voice. Wolf Fleishman? What was he doing here?

Wolf and I met when he was investigating a murder. We had dated for a long time but our relationship had come to an abrupt halt. Only a few months ago, I had unknowingly interfered with one of his investigations. I had learned my lesson, though, and planned to steer clear of police investigations in the future.

The audience broke into applause. Wolf left the podium and a guy stepped up to the microphone and thanked him. He announced a fifteen-minute break between sessions. Walking along the perimeter of the room, Wolf spotted me and headed in my direction. Hundreds of lawyers rose to their feet, some stretched, others rushed by me.

Wolf broke through the crowd, gently took my elbow,

and escorted me out of the meeting room into the crowded lobby. "What are you doing here?"

"I was going to ask you the same thing. Since when are you an expert on family law?"

"I wish I weren't. I've been called to too many domestic disputes. They can be very ugly. Hey, I'm glad I ran into you. I was going to give you a call. What do you know about a place called The Parlour?"

"It's a tearoom. Elegant, yet very comfortable. You would love their baked goods. Are you going to take tea?" I grinned at the thought. Wolf's passion for food kept him a little heavier than he would like to be.

Wolf groaned. "Sounds like a ladies' place."

"Only if you think tea and cake are for women. And, by the way, that would be fine with me because it would mean more for us. I think they have takeout if it's too girly for you. But Alex was there yesterday, so maybe it's like quiche. Real men do take tea?"

"Trust me, I won't be eating their food anytime soon. Neither will you. It's being closed down. Some guy died from botulism poisoning this morning, and his next of kin says he ate at this Parlour place yesterday."

CHAPTER TWELVE

Dear Natasha,

My father-in-law is insane. He takes the temperature of the water before he pours it over the tea. And he refuses to use tea bags. Plus, he calls the tea "liquor." I think he's gone fruity! He reads your column. Please set him straight?

—Biting My Tongue in Bagtown, Maryland

Dear Biting My Tongue,

You could learn from your father-in-law. Teas require different temperatures. In general, the darker the tea the hotter the water should be. And the correct term for brewed tea is liquor.

—Natasha

My throat constricted. "So did I. And a lot of other people! They hosted a charity auction."

Wolf studied me. I could see the fear in his eyes. "How do you feel?"

"Fine."

"Any uh, gastrointestinal discomfort?"

I grinned at his embarrassment in coming right out and saying what he meant. "No. I'm perfectly well, thank you." I grabbed his arm. "Wait a minute. The guy who died, what was his name?"

"Robert Johnson. You know him?"

"He died?" My voice broke when I spoke. I weaved a little bit as it sank in. I hadn't expected that. I thought the doctors would find Robert had a mysterious illness and would be able to help him.

"Soph? You okay?" Wolf placed his hands on my upper arms as though to steady me.

"I *found* Robert this morning and called the ambulance. I can't believe he died."

"I'm sorry. I didn't know he was a friend of yours."

"I hardly knew him. I'm just so shocked. He had botulism poisoning? I thought people didn't die from that."

"They tell me it depends on how much they ate and how soon they got help."

Velma would be devastated. What a bizarre turn of events.

"Maybe I should get you some coffee."

"That's sweet, but I'm okay. It was just so unexpected. I can't believe they're closing The Parlour. His sister-in-law said he felt sick yesterday."

"Hopefully they'll find the culprit in his kitchen, but it's a major public health issue. We don't want more people getting sick. They have to close the places he ate until they find the source." He stared over my shoulder for a moment. "Still seeing Alex?"

I nodded.

His eyebrows jumped ever so briefly. "I have to get back to work. If you feel even the slightest bit ill go to the hospital right away. Okay?"

I assured him that I would.

Wolf sighed and cocked his head like he pitied me. "Take care."

What was that about? I watched him walk away, turned

abruptly, and slammed into Alex, who spilled his jumbo-size coffee on the pretty brunette I had seen him with at The Parlour.

"I'm so sorry!" I gushed.

She brushed her ivory suit with one hand, holding her own coffee in the other hand. Alex's drink had a good bit of milk in it, but I suspected that the suit was ruined.

Alex fetched paper napkins from the coffee stand and handed them to her.

She wiped her skirt and looked up at me from under her long bangs. If looks could fry, I would have sizzled.

Alex, dressed in a well-cut suit with a white shirt and a burgundy tie, apologized to her profusely.

"Now stop that," she drawled in what had to be a North Carolina accent. "It wasn't *your* fault."

Oh! The nerve. It wasn't *my* fault that they were right behind me in a crowded lobby. But it did annoy me that they made a pretty couple, both with dark brown hair and more fit than I would ever be.

"Elise Donovan, this is Sophie Winston," Alex said.

She extended a hand and when I shook it I realized that she wore the sapphire I had bid on.

"What a lovely necklace."

"Thank you. It was a gift from Alex." She resumed wiping her skirt.

It wasn't as though Alex and I had an understanding of exclusivity, but at that very moment, I wasn't as sorry as I might have been about her ruined suit. I shifted my gaze to Alex, who didn't appear embarrassed about being caught with another woman. Was that his military training? Buck up and never show your discomfort?

"Elise was married to my law partner in Charlotte," he explained. "Their son, Kevin, is going to live with me and go to school here this year."

His sentence was ordinary conversation, yet so fraught with innuendo that I was taken aback. Wasn't she married to his partner anymore? Hadn't school started weeks ago? Had her son been with Alex that long but I hadn't known?

And why on earth would he be moving in with Alex anyway? This could mean only one thing—we weren't dating
anymore. We'd had some nice times together. I just wished
he would have told me.

I smiled as sweetly as I could muster. "Are you coming
to the cocktail party at the National Museum of American
History?"

Alex nodded. "I'm looking forward to—"

"Sweetheart, you've forgotten that we're having dinner
with Kevin." Elise looked me in the eyes and added, "Just
the three of us."

I was stunned. I recognized a barbed jab when I heard
it. Ohhh, this was not a nice woman. The truth was that Alex
and I weren't so close that I would make a fuss. If he had
moved on, I would wish him well. But I had a sneaking
suspicion that if Elise was showing her true colors, their
relationship wouldn't last very long.

"That's a pity. Alex and Kevin would have enjoyed it."
Determined to take the high road, I added, "Nice meeting
you, Elise." I walked around her and went in search of the
conference organizer.

～※～

For the next two hours, I pushed Robert's death and Elise
out of my mind and focused on the details of the special
events I had been asked to plan. In a way, they were easy
money. I had done them so many times for other groups that
it was almost like having a week off. Cocktails at the museum
tonight. A guided tour and luncheon for spouses at the Capitol tomorrow. And finally, a gala dinner at a restaurant overlooking the Potomac River.

On the lookout for Alex or the dreaded Elise, I left the
hotel. I had plenty of time to walk home, change shoes, and
let Daisy out before driving to the museum. But on my way,
a small crowd blocked the sidewalk in front of The
Parlour.

Martha consoled her regulars, assuring them she would
reopen as soon as possible. I made my way to her.

"I'm so sorry about this." Whispering, I asked, "Has anyone else reported feeling ill?"

"No. Not at all. Not that I've heard of, anyway. I'm horrified."

A tall gentleman with the same kind of erect military bearing as Alex joined us. His gray eyes sized me up like a mountain lion on the hunt. At first glance I thought he was bald, but soon realized that he shaved his head. He wore glasses shoved partway up his forehead.

"Sophie, this is my husband, Max. What did you find out?" she asked him.

"They're testing the contents of Robert's kitchen and his trash first," Max said. "It could be anything. It could even be something from a grocery store, which might mean a national outbreak. But apparently the most likely source is improperly canned foods."

"Robert doesn't really seem the type to be canning food," I said. I omitted my thought that it would more likely be takeout. "Can food that spoils in the refrigerator develop botulism? You know, the stuff that starts to look like a science experiment?"

They turned blank faces toward me.

Max shook his head. "I don't think so, but I haven't researched it enough yet. I think it has to be oxygen deprived."

Martha consoled another lady who begged to buy some macarons *on the sly*. "I can't do *that*. I could lose my business license!" Martha exclaimed.

"But it's my bridge club. I was counting on the macarons."

"Martha." Max uttered only her name, yet his tone carried layers of warning.

Martha looked worn out. Her hair was swept up. Her makeup was perfect. But deep furrows accentuated worry lines between her eyebrows, and her mouth puckered tightly as though she was struggling to keep it all together.

In a voice so soft I could barely hear it, she said to the woman, "I'm so sorry."

The woman left in a huff, prompting Max to hiss, "This will be the end of your business."

Martha rubbed the side of her forehead with three fingers but showed no other reaction to her husband's unhelpful observation.

"He's a single guy. It was probably something canned he bought at the grocery store," I said. "What a rotten break when you work such late hours and you've put so much effort into The Parlour. I'm sure everyone will come back as soon as you reopen."

Max's piercing eyes snapped to me. "Late hours? The Parlour isn't open in the evening."

"I suppose there's always work to do. I saw someone inside last night."

The muscles in Martha's neck tightened. "You must be mistaken, Sophie. I was home with Max last night."

CHAPTER THIRTEEN

Dear Sophie,

My best friend insists on leaving the tea bag in her tea as long as possible. Like half an hour! I think that's crazy. I steep my tea for 2–3 minutes. Who's right?

—Light Tea for Me in Steep Brook, Massachusetts

Dear Light Tea for Me,

You are partly correct. The proper steeping time depends on the tea and on your preferred flavor. Your friend, however, is way wrong. Allowing the tea to steep too long only results in the release of more tannins and may result in a bitter flavor.

—Sophie

Uh-oh. Had I stepped on a sensitive spot? "Maybe it was the cleaning crew." I tried to sound soothing.

"It was probably Callie. She's always forgetting something." Martha didn't meet my gaze.

Her husband snorted. "I don't know why you keep her. You shouldn't have such irresponsible employees."

"Callie is a talented baker, not a mess crank."

Alex was former military, too, but as tidy and precise as he was, Max made him seem like a lazy slouch. Granted, the situation was grim, but I wondered if Max could smile.

I had to get going or I would be late. "Lovely to meet you, Max. Martha, I hope you'll let me know if there's anything I can do."

"Thank you, Sophie."

I walked away but overheard Max say, "There's nothing anyone can do about this mess."

I hoped Max wasn't always so full of doom and gloom. At home, I let Daisy out in the backyard, swapped my flats for heels, patted Mochie, and let Daisy in again. I locked up, hopped in the car, and negotiated the traffic into Washington.

━━◆━━

The cocktail event at the National Museum of American History was a huge hit. I had guessed that lawyers would be particularly interested in history. I must have been right because they turned out in droves. By seven o'clock most of them had gone off to dinner, and I spent half an hour wrapping up before heading home.

I pulled into my garage wishing all events would go that well. My feet ached from the high heels, though. When I stepped into the covered porch that joined the garage, I stopped and stepped out of the shoes. While I was bending over, a warm wet tongue licked my cheek. Startled, I jerked away before I realized that Francie's golden retriever, Duke, was standing next to me.

"What are you doing here, sweetie?" I picked up my shoes and shrieked when I saw a shadowy person on the porch.

"Finally! Where have you been?"

"Francie? What are you doing out here in the dark?" I flicked on the tiny starlike lights overhead and realized that Velma was with her.

"It was peaceful in the dark. A little cold, but considering the day we've had it was nice." Velma sniffled and blew her nose in a hankie.

"I'm so sorry about Robert."

"You heard, huh? Velma has been walking around like a zombie. The death of a loved one is always hard." Francie looked over at her friend.

"It was so unexpected," Velma said. "I knew he was seriously ill when I saw him on the gurney, but it never crossed my mind that he would die."

"Would you ladies like to come inside? I think I could rustle up something to nibble on."

The two of them struggled to get to their feet. Velma carried a good-sized Vera Bradley bag with her.

I unlocked the living room door, and Daisy greeted us all with excitement, especially her pal, Duke. I let them play outside for a bit while the rest of us settled in the kitchen.

"What would you like, ladies? Hot cider, maybe?"

"Scotch. Have you got any Scotch? I could use a stiff drink tonight." Velma opened her bag, pulled out slips of paper and a fragile paper rose, and set them on the table.

Like magic, Nina appeared at the kitchen door. When I opened it for her, Daisy and Duke dashed inside.

At the commotion, Mochie lifted his head and yawned.

Nina stopped cold when she saw Francie and Velma. "I guess you already heard about Robert. Velma, I'm so sorry."

"Would you get them some Scotch? I'll put out a few goodies and build a fire."

In minutes, a crackling fire warmed my kitchen. Scotch had been poured in Waterford Irish Lace double old-fashioned glasses for everyone except me. It wasn't my preferred drink.

Given the odd pile of items on the table, I thought maybe I should stay alert. For all I knew, the two sweet old Peeping Toms had begun pilfering, too. I made a bracing cup of hot tea for myself with sugar and milk.

A quick raid of the fridge produced hard-boiled eggs, leftover plum tart, and a lovely brie. I popped a frozen baguette in the oven to warm, topped the brie with chopped pecans and apricot preserves, and slid it into the oven next to the bread. I cut the eggs in half and mashed the yolks with mustard and mayonnaise for deviled eggs. A quick sprinkle of paprika and I arranged them on a large platter, along with the warmed brie and black grapes. I sliced the baguette on a diagonal and tossed the pieces into a basket lined with a napkin.

I cut the leftover plum tart and placed the slices on vintage china dessert plates with white centers and pale green rims with a touch of gold around the edges. I carried a little crystal bowl of whipped cream for the plum tart to the table and found that Nina had very thoughtfully put out plates, forks, and pale green napkins that matched the color of the dishes.

The Scotch must have loosened Velma's lips because the second I sat down, she slathered a piece of baguette with brie and held it in her hand while she pronounced, "Robert's death wasn't an accident."

I nearly choked on my tea.

"I knew it!" Nina was so excited that she almost spilled her Scotch.

I tried my best not to appear skeptical or to belittle them. It wasn't uncommon for the bereaved to second-guess everything that had happened, sometimes even blaming themselves. It was a time when people asked *what if* and *if only* and sometimes *who could have?* Too many people lived with secrets about their health, and more often than I would have expected, about things they had done in their lives.

As sweetly as I could, I said, "Botulism isn't exactly a handy means of murder. I think it's highly unlikely that anyone slipped Robert some botulism on purpose."

"But that's exactly why it's so diabolically clever. No one would ever suspect it." Francie selected a little cluster of grapes.

"Why on earth would you even think such a thing?" I asked. "You'd have to plan far ahead, intentionally can something poorly, and then convince the person to eat it. I'm sorry, Francie and Velma, I don't think so."

Velma raised her eyebrows. "Why did you ask me if my sister's name was Rosie?"

I'd forgotten about that. "Robert said the word *rosy* to me. But I could have misunderstood. He could barely breathe, let alone talk."

Francie's eyes sparkled. "You didn't misunderstand."

Velma snapped her fingers and pointed at me. "He was trying to give you a message. What do they call that? Dying utterances or something?"

One by one, Velma held up items from the pile on the table. "A pretend rose tattoo, a withered dried-up rose, a rose made out of the pages of a book—"

"I want to know how they made that. It's so cute!" Nina peered at the paper rose.

"Where did you get these?" I asked.

Francie swallowed a bite of the tart. "From Robert's house!"

"So he had some roses. Maybe he liked roses." I sat back and listened.

"We went over to his house when the health department was collecting specimens. We found these on his rolltop desk." Velma produced scraps of paper from her bag. She read aloud.

> You will see my face in still waters,
>   And hear my voice in the wind.
>   I will curse you eternally,
>   A reminder that you sinned.

"Eww. Do you think he got that from a book or something?" Nina asked.

"Just listen." Velma picked up another one.

> In your darkest hour
>   Remember this,
>   You have created
>   Your own miserable abyss
>   And the devil awaits you.

Nina gasped. "Maybe he liked dark poetry."

I admit I was a bit taken aback, too. "Were these on his desk as well?"

Velma nodded. "You see? Someone had it in for him."

Suddenly, I didn't like that she was holding the small wisps of paper in her fingers. I retrieved a plain paper bag and some non-latex gloves. Handing them to her, I said, "Slip these on. Let's not get your fingerprints all over them."

The color drained from Velma's face. She dropped the paper she was holding. "You mean these could be real threats?"

"Isn't that why you showed them to us?"

"Well, sure. But I don't know . . ." Her voice faded. "Suddenly it's all very real. Do you think this person murdered him?"

Nina poured herself another Scotch. "Of course! Those are clearly threats."

"Come on," I said. "It seems very unlikely. Kind of like giving someone the flu and hoping that person would happen to die from it. Stabbing Robert with a knife would have been a sure thing and required a lot less planning."

"It would have been much messier," Francie observed. "Poisons are a rather tidy means of dispatching someone. And so much harder to track. After all, don't many of our neighbors have some kind of poisons in their homes?"

"I don't!" Velma recoiled at the thought.

"Really?" A sly smile worked Francie's lips. "You have no medicine that could kill in a large dose?"

"That doesn't count. Everyone has . . . I see what you mean."

"And that doesn't begin to include all the lovely poisonous plants in our yards."

"You're beginning to worry me, Francie." Velma scowled at her.

Oddly enough, that seemed to please Francie. "I've always had a fascination with poisons. Though I rather suspect that botulism isn't actually a poison per se. But it would be a very clever way to kill someone because no one would ever suspect that it was intentional."

"Are there any more of those weird notes?" asked Nina.
Velma slipped the gloves on and read aloud again.

> You can never escape your past.
>> It chases you wherever you go.
>> Until the day when at last,
>> You collapse from the weight of
>> your woe.

"Why do you think these had anything to do with him saying *Rosie*?" I asked.

Francie waved her fork at Velma. "Read her the one that gave us chills."

> Roses are blood red
>> Now I bid you adieu.
>> Rosie is dead
>> And so are you.

CHAPTER FOURTEEN

Dear Natasha,

I threw a tea party and served cucumber sandwiches, but it seems nobody liked them, because most of them were left on the serving platter. I spread margarine on white bread, added cucumber slices, and cut off the crusts. Where did I go wrong?

—Embarrassed in Bread Loaf, Vermont

Dear Embarrassed,

You erred by using margarine. The classic cucumber sandwich demands butter. The flavor and texture will be off with margarine.

—Natasha

The other messages were unpleasant, for sure, but that was a death threat. I rose from the table and phoned Wolf. Naturally, I got his voice mail. I left a message. "I'm sorry to call you so late but Francie and Velma found something you should know about. Can you please stop by my house?"

When I turned around, Nina had disappeared. "Where's Nina?"

"She's making copies of the notes in your office."

It didn't take her long. She was back in a flash, still wearing gloves. "They all look alike. Probably written on a computer and printed out, then cut into little slips." She handed each of us a copy of them.

I shared a piece of bread with Daisy and Duke while the other three leaned over the table, examining the notes. "Velma, did Robert ever mention anyone named Rose or Rosie?"

"Francie asked me the same thing. I can't remember him mentioning anyone named Rose."

Her sister had died in an unusual manner. "Are you sure he didn't call your sister *Rose* or *Rosie* as a pet name?"

"Positive. He called her Pookie. Don't ask me why. I found it a bit nauseating, but she loved it. It was probably some kind of private joke between them."

"What do you know about Robert's past?" Nina asked, helping herself to more plum tart.

Velma settled back in the banquette. "He came from a small town in Virginia, not too far from here. Graduated from college. He married my sister in a beautiful beach wedding and they settled in Charlotte, where he was employed by a company that manufactured furniture. He worked his way up, then opened his own furniture store. He and my sister dreamed of owning an antiques store in their retirement but she never lived to see it happen."

"Why did he move up here?" asked Nina.

"Because I was his only living relative. My sister wanted to live near me, so they always looked at houses when they came to visit. As you can imagine, they loved the ambiance of Old Town and all the antiques. After Livy died, I didn't think he would come. But you reach an age when you're grateful for family and friends who can lend a hand when you need it. They lived out in the country in a lovely house, but it came with some acreage and was a lot of work. I guess a town house in Old Town started to seem more attractive to him."

"They didn't have children?" I asked.

"No. And he was an only child. No siblings."

Daisy and Duke ran to the door. I saw Wolf before he knocked and got to my feet to let him in.

He grinned when he saw the table. "Looks like I'm in time for dessert?"

"Tea?" I asked.

"Sure. Can you make it decaf?" Wolf slid off his jacket and warmed his hands by the fire.

While I cut a piece of the plum tart for him and heated water for tea, Velma and Francie filled him in about the rose items and the threatening notes.

When we had dated, I was often frustrated by Wolf's poker face. It was a good thing for a police investigator, but it drove me crazy when I didn't have a clue what he might be thinking. He listened to them politely, as though they were explaining something less important, like a broken window.

I brought his tart and tea to the table, threw another log on the fire, and joined everyone.

"They're clearly threats," insisted Velma. "Don't you think that changes things? Someone wanted Robert dead."

"Thank you for bringing these to my attention." Wolf turned his focus to the tart.

"How can you be so calm?" Velma's eyes grew large. "This person obviously wanted to kill Robert."

Wolf took a sip of tea. "And he or she might have done exactly that if Robert had not died from botulism poisoning. I would be much more concerned if Robert wasn't already dead. There's not much anyone can do to harm him now."

"How do you know the person who left the notes didn't murder him?" demanded Francie.

"Botulism poisoning is an accident, not an intentional murder." Wolf remained calm and ate more of the tart with a generous dollop of whipped cream on top.

"I thought you were smarter than that." Francie seemed to be baiting him.

Wolf lifted his eyebrows. "How's that?"

"Botulism would be a very clever method of murder. Think about it. Whoever made the food that was tainted with the deadly botulism can simply pretend it was accidental. Better than that, there are no fingerprints, and virtually no way to follow the trail to the killer. You can find out where someone bought a knife or a gun. But how are you going to figure out where the poisonous food came from?"

"Yeah!" Velma's voice was loud and strong.

"Francie, I'm going to have to keep an eye on you," teased Wolf. "We can indeed follow the botulism to the source. That's what we're doing right now."

"Oh, please. You youngsters are so naïve. You see everything in technological terms. Can you even imagine how many cowering wives killed their husbands this way in the old days? Back then, the doctors probably wouldn't have even known it was botulism. Plenty of food spoiled on the prairie and on farms where they didn't have refrigeration. It wasn't uncommon for wives to slip nasty things into food to dispatch men who were cruel to them."

"Ugh." Nina stuck out her tongue. "That's scary and revolting."

"It's just the truth. The ones that do the cookin' have always been in a position to eliminate people."

"How did you say your husband died, Francie?" asked Nina.

We all burst out laughing.

"How long will The Parlour be closed, Wolf?" asked Francie.

"Probably just another day or two. Unless they find it's the source of the botulism."

"Velma and Francie go there every day," I explained.

Wolf looked at each of them. "Any symptoms? Nausea, vomiting, general weakness?"

"Not at all. I can assure you that Martha Carter runs a very clean establishment." Francie toyed with her fork.

"That's what the health department said. She hasn't

been open too long but her tearoom has passed their inspections with flying colors."

Suddenly it dawned on me that Francie could be worried about her birthday celebration. She might be a nosy Peeping Tom but I loved the old coot. "What if we had a birthday tea for you here? It won't be as fancy as The Parlour, but we could try."

Francie perked up for a second but soon sagged. "It wouldn't be right. Not when Robert just died. We need to bury him first, give him the respect he deserves."

Maybe she was right.

"Aww, I was looking forward to crumpets," Nina complained.

Velma looked confused. "Just what *are* crumpets? People always talk about them but I don't know what I would be ordering."

"I think they're sort of a cross between little griddle cakes and English muffins," I said.

"I'm having trouble imagining that," Wolf said.

"Would you make us crumpets sometime?" asked Francie.

"I can give it a shot."

Velma sniffled. "If Sophie is willing, I think we should celebrate your thirty-ninth birthday anyway."

Francie looked down at her fingers, decidedly unhappy.

"What's wrong?" I asked.

"You're so sweet to be doing this for me. I feel guilty asking for any other favors."

"Spill, Francie," I ordered.

"Would it be okay if we invited Callie?"

Velma gasped with excitement. "Oh, yes. She's such fun! She won't have to work if The Parlour is closed. And she might be glad to get out. Have you seen her place? I swear I have bigger shoeboxes."

Wolf carried his plate and mug to the sink. "I need to get going. Thanks for the notes, ladies."

"Don't you go throwing them out!" cried Velma.

"Trust me. I won't."

I walked him to the front door. "Thanks for being so nice to them. They're convinced that Robert was murdered."

Wolf sucked in a deep breath. His eyes met mine, dead serious.

CHAPTER FIFTEEN

Dear Sophie,

I'm not a terrible baker but those beautiful little macarons simply won't turn out right for me. What can I be doing wrong?

—Florrie on the Farm in Egg Harbor, Indiana

Dear Florrie on the Farm,

The answer may be in your eggs! Make sure your egg whites are at room temperature. And you'll have more success with older eggs. Don't use the farm fresh ones!

—Sophie

"Are you kidding?" I whispered. "You think that's a possibility?"

"Ordinarily? No. But no one else has turned up sick. Not even one report of it. The incubation period for botulism poisoning is twelve to seventy-two hours. Kinda makes me wonder. Let me know if you hear of any developments."

I was reeling when I closed the door behind him. I had dismissed Francie and Velma's theories as silly.

Of course, those notes were very odd. Stranger than odd, actually. Someone had been intentionally tormenting Robert.

And then he said *Rosie* to me. Why? What had the note said? *Rosie is dead*. If Rosie was dead, why would he say her name? Unless . . . she wasn't dead!

I dashed into the kitchen so fast that the dogs jumped to their feet and barked. "What if Rosie isn't dead? What if Rosie killed Robert?"

The three of them stared at me like I had lost my mind. "Velma, *think*! Who was Rosie?"

Velma sat back, crossed one arm over her abdomen, and touched the fingers of her other hand to the bottom of her chin.

"Did Wolf tell you that?" asked Nina.

"No. I just don't know why Robert's last word would have been *Rosie* if she's dead."

Nina's eyes went wide. "You think this Rosie could be alive? Was he trying to finger his killer?"

"Now, girls," Francie said. "I know I'm the one who thinks botulism would be a great way to kill someone, but there are some big flaws in your logic. In the first place, the killer was taking a chance that Robert might survive. If this Rosie"—she chuckled—"rose from the dead, she would surely have used an instantaneous method to kill him. Otherwise she would have run the risk that he would reveal to everyone that she was alive. Right?"

"Maybe she didn't care about that," Nina said.

"There's another problem. Nina, if you felt deathly ill today, would you blame someone?" Francie asked.

"I might if I knew what made me sick."

"You see? I doubt that he even knew who was responsible for the tainted food. He probably ate it without realizing that it would poison him. If he had known, wouldn't he have sought medical care sooner?"

"I think that supports my original theory that his death was an accident. But then why did he say *Rosie*?" I asked.

"Francie, I think we'll have to do a little more snooping around Robert's house." Velma threw her hands in the air. "Don't look at me like that. As his only kin it falls to me to clean out his house, doesn't it?"

Nina grinned. "It sure does!"

"You could help us, Nina," Velma said.

They made arrangements to meet at Velma's house in the morning. Nina, Daisy, and I walked the elderly ladies home. I left three eggs on the kitchen counter to come to room temperature while we were gone.

It wasn't too late to bake when I returned, so I set about making macarons, the fine, light cookies that were the delight of every tea party.

I cracked the eggs and separated the yolks from the whites. In my food processor, I ground almonds with powdered sugar as fine as I could and pushed them through a sieve to make sure there were no little lumps. After whipping the egg whites, I folded in the sugars as gently as possible, and added a little raspberry juice to give them a faint pink color. I piped the resulting dough in one-inch circles on parchment paper. While they were in the oven, I tackled the filling.

Around eleven, I placed the adorable little cookies in the fridge and headed up to bed.

Just past midnight, someone hammered the knocker on my front door. Daisy and Mochie flew down the stairs to investigate while I lumbered along behind them, half-asleep.

I peered through the peephole. Natasha? What did she want at this hour? I opened the door.

Natasha barged in. "I can't sleep."

"I was doing just fine."

"Sophie, I have a problem, and I don't know who else to go to. But let's be clear that I have not forgiven you for throwing yourself at Mars."

Great. This couldn't have waited until morning? I closed the door behind her. Maybe if I made her some hot milk she would get sleepy. I staggered into the kitchen and flicked on the lights.

"How about some hot milk?"

"Eww. A skin forms on top. How can you drink something like that?"

"Hot chocolate?"

"A glass of white wine, perhaps?"

I poured two glasses and sat down with her. "So what's the problem?"

"I guess you heard about Robert?" she sniffed and dabbed at her nose with a lacy hankie.

I felt ashamed for being a grouch. I'd forgotten that she was crazy about him. "I'm sorry, Natasha. I'm sure he was fond of you, too."

She bit her upper lip like she was trying to compose herself. "We were perfect for each other. Who knows what would have happened if he had lived?"

Natasha closed her eyes and paused. I thought it best to let her have a minute, so I sipped my wine and waited.

"I know how much you like my mother," Natasha said.

"I do."

She reached out a trembling hand. "I think she killed him."

Natasha couldn't have said a thing in the world that would have surprised me more. I spoke as soothingly as I could. "I'm sure that's not the case. Robert died from botulism poisoning."

"Exactly!"

"I'm not following you."

"You know my mom is a little unusual."

"A free spirit. That's what's so great about her!" I said.

"That's a nice way to put it. But I'm terrified. She was the last person to see him alive."

"Actually, I think the doctors and nurses were the last people to see him alive."

"Why are you being so difficult? She went out with him the last night of his life."

I nodded. "And?"

"And he didn't feel well," Natasha said.

"So he had already been poisoned."

Natasha almost shouted. "Would you just listen to me? She gave him some of her potions!"

"Oh, honey, they probably didn't contribute to his death."

Even though we were the only people in the house, she whispered. "How do you know they weren't tainted with botulism?"

Now I saw the problem. "She makes them herself?" I asked, even though I thought I knew the answer.

"Of course she does! She picks flowers and gathers weeds and weird pods and makes tea out of them. It's just like canning. She has all these little bottles of herbal potions. Mars used to be afraid to eat anything when she was visiting, because she'll pour some of that vile stuff right on your food and you won't even know it!"

"She wouldn't do that," I said.

"Wouldn't she? She thinks she's doing good. But, Sophie, what if her canning method went wrong? What if she gave Robert something to cure whatever ailed him and it was loaded with powerful botulism?"

I desperately wanted to assure her that couldn't be the case. What had Wolf said? *A twelve to seventy-two hour incubation period.* If Robert had felt queasy for some other reason and Wanda had given him one of her potions at dinner, twelve hours could have easily passed by the time I found him. Maybe Natasha was right to worry.

Horrified and now fully awake, I set aside the wine. What would happen to Wanda if she had poisoned him? It wouldn't have been intentional, of course. I would have to ask Alex what happened under that kind of circumstance.

"I don't know what to do," Natasha said. "I can't turn in my own mother. She may drive me nuts. She may be a little different from most people—"

"A free spirit."

"—but I'm scared to death that she murdered him. What do I do?"

"I don't know," I said. "But let's not be hasty. After all, we don't know for sure that she gave him anything. He could have already been sick from the botulism when she met him at The Parlour."

Natasha gazed at the floor.

"Natasha! You can't just go jumping to conclusions. Besides, wouldn't it have looked and smelled icky?"

"Not according to the Internet. It's odorless and tasteless. You can tell because a can is bent out of shape or the top on a jar has bulged."

"Surely Wanda knows that and wouldn't have given him anything that was tainted."

"Sophie," Natasha said gently. "What if Mom wanted to get rid of him? What if she thought he was scum for dating me?"

My breath caught in my throat. "Seems awfully drastic. She could have alienated him in some other way. Right?" Of course, if Wanda had used one of her magical potions, that would explain why no one else had gotten sick. But it didn't explain Rosie or the notes.

I told Natasha about them, concluding with, "So you see, most likely Robert's death was an accident. And even if it wasn't, it was probably connected to this Rosie person."

Natasha burst into tears.

I reached over and patted her shoulder. "There, there." It was stupid to say. Who said that? Yet somehow, it seemed appropriate under the circumstances. "Let the tears flow. You don't have anything to worry about."

She bawled even harder.

"Natasha! You should be happy. You should be relieved." I handed her a box of tissues.

With a totally congested nose, she blurted, "Wanda Rose Beasley Smith. Her middle name is Rose!"

CHAPTER SIXTEEN

Dear Natasha,

My foodie girlfriend turned her snooty little nose up at the lemon curd I made with lemon juice from a bottle. I think there's no difference in flavor. I can't imagine you wasting your time squeezing lemons! Back me up on this!

—Sour in Lemon Grove, California

Dear Sour,

I can't believe you used bottled lemon juice. Your girlfriend is right. Squeeze the lemons yourself for a pure lemon experience.

—Natasha

I felt like crying, too. Surely Wanda couldn't be the Rosie of the notes?

I stepped away on the pretense of washing my wineglass. It wasn't out of the question that something else had made Robert ill, and Wanda had fed him a potion that contained botulism to cure what ailed him.

"Okay, here's what we'll do. Where does she keep those vials of medicinals?" I asked.

"In an old-fashioned doctor's bag."

"It's in the room where she's sleeping?"

Natasha nodded.

I thought fast. What could I do to get Wanda out of the house for a little while? "Tomorrow morning, tell her to meet me at the grocery store on King Street at ten o'clock."

"Why would she do that?"

"Because you have no food in your house?"

"That might work," Natasha said.

"I'll buy her a latte and while we shop around, you grab the medicinals and take them to be analyzed. Okay?"

"What if they contain botulism?"

The answer seemed clear to me. Wanda would have to turn herself in. Clearly, it would have been an accident. I wasn't sure Natasha could take that news, though. "Let's wait until we have the results. Okay?"

Daisy and I walked Natasha home. "Any news on your attacker?" I asked.

"Wong says there weren't any fingerprints. Unless something is missing and it turns up somewhere, it's a dead file."

"I'm sorry. Are you scared?"

"Not as scared as I am for my mother. I forgot all about the man who attacked me when I ran over to your house."

I wished her a good night and watched to be sure she made it in the door safely before Daisy and I turned back. Daisy stopped dead on the sidewalk.

"What is it, Daisy?" I murmured. I peered into the night. Just past Nina's house, I thought I saw movement. Just a shadow, really. Why hadn't I brought my phone? I squinted and stared, alert for any sound or movement.

I didn't see anything. I coaxed Daisy across the street and ran for my front door. When we were inside, and it was locked, I sagged against the door with relief.

"Was there really someone out there?" I asked Daisy.

She wagged her tail and walked into the kitchen, where I kept the dog cookie jar.

"You're so smart." I fed her a cookie and, with the lights off, I looked out the bay window at the quiet street but saw no one. Still, I double-checked the doors to be sure everything was locked, and it took some time to fall back to sleep.

In the morning, after a strong cup of tea while taking care of Daisy and Mochie, I walked over to the hotel where the lawyers were staying.

The conference liaison was engaged in what appeared to be a heated conversation with the tour guide and bus driver. I couldn't make out what they were saying, but there was no doubt that something had gone awry.

"Good morning. Everything okay?" I asked.

The conference liaison turned weary eyes toward me. Dark blue rings hung under her eyes. "It's that Elise Donovan. The woman is driving us nuts. She thinks everyone is supposed to be her personal assistant."

Were they talking about Alex's new flame?

"Sophie," said the tour guide, "I hope you don't mind that I made a decision without consulting you. She asked us to take her little boy with us today, unaccompanied by an adult. Honey, it's hard enough keeping up with the adults. I am *not* a babysitter! How could I guide everyone if I was chasing after a little boy the whole time?"

"No problem. I understand completely." What kind of person would hand over a child to a bunch of strangers? "Aside from the fact that you have a job to do, everyone would have required a special liability waiver. I can't imagine what she was thinking. She should know better than that."

The hotel liaison groaned. "She's thinking she doesn't want to be saddled with that little boy."

The shock I felt must have shown on my face.

"The night before last I was up with him half the night." The liaison looked around and lowered her voice. "Her sweet boy woke up and realized his mommy wasn't in the room. He was scared out of his poor little mind and wandered downstairs to the lobby all by himself. They woke me because she was registered for the conference. I called and called her cell phone number but she never once picked up. A few hours later Elise waltzed back in and acted surprised that he was afraid because his mommy was gone."

The bus driver shook his head. "That mama is asking for trouble. Imagine all the things that could have happened. Some people don't have the sense God gave a donkey."

The liaison whispered, "She's paid more attention to that good-looking Alex German than she has to her little boy. If she wanted to cat around, why didn't she leave that child at home?"

I was of the same opinion. Somehow, it didn't seem right to divulge her intention to leave her son with Alex for the school year. I was sad for her child. He must be a real problem to make her want to pawn him off on other people.

Forcing a smile, I said, "I hope everything else is on track here?"

At that moment, a large crowd emerged from the hotel to board the bus. The liaison took off, but I stayed until the bus was in gear and I could hear the tour guide welcoming her passengers.

I strolled to meet Wanda, enjoying the glorious fall morning. The dreadful summer humidity had disappeared, leaving a fresh briskness in the air. Bernie stepped out of a drugstore only feet away from me. I called his name.

Clutching a white bag, he kissed my cheek. "How's my favorite neighbor?"

"I'm fine, thanks." I pointed to the bag. "I hope you're okay?"

"This is for Mars. He's got a queasy tummy this morning."

"No!" *Not Mars!* "Has he seen a doctor?"

"Sophie, it's just an upset stomach. I bought him some over-the-counter meds."

"He has to see a doctor. What if *he* has botulism poisoning, too?"

"Sophie, he'll be fine. It's nothing."

"Bernard Frei, you take Mars to the doctor this minute. Do you understand me? I saw the misery Robert went through. He probably thought it was nothing, as well. You can't take chances with this."

"All right, *Mother*," he said sarcastically. "I'll make sure he sees a doctor. But I'm telling you that it's nothing."

"Fine, let's hear that from the doctor."

Bernie grinned at me and took off in the direction of his house. I watched him go, thinking that I would call in an hour or so to be sure Mars actually went to a doctor.

At ten o'clock, I met Wanda at the grocery store. Dressed in a beige lace skirt, cowboy boots, and a denim shirt, Wanda already had several items in a cart when I spotted her.

I bought two lattes and grabbed my own shopping cart.

"Sophie!" called Wanda. "There you are. Are you familiar with this store? I'm lookin' for white sage. Fresh white sage."

I handed her a latte. "They have a nice selection of herbs—"

"Now, not the kind in jars. It has to be fresh."

"Then I think it might be with the vegetables. What are you cooking? One of Natasha's favorites?"

I selected some cucumbers, a bag of lemons, and my favorite spelt sandwich bread as well.

Wanda plucked a bunch of sage out of the display. "It's not white!" She heaved a great sigh. "I'm not cookin', I'm burnin' it."

I stared at her in confusion.

"To cleanse Natasha's house. I just hope green will work."

"There are a lot of cleaning products—"

"Bless you, darlin'. I'm not *cleaning* the house. Heaven knows Natasha doesn't let a speck of dust settle anywhere. I'm cleansing away any negative energy left by Robert and the person who attacked her."

If anyone had negative energy, it was Natasha. "Why do you think Robert left energy in her house?"

The corners of her mouth turned down. "Do you think he could be the one who whopped her over the head?"

"Robert? Why would he do that?"

"I don't know." She rubbed her hands and folded her fingers as though she was praying. "But there's somethin' not right about the way he died. Who ever heard of a person dyin' of botulism? I mean, it's not like he was cannin' anything. Not a man like Robert. I have a mighty bad feelin' about the whole thing." She paused and sucked in her upper lip. Whispering, she added, "I just have this terrible feeling that my Natasha is involved somehow."

I supposed it was nice that they were worried about each other. I glanced around to make sure no one could overhear. How could I phrase this so she wouldn't feel like I was accusing her of anything? In a low voice, I said, "Wanda, I know you didn't bring all of your elixirs. Did you give Robert any . . . herbs when he wasn't feeling well?"

"I had dandelion with me. I told him it eases the stomach."

Oh no! It was a good thing that Natasha was collecting the bottles. We should know within a few days.

Wanda peered into my cart. "What are you doin' with all those lemons?"

"We're having a little tea for Francie at my house this afternoon. Would you like to join us?"

"Now, that's how you treat somebody from out of town. I always feel like Natasha is hidin' me."

We finished shopping and walked home, stopping once on the way for a vase of pink, lavender, and white flowers that would serve as a centerpiece. Francie could take it home to enjoy after the tea. If I didn't hurry, there would be no tea.

Wanda continued on to Natasha's house, and I rushed into my kitchen to get to work but paused to make one phone call to check on Mars.

Bernie answered his cell phone. "We're at the doctor's office now, Soph. I'll call you when we're done."

I let out a deep breath, glad that Mars was in good hands.

I made the lemon tarts first so they could set. The crust rolled out beautifully and the luscious lemon filling was easy to make. Next I tackled the scones. I was at the point of shaping the dough when the front door knocker sounded, surprising me. I looked out the peephole in the door, but couldn't see anyone. With great caution, I opened the door and found a little boy, about ten years old, standing there.

"Hi. Is Alex here?"

I looked around. Surely he was accompanied by an adult. "No. I'm sorry, but he's not."

"Oh. Okay." Clearly disappointed, he shuffled his feet as though unsure what to do. He lifted his chin and sniffed. "Are you baking? I smell lemons."

"Good guess. Are you Kevin by any chance?"

"Yeah. And you're Sophie."

I stifled a chuckle. "Why don't you come inside?"

He didn't hesitate and immediately fell to his knees so Daisy could waggle and make a fuss over him. "Oh wow. You have a cat, too."

Mochie sniffed him politely while Kevin stroked his back.

All three of them followed me into the kitchen.

"Are you baking scones?" Kevin acted as though he was perfectly comfortable in a stranger's house.

"I am! Do you like scones?"

"Not really. They're always kind of dry. But I like the cream and the jam that comes with them. And I like cutting them. Hey, you have the mixer that my mom won't buy. Can I help?"

I stared at the little guy in amazement. With a very round head and straight hair the color of light brown sugar, he looked nothing like his mother. He must favor his father.

"Sure."

Without being told, he marched to the sink and washed his hands.

I picked up the phone and dialed Alex's number. "Hi. There's a cute fellow here looking for you."

"What are you talking about?" Alex sounded distracted.

"Kevin is here."

"What?"

That got his attention. "He's fine. He's helping me bake."

"I'll be there as soon as I can." He hung up.

"I like your fireplace. When I grow up I want a fireplace in my kitchen."

"Does your mom like to bake?"

"No. All she does is work. Are you a lawyer?"

"No."

"You're lucky. It's very boring. My mom doesn't like me baking. She says boys don't bake."

I was having trouble containing my laughter. Both of his parents were lawyers. "You can tell her that some of the finest chefs in the world are men."

"Is that true?"

"Absolutely."

I showed him the scones in progress. "So now we need to—"

"I know what to do." The island was a little bit tall for him, so he took the scone dough to the kitchen table. "Can I work here?"

"That's fine."

He whipped off the tablecloth, folded it neatly, and stashed it on the seat of the banquette. Why on earth would his mother want him to live with Alex? He was a wonder child! I had stupidly assumed that he was a troubled teen.

"Do you think it's wrong for boys to bake?" he asked.

"Not at all," I said.

"That's what I think. But my mom is very stubborn and says I have to be a lawyer."

"You could do both."

"I guess so."

He set to work without instructions and even checked to make sure the oven had been preheated. "Are you in love with Uncle Alex?"

He took me by surprise. I had to be careful. Anything I said would surely be repeated to his mother. "We're friends."

"That's good. I think my mother is in love with him. I wish she would go back to my dad. Do you know my dad?"

"I've never met him," I said.

"He's great. I like Uncle Alex okay, but I'd rather live with my dad."

Oh? "Maybe you can someday."

"Not if my mom has anything to say about it. She thinks my dad is a bad influence on me because his girlfriend is living with him. I already know that. It's not like I'll be surprised. And my dad says my mom is a bad influence because she's nuts."

"Sounds like quite a problem. How do you know all this?"

"I'm ten—I'm not deaf. They yell a lot." After a moment of silence, he asked, "What's an affair?"

Yikes! Alex was going to have his hands full with this little guy. "Well, one meaning is a party, like an event." Maybe that would satisfy him.

"I don't think so. Does it mean anything else?"

I chose my words carefully. "Sometimes it's used when a married person is in love with someone else."

"That's it!" He didn't even sound upset. "My dad said my mom was having an affair, and I know she didn't have a party. He must have meant she was in love with Uncle Alex."

So I hadn't been wrong about Alex and Elise. If that was the case, I was better off without him.

I watched the little guy with all kinds of thoughts running through my mind. "Kevin? How did you know where I live?"

He turned his face up to me, his eyes big. "I followed my mom."

CHAPTER SEVENTEEN

Dear Sophie,

My sister-in-law insists that you have to take the seeds out of the cucumbers for a cucumber sandwich or they'll get too soggy. I like the part with the seeds. Which is the right way? Tea at a very fancy place in Beckley is riding on this.

—Tea for Two in Cucumber, West Virginia

Dear Tea for Two,

Personally, I like to leave the seeds and the center part intact. Otherwise, the sandwiches can become too dry. The trick to reducing the amount of liquid is to salt them first and let them drain.

—Sophie

Now I was confused. "But your mom isn't here."

"Last night. I pretended to sleep and when she left, I followed her."

"By yourself? Alone? In the dark of night?"

"She was with me, kinda. She just didn't know it," Kevin said.

"And she came here?"

"Uh-huh."

"How did you know *I* lived here and not someone else?"

"Cause I saw you at your front door."

"But we've never met before."

"I knew it was you. Uncle Alex has a picture of you on his desk and my mom turns it facedown every time we go into his office."

I wasn't sure if I was more shocked by the fact that Elise had spied on me during the night or that Kevin had followed her. They must have been the shadowy figures I thought I saw. Did Elise think Alex was staying with me since he wasn't with her last night? "Why did you think Alex would be here today?"

"'Cause she said he spends too much time at your house and it would be good for him if I moved in with him."

My, my. Elise talked quite a bit in front of a certain impressionable young fellow. "Where *is* your mother?"

He shrugged. "Taking law classes, I guess. She got some lady to stay with me but it was boring so I left to find Alex." He wandered over to the counter. "What's that going to be?"

"Petit fours."

"Oh cool! I've never made those. Can I help?"

For the next half hour, Kevin and I iced the little cakes. He flipped out over the sugared violets that we placed on top.

He was licking his fingers when Alex showed up.

Kevin rushed to the kitchen door and opened it. "We're baking!"

"What happened to Mrs. Murphy? She was supposed to be watching you."

Kevin shrugged. "She fell asleep, and I was bored."

While Kevin answered Alex's questions about how he came to be at my house, I wrapped a package of scones and petit fours for Kevin to take with him.

"Kevin, could you do me a big favor and take Daisy out back for a few minutes? She needs a little exercise."

"Sure! Come on, Daisy."

I waited until the door closed.

Alex grinned at me and leaned in for a kiss.

I was blown away. The nerve of him! I placed my palm squarely on his chest and took a step back. "What is going on?"

"Elise is in continuing legal education classes, and I guess his sitter isn't used to taking care of a lively little boy."

"Did you know that Elise tried to pawn him off on the tour guide I hired?"

Alex's head jerked back in surprise. "I'm sure it's not true. Where did you hear that?"

My tone was droll when I said, "From the tour guide."

"There must have been some misunderstanding. You know, Elise is very pretty. She's always complaining that other women don't like her because of that."

I snorted. "Oh, Alex! You've been suckered by Elise."

He laughed. "Sophie Winston, I believe you're jealous."

Maybe a little bit. But I sure wasn't going to admit it!

"Don't you remember how upset you were with me when I complained about Wolf and Mars hanging around here all the time? You said they were friends. This is exactly the same. Elise is an old friend."

It wasn't the same at all. Mars and Wolf weren't trying to lure me into a relationship. "Apparently your old friend was prowling around outside my house last night."

"Sophie! Don't be silly."

"You can ask Kevin. He followed her. How do you think he found his way here? He didn't just knock on any old door."

Alex wasn't laughing any longer. "I don't get it. Why would she do that?"

"She also told him that you're spending too much time with me. Is it getting more clear for you?"

"That doesn't sound like Elise at all. Listen, she's having a really rough time with the divorce. Her husband is already shacking up with someone else, and she's taking it hard. It's always like that in divorces. The person who leaves has usually been thinking about it for two years, so in this case, her husband was ready to move on. But she got blindsided. You must remember how hard it was for you when Mars went right on with Natasha and you were all alone."

"In the first place, Mars and I agreed to an amicable divorce."

"Yeah, right," Alex said.

"Excuse me. You were not here then. And in the second place, this is not about *me*. It's about a crazy woman who wants you!" I pointed at him with my forefinger.

Alex smiled and laughed. "Oh, Sophie. Elise isn't interested in me. She just needs an old friend to listen to her and care a little bit."

"Ohh, men are so dense. Trust me on this."

"That's really not fair. You don't even know her."

"Look, Alex, I don't know why we're arguing about Elise. I know that she was with you her first night in town. If you want to date her, that's okay. I understand. No problem."

Alex appeared puzzled. "Did Kevin tell you that, too?"

"No. It seems he woke up in the hotel and was afraid, so other people had to take care of him." I stopped short of saying she was a lousy mother, but that's what I was thinking.

"No wonder you're so testy about her." Alex studied the floor for a moment. "Something must have been lost in translation. Someone must have relayed the situation incorrectly. Elise hasn't spent any nights with me, and she dotes on Kevin. She would never leave him alone."

Oh no? I could see Kevin on the stoop. No time to ask why she was leaving Kevin in Old Town. "Just be careful."

Alex shot me a look of incredulity as Kevin stepped into the kitchen. "Thanks for taking care of him. We're lucky nothing happened to him on the way here."

"Kevin is welcome anytime," I said. "I think we are in the presence of a future master pastry chef."

Kevin high-fived me. "Yeah!" He glanced at Alex, and

as they walked out the door I heard Kevin say, "But don't tell my mom that, okay?"

I checked the time. With Kevin's help, I was actually ahead of schedule. I was still thinking about Elise as I walked into my dining room and shifted my thoughts to the tea.

It was a rare occasion when I was able to use the fine bone china that I had lucked into at an auction. I threw a white tablecloth over my dining table and set it with the delicate pink-rimmed dishes and matching pink-and-gold teacups.

Mars's Aunt Faye had left us an antique silver server with three tiers and a handle on top. Each tier decreased in size and the edges had been worked with decorative piercings. We had received a similar server as a wedding gift, except it was very modern, with shiny unadorned square tiers. I planned to use them both and set them on the buffet.

Faye had collected Reed and Barton's Tiger Lily silver flatware. Every time I used it I felt like Faye was there with us in spirit. The wind howled outside as I placed forks and spoons at each table setting.

The phone interrupted me. I had rarely been so relieved to hear Mars's voice.

"Just wanted you to know that they're running tests. I'll call you when I have the results. And, Sophie? I'd prefer that you didn't mention this to anyone just yet. It's kind of embarrassing."

"No problem. I hope it's nothing." I hung up, glad that he'd seen a doctor.

I showered and changed into a periwinkle blue sheath and faux pearls. It wasn't a typical tea dress, but it was ladylike. Keeping a careful watch on the time, I peeled a cucumber and began slicing it as thin as I could.

Nina arrived wearing a turquoise dress with large white polka dots. The waist was cinched with a belt and the skirt flared. Very 1950s. When Nina entered my house, I always felt like a rush of energy had blown in the door. "Is that vintage?"

"Can you believe my mother used to dress this way? I thought the white gloves she wore with it were too much." She set a small grocery bag on the counter. "No peeking. This is my contribution. It will put those crummy little cucumber sandwiches to shame."

"But you don't cook." I could not imagine what it might be. I salted the cucumber slices lightly so they could drain.

"Mmm. But I shop."

She pinched a slice of cucumber. "I helped Francie and Velma at Robert's place all morning. Ugh. It's so sad going through a person's things and packing them up. Makes me want to clean out all my drawers and get rid of the junk I don't need."

"Did you find any more notes?"

"Nope. But he had a bad habit of stashing cash in weird places. Francie found two hundred bucks in a book! That slowed us down a lot. We had to look through every single item carefully. We're still working upstairs!"

"Sounds tedious."

"It was. But Francie is very excited about her tea today. Hey, did you know that Velma is going to inherit Robert's antiques business?"

"I hadn't given it any thought, but if she's his only living relative, I guess that's not too surprising," I said.

"Umm." Nina gazed out the window.

"What does that mean?"

"Robert moves to town, gets his business set up, has ladies chasing him every which way, and then boom. He dies."

"So?" I asked.

A tapping at the door made her shriek and jump.

Wolf opened it, his voice reassuring. "Sorry. I didn't mean to scare you."

Nina staggered toward him and collapsed into a comfy chair. She did her best imitation of Scarlett O'Hara. "We Southern damsels are delicate and easily spooked. I was looking out the front window. What are you doin' coming through the backyard?"

"Don't mind her," I said. "Everyone's jumpy because of Robert."

"Actually, that's why I'm here. Do you have a list of the people who were at The Parlour for the auction?"

"He was murdered! I knew it!" Nina exclaimed.

Wolf asked, "Why do you think that?"

"You wouldn't be here otherwise. Unless—" She glanced from Wolf to me and back again. "How's your wife?"

Thoroughly embarrassed, I rushed to say, "It's business, Nina."

"You see? I knew it was murder," Nina said. "How did he really die? Rumor says it was botulism poisoning but that would be an accident."

I started assembling the cucumber sandwiches and arranged them on the tiered stands.

"I hate to disappoint you, but I'm just doing the health department a favor by getting a list of names from Sophie. Were you at the auction, Nina?"

Nina groaned. "It really was botulism? Ick. I was there. I ate like a little piggy, but so far I feel fine."

"Glad to hear that."

"Wolf, I don't have the list of attendees," I said. "It was Natasha's gig. Would you like me to call her?"

"I can go over there."

"I'll call to let her know you're coming. Her mom is here, but she might still be a little skittish after being attacked."

"I heard about that. Can't blame *her* for being nervous." Wolf frowned at Nina.

"Are there any leads on her intruder yet?" asked Nina.

"Not that I know about," Wolf said. "Unless someone saw the perpetrator, that kind of crime is tough to solve."

I phoned Natasha, who said she would bring the list over.

Nina perked up. "First Natasha had an intruder who bashed her over the head, then Natasha hosted the auction at The Parlour. Robert was part of the auction, providing the pre-auction viewing, and now he's dead!"

"Come on, Nina. There's no connection. Right, Wolf?" I asked.

He didn't respond.

"I see Velma and Callie," Nina said. She rose and went to the front door.

I rushed to put the kettle on and spooned loose Lady Grey tea into a strainer.

"Uh-oh. Am I interrupting some kind of ladies' party?" asked Wolf.

"We're throwing a little tea for Francie's birthday."

"That's nice of you. If you don't mind, I believe I'll sneak out the kitchen door and intercept Natasha on her way over here."

"Chicken," I laughed.

In minutes, my dining room filled with a gaggle of ladies. I lit the fire in the fireplace, and they all took seats while Natasha explained in great detail that a proper hostess would have made place cards for a tea, but that I was to be excused as I obviously did not know any better.

I was tempted to spill tea on her dress. Gray at the top, it faded into cream on the bottom. Cream must be the in color this year. I was very ashamed when the thought that cream would stain well crossed my mind.

Nina excused herself for a moment and returned with a plate and a bowl. "Ladies, for your enjoyment, I offer you the ultimate Southern snack, warm pimento cheese dip with crackers."

"You don't serve pimento cheese at a tea!" Natasha clasped her hand against her chest as though she could barely contain her horror.

"Aw, darlin' git off your high horse. I haven't had delicious pimento cheese in forever. Did you make it yourself, Nina?" asked Wanda.

Nina shot me a sly glance when she said, "You might say I cooked it."

I suspected Nina's "cooking" had been limited to popping it into the microwave, but there was no question that it was a hit. In fact, I feared that our delicate cucumber sandwiches would taste bland after the tangy cheese dip. If the others thought that, they were kind enough to refrain from saying so. I noticed that Natasha refrained from eating the dip altogether.

When Callie expressed her delight over the pimento cheese, Wanda asked, "Where are you from, honey? You sound like people from my neck of the woods."

"Do I? I was just thinkin' the same thing about you," Callie said. "I haven't heard an accent like yours in years. I grew up in a little town in Virginia called Pike Creek. Have you ever heard of it?"

"What a small world," Wanda replied. "That's about an hour from Berryville, where I live. We used to drive past there for Natasha's beauty pageants in Forest Glen. We always stayed in a hotel near the college. And there was the best bakery."

"I remember that place," Natasha said. "Wyatt's? You always treated me to a doughnut after a pageant."

"I've been there! My uncle knew the owner." Callie beamed with excitement.

"Isn't that odd? I thought you were from Florida," Francie said.

"I'm from there, too," Callie said. "I fled to the sunshine to escape my first husband. We were so young. Of course, that's no excuse for beating on your wife. So one night when he was sprawled on the sofa, dead drunk, I packed my bags, took the only car we owned, which he woulda killed me for if he'd found me, and drove to Florida. Didn't know a soul down there."

"You're here today, so I guess he didn't find you?" asked Nina.

"I'm no dummy. I traded that car for another one at a scuzzy used-car dealership in Georgia so he couldn't trace it to me. He never did come lookin' for me. Last I heard, he got rough with the wrong woman. She shot him in the knee with his own gun." Callie dabbed her lips and chuckled "'Scuse me for laughin' but he sure deserved it. I hear he walks with a cane now and is real polite to the ladies."

No one looked appalled. In fact, every single one of them smiled, and Wanda guffawed like it was the best story she'd heard. No wonder Francie and Velma found Callie so interesting.

"Did you remarry?" asked Wanda.

"I did. I just have the worst luck with men. Seems like I've spent my life running from lousy husbands. After Florida, I ran to Charlotte in North Carolina, then I ran here. I thought about New York City but I figured I'd blend in better in these parts."

"And now you have a lovely man interested in you!" Velma cooed.

"You mean Hunter Landon? Aww, he's just a customer."

"Callie, you know as well as I do that most men don't hang out in tea parlors every day." Francie grinned at her.

"He comes in because he's particular fond of the bacon-cheddar scones. He's awful cute, but I don't need man trouble again."

"You don't have to tell *me* about lousy husbands," Wanda said.

"Mom." Natasha's voice was stern.

"You've got nothin' to be ashamed of, baby. It was your daddy who left us, not the other way around."

Even Natasha's heavy makeup couldn't hide the flush of red that flooded her face.

I was thinking I had better change the subject when Wanda said, "These lemon tarts are wonderful! You know what I think of every time I hear about Forest Glen? That girl, Rosie, who went missing."

CHAPTER EIGHTEEN

Dear Natasha,

My know-it-all sister insists that it's not a proper tea if cucumber sandwiches aren't served. Is that true?

—Hostess with the Mostess in Sandwich, Illinois

Dear Hostess with the Mostess,

Personally, I loathe the little tasteless things. It may be a British tradition but we Americans need not adhere to it. I was appalled to learn that American scientists dubbed the homely cucumber sandwich the best food to eat during a heat wave.

—Natasha

Velma choked on her tea. Francie gasped. Nina's eyes met mine.

"Rosie?" I asked.

"It was years ago," Wanda said. "She disappeared. I remember seeing her picture in the paper day after day. Such a pretty young woman. They searched for her everywhere. I heard they found some bones partly buried in the riverbank a while back and confirmed they were hers. Did you know her, Callie?"

Callie chose a macaron from the server. "Never met her. I heard what happened, though. They said she fell in the river."

Velma heaved a sigh of relief. "It's not our Rosie, then."

While I enjoyed the sour sweetness of a lemon tart, Velma and Francie told the story of Robert and the curious notes about Rosie.

Natasha stiffened. She'd been pushing the same macaron around her plate since we sat down. She sipped her tea, holding the cup oh-so-properly with her pinkie in the air. But she took it plain. No sugar, no cream, no lemon.

Wanda shook her head. "Not a one of us knows when the grim reaper will come callin'. Some things are best not kept for our loved ones to find. Back in Berryville, Elmira Grimley surprised everyone when she passed. She kept to herself, had a vegetable garden that was the envy of the town, never missed church on Sundays, and doncha just know when she died in a car accident and the church ladies cleaned out her house, it turned out she'd been entertaining men on the computer for money. She wore naughty black leather and snapped a whip at 'em!"

"Mom!"

"Well, it's true, honey. We're among friends anyway."

Velma set down her fork. "Goodness gracious! There's no telling what people are up to. But don't you think those notes are odd? Sounds like someone was after poor Robert."

"Now that he's dead I guess it doesn't matter anymore." Callie helped herself to jam and cream. "I wish I had a backyard to plant a few things. I miss that about country life."

"We have a lovely farmer's market," Francie pointed out.

"I know!" Callie said. "I worked there this past summer

in exchange for some vegetables and fruit that I canned for winter. But it's not the same as digging in the dirt and growing it yourself."

Wanda's cup clattered to the saucer. "Natasha! I just had the most brilliant idea. Darlin', I know it has been your goal to be the Martha of the South, but I believe you have been goin' about this all wrong." Wanda snapped her fingers. "Instead of Martha, you should be like that Pioneer Woman, Ree. But she's out west. You could set yourself up as a country girl of the South. I can even help you. I've been cookin' gravy and grits for years. And you know how good my apple fritters are."

"Mom, do I look like a country girl?"

I hoped no one would laugh.

"Don't worry about that. I can fix you up. You just need to wear some jeans and boots. We'll get you some pretty clothes instead of those things you wear that look like they were made out of bargain-bin upholstery material."

"I pay a lot of money for my clothes."

"Well then I have no idea why you look so plain all the time," Wanda said.

Natasha's eyes narrowed and she studied me. "Hmm. Maybe you're onto something. Even Martha likes to wear big shirts. Maybe I do look too perfect."

Francie coughed so hard that I patted her on the back.

Between Wanda and Callie and their colorful stories, the afternoon passed too quickly. Before I knew it, I was handing everyone little packets of leftover goodies to take home with them. And I still had a packed fridge.

Before leaving, Nina pulled me aside. "I'm rushing home to change, then I'm picking up a foster puppy. Would you have time to meet me in an hour or so? It would be helpful if Daisy walked to my house with the puppy."

I agreed, suggesting we meet at the hotel because the bus would be back soon. As I closed the door, the phone rang. I picked it up.

"I hate it when you're right," said Mars.

"What? You must not be feeling too bad if you're up to teasing me."

I could hear Bernie shouting in the background, "You saved his life!"

"It's botulism poisoning."

"No!" I said.

"You bet it is. Looks like it's pretty mild. They don't think I need the antitoxin. So I will probably live to tease you in the future."

"What about your travel schedule?" I asked.

"I'll be hanging around here for a bit, doing what I can from Bernie's house. I don't relish the notion of flying and being in crowded places with a gastrointestinal upset."

I would feel the same way. "Let me know if you need anything, okay? Hey, Mars? Where do you think you got it?"

Mars lowered his tone. So Bernie wouldn't hear? "Probably at The Laughing Hound. That's the only place I've eaten since I had breakfast at your house. Bernie brings home leftovers, and I went over there for dinner a couple of nights."

Oh no. I hung up the phone. Poor Bernie. The Laughing Hound was his baby, his life!

I dashed upstairs, and changed into comfy elastic-waist trousers. A dark green, they suited the season better than my dress had. I slid a rosy-pumpkin-colored long-sleeved T-shirt over my head. It covered the forgiving waistband of the trousers. Boots would have given the outfit a touch of style, but if I was going to walk, Keds were my preference.

I washed the delicate cups and dishes by hand, noting through the window over the sink that the darkness of fall was descending upon us earlier each day. With the cups, saucers, and dishes neatly stacked away in the breakfront, I donned a warm forest-green vest and headed toward the hotel with Daisy.

The passengers wearily dismounted from the bus. They clutched souvenirs, and bags with Smithsonian museum

logos on them. They passed me quickly, undoubtedly eager
to get to their rooms and rest.

The tour guide stepped out for a quick chat. "What a day!
I think everyone had a great time, though. A few congress-
men and congresswomen stopped by to chat with them when
we toured the Capitol, which excited them no end."

I thanked her and the bus driver for their help, tipped
them both generously, and they departed.

Lights glowed inside the hotel, casting a warm welcome. Daisy and I watched the evening bustle of Old Town
from the sidewalk. We didn't have to wait long for Nina.
A beagle puppy trotted along beside her, taking in everything. That puppy could warm the coldest heart. With typical floppy brown ears and a white muzzle, he also had a
white blaze that ran up between his eyes to his forehead.

"Who is this?" I asked. I kneeled to pet him and was
immediately rewarded with a puppy kiss on my nose.

"We're calling him Peanut. His mom was a stray who
was brought into the shelter pregnant. This is his first night
away from her."

"You won't be getting much sleep tonight!"

"He's such a cutie that I couldn't resist. Besides, my
husband is away on business *again*, so I have lots of time
to teach this little guy how to behave. Thanks for helping
me show him what to do, Daisy."

Peanut and Daisy made friends right away. The four of
us walked along the brick sidewalk, the dogs sniffing gates
and bushes with enthusiasm. Lights turned on in houses as
people arrived home from work. In spite of the attacks on
Natasha and Callie, I didn't feel threatened or afraid. I stayed
on the alert, though.

Nina chattered about Callie and Wanda. "I'm scared to
death to see what Natasha might do next. She has always
taken such pride in being a city slicker. Think she'll do the
country gal thing like Wanda suggested?"

"I have a little trouble imagining that myself—" I stopped
and listened. "Did you hear something?" I whispered.

"The dogs did."

Both of them raised their noses.

Nina grabbed my arm when a low-pitched moan came from our right somewhere. "Good heavens. It's not Halloween yet. What do you think that is?"

"I have no idea." But the dogs appeared to know where it originated. They tugged on their leashes, and we followed to the entrance of an alley.

It was darker than pitch, and I wasn't sure we should go in.

Nina pulled out her cell phone and flicked on a beam of light. "Flashlight app. Drains the batteries but it's mighty handy."

She shone the beam into the alley, and we heard another terrible moan.

And then the light landed on a person who was sprawled on the ground.

I grabbed my cell and dialed 911 as fast as my shaking fingers could move. Nina ventured into the alley a few steps. She raised the light, probably to see if anyone else lurked there. I didn't see anyone.

The dispatcher answered. I told her where we were and that someone appeared to be ill or injured. I hung up and followed behind Nina.

"Hello?" I called. "Do you need help?"

Nina appeared to have reached the person. "Sophie!"

I hurried to her and looked down into the contorted face of Elise Donovan. Dropping to my knees, I leaned over her. "Are you okay? Can you sit up?"

Nina nudged me with her foot and moved the light. There was no mistaking the pool of blood in which Elise lay. Her suit jacket had fallen open and the stain on her blouse frightened me. She had lost a lot of blood.

"We've called for help. The ambulance will be here any second." I picked up her hand. "Hang on. For Kevin's sake, hang in there. You have to be strong for him."

She gazed up at me and moved her lips.

"Conserve your strength. They'll be here any moment."

Almost like magic, I heard the first bleat of a siren.

"Not much longer. Did you hear that?"

Nina kept the light steady, and I could see Elise waning. "Hold on, Elise!" I shouted. "Stay with me!"

Elise's eyes met mine. With a huge effort, she spoke. "Rosie."

CHAPTER NINETEEN

Dear Sophie,

The wife of my husband's boss called the china I inherited from my grandmother "transferware"! It's extraordinarily beautiful but the way she said it sounded like she was putting it down. What is transferware?

—Not Sure If I'm Offended in Transfer, Pennsylvania

Dear Not Sure If I'm Offended,

Transferware arose to fill the demand for lower-priced tableware for the middle classes. The pattern was transferred from a metallic plate to pottery. It is highly collectable and some patterns are so popular that they are still produced today.

—Sophie

Suddenly, there was no life in her eyes anymore. They stared blindly upward.

"No!" I grabbed her shoulders and shook her gently. "No, Elise! Stay here. For Kevin. Elise!"

"They're here, Sophie," Nina said.

I moved out of the way, yelling, "She was just with us. Bring her back. CPR! Do something!"

I heard one of the EMTs say to Nina, "Can you get her out of here, please?"

I stepped aside but remained in the alley watching. "She has the sweetest little boy. She can't do this to him."

They started CPR, and I realized that I was holding my breath. She had to come back. She just had to!

But I had been around enough deaths to know how it worked. They would keep trying until a local medical examiner came and declared her dead. I looked up at the sky, wishing a bolt of lightning would zap life back into her.

"I think she's gone, Sophie," whispered Nina. She squeezed my hand tightly.

We stood there for what seemed a hopeless eternity, waiting and praying that Elise would return to the living, knowing with each passing moment that it was less and less likely.

Wolf arrived before the medical examiner. He assessed the situation quickly. In minutes, Wong was there with him, stringing up crime scene tape and shooing us out of the alley to the sidewalk. I hadn't even realized that crowds of neighbors had gathered on both ends of the alley.

"Do you think she was shot?" asked Nina.

"I don't know. There was so much blood. Alex! I have to call Alex."

I punched his number on my cell phone. "Alex? Something happened to Elise." I told him the location but didn't feel I should go into details. "And, Alex, do *not* bring Kevin. No matter what you do, *do not* bring Kevin with you."

I hung up, covered my face with my hands, and took some deep breaths.

"Soph? You okay?" asked Nina.

I moved my hands and nodded. "I just can't get that darling little boy out of my head. She was a terrible mother.

Absolutely awful! But losing her will leave scars on that sweet boy that will never heal."

Wong was still working at pushing back the onlookers. We moved under a streetlamp. The woman next to me screamed and stepped back, pointing at me.

"No. No. You don't understand. She was helping the—" Nina looked at me, clearly at a loss for words, which never happened to her.

"The victim," I said. Because that's what she was. Some terrible person had taken a mother from her little boy. Someone who probably didn't even know about Kevin's existence. Not that such knowledge would have necessarily stopped him.

Wong rushed over. "Sophie!" She shook her head. "Honey, you have blood on your face."

"It's okay, Wong. I called it in and tried to comfort"— my voice broke—"Elise."

"Stay here, okay?"

I watched as Wong fetched Wolf. He glanced in our direction and strode over to us. One look at me, and he crooked his finger.

We ducked under the tape and followed him to a quiet spot in the alley.

"So what happened?" he asked.

We told him about hearing her moans.

"How did Elise die? Was she shot?" I asked.

Wolf's eyebrows rose. "You know her?"

"Not well. She's Elise Donovan, a lawyer from Charlotte who's here for the family law convention."

Nina whispered, "She has a thing for Alex."

I stared daggers at her. What kind of friend says something like that? Didn't she realize that she was incriminating me?

"What? I was with you. You have an alibi!" Nina tilted her head at me like a confused puppy.

Wolf pulled out a flashlight and trained it on me. "You've been together for the last couple of hours?"

I had to tell him the truth. "Nina was picking up this puppy, and I had to meet a tour bus at the conference hotel.

I tipped the driver and the tour guide. They probably remember that."

"And before that?"

My heart sank. "Wolf, you *know* me. I did *not* shoot that woman. I don't even own a gun. Don't put me through this."

He didn't speak and appeared to be waiting for an answer.

"I washed the dishes from Francie's tea party and then walked over to the hotel," I said.

At that moment, Alex broke through the crowd. He stopped at the crime scene tape until he saw me. Ducking under it, he ran toward me.

"Where's Elise?"

"I'm so sorry, Alex." There wasn't anything else I could say.

"What?" He glanced at the body on the ground. "What happened?"

Wolf grabbed Alex's arm before he could dash over to Elise's body. "Go home and clean up, Sophie. Alex, I'd like a word with you."

Nina and I slipped away quietly.

When we were on the street, Nina said, "We're lucky Wolf responded to the call."

"Thanks for telling him Elise was chasing Alex. Didn't you think that might implicate me?"

"Sorry. I was trying to be helpful!"

"To whom?"

I was shivering as I unlocked the door to my house, though I wasn't sure if it was from shock or from the chill in the air.

"I'll make us hot drinks while you change," Nina said.

I took her up on the offer, grateful to hop into a hot shower. I dressed in warm, sloppy pants with a drawstring waist and a comfortable, oversized shirt. I really wanted to wrap up in a big fluffy bathrobe, but this was the next best thing for feeling comforted. The clothing equivalent of mac and cheese.

I padded down the stairs barefooted, surprised to hear voices. A fire blazed in my kitchen fireplace, and Mars and

Bernie had made themselves comfortable at my kitchen table.

"Mars! You look pretty good. How do you feel?"

"Better than Bernie."

Bernie scowled. "What a bloody nightmare. The health department shut us down in an instant. It was utterly humiliating. I can't believe my place is the source. Expect to hear about some of our friends getting ill."

The Laughing Hound was so popular. Half the town could be affected. "Like who?"

"Alex, for starters," said Bernie. "He was there with"—he coughed intentionally—"the other woman. Martha Carter and her husband had dinner a couple of times this week. The list goes on and on."

"Elise." And then a horrible thought sprang to mind. "Did Alex and Elise have a little boy with them?"

Bernie looked at Mars. "Cute little fellow. He asked for a tour of the kitchen!"

"So a family dinner, huh?" I said.

"Sorry, Sophie." Mars bit into a cracker.

Nina handed me a mug of hot cider. "Is it okay if we eat some of the party leftovers? I already reheated the pimento cheese dip."

"I might start serving this as an appetizer at the restaurant. It could be very popular in the winter months and none of the other restaurants in town are offering it." Bernie popped a cheese-coated cracker into his mouth.

Nina grinned at me. "And to think that my mother-in-law once called me the anti-diva."

"Did she tell you?" I asked, taking leftover cucumber sandwiches, lemon tarts, scones, and petit fours out of the fridge.

"I didn't tell them the important part." Nina pulled red-and-white transferware dishes with ornate flowers and birds from the cabinet and stopped midstep with a gasp. "I forgot to tell Wolf!"

Mars and Bernie stopped eating.

"So did I. He has to know!" I said.

While I phoned Wolf, Nina brought Mars and Bernie up to speed about the strange notes found at Robert's home.

Naturally, Wolf didn't answer. He was in the middle of a murder scene, what had I expected? No wonder he wasn't taking calls. I left a message telling him I had important information about Elise.

When I hung up, Bernie was saying, "Hold it. Are you telling me that someone *murdered* Robert and my restaurant is closed for no good reason?"

Nina scowled at him. "Hey! Don't blame the messenger. Besides, Mars got sick, too."

"Do you know how much perfectly good food is going to waste?"

"We're talking about murder, and you're worried about losing money?"

Bernie ran his hand over his scruffy hair. "Yeah, sorry. You're right. Lost my head there for a minute, but it's still a big inconvenience."

I sat down at the table. "Here's the thing. The last word Robert said was *Rosie*. And the last word Elise said was *Rosie*."

Mars put his fork down. "Soph, are you sure you didn't imagine that? Seems like an awfully big coincidence. Maybe you had it on the brain and just thought that was what she said."

"Only one problem with that, Mars," said Nina. "I was there, too, when Elise spoke. I heard it just like Sophie did. No question about it." She crossed her arms over her chest and leaned back in her chair.

"This is a little bit creepy." Mars glanced out the bay window at the dark night. "If Rosie is supposed to be dead, how could she be running around killing people?"

Bernie shook his head. "Unless the authorities are lying to us, and I seriously doubt that the authorities would want to start a health panic unnecessarily, Robert died from botulism. You can't murder someone with botulism. It's not as though someone named Rosie walked up to Robert with something disgusting and forced him to eat it. I'll grant you that it's odd they both said something that sounded like *Rosie*, but there cannot be a connection. That wouldn't make any sense."

"Maybe Robert didn't know how he got sick, but he was afraid of this Rosie, because of the notes," I suggested.

"But the note said Rosie was dead. Right?" asked Mars.

I retrieved my copies from my office and handed them to Mars and Bernie.

"Assuming these notes are accurate, we know that Robert sinned and that Rosie is dead," mused Mars.

"Revenge. If Rosie is dead, maybe someone wanted him to pay for his sin?" I asked.

"Then why would Elise say Rosie's name?" Nina grabbed a petit four and ate it in two bites.

"Ahh." Bernie slathered a scone with cream. "Perhaps it was this Elise who killed Robert to avenge his sin."

"Then who killed Elise?"

That brought our speculation to an abrupt halt. Only the sound of the crackling fire broke the silence. The flames threw shadows against the walls. Daisy and Peanut snoozed near the fire. But as I watched them, Peanut raised his head and howled mournfully.

Someone banged on the door and Nina shrieked again.

CHAPTER TWENTY

Dear Sophie,

I hope you can help me. My husband hates green tea but I heard it helps people lose weight. He likes regular tea okay. What is the difference between green tea and black tea?

—Mrs. Tubby in Green Acres Valley, New York

Dear Mrs. Tubby,

Green tea is fresh tea while black tea has been fermented. Because it has not been processed much, green tea is loaded with antioxidants. Some people feel it may stave off food cravings, thus helping them lose weight.

—Sophie

I flicked on the outdoor lights. "You're awfully jumpy, Nina. It's only Alex."

I opened the door, and he stumbled inside. He fell into a

chair and slouched as though he couldn't hold himself erect any longer.

The man who had such perfect military posture, the one who was rarely flustered and never wore wrinkled clothes or had a five o'clock shadow, the seemingly imperturbable, unflappable Alex that I knew, had descended into a quivering mess.

"Alex, are you okay, man?" Mars observed him, clearly shocked by his appearance.

I rushed to the pot of hot cider that sat on the stove, poured him a mug, and didn't object when Nina added a hefty dose of rum.

Alex held the top of his head with both hands and muttered, "What have I done?"

I handed him the cider, fearful for him.

All eyes were on Alex. He drained half the mug before saying, "This is all my fault."

I tensed, slightly confused because I was certain Alex was far too sensible and kind to have murdered Elise.

He set the mug on the table and sank back in the chair as though he had used his last ounce of energy. "I called Elise's husband, Rosey." Alex snorted. "Turns out she abducted Kevin—"

"Rosey?" All four of us said it at the same time.

"Yeah, like Rosey Grier, the football star. I know, it's an unusual name for a guy, but he's used to it."

I tried to sound casual. "He lives in Charlotte?"

Alex nodded. "Apparently he was supposed to get Kevin for visitation, but Elise never showed. Rosey has been looking for her all weekend. He had no idea she brought Kevin up here or that she intended to leave him with me." Alex reached for my hand. "You tried to warn me. I bought into everything she said. That they wanted to get Kevin away from the ugly divorce and the squabbling for a while. That they didn't want him to be scarred by all the hostility. I've known them for so long that I never questioned what she was telling me."

"Alex, are you sure this Rosey isn't in the area?" asked Mars.

"Did you phone his landline or his cell?" asked Bernie.

Alex appeared to come out of his stupor a bit. He sat up and studied our faces. "No, no, no. You think Rosey could have murdered Elise?" He shook his head. "Not a chance. In the first place, that would be totally out of character for him. In the second place, no matter how awful Elise might have acted, Rosey would never have killed her. He loves Kevin too much to do that to him. Rosey is on his way here right now to pick up Kevin."

Nina's mouth twitched as though she was trying not to blurt what she thought. "And yet divorcing spouses do often kill with disregard for their children. Sometimes the kids even find the corpse of the murdered parent. Do you know how many times my husband has been called to testify about cases like that?"

Alex gazed at her and muttered, "I always forget that your husband is a forensic pathologist." He waved his hand through the air like he was erasing invisible words. "No. There's no way Rosey would do anything like that."

"Chances are pretty good that Rosey didn't know Robert," Bernie observed.

"Robert Johnson? What's he got to do with this?"

Nina explained Robert's connection to Rosie.

I waited patiently while Alex read my copy of the bizarre notes Francie and Velma had found. "Why didn't you tell me about this?" he asked. "Clearly it's not the same Rosie. It's spelled differently, and I just talked to my Rosey, so he's definitely alive."

"There is one tiny connection, though." They all looked at me. "Elise lived in Charlotte, and that's where Robert resided before he moved here."

Alex seemed to be recuperating. "I'm not sure that's relevant, unless you're implying that they both knew someone named Rosie who died. What are the odds that they would both know the same person named Rosie and someone who would want to kill both of them because of her?"

"Alex, I hope you won't be upset with me for asking you this." Nina smiled at him.

I cringed, imagining the worst.

"It was quite apparent that Elise was chasing you—"

"That's just not true," he protested. "Did Sophie tell you that?"

"Really?" Nina said. "She conned you into thinking that it was okay with her almost-ex-husband for Kevin to live with you. And you don't think she could have been conniving enough to ask that because she wanted *you*?"

Alex's expression was so funny that Nina and I giggled at him.

Alex held up his palms to Mars and Bernie, as though he hoped they would back him up.

"Women!" Mars said, shrugging.

"And Sophie didn't have to tell me, by the way," Nina continued. "I saw Elise with my own eyes at the charity tea. You bought right into her game. You even purchased that sapphire necklace for her. So back to my question—is it possible that Elise might have been chasing someone else as well?"

"I wouldn't know," Alex's tone conveyed his dismissive opinion. "I can't imagine that was the case."

"Not so fast!" I pondered how to put it, but went for the simple truth. "The night she arrived in town, Elise left Kevin alone in the hotel room while she went out."

"That's nonsense!" Alex shook his head. "I already told you that she wasn't with me that night."

"I have it on very good authority that she went out. I hardly think Kevin would have been wandering in the lobby if Elise had been with him."

Nina's eyes sparkled with excitement. "That's it! If she wasn't with you, Alex, then where did she go?"

CHAPTER TWENTY-ONE

Dear Sophie,

My doctor has taken me off coffee because of the caffeine. I really miss my morning fix. Does tea contain caffeine?

—Coffee Addict in Coffeeville, Alabama

Dear Coffee Addict,

Tea does contain caffeine. The amount varies with each type of tea, but generally, it contains about one-third of the caffeine in a similar amount of coffee. For a caffeine-free diet, drink herbal tea or a coffee substitute.

—Sophie

After a sleepless night, I gave up and stumbled down the stairs for coffee. It was still dark outside when I opened the door for Daisy. She sniffed the air before going out, as if she couldn't believe we had risen so early, and she wasn't sure she wanted to start the day.

I was running water into the kettle when Wolf tapped on my kitchen door. He opened it a crack. "I saw your light on. Is this a bad time?"

I tightened the belt on my bathrobe. Naturally, I was wearing the fuzzy lavender one that made me look like a chubby purple bear. "Not at all. Come on in. Coffee?"

"That would be great. I got two hours' sleep last night. I'll be running on caffeine all day."

He probably hadn't had a decent meal, either. "How about crispy hash browns, eggs sunny-side up, and bacon?"

"Oh, Soph. I don't want to put you to any trouble."

"Not to worry. I'm making them all the easy way."

I ground coffee beans, pulled out the French press, and spooned them into it.

"Can I help?"

"Sure. Why don't you get down some mugs and set the table?" I preheated the oven, draped bacon over a rack in a pan, and slid it inside.

"So what was this pressing information about Elise?"

I switched on the panini press to heat it up and set a pan over medium-low heat on the stove.

Wolf stood across the island from me. I looked him in the eyes. "The last thing Elise said before she died was *Rosie*."

He simply nodded. "Figures. Thanks, Sophie. You may be called to testify."

"Nina heard her, too."

"Good to know."

I paused for a minute and studied him. He'd taken the news about Rosie as though he'd expected it. "Does that mean you have a suspect?"

"Let's just say we have someone of interest."

I laughed at him, cracked eggs into the pan, and covered them with a tight lid. "That's the new cop lingo for 'we're not ready to arrest him yet,' right?"

Wolf poured the coffee, adding sugar and cream to mine, just the way I liked it. He hadn't forgotten.

"More or less," he said.

"Can you tell me who it is?"

Wolf looked at me as though I had asked a stupid question.

"Oh! Testify—someone named Rosie. Her husband! It was her husband, Rosey!"

Wolf only raised an eyebrow.

"But . . . why would he murder Robert?" I asked.

Wolf set the table and brought two plates to the island to be filled with food.

Hmm. He hadn't responded. I tried my question a different way. "Surely you don't think there's a connection between Robert's death and Elise's?"

Using my cookie spatula, I slid the eggs onto the plates, added hash browns, nicely crisp from the panini press, and slices of bacon that smelled so heavenly I wanted to eat them all.

I delivered the plates to the table. "You didn't answer me," I said.

"You know I can't talk about cases."

"Neither can Alex. It's infuriating that you guys know information that you can't share."

"Soph, you don't really need to know. This is one time you won't feel obligated to go prowling around."

I bit into a slice of salty bacon. "I have a natural curiosity. And I come by it legitimately. I think there's a snooper gene in my family." My big fuzzy robe had become too hot, but I couldn't just shed it with Wolf there.

"Then Nina must be related to you, too." Wolf grinned before gulping coffee. I rose to make more.

We heard a little commotion at the door before Francie and Velma burst into the kitchen.

Francie could scarcely contain herself. "There's been another murder—a woman from out of town! We think the killer mistook her for Natasha."

Velma unfolded a local newspaper. "Look at her picture. Tall, thin, dark-haired. Isn't this the woman your boyfriend is dating?"

"If you're talking about Elise Donovan, we already have a person of interest and it has nothing to do with Natasha," said Wolf.

Francie gasped, evidently not having noticed Wolf in the banquette behind her. She looked from him to me and frowned as she took in my fluffy bathrobe. "I hope we're not . . . intruding . . ."

"Of course not. Could I make you some eggs?" I said.

"Yes, please," said Velma. "I'm ravenous. When Francie heard about the second murder, I came straight here. I haven't even had my morning coffee!"

I felt shabby in my bathrobe. I hadn't even brushed my hair yet! Meanwhile, Velma's coif was hairdresser perfect, and she even wore makeup.

Francie gazed at Wolf again. "You know, I'm modern enough not to hold anything against you two. I suppose we should keep this quiet?"

"Oh, please!" I cracked more eggs and revved up the panini press again. "If it were romantic, don't you think I'd be wearing a more becoming bathrobe?"

Francie appeared skeptical, but in a very loud voice, Velma said, "Honey, I sure hope so. That is *not* a man-catching outfit. Though I must say that I admire you young women for bravely wearing what's comfortable instead of squeezing yourselves into girdles like our generation did. There wasn't a day in the first twenty years of my married life that I didn't have that awful girdle on, even to serve breakfast."

"Isn't that the truth?" said Francie. "I love the new freedom to wear whatever dreadful thing one likes."

I brought their plates and coffee to the table. "Do I dare leave the two of you alone with poor Wolf?"

Velma salted her eggs. "Please do, sweetheart, we have to pry some information out of him."

"Yeah, good luck with that." I walked toward the stairs but heard Velma ask, "Was that sarcasm?"

Upstairs, I quickly pulled on jeans that stretched every which way thanks to a touch of spandex, and a scoop-neck purple top with three-quarter length sleeves. Pearl earrings that dangled made me look just a tad more put together. I swept my hair up into a loose twist and fastened it with a big clip.

When I reappeared in the kitchen, Francie and Velma had the nerve to applaud.

"I had no idea Wolf was married or that you two used to be an item," Velma said, waggling her forefinger at me.

"He just caught me by surprise, all right, ladies? There's nothing inappropriate going on."

"In fact, I have some news that might make you feel better since you were at The Parlour for the auction," Wolf said. "Martha's getting the all clear to reopen this morning. They didn't find any problems at her place."

Francie dabbed her mouth with a napkin. "Wonderful! Sophie, can you come to The Parlour this afternoon? We need to fill it with people so it will look full. Martha's afraid people won't patronize it anymore because of what happened to Robert. She gives etiquette classes to children and their parents have been canceling by the dozen!"

"Sure. My family lawyer group has a free day today. I'd be happy to help."

"How about you, Wolf?" asked Francie.

Very politely, he said, "Sorry. I'm afraid I'm busy."

"Francie! You know he has to make an arrest," Velma sounded eager. "I'd like to be a ladybug on his shoulder, hearing all the details. Are you going to grill your suspect behind two-way glass like they do on TV?"

"I would guess that it won't be nearly as exciting as anything on TV. Soph, I hate to eat and run—"

"You go right ahead, Wolf. You *get* that awful criminal!" Francie smiled sweetly.

"Thanks for breakfast." Wolf let himself out.

I refilled everyone's coffee and settled into my banquette, holding my warm mug in both hands.

"Is he gone?" asked Velma.

Francie rose to peer out the bay window, where Old Town was coming to life. "Yep. I see him out on the walk. Looks like it's going to be a beautiful fall day."

"Yeah, yeah, yeah. Forget about the weather." Velma turned toward me. "Wolf is wrong."

CHAPTER TWENTY-TWO

Dear Sophie,

Our school is hosting a tea party fund-raiser. Some of the parents think the cucumber sandwiches should contain eggs or mint. Not everyone is in agreement on this issue. We're letting you decide.

—Lizzie's Mom in Mint Hill, North Carolina

Dear Lizzie's Mom,

Eggs in sandwiches are egg salad sandwiches. And mint would only overpower the delicate cucumber flavor. I prefer to stick with the traditional recipe.

—Sophie

I almost spilled my coffee. Had they found something else? "How so?"

"For starters, he's ignoring Robert! I don't want to besmirch Robert's reputation." Velma wriggled with discomfort. "I had the highest regard for him. My whole family did! Well, almost. My parents thought he was wonderful. But my husband never cozied up to Robert. What I saw as genteel and refined, my husband, rest his sweet soul, interpreted as a façade. He thought Robert had carefully crafted an image as a distinguished gentleman but he felt something else simmering underneath."

"That's no reason—"

Velma held up her hand. "As you know, Francie and I had been keeping an eye on Robert. Honey, a stream of widows and divorcées visited him."

"We tried to tell Wolf," Francie said, "but he wasn't a bit interested in our logic. Here's how we see this. The incubation period for botulism is twelve to thirty-six or seventy-two hours, depending on your source."

I nodded. That was consistent with what Wolf had said.

"And now we know they're opening The Parlour again, so he clearly didn't get it there."

Velma picked up the thread. "Consequently, he must have eaten something that was home canned, which we have suspected all along. We know for a fact that Robert wasn't into canning. He wasn't much of a cook at all. That means one of the ladies who visited him was probably the murderer."

I tried to interrupt them but they chattered at me and didn't give me a chance to say a thing.

"I don't mean to be trite," said Velma, "but there's a lot of truth in that saying about a woman scorned."

"But—"

"Ahh, my little chickadee"—Francie winked at me—"you overlook the obvious. If he had eaten something in a restaurant, then more people would surely be ill by now."

"And we have a source with intimate knowledge," said Velma, "who confirms that no such unlucky person has turned up. Thus, we return to our original theory that one of Robert's many admirers slipped him the poison."

"Ladies!" I raised my voice just enough to get their attention. "I hate to disappoint you, but they shut down The Laughing Hound yesterday. Mars has botulism, too. Looks like The Laughing Hound is the culprit."

"But we made a list—" said Francie.

"And checked it twice," said Velma, who withdrew a folded sheet of paper from her pocket. "These are all the women we saw coming—"

Francie interrupted her, "—or going—"

"—from Robert's house."

I set my coffee on the table and examined the list to humor them. "Ladies, you have married women on here."

"We are fully aware of that. We're simply reporting that they were seen." Velma sat back, satisfied.

"We can't account for what might have gone on *inside* the house." Francie smiled at me sweetly.

"What do the stars mean?" I asked.

"Those are people who cook. The others are less likely to have canned food themselves." Velma gazed at the list. "Seriously, I don't think Angie Lowenstein has ever stepped foot in a kitchen, much less tried canning. There are some others like that. We visited each of them and peeked in their kitchens for any evidence of home canning."

"You did what?"

"Don't worry, they didn't know what we were doing," Velma said.

I looked from one to the other in astonishment. They went to people's homes and snooped? "I don't believe you two."

"I know! Who'd have thought we would make such great sleuths?" Velma flexed her fingers in delight. "We've narrowed down the list considerably."

"Natasha and her mother are on here!"

"Naturally. We didn't play favorites." Velma was so earnest that she was beginning to scare me.

Francie pointed at the list. "Beverly Hazelwonder and Patty Conklin are on there, too. Velma plays bridge with Beverly, and Patty is in my garden club. You see? We're covering all our bases and being very thorough."

"I'm not on the list."

"Well, of course not! We never saw you stopping by Robert's place." Velma's eyes narrowed, and she pulled a pen out of her purse. "Did you?"

"I did *not*. I didn't even know where he lived until I saw you two spying on his front door. But that raises some questions. What if someone went in through his back door? And for that matter, what about women who visited him in his store? Someone could have brought him a tasty treat that he ate on the spot."

The startled looks on their faces almost made me feel guilty for ruining their fun. *Almost*. "Look, I got into a lot of trouble a few months ago when I unknowingly interfered with an investigation. Wolf just assured me that he has a suspect in Elise's murder. I hope they'll have enough evidence to make an arrest today or tomorrow, so I really don't think you need to go to all this trouble."

"But don't you see? He'll arrest the person who killed that woman." Velma clutched a hand to her chest. "Robert's murderer will get away with it."

What did it take to convince them? "Now that Mars—poor guy—is sick, too, Robert's death was obviously accidental."

"I told you botulism poisoning was a brilliant way to dispatch someone." Francie folded her arms over her chest, signaling her determination.

"Do you think the person who poisoned Robert intended to murder Mars as well?" I asked.

Velma leaned toward Francie. "I thought you said Sophie would understand. She doesn't appear to get what we're saying."

"She's just being stubborn," Francie responded.

They were impossible! "I'm still here, you know."

They avoided making eye contact with me.

Hah! I knew how to dissuade them. "Okay. Suppose you're correct."

They perked up immediately.

"Which of the people on this list had a motive to murder Robert?"

"Any of them who were jealous of the attention he lavished on other women." Velma shot Francie a quizzical look.

"Fine. Which ones?" I pressed them a little, hoping they

would realize that they didn't really have a reason to pursue anyone.

I hated to admit it, but I was happy when they looked at me, dumbfounded. "I'll make a deal with you. We'll let Wolf handle this. After all, it's his job, and he's the expert."

"But he's wrong!" Francie protested. "Robert's death was intentional. You saw those notes."

"How do you know that? And how do you explain that Mars also ate whatever had gone bad? Give Wolf a chance to interrogate and arrest his suspect. If you're not convinced after he makes an arrest, then I'll reconsider. Okay?"

They looked a little glum when they left but I heard Velma say, "Good thing we have to hang out at The Parlour this afternoon to assist Martha. It will help kill time while the Mountie gets the wrong man."

My morning passed rather quietly. I wrote some advice columns and around noon, I took Daisy for a long walk. Our path took us by The Parlour, which was open but didn't seem to be doing much business. We wound around toward Robert's house, where the front door stood open.

Either Velma was airing out the house or planned to carry something in or out.

I walked inside, remembering the morning I had found Robert near death. The main floor appeared much the same. None of the lavish paintings had been removed yet and the furniture was still in place.

"Francie? Velma?" I called.

I stopped dead at the dining room, surprised to see Hunter Landon, who allegedly had a thing for Callie. He appeared to be equally surprised. He had the decency to flush and seem slightly embarrassed at being caught. Of course, I had no more right to be there than he did.

I could see what Francie and Velma liked about him. Neither slim nor chubby, he had a friendly oval face with a very slightly receding hairline. His eyebrows appeared to be stuck in perpetual worry. And there were tiny dents at the tops of his cheeks. I wondered if he really was a worrying type. In any event, it gave him an air of approachability, like a nice guy who tried to do his best. He wore jeans with a sport coat—informal, yet sufficiently put together.

"Are you looking for Callie?" I asked.

His thin lips spread into an embarrassed grin. "Actually, you caught me having a sneak peek. The door was open, so I hope no one minds. This is an amazing house. I knew Robert was an antiques dealer, but he obviously had an eye for the better things in life."

"I would have to agree. He had excellent taste."

Hunter gestured toward large paintings of men and women from another era. "Think these are family portraits?"

I walked closer to study them. "I really couldn't say. I don't know anything about Robert's background. They look like they belong in a castle, don't they?"

Hunter pointed at a particularly stern woman in a brown gown adorned with lace. "I think her eyes are following me around the room."

"She *is* a little scary."

"Probably the wicked governess who married the widowed father."

I couldn't help laughing. He had nailed her! "I guess we can both be glad we're not related to *her*."

"So what are they going to do with all this stuff?" Hunter asked.

"I suppose Velma will sell the house, but I understand she intends to keep the store."

"I'll be interested in seeing who buys the dreaded governess."

"Do you live in Old Town?" I asked.

"I'm renting at the moment. I didn't think I would want to stay here because the houses are packed in pretty tight for a country boy. Turns out that's not a big deal for me after all. But sometimes I do think I'd like to sit out on the front porch on a summer night, watching the fireflies and looking out over the fields. Not a sound except for a distant owl. Who knows? Maybe I'll get a little mountain cabin somewhere for weekends."

"Do you work for the government?"

"Not directly," he said. "I'm self-employed. I do search and rescue training, so governmental agencies often contract me."

That explained how he had time to hang out at The Parlour on occasion. "You mean with dogs?"

"No, I train people. They have to be certified, and municipal governments have to come up with plans for managing big emergencies, so I help them do that."

"Are you interested in buying this house?"

Hunter gazed around. "I think it's probably way out of my league. I'm fairly handy, so I had a fixer-upper in mind. Robert's place sure is impressive, though. He obviously lived the good life."

"I saw The Parlour opened back up," I commented.

"Yeah. I'm sure Martha is happy about that."

I felt a little bit awkward—the two of us having no real business in the house. He didn't appear eager to leave, though. "Is Velma around?"

"Did I hear my name?" She came barreling along the hallway from the kitchen. "Was taking out trash. Good heavens, I never imagined there would be so much to throw out." She looked from Hunter to me. "Did y'all come to help?"

Hunter set his briefcase on a chair and removed his jacket. "Sure. Why don't I give you a hand with the heavy stuff? You tell me what needs to be done."

"You're like an angel from heaven. I thought I'd have to hire a handyman."

"I could pitch in for an hour or so," I said. "If you don't mind Daisy helping."

She set us to work right away. "Hunter, how about you bring boxes downstairs, and, Sophie, maybe you can empty the linen closet?"

We worked steadily for an hour. Hunter didn't complain once about lugging all the boxes downstairs. He whispered to me, "Velma reminds me of my mother. She thinks these boxes are heavy but they don't weigh a thing."

I slid a stack of pillowcases into a box. "Does your mom live around here?"

"No. She still lives in the little house I grew up in. Never budged from it."

"Where's that?"

He hoisted a box and paused, almost as if he was wondering if it was safe to tell me. "A little college town called Forest Glen."

CHAPTER TWENTY-THREE

Dear Sophie,

I inherited china stamped Rose China on the back with a picture of a rose. People tell me it's Noritake. If that's so, then why does it say Rose China?

—Confused Collector in Rose Hill, Kansas

Dear Confused Collector,

Rose China was made by Noritake immediately after World War II. Some speculate that post-war production was difficult and not up to Noritake standards, so they used the Rose China name instead. Others believe it was a method of circumventing limitations on Japanese imports or that the company did not use its famous name because Japanese products were not in favor with Americans after the war. Rose China also often carries the words Made in Occupied Japan.

—Sophie

"I've heard of that!" All too recently, I thought.

"You have?"

I covered quickly. "I grew up in Berrysville."

"No kidding! Small world, huh?"

Indeed it was. I presumed he knew that Callie had come from a town near Forest Glen. It didn't mean anything. Clearly I was on edge for no good reason. In fact, maybe that was the reason they were attracted to each other.

Velma bustled toward me. "Look what I found!"

She held out a newspaper clipping with the title "Tea Parlor Coming to Town." Martha smiled in a photograph.

"She's quite photogenic, isn't she?" Velma said.

I had to agree. Her trademark upswept hair imparted a distinctive elegance. "She's very attractive. Where did you get this?"

"It was in Robert's things. He has piles of papers. I do the same thing. I think I'll need a letter or a note or a clipping. Of course, when I want it, I never can find it. I'm terrible about filing. And where do you file something like this anyway? It's not like a bill or a contract or something important. I guess he was like me in that respect. He has stacks of papers but I'm afraid to throw them out without going through every one of them. There could be something important!"

I felt a little bit guilty about a few piles of papers in my own office and resolved to keep less. Maybe I would buy one of those things that scanned them into the computer.

"Say, Velma," Hunter said, "Robert told me about an old necklace he used to wear in the sixties. A carving of an old ship. Have you found it? It sounded kind of cool."

"I've been through his valet but there was nothing like a ship. I can't imagine him wearing something like that. Oh my! The sixties were grand, weren't they? I wore my skirts so short I got sent home from school once!"

Before long, the linen closet was empty. It hadn't produced anything of interest. Comforters, towels, the regular items except for some lace tablecloths that were probably antique. I had packed them in another box that would likely go to the antique store.

Then Velma locked up and sent Hunter, Daisy, and me home to clean up so we could meet her at The Parlour to make it look busy. Velma peeled off to her house, but Hunter walked another block with Daisy and me.

Hunter asked me about Daisy, who got along very well with him. He'd even played some doggy games with her at Robert's house. "As soon as I buy a place, I'm heading to the shelter. I've missed having dogs and cats."

"Nina works at the shelter. In fact she has an adorable foster puppy right now. A beagle named Peanut."

"Wonder how fast I can find a place?" He grinned and said, "See you at The Parlour," before turning right. I kept walking toward home.

I had walked only a few steps before I heard someone call, "Ed! Eddie!"

I turned my head, and saw a blond man. It appeared that he had meant Hunter, since he jogged over to Hunter, who greeted him as though they were acquaintances. How odd. Had I misunderstood? Maybe it was a nickname or a middle name. Maybe I would Google Hunter when I got home.

On the way, I passed The Laughing Hound and spotted Bernie sitting outside on the patio all by himself with a beer and a stack of papers.

"Sophie!" He opened the gate for Daisy and me.

"Looks kind of lonely around here."

"It's pathetic. Would you care for a drink?"

"No, thanks. Taking care of paperwork?"

We sat down at the table. "Soph, Mars is like a brother to me. Next to my mum, you and Mars are my closest friends. I'm *crushed* that he got sick from my food." Bernie placed his elbows on the table and leaned toward me. "Here's the curious thing. You know how many people have been sickened by this?" He held up two fingers. "When the health department came to collect samples, they told me that Mars was only the second known case."

I thought I could see where he was going, and I certainly

didn't want to burst his balloon, but I had to say it. "Mars's symptoms were so mild that you didn't think he needed a doctor. There could be others in the same situation."

Bernie slapped his iPhone on the table. "I know a few of the regulars well enough to call them and see how they're doing. No one is sick."

"Do you think Robert ate here?"

"We do a pretty good business, so I don't see every single person who dines here. But none of the employees recalls seeing Robert during the last few days."

"Velma said he didn't feel well the day of the auction," I said. "I guess there's no way of knowing if that was already the botulism at work, or something else. Maybe someone brought him takeout?"

"I doubt it. Here's why. From my research on botulism, it doesn't often occur in acidic foods or fresh foods. That's why it doesn't happen much with things like pickles. We cook everything fresh. We use very few items that come in jars or cans. So there's almost no chance for botulism to be in the food we serve. Mars got botulism poisoning, but I'm convinced that it wasn't from my food."

"Where else did he eat?" I asked.

Bernie shook his head. "According to Mars, only at your house."

"My house!" Oh no! I would be the next one raided by the health department!

"Don't look so worried. Your food was fresh, wasn't it?"

I relaxed a little. "The pumpkin you used in the pancakes was from a can. But I feel fine and so do you. Mars must be mistaken. Maybe someone offered him a little treat, but he doesn't remember."

"According to Mars, he didn't even stop to grab a drink somewhere or nosh on a candy bar."

"That makes no sense."

Bernie sat back in his chair and crossed his ankle over his knee. "Precisely. We serve two to three hundred people a day, but only one is sick?"

"What are you going to do?"

"I'm planning to talk with the health department. I doubt that they'll listen to my reasoning but they are going to come up empty-handed in my kitchen. The Laughing Hound is not the source of the problem."

I walked home wondering if Francie and Velma could be right. Maybe one of the ladies chasing Robert had been the source of the tainted food after all. That didn't explain how Mars would have been exposed to it, but it would be more logical since there didn't appear to be a big outbreak of botulism poisoning.

I swung open the gate to my property and discovered a sad little figure sitting on the stoop of my kitchen door.

Kevin's eyes were red from crying. Tears stained the apples of his cheeks. When he saw me, he ran toward me and flung himself at me, clutching me and burying his head in my abdomen.

Daisy nuzzled his face, trying to lick him. There was nothing I could do but hug him and stroke his hair. We stood that way a long time. Nothing would bring his mom back. The least I could do was hold him tight as long as he needed.

When he let me go, he asked, "Did you hear about my mom?"

I nodded. "I'm really sorry, Kevin." I didn't know what else to say to him. "Why don't we go in the house? Would you like a glass of milk?"

We walked toward the door.

"Have you got anything stronger? I got troubles."

I tried to hide my smile. Where had he picked that up?

"How about hot chocolate? With whipped cream *and* marshmallows?"

For one split second, I saw a gleam in his eyes and knew for that instant, he'd thought about food instead of his mom. Whipped cream and marshmallows was an overload, but if ever a child deserved a whopper of a treat and a sugar over-load, it was this little boy right now.

I unlocked the door. He played on the floor with Daisy and I excused myself for a moment. I hurried to my office and called Alex. "Your little buddy is here again."

I heard him shout, "Found him!" Into the phone he said, "Is he okay?"

"Seems to be. But he's one sad kid."

"Poor guy. I'll be there ASAP."

I returned to the kitchen and whisked powdered chocolate into a little water, which I added to the milk and heated. I poured it into two mugs, added marshmallows and the promised dollop of whipped cream. I brought them to the table along with a few leftover macarons and petit fours.

Once again, without being asked, he washed his hands and dried them before crawling into the banquette on his hands and knees. He settled in and licked the cream on his drink. "They're going to send me to reform school."

I bit my upper lip to keep from grinning. "I'm sure that's not the case. That's where they send bad kids."

He smacked his palm against his forehead. "Oh great. That's all I need, being locked up with all the bullies."

"Honey, no one will send you to reform school or lock you up. Believe me."

"You don't understand. It's all my fault," Kevin said.

"What is?"

"My dad killed my mom because of *me*. He wanted me back."

"Where did you hear that?"

"My grandparents. And they're afraid the court won't let them keep me because they raised a killer and they're incontinent."

That gave me pause. I hoped he meant incompetent. "I'm sure they're very nice people."

"Um-hmm." He nodded his head. "I'd rather be with my dad but they're going to lock him in jail and throw away the key!" His voice rose with hysteria.

People really ought to be more careful what they said around this child. "That's just an expression. No one will throw away the key. And Alex is going to do his very best to make sure your dad doesn't go to jail. You trust Alex, don't you?"

He thought about it. "Will you help him?"

"I'm not a lawyer. Remember?"

"Can't you find the real killer? Alex told Mom you solve murders."

"Not professionally. I just got lucky a few times."

"Do you cost a lot of money?" He pulled a few wrinkled dollar bills from his pocket.

"Kevin, I don't charge anything—"

He interrupted. "I can afford that. Then you'll do it? You'll help me?"

I couldn't help him, of course. And he would think I was a traitor when he found out that his mother said his father's name to me when she was dying. Why hadn't she said Kevin? Then I could tell him how much she loved him. I could do that anyway, I supposed.

He focused on his drink, trying to catch melting marsh-mallows with his tongue.

I desperately wanted to help Kevin. He clearly loved his father and being raised by his dad was probably his best shot at normalcy. On the other hand, if his dad really killed Elise, he was a dangerous man.

But something else was bothering me. I'd been okay with Wolf's take on Elise's murder. Certainly Rosey was up to his ears in trouble. But it *was* peculiar that both Elise and Robert had said the same thing to me. The odds of anyone saying *Rosey* as a final word were pretty slim.

And then it hit me. Two people had trusted me with their last breath. They were on the verge of death but they had rallied enough strength to say one word before they left this world. And they had said it to me. Didn't that create some obligation on my part to be sure we knew what they were trying to say? Especially Robert. Between Wolf and Alex, the mystery of Elise's murder would surely be solved. I glanced at Kevin. Unless, of course, it wasn't Rosey who killed her. For Kevin's sake, I really hoped that was the case. Why had they said Rosey, or Rosie, or Rosy?

"So? Will you help my dad?" Kevin wore a whipped cream mustache and licked his fingers.

Once again, I didn't know what to say to him. I didn't

want to create false hope. I couldn't make promises. "I'll make a deal with you. If you stop running off, I'll see what I can find out."

"Really? Yippee!"

"Don't get too excited. Kevin, sometimes these things don't turn out the way we wish they would."

"What do you mean?"

Well now I'd done it! I couldn't exactly say *maybe your dad really did kill your mom.*

CHAPTER TWENTY-FOUR

Dear Sophie,

The last time my mother-in-law came to visit from China, she said I wasn't making her Pu-erh tea correctly. It's obnoxious to have to pry the old compacted leaves loose in the first place, but I did it. Then I put them in a tea ball and steeped them. Do you have any idea where I went wrong? I'd like to get it right this time.

—Inept Daughter-in-Law in Chinatown,
Washington, DC

Dear Inept Daughter-in-Law,

Pu-erh ferments in a tightly compressed cake or brick. You use a Pu-erh knife or a tea pick to make three holes in the cake or brick to break off a piece. Instead of using loose leaves, you steep a still-compacted chunk of the tea. Each layer is thought to infuse the tea with its own flavors. Leaves that fall off are discarded. You were making the tea with the parts normally discarded.

—Sophie

"Honey, I mean that sometimes we wish we didn't know the truth because it's not what we hoped for."

He was mulling that over when Alex appeared at the kitchen door. He opened it and gave Kevin a stern look. "I have a bone to pick with you, young man. Why do you keep running away?"

Kevin didn't appear to be the least bit distressed. In a most logical tone, he said, "I had to talk to Sophie, and I didn't have her number."

Alex blinked hard and looked at me. I did my level best not to smile or laugh. "Maybe I should give you my number."

I fetched a pad of paper and wrote it down for him.

Kevin emptied the last of his cocoa. He folded the paper neatly and tucked it into his pocket. "Thanks for the stiff drink, Sophie."

Alex's eyes opened wide. He looked at me, his expression incredulous.

Kevin walked by him, looked up and said, "I needed that."

Alex followed him out the door. I closed it behind them, imagining the interesting conversation they would be having on the way back to the hotel.

I changed into a skirt, nothing terribly fancy, just an A-line in a camel color. It seemed more appropriate for The Parlour. I topped it with a sleeveless dark red mock turtleneck that matched a cardigan in all the glorious colors of fall leaves.

Once again I walked along the brick sidewalk, glad I'd worn a sweater. The days were definitely getting cooler. At The Parlour, Velma greeted me at the door and quickly ushered me to a love seat grouping at a window. Nina and Francie were already seated.

I greeted them and as I sat down in a comfortable French-style armchair, Francie said, "We're trying to seat everyone near the windows so passersby will think it's busy in here."

I gazed around the room. It was mostly empty. I had a great view of the ugly face on the sideboard that no one had wanted. Martha had done her best with it by placing identical thin candlestick-type lamps on each end. A stunning elaborate silver tea and coffee set took center stage, drawing the eye away from the evil face. If it hadn't been for the horrible carving in the middle, it would have been a lovely piece of furniture.

Hunter enjoyed a window seat all to himself. He was the picture of modern contentment with his laptop open and a Spode Woodland teacup. Nicely masculine, it bore brown sketchings of flowers around the top and featured what I thought was probably a quail.

He worried me a little, though. I considered calling him Ed or Eddie to see how he would react.

I recognized two of Velma and Francie's friends at the next window. They had called in everyone they could.

Our table had been set with blue-and-white china. Morning glories were painted on the interiors of the cups. Blue arcs adorned with gold circled the dishes with more morning glories toward the middle.

"They're from Germany," said Francie. "Vintage Bavaria. Aren't they stunning?"

"I'm surprised you don't collect teacups, Francie. You certainly know a lot about them."

Martha delivered a platter of little cakes as Francie said, "They're just so beautiful. You know how I love flowers and gardens, which seem to be a main theme of teacups. But heaven knows I don't need anything more to dust. I'm much happier admiring them here." She squeezed one eye partially closed and tilted her head. "Don't you girls go buying me any as presents. I'm not kidding about that!"

"Such willpower!" exclaimed Martha. "I'm afraid china is my weakness."

Callie brought more goodies to our table. "Martha's husband and I think she should write a guide to china patterns."

"I might do it, too," said Martha. "Not a guide so much, but something of a history. There are such fascinating stories about china that tie to politics and history. For my personal use, I collect Schumann china from Germany. You've probably seen Schumann. It's very elaborate with flowers and gold. But after World War II, it was marked on the back with *US Zone* when Bavaria was occupied by the United States. It was a short period of time, but that's the china I collect. I find it fascinating."

Callie waited politely for Martha to walk away before saying, "The open-faced sandwiches are smoked salmon with just a hint of a dill cream. The heart-shaped ones are watercress. Because of the season, we're trying out pumpkin scones, and those slices are apple bread. Martha would like your opinions on those."

"Callie, can you take a break and have a cuppa with us?" asked Francie.

Callie glanced toward Martha. "Thank you for asking me, sweetie, but I'd better not."

"It's not very busy," Velma protested.

"Velma, don't go getting her into trouble." Francie plucked a salmon sandwich off the tray.

"Make sure everyone has what they need, Callie. I know how to handle this." Velma winked at us and left for a little chat with Martha at the cash register.

Martha returned with her and pulled up two additional chairs. "Callie, have you seen the Pu-erh knife? Beverly Hazelwonder has ordered Pu-erh tea again."

"I wonder where that thing disappeared to. I haven't seen it in days," Callie said.

Martha excused herself and returned after brewing the special tea for Beverly. "Thank you, ladies, for including Callie and me. I hope there won't be many days when we can take a break."

Callie brought another teapot and additional china.

"I'm sure people will start coming back," I said. "We tend to have short memories about little scares like this."

Nina shook her head. "It would help if they could identify the source of the botulism."

"I doubt that would make a difference." Martha grimaced. "A lot of people will only remember that they shut us down and will never hear about the restaurant that really provided the tainted food."

"Martha, Martha," Callie said sympathetically. "You

shouldn't listen to your husband. I know you think the
world of him but he's a bit of a pessimist."

A smile crept to Martha's lips. "He is, isn't he? I love him
to death but that man can see the worst in everything."

"How did you meet him?" asked Velma. "I bet it's a
romantic story."

Martha smiled broadly and for the first time since I'd
met her, all the little worry lines left her face. "It's nothing
that special. My parents cobbled together every cent they
had to send me to Italy, to my great-aunt, Antonella, to learn
to speak Italian. She was a dear. But she was *very* concerned
about a twenty-year-old woman who wasn't married. She
paraded every eligible male in the village by me. From sixteen to sixty, if they weren't married, I was forced to meet
them. Word spread to the surrounding villages and every
old widower who needed a housekeeper or a farmhand came
to check me out. Of course, I wasn't having any of it. Imagine me stuttering through Italian. I could hardly understand
what any of them were saying!"

She had us all in stitches.

"And then one day, Great-Aunt Antonella was at the
butcher shop complaining that I was already a dreaded *zitella*."

"What's that?" Nina bit into a pumpkin scone.

"The most horrible thing imaginable to an elderly Italian
woman—*a spinster*! The butcher's wife gave her the
don't-I-know-it speech because her twenty-two-year-old
grandson wasn't married yet. Great-Aunt Antonella couldn't
believe there was a man within fifty kilometers that she had
overlooked. It was because he was an American in the military. Alas, he was assigned to a post in Frankfurt. But the
two crafty ladies put their heads together, and one day, when
he came for a visit with his grandmother, Great-Aunt
Antonella gave me a package of cannoli to deliver to the
butcher's wife by bicycle. It was a gorgeous day, and I didn't
mind riding out in the beautiful countryside one bit. What
I didn't know was that Great-Aunt Antonella had pricked
the back bicycle tire so that it had a slow leak. About halfway there, it was flat as a pancake. There was nothing to do

but walk. And along came this tall young man with the prettiest gray eyes I had ever seen. It was love at first sight. He happened to be riding a tandem bicycle and offered me a lift. When we realized that my destination was his grand-parents' house, we knew that we had been set up. In spite of that, we married six months later."

"What a great story!" I sipped my apple spice tea. "How did you end up here in Old Town?"

"We lived all over the world with the army. Max's last post was at the Pentagon, and we liked it here. Now he has his own company with military contracts, so this seemed like the perfect place to stay. And I always dreamed of open-ing a tea parlor, so everything came together as though it was meant to be."

"We're certainly glad that you landed here!" Velma dabbed her mouth with a pristine white napkin. "And that you discovered Callie. These pumpkin scones will be a huge hit."

"That was a very lucky break for me. I don't know what I would do without Callie." Martha shot her a fond look.

"It was fate," Callie said. "The restaurant where I wait-ressed for a year and a half went belly-up, and I didn't know what I would do. I was walking by and saw a *Waitress Wanted* sign in the window."

"And when I found out she could bake, well, that sealed the deal!"

Velma cast a glance at Hunter. "Funny how people come together from all over. You never know what life holds in store." She leaned forward and whispered, "How are things going with Hunter?"

"Velma, Francie, don't get any ideas about puncturing bicycle tires!" warned Callie.

"Callie!" whispered Martha. "Customers!"

As they rose, Francie joked, "Approach them slowly. You don't want to frighten them!"

They seemed like tourists to me. But any customers were surely welcome.

Nina looked at the apple bread in her hand. "It would be

nice to know what made Robert so sick. I know the health department was here and all, but there is just a hair of a stigma."

I noticed that didn't stop her from eating the apple bread.

"You have nothing to worry about, Nina," Francie assured her. "No one else except Mars has reported being ill, and Mars never ate here. If The Parlour were the source, Velma and I would be dead right now, too."

She glared at me. "Velma and I have been doing our level best to convince Wolf and a certain other person present at this table, whom we won't name, that someone murdered Robert, but they simply won't listen."

Nina focused on me. "Alex and Wolf questioned me about finding Elise. I don't think Alex was very happy with me. But clearly, we have to tell the truth. She said *Rosey.*"

"Wolf arrested him today. But exactly as we suspected, nothing was filed against him for Robert's death," Velma said.

"Why would there be?" asked Nina.

"Precisely!" declared Francie.

Velma pulled a sheet of paper from her purse. It was their list of women who had visited Robert, presumably whittled down to those with plausible motives. "Well, Sophie?"

I had had the best intentions of staying out of this matter entirely. But Bernie and Kevin needed help. I took the list of names and perused it. Nina leaned over my shoulder to read it.

"Okay," I said. "I'll look into it. But I can't make any promises."

Francie and Velma lifted their teacups to each other in a mock toast.

Leaving the list with Nina, I stopped by the table where Beverly Hazelwonder and Patty Conklin were seated. "Thank you so much for helping us out today. We need to restore confidence in The Parlour again. And Bernie will need the same thing at The Laughing Hound when he reopens."

"I was so shocked to learn that's the source of the poisoning," said Beverly. "My husband and I go there all the time. In fact, that's where we like to take out-of-town guests!"

"Well," I said as if I were confiding a big secret, "I have it on excellent authority that the health department didn't find a thing there!"

Patty gasped. "I have to tell my friends. We had a big club meeting at The Laughing Hound the day before Robert died. We've all been watching and"—she crossed her fingers and held them up—"hoping none of us would get it."

"And?"

"Not a one of us came down with it. The health department told us we would know by now if we had any ill effects."

Continuing to pretend to gossip, I said, "I've heard rumors that Robert was seeing some ladies in Old Town, if you know what I mean."

"That's just not true," declared Patty. "I don't know how he developed that reputation."

Beverly shifted in her seat uncomfortably and peered in her giant purse for something.

I nudged them a little more. "They say his refrigerator was packed with food from his admirers."

"Oh?" Patty frowned. "We were dating, you know."

"I did *not* know that!"

Beverly scowled at her friend. "I don't think hanging out at his favorite bar in the hope you might see him constitutes dating."

"That's how it's done these days, Beverly. You've been married so long that you don't know about the in scene. Things have changed, sweetheart."

"I can tell you where they haven't changed." Beverly looked like she might pounce on Patty.

What had I started? *Yikes!* I floundered for something to distract them. "Did you hear they're arresting someone for the murder of that young woman?"

Beverly clapped a hand against her chest. "Thank goodness for that. It's gotten to the point where I'm on the alert all the time. That could have been any one of us."

"A bar date counts as a date!" Patty wasn't letting go.

I said good-bye and felt like a terrible weasel. Not only had I caused friction between friends, I hadn't learned a single helpful thing.

A larger group entered when Nina and I left. I was hopeful that business might pick up.

Nina and I were almost home when we saw a police car parked on our block. We broke into a jog. As we neared, it became obvious that it was outside of Natasha's house.

CHAPTER TWENTY-FIVE

Dear Natasha,

My best friend forever is getting married. My mom and I are giving her a tea party bridal shower. Much as I love my friend, she has the worst taste in the world. Her color scheme is pinks. It's so pastel that I gag from the sugar rush. Please tell me that I can decorate for the party in grays and blacks.

—The Maid of Honor in Weddington, Arkansas

Dear Maid of Honor,

You owe it to your friend to decorate tastefully in grays and blacks. With any luck, she will learn from you and appreciate your effort to educate her.

—Natasha

Panting, we rushed toward Mars, who spoke with an officer.

"Did someone try to break in again? Is Natasha okay?" I asked.

Mars responded wryly, "Physically or mentally?"

I headed for the stairs.

"Not that way!" called Mars. He pointed to the gate that led to the backyard. "That way."

Nina and I raced along the side of the house. When we reached the backyard, I stopped so abruptly that she bumped into me.

Natasha wore a glittery beaded bronze top under black leather overalls that were skin tight on her long legs. The spiky heels on her shoes made her stagger like a drunk as they pierced the ground and lodged in it. A dozen full-grown chickens pecked at the grass she didn't allow Daisy to step on, and she seemed to be trying to catch one of the birds.

A turquoise-blue chicken condo had appeared in the back corner of her lot.

A police officer appeared to be losing his patience with her. And in the middle of the chaos, Wanda flung handfuls of something at the policeman.

"Ma'am, will you *please* stop doing that?" He uttered it at Wanda tersely.

I scurried over to her. "Wanda, I think you're making him angry."

"Then we're even, 'cause I'm hoppin' mad!" She leaned toward me and whispered, "It's to make him go away."

The officer looked at Nina and me. "Do you live here, too?"

"No. We're just friends. Natasha, what's going on?"

Her thin lips tightened. "Do not steal this from me. You're much more believable as the country diva than I am, but I call dibs on this gig."

"He wants to take away our chickens," said Wanda.

Natasha was busy trying to scrape chicken poo off her shoe. Were those Louboutins?

"I'm pretty sure there must be ordinances about chickens."

"Thank you," shouted the officer, raising his arms in joy. "Two hundred feet. You cannot have chickens within two hundred feet of another dwelling."

I wasn't the best judge of measurements but I had a hunch

Natasha's backyard wasn't even two hundred feet wide. "And where exactly would that line fall from the house on the side?"

"It would be across the street and over on the next lot somewhere. Which would tell most people"—his eyes got very big—"that even if there were two hundred feet from one side, there wouldn't be two hundred feet from the other side."

The lots in Old Town were definitely narrow. Very few homes would meet the two-hundred-feet requirement. Maybe some of the mega-mansions, but those owners probably weren't particularly interested in raising chickens. "Natasha?"

"I told him to call Wolf. He always gets *you* out of trouble."

"Ma'am, I told you before. Wolf is not going to come to the rescue. You have illegal chickens. I'm sorry, but if you don't remove them, I'll be forced to bring animal control out here."

"Who complained?" I asked.

"Six neighbors! Will you stop throwing that stuff at me?"

I grabbed the bag from Wanda. The aroma of the contents wafted to me. I peered at it. "Is this dill?"

"Marjoram and dill." She lowered her voice to a whisper. "To ward off the evil man."

I sealed the bag, noting that Mars looked on with amusement.

I debated who would be more sensible and appealed to Wanda. Grabbing her arm to get her attention, I said, "Wanda, there are laws against raising chickens here. Honey, look around. You know there's not enough room for livestock. If Natasha wants to be the country diva then she should live in the country. Maybe near Berrysville!" That should do it. Wanda would be thrilled if Natasha lived closer to her.

Natasha eyed me. Her chest heaved. "Oh no, you don't. I thought you were my friend, but I see what's going on." Her gaze drifted to Mars.

"Sophie, that's a wonderful idea. I'll call Harvey

Gooch. Nat, I bet he'll keep your chickens while you move down to Berrysville."

"Mom!"

Mars finally stepped in. "Nat, I'm sorry. Sophie is right. You had your photo shoot and now it's time to send the chickens someplace else. You would be the first person to complain if the neighbors kept pigs or cows in their backyards."

"That's not the same at all. Those are big animals."

"Natasha, you had a country house," I said. "Remember? But you sold it to move here. Why did you want to live in Old Town?"

"For the same reason you do. It's so chic and elegant. I love walking the streets of Old Town. What a stupid question." She bent to pick up a chicken that pecked near her shoe, slid, and fell face-first on the lawn. The officer helped her up. She wiped chicken poo off her leather overalls but evidently didn't know it was on her cheek as well. Holding her hands in the air, her fingers stiff with revulsion, she said, "Go ahead and call Harvey, Mom." She shook a finger at the police officer. "But I want to be clear that I'm not doing this because of some stupid regulation. I just don't like a messy yard." She strode toward the house holding her head high.

Wanda hurried after her.

"Is that satisfactory?" I asked the officer.

"Yeah. But I'm coming back in the morning. If the chickens are still here, animal control will remove them."

Dusk was settling on Old Town when I returned home. I'd been in the house for less than one hour when Alex knocked on the kitchen door.

I opened the door, and he held up white bags. "I brought a peace offering."

"Come on in!"

He set the bags on the kitchen counter. "Chinese okay?"

"Sounds great." I fetched square white plates and set the table. "White wine?" I asked.

"Sure. I could use a drink." He chuckled. "I'm starting to sound like Kevin."

"He's such a funny little guy."

"Did I tell you he's my godson? I'm almost sorry he won't be living with me for a while."

"About that . . ." I said.

Alex winced. "Sophie, I wasn't keeping anything from you. I swear! Elise showed up and sprang it on me." He leaned against the island while I poured the wine. "There isn't much I wouldn't do for Kevin, so when she asked if he could stay with me, I was surprised but willing. It never occurred to me that she wouldn't have discussed it with Rosey first. They're old friends. You know what that's like. You're surrounded by friends all the time."

I could understand that. Kevin was a very special little kid. I'd have wanted to help him, too. "But what about the necklace and cozy family dinners?"

"Cozy family dinners?" Alex's brow furrowed. "I'm an idiot. I can see how it might have seemed that way, but it was nothing more than showing an old friend a nice time while she and my godson were in town. You'd have done the same."

Reluctantly, I conceded that he was absolutely right. I would have.

"If the situation had been reversed, I probably would have come to the same conclusions. Although you should know me well enough to realize that I never would have spent the night with her and left Kevin by himself. And if he had been at my place, trust me, there wouldn't have been any hanky-panky."

I couldn't help grinning. It *would* have been out of character for him. "She had us both going. Why were you friends with someone who was so deceptive?"

"I never saw that side of her before. Rosey insists it was there all along. He was married to her but didn't see the crazy, manipulative side for a few years. Apparently, some people warned him, including one of our professors, but he just didn't believe it."

Alex brought containers of food to the table. "Kung-pao chicken, shrimp lo mein, moo-shu pork, garlic beans."

"How many people were you planning to kiss up to?"

"I wasn't sure what you would like. Thought I'd just take

a chance. And Chinese leftovers are always good. Shall I light a fire?"

"That would be great."

Alex lit kindling while I added candles to the table and dimmed the lights.

"Sophie?" Alex rose and faced me. "I didn't know you were at the tea auction. The truth is that I bid on the sapphire necklace as a surprise for you."

"It was a surprise, all right! Kind of funny, though, that you were bidding against me."

Alex wrapped me in his arms and kissed me.

I savored his kiss for a moment then pushed him away. "Hold everything! If you bought the necklace for me, then how did Elise end up with it?"

Alex groaned. "I guess she misunderstood. She was so excited about it and things were going so rotten for her because of the divorce and all that I didn't have the heart to take it away."

"You're a big softie." I didn't mention that I happened to find that a very attractive quality in a man, but he might have guessed by the lingering kiss that followed.

With our issues cleared up, we nestled in the banquette. The fire crackled and the warm glow made our world seem cozy and calm.

We ate with chopsticks, digging into the savory dishes. It was almost hard to remember that Elise had been murdered.

"How are things with Kevin's dad?" I asked eventually.

Alex drew a deep breath and sipped his wine. "It's been a rough day. Rosey was formally arrested for Elise's murder."

"So I heard. Did you bail him out?"

"Working on it. The bail is high because of the grisly nature of the murder and the fact that he's not local. He's a flight risk. And his funds are a little complicated because of the pending divorce."

"Kevin is with Rosey's parents?"

He nodded. "And now Elise's parents have arrived because they want him, too. It's all a big mess."

I picked up lo mein with the chopsticks and took a bite of the warm noodles.

"I never thought I'd end up representing Rosey in a murder case. Funny, people always say to me that so-and-so couldn't have done it. And now I find myself thinking the very same thing. There's no way the Rosey I know would have killed Elise." He studied the container of kung-pao chicken. "You know what a great kid Kevin is? He gets it from his dad. Rosey is a good egg. He *never* could have been violent toward Elise."

Alex placed his chopsticks on his plate and looked at me. "Listen, I think they're going to base their case, at least in part, on what Elise said to you. Are you certain that she said *Rosey*?"

He stared at me with hopeful intensity.

I understood how much was riding on my correct memory of what she'd said. I tried to go back to that moment in my mind. Elise, laying on the ground in the dark, saying *Rosey*. Was there any possibility that Elise had said something else? "I'm sorry, Alex. It sounded like *Rosey* to me. Maybe there are other words that you could argue would make more sense? Mosey? Cozy?" Even as I said them I knew they didn't sound enough like Rosey. "Nina heard her, too."

"I know. I already talked to Nina. She's even more sure than you seem to be."

That sounded like Nina. "What about the police where they live? Didn't Rosey report Kevin missing? Can't they confirm that Rosey wasn't here when she was murdered?"

Alex sucked in a long breath. "He didn't go to the police. Both of them practice law, and Rosey didn't want their marital problems made more public. If they lose their clients, it will only exacerbate the situation."

"Surely *someone* saw Rosey where he lives so you can prove he wasn't here in Old Town. What about his girlfriend?"

"The girlfriend has been in London on a business trip. But it's even worse than that." Alex loosened his tie and slid it off as though it was strangling him. "Rosey was driving all over creation looking for Elise and Kevin. He went to her mom's house, a cabin that a friend owns, her best friend's house. He's been sitting in his car staking out these places, hoping to spot Kevin."

"He probably used his cell phone. Won't that show he wasn't anywhere near here?"

"Maybe. We're getting the records." He didn't seem any happier.

To me, that seemed like it would solve the problem. Unless . . . "Some of those places were close to here, weren't they?"

Alex didn't respond.

"Close enough to drive in and kill Elise?"

He winced like I'd punched him in the stomach, but he nodded.

"But Rosey is a lawyer, right? Wouldn't he have been smart enough to set himself up with an alibi? Wouldn't he have planned it better?"

"You'd think so, wouldn't you? I think that speaks to his innocence. He didn't plan to murder Elise."

Or he was so nuts about Elise stealing Kevin that he wasn't thinking straight. It didn't look good for Kevin's dad. "I know what I heard, Alex. But maybe she was slurring her words or unable to move her tongue or her lips. I thought that could be the case with Robert."

Alex rested against the back cushion of the banquette. "I've been thinking about Robert. It's Rosey's only chance. I have to build a case linking their deaths to this other Rosie. Do you still have your copy of the notes?"

I fetched them and brought them to the table.

Alex pointed at the most dire message and read it aloud.

Roses are blood red
    Now I bid you adieu.
Rosie is dead
    And so are you.

"I think it's significant that this Rosie is spelled differently." He said it almost triumphantly. "And it says that Rosie is dead."

"A dead Rosie, spelled any way you like, could not have stabbed Elise."

"First of all, we don't know that Rosie with an *ie* is really dead. And second, they didn't tell you Rosey with an *ey* killed them. They just said *Rosie*. Right?"

"Right. But I don't know how you're going to connect Robert and Elise."

Alex groaned. "There's something you don't know."

CHAPTER TWENTY-SIX

Dear Natasha,

I have always served jasmine tea with Chinese food. But now someone has suggested to me that jasmine tea isn't real tea at all but an herbal tea. I'm mortified! Which is it?

—Always Proper in Jasmine, Arkansas

Dear Always Proper,

You are a hostess after my own heart. True tea comes from the leaves of the Camellia sinensis tree. Fortunately, you have not committed a gaffe. Jasmine is usually added to real tea, green or black, as a flavoring to create jasmine tea.

—Natasha

"Elise had an affair with Robert."

I nearly choked on a bite of chicken. Alex patted me on the back and held out my wineglass to me.

"I'm having a lot of trouble imagining that. How do you know?"

"Rosey found out. He was suspicious and followed Elise one day."

"Let me guess. That's what broke up their marriage?"

"I gather that started the downward spiral," Alex said.

"So Elise was the one who broke up the marriage? Not the evil girlfriend?" I coughed and drank some wine. "Oh! Maybe that's where she went her first night here. She couldn't exactly take Kevin to see her former lover."

"Possibly. I wish I had a witness. If only someone had seen her there."

"How would that help?" I asked.

"It would confirm the connection between them and that their deaths might have something to do with the other Rosie."

"You don't suppose Elise brought Robert something that was contaminated by botulism?"

"What?" Alex said. "I thought Bernie's place was the source of that."

"Probably not. Elise was acting strange if you ask me. If she wasn't dating you, then she was spouting a lot of lies. I heard her talking about you."

"I've given that some thought. I think she wanted to make Rosey jealous, and I happened to be handy."

"I guess that's not totally implausible," I said. "But Rosey wasn't around to hear her. Why tell other people who didn't know or care?"

"I think that might have been for your benefit."

"Or for Robert's! He was watching her like a hawk."

"Soph, were you serious about helping Kevin?"

Uh-oh. Here came the real reason for his visit. "Yes. It breaks my heart to imagine that he'll lose both his parents. His mother's death is a tragedy but to have his dad in prison, too? That's horrible. No kid should have to go through that."

"You know Velma and some of her crowd. Plus you're kind of nosy."

"Thank you. I'm so flattered," I said drolly.

"Would you snoop around? See if you can dig up anything about this Rosie?" he asked.

"How am I supposed to do that? It's not like I can ask Robert, and Velma says she doesn't know anything about a Rosie. Hey, is Rosey going to be charged with *Robert's* murder, too?"

"I don't know yet. Word is that unless the prosecutor can find some decent evidence, the only thing they have is his last word."

"If Rosey was jealous of Robert, I guess they have a motive," I said.

"You think a jury is going to buy that Rosey brought Robert some tainted soup or something? There's no evidence of that."

I saw his point. Wolf had said all along that botulism was an accident. Even if they knew what he had eaten, convincing a jury that it was intentional might be tough. "All right. I'll be my usual nosy self. If finding out about Rosie is the only way to prove that Kevin's dad is innocent, I'll do my best to help you."

"Thanks, Soph. More lo mein?"

Alex left early. I wasn't surprised. It had been nice of him to stop by with dinner, even if he did have an ulterior motive. I just didn't know quite where to start my search for the elusive Rosie. I checked out Hunter Landon and Edward Landon on the Internet but found nothing of interest.

When I rose the next morning, a clatter outside drew my attention. I threw on warm sweats and stumbled downstairs. Daisy waited at the front door, eager to go out. I snapped on her leash and stepped outside.

A green pickup truck that had seen better days was parked in front of Natasha's house. Daisy tugged me in that direction.

She sniffed her way through Natasha's service passage, where Wanda and an unfamiliar man were trying to catch chickens.

"Good mornin', Sophie! Do you know Harvey Gooch?" asked Wanda.

"I don't believe I do."

"Mornin'!" the man said. "That looks like a mighty fine hunting dog—let her drive these chickens over my way."

Even on the leash, Daisy's curiosity about the chickens was enough to send them toward Harvey. It didn't take long for all the chickens to be in cages.

"Where's Natasha?" I asked.

Wanda stretched. "That girl! I don't know what to do with her. Shush now. Here she comes."

Natasha carried a tray of coffee mugs so hot that they steamed in the chilly fall morning. "Thank you, Daisy. I saw how you helped. You're better at dealing with chickens than I am."

I couldn't help noticing that Natasha had returned to her usual style of dressing. Her sleeveless asymmetrical dress wasn't made for rounding up chickens, or collecting eggs for that matter. Burnt red, it followed her figure nicely without being tight. She was a knockout in it. "That's a great color on you," I said.

"It's new to me. I much prefer blues and browns."

We stood on her patio to drink our coffee. I guessed she didn't want us to bring the chicken mess into her house.

"Harvey, do you remember that girl Rosie?" asked Wanda. "I was telling Natasha and Sophie about her the other day."

"Rosie Barnes! There's a name I haven't heard in a long time. Poor kid. I was young and new on the volunteer fire department when she went missing." He shook his head. "A sad, sad business. That fellow got away with murder. You know a couple of us spotted Rosie's daddy on his way to pay that guy a visit. Had his rifle with him, and it sure wasn't hunting season. It was just a good thing we stopped him when we did or he would have spent his life in the slammer for killing the man who murdered his daughter."

"Murder? I thought she disappeared."

"You got it part right. At the time, everybody thought her boyfriend did her in and hid the body."

How I wished that were our Rosie. "Do you recall the boyfriend's name?" I asked.

"Aw, honey, that was years ago. It will come to me in the middle of the night. Well, I best get these chickens packed in the truck. It's awful nice of you to give them to me, Natasha."

"I know you'll provide them with a good home, Harvey. And you can bring 'round some fresh eggs sometime," said Wanda.

"Sounds fair."

I went home, showered, and dressed. The phone rang at the exact same time as Bernie and Mars showed up at my kitchen door.

I opened the door as I said *hello* into the phone. It was the conference organizer.

"Sophie, honey, I hate to do this so last minute but we're canceling the banquet tonight. Over half our attendees are checking out this morning. Elise's murder and the rampant rumors about botulism poisoning put a damper on everything. They don't want to eat anything here and way too many of them are concerned about being outdoors after dark. I've looked at the cancelation clauses in our contracts. Please assure the restaurant that we'll uphold our end. And you'll be paid, too. There's just no point in fighting it."

And that was that. I couldn't blame them. They were from out of town and who knew what kinds of gossip had flown around the conference? Elise was one of *them*. No wonder they were scared.

I phoned the restaurant. They weren't nearly as upset as I feared. Turned out they thought they'd have a good crowd anyway because Bernie's place was closed.

When I hung up, Mars was brewing Yorkshire Gold tea, and Bernie was in the middle of poaching eggs.

"Okay if I use up the ham, Soph?"

"That's fine!"

I felt thoroughly spoiled. I flung a fresh gold-and-blue country French tablecloth over the table and set it with square lapis Fiesta ware plates. Mars handed me a mug of tea and whisked a platter on the table that made me yelp— chocolate-iced Krispy Kreme doughnuts!

I turned to look at them. "Okay. What's up? I know when I'm being buttered up for something."

They laughed at me. It wasn't until we sat down to eat that Mars pulled out a sheet of paper and a pen.

"We don't know where to start," he said.

"Neither of us knew Robert very well," explained Bernie. "Finding the source of the poisoning may be the only way to restore The Laughing Hound's reputation."

"We have to begin with the facts," I sipped my tea. "The things we know for sure."

Mars held his pen poised over the paper. "And what exactly would that be?"

I saw his point but was savoring the hollandaise sauce Bernie had made. Bernie certainly knew how to make perfect eggs Benedict.

"Let's begin with Robert eating at The Parlour," said Bernie.

"I think you have to go back farther than that. Velma said Robert had an upset stomach at the auction. So he had probably already eaten the tainted food."

Bernie placed his fork on the side of his plate. "That's just aggravating. There was no need to close me down."

I didn't remind him that Mars might have been poisoned by something from his restaurant.

"But he's dead," Mars said. "How will we ever know where he went that day or the day before?"

"Velma and Francie might know," I said. "Let's stick to what we know for sure. Elise was at the auction, making a big fuss about dating Alex. Then Robert appeared to be quite taken by Wanda."

Mars wrote that down. "That's just weird. I like Wanda, but those two look like opposites. I don't get it."

"Maybe she reminded him of someone he liked?" suggested Bernie.

"Then Natasha refused to go to dinner with Wanda and Robert because she had eyes for Robert."

Mars shook his head. "As long as I live I will never understand Natasha. What did she see in him?"

I wasn't going *there*. "Wanda walked Robert home. And then I found him in the morning."

"Sorry, Sophie. I don't mean to criticize, but this isn't helping at all." Bernie looked so glum that I wanted to hug him.

"We do know that Elise left the hotel at night before Robert died, and she had had an affair with Robert in the past. I think she might have paid him a visit," I said.

"Elise had an affair with Robert? What was it about that guy?" said Bernie.

"Unbelievable. Wanda, Natasha, Elise. He was a chick magnet." Mars shook his head. "Maybe Elise poisoned him? And that's why someone killed her?"

"Velma," I said softly. "She adored Robert. She thought the world of him and was crushed by his death. All along she's been upset because the police aren't treating Robert's death as a crime. Maybe she took justice into her own hands."

"Are you joking?" Bernie licked hollandaise off his fork. "Elise was young and strong. She could have pushed Velma over with one finger."

I nodded my agreement and sank my teeth into an impossibly soft doughnut. *Heaven!*

"We didn't go back far enough." Mars picked up a doughnut. "What about the person who attacked Natasha?"

"So much has happened that I keep forgetting about that," I said. "There's only one thing I'm sure of. Well, sort of sure—Rosie seems to be the key."

~≈~

After the guys left, I headed to Robert's house with Rosie on my mind. As I had hoped, Velma and Francie were there, hard at work packing china and crystal.

"Would you mind if I poked around upstairs a bit?" I asked.

Francie almost dropped a glass. "Really? You mean you've come to your senses? You think Robert was murdered?"

"Don't go getting excited. I just think we should find out more about this mysterious Rosie and the notes." And then

I told them all about Kevin. "It seems Elise had an affair with Robert. Did you find any mention of her in his stuff?"

They dashed up the stairs faster than I had ever seen them move. They had already emptied most of the drawers in his desk. Still, I poked around. It was an antique rolltop. "Did they put hidden drawers in these things?"

Francie and Velma crowded in. We removed every drawer, checking the bottoms in case Robert had taped something to one of them.

We didn't find anything of interest. While I reinserted all the drawers, Velma gushed over a framed photograph.

"This must be the day they opened the store in Charlotte. Robert has big scissors in his hand."

"You look a lot like your sister," said Francie.

"You think so? She was so delicate. I always felt like a rhinoceros around her," said Velma.

I peered over their shoulders. "There's definitely a family resemblance. Robert looks very distinguished."

They chattered on but I saw something that made my skin crawl.

CHAPTER TWENTY-SEVEN

Dear Sophie,

I'm so confused. At the grocery store, I found parsley tea, lemongrass tea, and (I'm not joking!) spinach tea. Hello? Those aren't real teas, are they? What happened to plain old tea?

—Where's My Tea? in Parsley, West Virginia

Dear Where's My Tea?

Unless they have black or green tea added, those would fall in the category of herbal teas. Spinach might even be a vegetable tea. Black tea is what most of us grew up with and it's probably still in your grocery store, though you may have to hunt for it.

—Sophie

"Francie, Velma, take a closer look at that picture. Do you recognize anyone?"

They peered through their reading glasses. Velma gasped first. Francie slapped a hand over her mouth seconds later.

"So I'm correct in thinking that's Callie over there on the right?" I asked. She stood apart from the jolly group cutting the ribbon.

"To think that we've been walking by this picture hanging on the wall, and we never noticed." Velma took another look. "What does this mean?"

"What it means is that our beloved Callie murdered Robert!" Francie said.

"Francie, don't go jumping to conclusions," I said. "But it certainly means she knew Robert before she ever showed up in Old Town."

Velma staggered to a chair and fell into it as though her knees gave way. "That's why he moved here. To be with Callie! Oh my. That little trollop never said a word."

"Did your sister mention suspecting Robert of having an affair?" I asked.

"Not a thing. She always was the one with the stiff upper lip, though. She might have perceived that as a failure on her part somehow. Or maybe she never knew!"

Francie leapt to her feet. "I believe it's time to pay Callie a visit. Let's go. Her place is practically next door."

"Wait a minute, Francie." Velma frowned at us. "I never saw her going into Robert's house. Or him into her house, for that matter."

"We couldn't watch day and night, you know. And he had a back door. Maybe she visited him that way. Come on, let's go!" Francie said.

"Won't she be working at The Parlour?" I asked.

"Even better!" Velma recuperated quickly.

I hadn't expected to be back at The Parlour so soon.

Martha greeted us when we walked in. "You ladies are just the best! We had a little flurry of takeout this morning, but it's been dead since then. Hunter hasn't even been in today. Would you mind sitting by a window again? Maybe that will encourage other people who walk by."

Velma picked a location, and we settled into the comfy chairs and love seat. Callie arrived with the serving cart immediately.

Velma and Francie stared at her.

To break the awkwardness, I said, "What service! You're so prompt."

Martha hurried over. "Callie, everything is on the house today for our good friends. It's the least I can do to thank you for coming. I have a little errand to run. Think you can handle the bustle in here?"

We thanked Martha profusely and she left.

Callie was her usual cheerful self, chattering as she set the table with lavish china. "I hoped Hunter would be by. He likes this china."

Dark red, pink, and apricot roses adorned the china. Gold accented the rims and the handles of the cups. They were beautiful.

Breaking out of her funk, Francie said, "This is his favorite pattern? I'd have expected him to like something more masculine. Of course, Royal Albert Old Country Roses is one of the most popular china patterns of all time."

"I'll never tell his secrets." Callie said it flirtatiously.

I couldn't help looking at all those roses. "Callie? What do you mean by Hunter's secrets?"

"I was just teasing. Sophie, I can't believe I got so lucky. He's about the most decent man I've ever met."

"Did you know that he grew up in Forest Glen?" I asked.

"I think that's kind of cool. The two of us lived in towns a half-hour drive from each other. We went our separate ways and now we've met up. Actually, I think that's what attracts me to him. We grew up with the same kinds of things. The same values, you know?" She set a tiered server on the table. It was loaded with scones and sandwiches, little cakes and fruit tarts. "We like to garden and love the countryside. And he's got the sweetest tattoo on his upper arm, which proves his gentle nature. It's a rose. Doesn't that mean he's tenderhearted?"

I shuddered a little. Roses were very common tattoos, I

reminded myself. It didn't mean anything. Still . . . Callie might think he was a great guy, but given what she'd said about her previous relationships, she was obviously a terrible judge of character. I wanted to like him. He'd been so nice to Velma. He didn't have to pitch in and help her. Maybe I was just imagining things. But why had that man called him Eddie?

"Since the cat's away, won't you join us?" asked Velma, finally coming to life.

As soon as Callie was seated, Velma pulled the framed picture from her giant purse. I hadn't even realized that she brought it with her. Velma showed it to her. "Look what we found when we were cleaning up Robert's house." She passed it to Callie.

I held my breath.

"How nice! This must be Robert's old store—" Her voice faltered, and she looked up at us with fear in her eyes.

"You knew Robert, didn't you?" asked Francie.

"Oh, Velma," Callie said. "I know how you admired him. I'm so sorry, but Robert was not a nice man. That man I was runnin' from in Charlotte? It was Robert."

That was way different than I had expected. I sat back with my teacup. "Why don't you tell us what happened?"

"When I lived in Charlotte, I got a real good job working as a receptionist in a furniture factory. I went to school at night and was eager at work, and I moved up in the company. So when my boss was leaving to open his own furniture store, he asked me to come with him."

"Robert." I said it as a fact. I didn't have to ask.

"Right. I took the job, that's why I'm in the picture. For a long while, he was as nice as everybody thinks. He was polite and considerate, and he paid me well. Velma, honey, I don't know if you should hear this."

Velma sat up straight. "I want to know the truth, Callie. Even if you did something wrong."

"One afternoon, Robert and Livy were supposed to sign some papers. I called them, and Livy asked if I could bring the documents out to their house. I'd been there before when

they hosted parties for their employees, like at Christmas."
She looked at me and Francie when she said, "They lived
out in the country a bit, off a little windin' road."

Callie closed her eyes and shuddered. When she opened
them, she took a deep breath, as though the memory was
disturbing. "I guess she didn't tell Robert I was coming,
'cause he sure didn't expect me. Nobody answered the front
door. I thought I heard voices, so I walked around back.
Robert's wife was kneeling on the ground, pulling weeds
from her garden and talking with some woman. Robert
walked up behind her. She looked around, and he bashed
her in the head with a rock. I'm so sorry, Velma."

"He killed my sister? Robert? I don't believe this." The
horror on Velma's face turned to anger. "It's not fair to
malign a dead man. He can't defend himself. Why would
you lie to us, Callie?"

Francie watched her friend with concern. "Velma, I'm
terribly sorry. And you were so good to Robert, too."

Velma closed her eyes a moment and opened them when
Callie spoke again.

"I can't forget the shock on her face. That poor woman
never saw it comin'." Callie's voice petered to a bare whisper.

Velma moaned. "My Livy! Do you think she suffered?"

"She fell to the ground and was so still. I'd never seen
anybody die instantly like that before. I could tell. I knew
she was dead."

Callie took a moment to compose herself. "But Robert
and the other woman had seen me. He ran toward me, and
I guess I was in shock. I stood there a few seconds too long
until he got close enough for me to recognize the hatred in
his eyes. It was the same madman look that my two husbands used to get right before they commenced beatin' on
me. So I ran like the dickens but I swear he was so fast that
it was like the devil himself was standin' in front of me."

She paused and gulped tea as though she was fortifying
herself. "I knew it was wrong then, and I know it now. Please
don't judge me. They call it survival instinct. And I got it
real strong. I knew better than to fight him. We were all

alone out there, the three of us. I would be as dead as his wife if I wasn't careful. Two against one is not good odds. He made me help him move her a little to make it look like she fell. I guess the woman had gone in the house because I didn't see her anywhere. Velma, I checked—your sister didn't have a pulse. Robert made me pick up the rock he used to kill her. And then he laughed at me and said what a dope I was because if I didn't keep my mouth shut, they now had *my* fingerprints on that rock, and they would say *I* was havin' an affair with Robert, and that *I* had killed Livy to get her out of the way." A shuddering sigh escaped from her mouth.

"When he turned for a minute, I took my chances. I was still holding that rock thinking I could use it as a weapon against him, and I ran for my life. I barely made it into the car, locked the doors, and gunned the engine. I didn't care if I ran over him."

"What about the woman?" I asked.

"I only saw her from a distance. I could see her in the rearview mirror as I pulled onto the road. Well, I didn't know what to do. I drove straight back to the store because I knew the other employees were there, and I wouldn't be alone. I had to hide that rock. He was sure to come after me when he noticed it was gone. We had the ugliest piece of furniture for sale. Mostly we sold new stuff but Robert always liked antiques, so he'd pick them up now and then at estate sales and whatnot. It had real pretty carved fruit on it but there was a devilish face in the middle."

"The sideboard!" I exclaimed.

"Right. My granny had one just like it. What Robert didn't know was that they were made to protect your valuables. That was the reason for that mean face carved into it. It was meant to ward off evil. On the right and left sides, when you opened the doors and removed the shelves, if you reached all the way in and pressed just so, a back panel opened up. That's where folks kept their gold coins or silver platters or pistols. It was a right sizeable space. So I hid the stone there. Insurance, you might call it. But then I realized how stupid I was to even be at the store. Where could I go? I knew I had to run or I would live in fear every day of my life. I went home and packed what I could fit in the car. But I saw his car parked outside my place almost right away. I had figured on a couple of hours while they notified 911 but I guess they left her lyin' there, 'cause he was watchin' me."

Tears rolled down Velma's perfect makeup. She dabbed at them with a napkin. She might not have wanted to believe that Robert killed her sister, but Callie's story was too detailed not to be true.

"So I called the local police and told them kids were ridin' in our neighborhood slamming bats against mailboxes. We had a real problem with that. Sure enough, a squad car came rolling along and Robert took off. I didn't dare take the time to go back to the store to get the rock. He woulda killed me if he got me alone there. I hopped in the car and disappeared from his life."

"But, Callie, why didn't you report him?" asked Francie.

"I know how it works. I'd been through it twice before. You report a guy. They take him in for questioning, and a few hours later, he's on the street lookin' for you."

Callie unbuttoned the top of her blouse and pulled it aside to reveal a long, horrific scar. "I've been through it twice. And I've got the scar to prove it. Nobody was gonna save *me*."

"I'm so sorry." It wasn't adequate, but I didn't know what else to say. She'd had a terrible life.

"Well I liked to have died the day he walked into The Parlour. And right across the street, a big ole sign was goin' up that said *Robert Johnson Antiques*. I mean, really, what were the odds of that? A year had passed. I thought I was done with him and home free. I managed to shake two husbands, but Robert found me. It was a major miscalculation on my part. You see, I had gotten away from two mean drunks. It's hard to make sense when you're drinkin'. It never occurred to me that Robert was different from them in an important way. He wasn't a drunk, he was just evil. One of them wolves in sheep's clothes. I didn't know what to do. He let me know he was watchin' me again. He followed me home so he knew where I lived. And I started thinking about runnin' again. And then I said to myself, *Callie, he found you once, he'll find you again.* To be honest, I'm getting tired of runnin'. I like Martha. I love baking. I even like my teensy little apartment and Old Town. About that time, Hunter turned up, and I thought, *Callie, you finally have a chance at dating a decent guy.* Probably for the first time in my life! So while I was packing, I changed my mind. I wasn't gonna let another man run me off. I'm older, and smarter, and I've had it with men who beat up on women."

"You're braver than I am," I said, wondering what I would have done. My instinct would have been to turn him in. But would I have felt the same way if I had a five-inch scar, courtesy of my ex-husband?

"I'm not that brave. In life we all do what we have to, you know? But I started wonderin' whatever happened to the sideboard where I hid the rock? Maybe I could control him with the knowledge that he didn't have it. But where had it gone? I could not believe my own eyes when I saw it in his store! He brought it up here with him because he never did sell the ugly thing."

"That's the same one?" I pointed to the sideboard Martha had won in the auction.

"Ironic, isn't it? He didn't realize that he brought that telltale rock right to me!"

"Did you know he planned to retire here?" asked Velma. "Why would you move here if you knew he was coming?"

"Your sister talked about Old Town all the time. How nice everyone was and how pretty it is. But behind her back, Robert always made fun of it, saying they would move here over his dead body. That was my second miscalculation. I figured now that his wife was gone, this was the last place he would move."

Callie shook her head. "I'm sorry, Velma. But I was mighty relieved when Robert died. Remember the night I ran into you on the street, Sophie? I thought it was Robert who was chasing me. I felt like such a fool for imagining that I could stand up to him. And then he died the next day. I felt free as a bird. Like I could breathe again and didn't have to look over my shoulder anymore."

And there it was—hanging out there in the air like an ominous thundercloud. Could Callie have murdered Robert? But then, how would Mars have gotten sick?

CHAPTER TWENTY-EIGHT

Dear Natasha,

Why is china called China if it comes from Europe?

—Curious in Potter Hill, Alaska

Dear Curious,

The first porcelain came from a pottery town in China. The name of the town sounded a bit like the word China and over the centuries it eventually morphed to China.

—Natasha

I took a big chance. "At least Robert is with Rosie now."

I watched Callie's reaction carefully. She lifted her teacup to her lips. Her expression didn't change, but the tea in the cup sloshed slightly from her trembling hand.

Francie and Velma, on the other hand, stared at me as though I had lost my mind.

I tried again. "Poor Rosie. At least she can finally rest in peace."

Callie carefully returned her teacup to the saucer. "You mean the girl in those notes? I don't understand."

Either she was a pretty good actress or she really didn't know.

"Thank heaven," declared Francie. "I knew you couldn't have murdered Robert!"

It was my turn to glare at her like she had lost her marbles.

"Killed Robert?" Callie seemed genuinely surprised. It was a good thing the place was empty. She said it loud enough for half of Old Town to hear.

"I haven't ever killed anyone." Callie laughed bitterly. "I just run away. But I'd be lyin' if I said I was sorry he was dead." Callie sagged into her chair like the air had gone out of her. "If ever there was someone who deserved a terrible end to his life, it was Robert. I hope he's burnin' in hellfire. I guess there weren't many people with a better reason to knock him off than me." Her head rose slowly and turned as she gazed at Velma. "Except for you."

I could feel a rosy flush creeping up my face. Callie was right. Velma was the one with the most compelling motive. Had she suspected Robert of murdering her sister all along? Had she been playing a role?

She had been spying on him from her window. I glanced at Francie. Was Velma using her? The two little old ladies seemed so darling. Could one of them be a crafty killer exacting revenge for her sister's death? How could I have been stupid enough to overlook the obvious?

Velma hadn't said much. I had assumed she was in shock from the revelation about her sister's demise. Or didn't she know how to play this scene? We waited for her to say something.

When she did, it was little more than a whisper. "If I had listened to my husband, my sweet sister might be sitting here with us today."

Velma held on to the arm of the sofa as she rose to her feet. She took two steps, bent over as though she'd aged ten years. "Sophie," she said softly, "I don't think we need to look for Robert's killer anymore. He got what he had coming. Whoever fed him that stuff deserves a commendation."

Francie jumped to her feet and hooked her arm into Velma's. "I'll walk you home."

When the door closed behind them, Callie said, "Maybe I shouldn't have told her the truth. She would have been happier if she had never known."

"It's hard to know what to do in a situation like that."

"I spared her one thing. When Robert talked about how he wasn't going to move to Old Town, he always mentioned the annoying sister-in-law that lived here."

One thing was bothering me. "You never met Velma before?"

"Maybe. She seemed slightly familiar but I didn't know she was the annoying sister-in-law until Robert showed up. I worked in the back office of his store, so when people came to visit, I didn't usually see them. And let's face it, sweet as she is, Velma has that permed, well-fed look like so many ladies her age. Now, if Wanda had come by, I might have remembered *her*!"

I thanked Callie for sharing her story with me and left a generous tip. I insisted on paying, too. The Parlour must be losing a lot of money as a result of the bad publicity. I was pleased to see a cluster of shoppers enter as I left.

～≈～

I was home closing my file on the family law group when someone pounded on my front door with such anger that fear coursed through me. As I ran through the hallway, I could hear Natasha outside yelling. I flung the door open and pulled her in, locking the door behind her. I peered through the peephole. I didn't see anyone. "What's wrong?"

She pumped her fists on her hips and glared at me. "Why did you turn me in?"

"What?"

"I thought we were on the same page on this. I thought I could trust you. First Mars and now this!"

"Natasha, come in the kitchen. How about a cup of tea?" I had to calm her down. I had no idea what she was ranting about.

"Tea, schmee. I am not interested in tea. Sophie, you were one of the very few people in this world that I trusted. I want you to know that our relationship is over. Do you understand me? I can't believe you would betray me this way. Oh, and while I'm at it—hands off Mars. I want him back!"

I didn't know where to begin. I tried to speak softly so she would have to calm down and listen. "I still don't know what you're talking about."

She matched my tone but managed to sound irate. "Mars, your ex-husband. I made a mistake. I want him to come home."

"I understood that part. But I didn't turn you in for anything."

She stared at me. "Then who did?" Her eyes narrowed to slits. "Liar."

I would have asked, *Have I ever lied to you before?* But I probably had. I tried a different tack. "What did you do?"

"You know perfectly well."

"I give up. I'm making myself some tea."

She grabbed my arm. "How can you be so calm after what you did? Don't you see the terrible position you've put me in?"

"Maybe you could tell me exactly what that is."

"They found a knife in the river," Natasha said.

"A knife? Is it the knife that was used to kill Elise?"

"Apparently. Of all the lousy luck. They never would have wanted to question me if you hadn't told them I was at the river. This is all your fault."

"When were you at the river?"

She cocked her head impatiently. "Why are you pretending you don't know? You were there."

I was getting annoyed. "Natasha, let's start at the beginning. When were you at the river?"

"Did you hit your head or something? You turned me in. How is it possible that you suddenly don't remember? It was the night I came over here."

"You couldn't sleep because you were worried about Wanda."

"Exactly. And you told me to throw her elixir bottles in the river so no one could track Robert's death to her."

"I did no such thing!" I said.

"Of course you did. Maybe you should take memory supplements."

"Natasha, I walked you home."

"And then you followed me to the river. I saw you, Sophie. You can dress in black all you want, I knew it was you who was there to make sure I was safe."

"Natasha, someone broke into your house and conked you over the head. What on earth would possess you to walk down to the river by yourself in the middle of the night?"

She let out a long breath. "I didn't have any choice. No matter the consequences, I had to do it. I had to protect Mom, Sophie. She's all I have. I couldn't let her go through a trial or rot in prison. I had to get rid of those containers. They can throw *me* in the slammer, but I'm not going to rat on my mom."

It was wrong of her to get rid of evidence, of course. But I had never liked her more than I did at that moment. I reached out my arms and gave her a big hug.

"Natasha, that was not me you saw at the river that night. I was at home in bed."

Her left eye twitched twice. "That's not funny."

"I know. But it's true."

She grasped behind her for the doorway and leaned against it. She breathed heavily through her open mouth, like she'd finished a long run. "I could have been murdered. Sophie, do you think the person who killed Elise could have been my attacker?"

Francie had thought someone might have mistaken Elise for Natasha. "Natasha, what does the word *rosy* mean to you?"

"Rosy? You're being weird again, Sophie."

"It was the last thing Elise said before she died. Her soon

to be ex-husband is named Rosey, and they're blaming him for her murder."

"That's ridiculous. What if she said it because she loved him more than anything else in the world, and she wished she could tell him that?" Natasha shook her finger at me. "Now that we're friends again because you didn't turn me in after all, that doesn't change the fact that I want you to stay away from Mars. I claim dibs on him."

"Yeah, I got that." She had enough troubles. I wasn't going to argue with her about Mars! Besides, you couldn't claim dibs on a person. I wondered, though, if Mars wanted *her* back.

Her take on *Rosey* was interesting. Funny that I had jumped to the conclusion that Rosey had something to do with her killer. She was right—sometimes a person's last word was a spouse's name or the name of a child because the person loved them.

"Sophie? Promise me you'll take care of Mom if they convict me of murder?"

"Natasha! Stop that." Surely she hadn't . . . "Did you kill Elise or Robert?"

"No! How can you even ask such a thing?"

"Just checking," I said. "If you didn't murder Elise then chances are pretty slim they'll go after you. Even if they ignore the fact that Elise said *Rosey*, they'll need more than an eyewitness that you were at the river. Think back, Natasha. Who could that have been?"

"If I knew, I would be at that person's house right now, wouldn't I? Will you bail me out if they arrest me?"

"You bet." I meant it, too. Even though I didn't think she would be arrested. Wolf wasn't that stupid. He could make a better case against Elise's husband.

"Sophie? I'm scared."

It was hard to imagine her being scared. Stubborn Natasha went headlong into everything without much thought. "It will be okay, Natasha." I stopped short of mentioning that she might actually have to tell the truth about what she did that night.

She opened my front door, and we stepped outside.

Wolf waited on the sidewalk with Wanda and Harvey, the chicken farmer.

Natasha squared her shoulders and walked out to meet Wolf like the beauty queen that she was. No one would have ever known that she was quaking inside.

"Shall we talk in my house?" Natasha asked.

"No!" Wanda and Harvey said it together.

"You're welcome to use my living room," I offered.

Wolf gave Wanda and Harvey quite a look. I couldn't blame him. I wondered what they were hiding, too.

The second Natasha and Wolf disappeared into my house, I whipped around to Harvey and said, "I thought you left." As soon as the words were out of my mouth I suspected they sounded rude, like I meant to get rid of him.

"My truck broke down about a half hour from here. Wanda had to come pick me up."

"Where are the chickens?"

They looked at each other and burst out laughing. "We loaded them into Natasha's car, drove it into the garage, and opened the car doors," Wanda said.

"Natasha doesn't know?"

"Nope. She must suspect since Harvey returned, though."

"I don't know what's wrong with her," Wanda said. "Seems like she hasn't been right since Mars left her."

"Are all those antiques still in her garage, too?"

"Yup!" Harvey laughed like he thought it was the funniest thing in the world. "Hey, young lady, I never did remember the name of the fellow who murdered Rosie, but her daddy's name came to me—Eddie. Eddie Barnes."

CHAPTER TWENTY-NINE

Dear Sophie,

Is it inappropriate to serve wine or champagne at a tea party? My sister is throwing a fit about a party without alcohol.

—Feeling Dumb in Champagne, Louisiana

Dear Feeling Dumb,

No need to feel dumb! No one was born knowing this. There are no hard and fast rules. Serve what you like! A delicious sweet dessert wine is traditional, but if the party is a celebration, what better way to enjoy it than with a glass of champagne in addition to tea?

—Sophie

I felt like I'd been hit by lightning. Eddie? Could there be a connection to Hunter? Was it remotely possible that the Rosie I had been looking for was Rosie Barnes? I rushed to my house to tell Wolf.

But when I placed my hand on the door handle, I paused. There were probably millions of people named Eddie. And in any event, Hunter was far too young to be Rosie's father. I was grasping at anything in desperation.

Wolf probably wouldn't be questioning Natasha for very long. Still, I ought to make them some tea. I let myself in and very quietly put the kettle on.

Natasha needed a tea that would relax her. I selected a gentle spiced orange tea. I poured it into teacups on a tray, added napkins and a plate of macarons, and carried it into the living room.

Wolf sounded very patient but Natasha was giving him bizarre responses. She wasn't helping herself!

"Approximately what time did you go down to the river?" Wolf asked.

"I don't really know. I didn't look at my watch," Natasha said.

Wolf didn't say anything for a moment. I assumed it was because of my presence, so I scurried out of the living room, but lingered in the foyer where I could hear what was being said.

Finally Natasha blurted, "There's nothing illegal about walking down to the river!"

Wolf's voice was calm. "That's true."

"This is America. I can take a walk at night if I want to!"

"You were seen pitching something into the river."

I wasn't sure if that was true or he was making it up. She *had* thrown Wanda's bottles into the water. But in the dark of night would anyone really have been able to see that?

With a start, I realized that I was holding my breath.

"Why would I do that?" Natasha asked.

"Maybe you had something you wanted to get rid of."

"I doubt that was the case."

"You *doubt* it? Don't you know?"

"I couldn't sleep."

Hah! She dodged answering by changing the subject. Maybe I didn't give her enough credit.

"Who was with you?" Wolf asked.

"Why would you ask that when you clearly know who ratted on me?"

"Why do you call it *ratting on you*?"

"Look, Wolf. You must be a nice guy or you never would have put up with dating Sophie."

Oh! The nerve of her!

"I heard you found a knife. I would assume that you want to pin the murder of that woman on me. I hate to disappoint you, but I didn't even know her, much less murder her."

"Ah, but you see, Natasha, your presence at the river might make you an important witness. Someone threw the knife in the river."

Wolf was smooth. How clever of him to make her feel important. Now she wouldn't be on the defensive.

"Why didn't you say so? There was someone else there. I thought it was Sophie."

I leaned my head against the wall. Maybe that was the truth, but now *I* might be in trouble. After all, Elise had told everyone she was dating my boyfriend, and I had found her. Thank goodness Nina was with me! Still, if it wasn't Wolf who was on the case, I knew the police would be looking at me more closely.

I heard them coming and skedaddled into the kitchen. Picking up a mug of tea, I leaned casually against the island, as though I'd just been hanging out.

Natasha left but Wolf spied me in the kitchen.

"All done?" I asked brightly.

Wolf appeared somewhat tired. "Were you down by the river?"

Ouch. He cut to the chase. "No. It wasn't me."

His mouth twisted to the right. "The witness says you were there."

"Oh, very nice. You're lying to scare me into admitting it. Hah!"

"Sophie, look into my eyes. Were you down by the river with Natasha?"

I looked straight into his eyes and craned my neck forward. "No."

Wolf looked down and scratched his neck. "See, the problem is that I'm not lying. The witness specifically named you."

"It doesn't change the fact that I was not there. Your witness must be mistaken."

He sighed so hard his shoulders heaved.

"Sophie, I'm not trying to pin this on you. Did you see anyone else down at the river that night?"

"Wolf, I wasn't there. Besides, anyone could have tossed the knife into the water."

He nodded but I could see that he was frustrated. "I think we have our man. They're checking for fingerprints now. I just need to put all the pieces together. I'd hoped you or Natasha might have seen him. Thanks for the tea and cookies. Not many people would do that."

"That's because they're nervous when you come to visit."

Wolf nodded. "Makes a cop wonder what Natasha had to be nervous about."

I wasn't telling!

When Wolf left, I grabbed a jean jacket and my purse, and hoofed it down to The Parlour even though it closed at four in the afternoon. Sure enough, The Parlour was already locked up. A sign on the door said *See You Tomorrow!*

It figured. Of course, Hunter hadn't been there earlier. Maybe he skipped a day. The issue of someone calling him Eddie wasn't really a big deal, but I had so few leads to follow that I was becoming obsessed with getting to the truth about him.

I strolled over to Callie's place. It wasn't as though I thought I'd see Hunter hanging around on the street. Would it be rude to knock on the door and ask Callie if he happened to be there? Or maybe she knew where he lived.

I was standing on the sidewalk debating when I heard someone say, "Psst. Sophie!" I turned around to see Francie and Velma beckoning to me from Velma's front door.

I dashed across the street to them. "Don't tell me you're spying on Callie."

"Spy? We've never spied on anyone, have we, Francie?"

"Never!"

"You just happened to open the door when I came along?" I asked.

"That was just a nice coincidence," Francie said. "What do you want with Callie? She has company."

"We think they're going out for dinner," added Velma.

"Hunter is with her?" I asked. "I was hoping to talk to him."

"Oh, marvelous!" Velma started across the street.

"I knew it was a fortuitous coincidence." Francie hurried after her.

They stopped traffic, waving their hands at cars as though they owned the street. By the time I caught up to them, Velma had knocked on the door.

Callie opened it and seemed quite surprised to see us. "Ladies! Oh my. Won't you come in?"

Hunter rose to his feet and nodded in greeting. "Ladies."

Velma had been correct when she said Callie's home was small. One tiny room with a large bay window served as both dining area and living room. It was the ultimate of shabby chic. A beat-up wood door in faded turquoise hung on one wall and a stunningly beautiful quilt in pastels hung on another wall.

Francie admired it.

"My mom made that," Callie said. "She calls it the square dance pattern."

A love seat and a chair had been draped in a creamy muslin. A small brown table with two matching chairs that had been painted turquoise occupied a corner near a tiny fireplace. Throw pillows picked up on the turquoise and cream theme.

The kitchen, barely large enough for one person, was separated from the living room by a counter. All the cabinets had been replaced by rustic shelving in turquoise. Delicate flowers and butterflies on her dishes and mugs could only be Lenox's Butterfly Meadow pattern.

Callie's home was enchanting. Like a little cottage one might find out in the woods somewhere. It made me wonder if that was where she longed to be.

Velma and Francie sat on the love seat. Hunter took one of the turquoise chairs.

I could barely squeeze by the love seat. I stumbled over Velma's feet and caught my balance just before I fell. But not before I saw a briefcase that I thought belonged to Hunter.

The initials on it were EAB.

"Who *are* you?" I blurted.

Was that anguish or horror I saw on his face? He gazed around at us uncomfortably, his breath coming fast.

"Honey, are you all right?" asked Francie.

He nodded. "I guess it doesn't matter anymore now that Robert is dead."

Velma leaned forward on the love seat. "What's this about Robert?"

"Hunter's briefcase, or should I say *Eddie's* briefcase says his initials are *EAB*."

"Edward Allen Barnes. Eddie." Hunter took a deep breath. "Robert murdered my sister."

CHAPTER THIRTY

Dear Natasha,

My father-in-law insists that tea should not be in bags. He says loose tea should be placed in a tea strainer and hot, not boiling, water should be poured over it. I think he's making a fuss about nothing. I can just microwave his mug and dunk a teabag into it.

—What's the Big Fuss? in Strain, Missouri

Dear What's the Big Fuss?

Your father-in-law is quite right about traditional tea. However, times have changed. Don't let him see you microwave his tea, and he'll never know the difference.

—Natasha

Eddie, if that was his real name, appeared miserable. "I'm sorry I couldn't tell you. The reason I've been hanging out at The Parlor, well, at the beginning, anyway"—he smiled at Callie—"was to spy on Robert. He, uh, he got away clean. My family has been looking for him for years."

"Your sister?" asked Callie. Evidently confused, she looked at Velma and back at Hunter. "Are you two related?"

"No," I said. "He's Rosie Barnes's brother."

"Excuse me?" Velma was clearly outraged. "I'm sorry if you think me audacious, but how dare both of you come along after Robert is dead and accuse him of murder?" She gazed at Francie. "I don't believe this. What's that saying about not speaking ill of the dead? You could accuse him of anything. He's not exactly in a position to deny it, now is he?"

Eddie/Hunter didn't seem bothered in the slightest by her outburst. "It's not an accusation. It's a fact. I wish I had said it to his face. It's my only regret—well, other than having to fool you lovely ladies."

"What happened? Why do you think that Robert was the person who killed her?" I asked.

"Let me be very clear. I don't *think* he did, I know he killed her. Rosie was seventeen when she got pregnant. She'd been seeing a local college student named Robert Johnson. Apparently, he was engaged to be married to someone else. My parents were very pleased when he called off the wedding and promised Rosie he would do the right thing by her and the baby. And then she disappeared."

"Wanda told us about her. She said it was in the newspaper every day," said Francie.

Eddie swallowed hard. "It was. We were crushed. You can't imagine what it's like when a member of the family doesn't come home. Rosie was a good kid. She was never in trouble, didn't do drugs or anything. My dad and I went out looking for her that night. We checked out all the college hangouts, and her friends' houses. No one knew where she was. But one of her girlfriends told me Rosie was supposed to meet Robert at a spot on the river. It was somewhat secluded and popular among the college crowd for necking. There was no sign of her. I tracked down Robert at his dorm room. He pretended he didn't know where she was, either. Of course, my parents went to the police. We did everything possible. We searched fields and parks. The whole town turned out to look for Rosie. Everyone loved her."

"How awful that must have been for you. And your poor parents!" I said.

"They aged ten years in ten days. You know, we were pretty simple people. From the wrong side of the tracks you might say. We all knew Robert was behind it. It wasn't hard to figure out that he didn't want her, and he didn't want the baby."

Eddie stopped talking and raised his hand, palm out. "There are no words to express the terror. You can't sleep. You can't eat. And worst of all, you can't think of anything else. You imagine the most horrific things. Is she lying somewhere injured or dying? Is she alone? Is she locked up?" He closed his eyes. "It's the worst nightmare you can imagine. Except it's real. You never wake up."

We all listened in silence, shattered by the mere thought of a loved one who had gone missing.

He opened his eyes. "The second day, my dad went to Robert's dorm room to beat it out of him. If the police weren't going to do it, then he would take things into his own hands to find Rosie. But . . . Robert had left. Everything that belonged to him was gone. There wasn't even a pencil or a piece of trash left in his room. One of the kids told my dad two guys came and packed everything up. Turned out Robert came from money. He lived in a town not too far from ours. I used to drive over and hope I'd catch a glimpse of him coming out of the house. Big place with a brick fence and one of those automatic gates. Their lawyers circled the wagons and even though the police questioned Robert, he was never arrested."

"But I thought Wanda said they found Rosie," said Callie.

"Years later a fisherman found some bones washed up along the riverbank. That's all that was left of our sweet Rosie and her baby, just a few bones. Our lives have never been the same."

Velma jumped to her feet, knocking the love seat against the wall. Pointing her forefinger at Eddie, she said, "Rosie is dead and you are, too. *You* murdered Robert!"

Eddie stood up. "I think I'd better go. I'm sorry if I upset you, Velma, but your brother-in-law was a vile man."

Eddie left in a flurry, and Velma looked like she might have a meltdown.

Callie made her sit down. "Could I get you some tea, Velma? It will calm you."

"I don't want to be calm. He's the one. He all but admitted to killing Robert. And how dare he make up stories about him like that? Did you notice that he didn't have any evidence? Not a shred. Did you hear any? I didn't."

"Velma, dear!" Francie seemed genuinely worried and patted her hand.

Callie swallowed hard. "I believe Hunter, er, Eddie. Poor Rosie got in the way of Robert's plans. Just like Livy did."

Velma trembled. I was afraid it had all been too much for her. "There's no proof," she whispered. "No proof."

Francie helped her home. The two of them shuffled across the street. Callie and I watched from her doorway.

"Think Velma will be all right?" asked Callie. "Maybe I'll look in on her later on."

"She'd probably appreciate that."

"Well," Callie said, "once again I have fallen for a liar."

"You think he's a worm?"

To my complete surprise, she started chuckling. "I guess I can't hold it against him. I ran away from Robert and kept it a secret from everyone when he showed up. I'm not exactly in a position to criticize him."

I said good-bye and walked away thinking that Callie was right when she said Robert got rid of the women who were in his way. I headed for home, but stopped by the grocery store and discovered Hunter, who was really Eddie but would probably always be Hunter to me, sitting at a table drinking coffee. I bought a latte, summoned courage, and sat down at the same table.

"Had enough of tea?" I asked.

"I like to switch it up. Keeps things interesting."

"I hear you have a tattoo." I tried to sound casual about it.

His eyes met mine straight on. "A rose in memory of Rosie."

There wasn't anything sinister about that. In fact, it was sort of sweet and sentimental. Still, that didn't mean he hadn't murdered Robert. "So you just happened to find Robert here in Old Town?"

A glimmer of a smile danced across his mouth. "I've been looking for him since the day Rosie disappeared. Did a couple tours in the army when I couldn't search, but I never forgot about him. Do you know how hard it is to track down someone named Johnson? There are millions of them."

"Robert is a popular name, too."

"Exactly. I figured he would have changed his name or used his middle name or just his first initial. There were a lot of variables."

"So how did you find him?"

"There was a little column in the newspaper. New stores and restaurants around the area, something like that. And there was his name—Robert Johnson Antiques. I lived in Arlington, not too far away, so I came over and realized that The Parlour was perfectly positioned to watch him. I didn't think it could possibly be the Robert Johnson I had looked for. Surely the man who murdered my big sister wouldn't broadcast his name by posting it on his store."

"How do you know it was the same man? He's a few decades older," I said.

He took a swig of coffee. "I knew it in my gut the first time I saw him. He was the right age and even though he was older, he had a certain swagger, a confidence, like he thought he ruled the world. Funny, once you have a little information, it leads to a whole lot more. Before I knew it, I had the story of his life. He changed colleges. I guess he couldn't go back to the one where he killed Rosie. Or maybe he was afraid of running into us Barneses in town. He married Olivia and went to work for a furniture company before he opened his own store in Charlotte."

"He never recognized you?"

"I don't think so. Remember, I was just a kid, and he only saw me once. I don't look much like the teenager he met anymore. But I didn't care if he knew. For a long, long time, my biggest fear in life was that Robert would die before anyone could make him suffer for what he did to Rosie."

CHAPTER THIRTY-ONE

Dear Sophie,

We're having a tea party outdoors. It's going to be very pretty in the shade of trees by a lake. But we don't know if we can serve iced tea. Somehow that seems wrong but when it's hot, will anyone want to drink hot tea?

—Overheated in Hot Spot, Kentucky

Dear Overheated,

Why don't you serve both? That way your guests can choose what they prefer.

—Sophie

I grew so cold at his words that my latte didn't even warm me.

"Why you were in Robert's house?" I asked.

"We knew Robert came from a wealthy family. If I had killed a girl like he did, I would have spent my life in prison. I wanted to see how Robert spent his life. I wanted to see what Rosie's life would have been like if Robert had been a decent man. Looked pretty comfortable to me. I heard you found him. Is that true?"

I nodded.

"Did he suffer?" He whispered it and looked at me with hopeful eyes.

I was cognizant of the people surrounding us. The shoppers and the store employees. I feared I was facing the man who murdered Robert. Nevertheless, I told the truth. "Yes. I think his was a terrible and frightening death."

I expected an evil grin or satisfaction, but he didn't seem outwardly happy. We were in a public place, so I dared to confront him. "Hunter, did you murder Robert to avenge Rosie's death?"

His eyebrows jumped. "Wish I had. Few have ever deserved it more. And now, after a lifetime of hunting the elusive Robert Johnson, it has almost come to an abrupt end." He leaned back and tossed his coffee cup into a trashcan as though he was throwing a basketball. "Now that he's gone, I find myself oddly free to do whatever I like. I've never felt this way in my adult life."

He stood up. "See you around, Sophie."

I sat there for a time, sipping my latte and thinking about Rosie's family and Callie living their lives in quiet desperation. The rest of us went about our business, none the wiser about their troubles.

I finally snagged a shopping cart and picked up a few items. Thick pork chops were on sale. Mars and Bernie probably had an empty fridge now that Bernie wasn't bringing home leftovers from The Laughing Hound. I bought extra pork chops in case they came over for dinner. I could always freeze them if they didn't. I didn't have my grocery dolly with me so I couldn't buy anything too heavy, but I couldn't resist buying a few apples now that the new crop was in. And the fresh figs were a rarity. I had to have those! I added a package of mixed baby greens, paid for my food, and walked home as darkness fell over Old Town. I checked behind me several times. It was best to be wary.

A block away from my house, I saw Nina walking Peanut.

"Dinner at my place?" I asked.

Nina took one of my bags and fell in step with me. "Did Wolf find you?"

"When? I saw him a couple of hours ago."

"He wanted to ask you something about tea," Nina said.

"I bet the ringer on my phone turned off again. We'll be home soon."

As we passed Bernie's house, he and Mars fell in step with us. I was beginning to feel like the Pied Piper.

"Soph," Mars said, "I've been wondering if I can start visitation with Daisy again when I'm home. Bernie's okay with her sleeping over."

I unlocked the door. "I bet she'd be very happy if you walked her right now!"

Mars grabbed her leash and said, "C'mon, Daisy."

Nina handed him Peanut's leash. "Since you're going anyway . . ."

Bernie started a fire while I unpacked the groceries and filled a pot of water for country-style mashed potatoes. With all the odd things going on, I craved comfort food and the sad truth was that I would happily hop into a vat of mashed potatoes and eat my way out.

Nina retrieved martini glasses. She and Bernie launched into a discussion of how to make caramel appletinis while I sliced juicy pears and chopped walnuts for a crunchy fall salad, and popped halved red potatoes into the boiling water.

I waited for Mars to return before starting the pork chops because they cooked quickly. In the meantime, I tossed cold butter, and flour in the food processor and whipped together a quick pastry for an apple galette. I rolled out the dough and arranged the apple slices in the middle. A dash of apple pie spice and a little brown sugar were all the fresh apples needed. I folded the dough up around the edges, leaving the center exposed, and slid it into the oven to bake while we ate. I sliced one of Mars's favorites, zucchini, and cooked it gently with nothing but butter and a dash of salt.

Mars barged inside muttering, "Cold snap! It's freezing outside tonight. I'm not ready for it to be so cold."

I tossed the salad with an apple-cider vinaigrette and started the pork chops. Next I put on the kettle and filled a tea infuser with a caffeine-free blend of rose hips, hibiscus, and a hint of mint.

I looked over at my friends, gathered around the table they had set. There was something reassuring about the warmth of my kitchen and their friendship. It pained me to think of Hunter/Eddie, Callie, and Velma, all suffering from Robert's callous actions. Not to mention poor little Kevin. It brought a smile to my face to think how much he would enjoy our dinner. He would have wanted to cook it, too!

Bernie divided the salad among plates and carried them to the table.

Using tongs, I placed a thick pork chop on each dinner plate and spooned the sauce over top of each one. A generous dollop of the mashed potatoes with the skins on, a little zucchini, and we were ready to eat.

The conversation quickly turned to botulism, which didn't seem appropriate for a dinner discussion at all. "Just to be clear, I didn't use any canned foods in this dinner," I said.

"Not even in the salad?" asked Mars.

I chuckled. "The vinegar and the oil I used in the vinaigrette, I guess. But vinegar prevents botulism from forming. So we're down to the oil."

Nina looked at her fork, which held a bite of mashed potatoes. "I read you can get it from canned potatoes."

Bernie nodded. "Non-acidic foods usually."

"Have you heard from the health department?" I asked.

Bernie groaned. "So far everything looks fine. Which brings me back to my belief that Mars ate something somewhere else." Bernie shot him a look of exasperation. "If only he could remember!"

"Bernie, you know I would be the first to help you out of this mess if I could," Mars said. "I'm telling you for the nine hundredth time that I haven't eaten anywhere else."

"Any luck on finding the elusive Rosie?" asked Bernie.

I filled them in about Hunter/Eddie, Callie, and Velma's sister. "Robert may have turned a lot of ladies' heads, but the ones who had the misfortune of being involved with him came to violent ends. Callie was lucky to escape him."

"Maybe it *was* Robert who was following Callie." Nina said.

I shook my head. "He had dinner with Wanda that night."

"He could have done it afterward. Didn't he make an excuse about not feeling well?"

"I guess that's possible, but we know he wasn't the one who killed Elise." I savored a bite of the creamy mashed potatoes.

"They died in the wrong order," said Nina. "It all would have made more sense if Elise had died first. We would be thinking that Robert had murdered her."

"Does anyone else think it's suspicious that Hunter and Callie are an item?" asked Mars. "What if the two of them are lying? What if they knew each other before?"

"That's not out of the question. They grew up in neighboring towns," I said.

Bernie sniffed the air. "Is your galette ready? I smell baked apples."

I pulled it from the oven and set it on a rack to cool while we finished dinner.

Mars pulled his list out of a pocket. "First Natasha was attacked. Then Callie."

"But that might not have had anything to do with Robert or Elise," said Nina.

Mars scowled. "I don't understand how Natasha figures into the equation, but it seems to me that the attacks on Callie and Elise might have been similar. Callie might have been his first victim if Sophie and I hadn't happened along."

Bernie cut a bite of pork chop. "But she didn't know Rosie."

"Unless she's lying," I said.

"You know who's missing from this grisly scenario," Bernie said, "is the fiancée."

"Callie!" I blurted.

They looked at me like I had gone nuts. "How old do you think Robert was?" I asked.

"Sixty-seven," said Nina.

"You sound so sure. How do you know that?" asked Mars.

"I helped Velma and Francie clear out some of his stuff."

"How old do you think Callie is?" I asked.

Nina shrugged. "Sixty-five?"

"What if she was the one Robert was engaged to when Rosie got pregnant?"

Nina perked up. "And Hunter knows that! Maybe he's not interested in dating her at all. He wants revenge or something."

"Then why would she have been running from someone on the street that night?" asked Mars.

"I didn't see anyone. Did you?" I asked.

"You're saying she made that up?" Mars asked.

Bernie finished his dinner and lay his knife and fork neatly on the edge of his plate. "Let me get this straight. You're suggested that Callie was engaged to marry Robert. He murdered Rosie so he could be with Callie? Then why didn't they marry?"

"Good question," I said. "Maybe they thought it would be too obvious if they were together? Or maybe the strain of murdering Rosie came between them."

"And then she found Robert in Charlotte and went to work for the same company," said Nina.

"Stalking him?" asked Bernie.

"Or resuming her relationship with him, and maybe she's the one who murdered Robert's wife?" I said. "He followed her here. All that baloney about why she moved here was lies. And she bakes. She probably brought him goodies to eat all the time. He had no reason to suspect she would poison him."

"Then why did she kill him?" asked Mars. "She finally had what she wanted."

"Maybe she didn't," I said. "Maybe he refused to marry

her. He lived in a fancy house, and she had that teensy little place. If they had married, she could have had a life of leisure." I could feel my face flushing with excitement.

"And she murdered Elise because she was jealous of Robert's relationship with her." Bernie nodded in agreement.

Mars cleared the table while I fetched dessert plates, whipped cream, and the apple galette. I was cutting the galette when Mars said, "There are two very big holes in this scheme. The first question remains, why break into my house and attack Natasha? And why did Robert and Elise say *Rosie* when they died?"

CHAPTER THIRTY-TWO

Dear Sophie,

Why is it that I drink black tea in the morning to wake up, yet I also drink black tea when I'm upset and need to calm down? That doesn't make sense to me.

—Anxious in Blacksburg, Virginia

Dear Anxious,

A study by scientists has concluded that black tea reduces cortisol, the stress hormone. It doesn't actually reduce the stress, of course, but it makes you feel calmer.

—Sophie

Mars had poked a big fat leak into my balloon. I didn't have answers.

Even the tempting warm apples in a flaky crust on the plate in front of me didn't make me feel any better.

Very quietly, Nina said, "Because it was Callie who murdered Rosie, and Elise knew it?"

"That actually makes sense," I said. "Robert could have confided in Elise. Velma has been having a hard time accepting that Robert killed anyone. Maybe Callie murdered Rosie and Velma's sister, and Elise. All out of a deranged love of Robert."

Mars and Bernie exchanged a look.

Mars said, "This doesn't work from Robert's perspective. If what you're suggesting is true, Robert was engaged to Callie. One of them knocked off Rosie, but they married *other* people. Why wouldn't they have gotten married after killing Rosie? Then they got back together and had a years-long affair until someone killed Robert's wife. Meanwhile, Robert was also having an affair with Elise? What was he? Some kind of sexual superhero? I don't think so."

"Men have been known to have more than one lover before," Nina insisted.

"Maybe we're overlooking something. I think it's Callie." I finally took a bite of warm apples topped with whipped cream. "Mmm, I love baked apples."

A knock on the door surprised us. I unlocked it and let Wolf in. "Hope I'm not interrupting."

"How about a pork chop and some potatoes?" I asked.

"I've eaten, thanks. But I wouldn't turn down some of the apple thing you're eating. How come it's freeform and not in a pie pan?"

"Just for fun. Hot tea?"

"Sounds good. It's cold out." He sat down next to Bernie. "Sorry about your restaurant. I hear they haven't turned up anything."

"I guess that's the good news. It would be worse if they had found something," Bernie said.

I set the teapot on the table along with cups for everyone.

"How are you feeling, Mars?" asked Wolf.

"Okay. The stuff they gave me worked right away. Anyone else get sick yet?"

Wolf let out a deep breath. "No. We're past the likely time that anyone would get sick, so either people had a mild case, like you, and didn't see a doctor, or . . ."

"Or what?" I handed Wolf a plate with apple galette.

He spooned whipped cream onto the top. "There are several possibilities. The most likely situation is that only Robert ate the contaminated food. Mars could have gotten it from something else entirely. Or the contaminated item is something that is being doled out slowly—"

"Huh?" Nina sipped her tea. "I don't get that."

"This whipped cream, for instance," Wolf said. "It's rich so you wouldn't eat it all at one time. If it were contaminated, you might get a little sick, like Mars. Then I might come along and have some two days later and feel ill."

"I can be a piggy about whipped cream," Nina jested.

"You're kidding, but that could be what happened. Robert ate more of it and didn't get help in time," Wolf said.

I could see irritation simmering on Bernie's face. "Wolf, they didn't even eat at the same place."

"I don't know what to tell you, Bernie. We're doing our best to locate the source. Actually, I'm glad you're here." Wolf pulled a sheet out of his pocket and unfolded it. "Two experts are better than one. Is this some kind of kitchen knife? We thought it was a hunting knife at first but apparently not."

The sketch showed a blade with three semi-circular notches on each side and a handle with a rope around it.

Bernie's eyes met mine. Together we said, "It's a tea knife."

"What would you use a tea knife for? To open tea bags?"

"There's a kind of tea—" I started.

"Pu-erh," said Bernie. "I had a nanny who insisted it kept her brain sharp because it was aged."

"It comes in a compressed cake or a brick. The knife is used to wedge a portion loose to make tea," I explained.

"You said it's aged?" asked Wolf.

"Right. All black tea is fermented, but Pu-erh tea matures and is actually labeled with the year and area of production. Kind of like wine. There are years that are coveted and some that are considered less desirable," I said.

"Could it form botulism?"

Bernie shrugged. "I don't think so. It's exposed to air. More likely it would grow mold."

Wolf looked at Mars and Nina. "Have you ever heard of this tea?"

Mars shook like a wet dog. "Ugh. I don't think that's anything I'd like to try."

"Me, either," said Nina. "How come you know about it?"

"Someone asked a question about it on my advice column," I said. "Have you ever noticed that you hear about something new and then it pops up all over the place? Apparently, Beverly Hazelwonder is a big fan of Pu-erh tea and orders it at The Parlour."

Wolf ate calmly, but I was putting two and two together. "Not many people around here would have a tea knife. Is this the knife that killed Elise?" I asked.

Wolf drank his tea and refilled his cup. "Beverly Hazelwonder, you said?" He jotted her name on a pad. "And clearly The Parlour must have such a knife if they serve the tea."

"Wolf! It's gone. It went missing the day of the auction. I was admiring the huge array of teacups, and I remember Martha searching for it," I said.

Wolf raised one eyebrow. "Who else was there?"

"Half the town," said Nina.

"Robert, Natasha, Elise, Beverly Hazelwonder, Hunter Landon—" I said.

"I can confirm," Nina said. "I was there the other day when Martha and Callie were talking about not knowing where it was. Callie again!" She shook her head. "It all fits together. Who would have thought it?"

We told Wolf our ideas about Callie.

He didn't say anything. I hated not knowing what he was thinking.

"Well?" Nina demanded.

Wolf cleared his throat. "I think you've cobbled together an interesting theory. I can make a phone call to the Forest Glen Police Department tomorrow morning, and then we'll know the identity of the fiancée. It might take them a few days to find the old file, though."

Nina pulled out her cell phone. "Wait a minute." She keyed in some words. "Meh. Not much here. Just a paragraph. Rosie

Barnes disappeared . . . She was supposed to meet her boyfriend, Robert Johnson . . . Some bones found. Murder unsolved."

Bernie asked, "Do we even know for sure that Rosie was murdered? How do we know she didn't fall into the water and get swept away by a current?"

Wolf thanked me for the tea and galette. "As I said, many theories. I have to work with facts."

When Wolf left, Mars said, "Pour another round of tea and let's look at those facts."

Bernie tossed another log on the fire, while Nina and Mars helped me wash and dry dishes.

When we sat down again, Mars said, "Natasha was attacked. Then Robert ate something with botulism."

"Which may or may not have been intentional poisoning," I pointed out.

"Then Callie was chased, but that might not be true," said Mars.

"And Elise was murdered." Mars toyed with his tea. "Good grief. No wonder Wolf is skeptical. When we cut this down to facts, we've got nothing."

"Who would want to get rid of Elise besides her husband?" asked Bernie.

They all looked at me.

"Thank you so much. I'm flattered to be your suspect, but I did not kill Elise," I said.

"Alex?" mused Nina. "I guess that's kind of far-fetched. What about Hunter/Eddie?"

"Did she even know him?" asked Bernie.

"Martha Carter? They talked a little bit the day of the auction," I said.

"You're grasping at straws! Be serious," said Mars.

"Okay, how about this?" I offered. "Rosie is definitely dead. And someone wrote those threatening notes to Robert. I can think of one person who would do that—her brother."

"Hunter/Eddie?" Nina sat forward. "There would only be two reasons to do that. To torture Robert, or to make sure he didn't think he got away with her murder."

"How would this Hunter/Eddie fellow get hold of botulism?" asked Bernie.

Nina poured herself more tea. "The same way I would. He could have bought something, opened it, and realized it had gone bad."

"But wouldn't other people have bought the same thing?" Mars frowned at her.

She shrugged. "So they threw it out."

"What about Velma?" Mars leaned back in his chair. "She's the only one who was definitely linked to Robert."

"And she *was* spying on him," Nina added.

"Why would she want to get rid of him?" I asked. "She seemed to like him."

"*Seemed* would be the operative word there," said Bernie.

"Perhaps she's been play-acting all along," suggested Bernie. "What if she always suspected Robert of killing her sister? What if her sister confided Robert's infidelity to her?"

I shuddered. "That would give her the motive to murder both Robert *and* Elise! And botulism would be such an easy way for an older woman to dispatch a man. Francie was right about that."

"Do you think she could have stabbed Elise? Is she strong enough to do that?" asked Mars.

"Maybe." Nina got up and broke off a piece of the galette on the counter. "Adrenaline can give people amazing strength. They can lift cars and all kinds of crazy things."

"Perhaps she caught Elise unaware?" Bernie tilted his head.

"So we have four people with motives." Mars tapped the pen on the paper.

"Four? I only count two?" Nina looked at me.

"Callie, Velma, and Rosey," Bernie speculated. "Rosey had reason to kill his wife and her lover, Robert. But who is number four?"

"Hunter," muttered Mars. "Hunter didn't have a motive to kill Elise, though."

Nina gazed around the table. "Not that we know of."

﹌

I didn't get much sleep that night. I prowled through my house in the dark, Mochie and Daisy underfoot. I finished the apple galette while Mochie and Daisy chowed down on treats.

I believed that Hunter/Eddie was Rosie's brother. If someone had murdered my sister or brother, I would have hunted them down to the ends of the earth, too. Ohh. Maybe that's why he called himself Hunter. Had Elise discovered that Hunter killed Robert? Was that why he murdered her? Was that why she had said *Rosie*, too? Or were we overanalyzing everything? Had Elise's husband, Rosey, rolled into town and murdered them?

When it came to Callie and Velma, I wasn't sure who to believe. But what reason would Callie have to make up such a horrible story about Robert if it wasn't true? And I had seen Velma's face when Callie described Livy's death. Not many people were that good at acting.

The next morning, I didn't know anything more, except that I felt the need to protect Francie. If Velma or Callie was the murderer, and Francie stumbled upon that fact, she could be in danger, too.

I phoned Francie when I rose. She was planning to meet Velma at Robert's house. I walked over with her, worried because I couldn't protect her around the clock.

Velma was in a tizzy when we arrived. "The Realtor is coming! Can you two help me get some of the boxes and papers tidied up?"

I stacked boxes for them, and we did our best to bring a little bit of organization to the house. Luckily, they were working slowly and the entire downstairs was still intact and would show well.

In Robert's office, I stacked papers that Velma had been going through until my hand fell on a newspaper clipping announcing that The Parlour was coming to town.

I glanced at the date. It was before The Parlour opened.

Before Robert had moved to Old Town. Why would this have caught his attention? If he didn't want to move here, then why clip this out? Unless he knew Martha. Was that possible? There was only one way to find out.

~~~

I phoned Wolf. For once he actually answered his phone. "Meet me at The Parlour."

I beat a hasty exit past the Realtor, and waited for Wolf outside The Parlour. I started talking as soon as he showed up. "I think Martha Carter knew Robert before he came here. It's only a guess but"—I held out the newspaper clipping to him—"you'll note the date? It was about six months before he moved here."

Wolf sounded very kind, like he was speaking to a child. "That doesn't prove anything. Maybe he thought a town that could support a tea parlor was a town that would also support antiques stores."

"True. Ordinarily I would agree. But he had been here to visit numerous times. He and his wife had planned to open a store here. So why this article? What interested him?" I smacked my finger on the photo of Martha.

"Sophie, I'm going to indulge you this time, okay? But I have police work to do. I can't be running over every time you get a crazy notion. This is nothing but wild speculation. I need facts."

"Then let's just act like this is my treat." I opened the door and led the way inside.

I selected a cozy spot where we could talk privately with Martha.

Wolf sighed. "You do remember that we're not dating? Soph, I can't be seen having tea or lunch or hanging out with you like this."

"This is business, Wolf. What if I'm right? Do you want her to stab me, too?"

"I hardly think that will happen over a newspaper clipping, nor would it happen here, in public. Not in front of other people, in her place of business. He gestured around the room, forced a smile, and waved to a woman who was leaning back so far to watch us that she fell out of her chair. "Oh no. Sophie, I'm really sorry but I can't do this."

Wolf rose and walked out.

I could tell from the heat in my face that I was flushing with embarrassment. That's the trouble with dating a cop and breaking up. They always think you're trying to get things going with them again. Not that I was totally unsympathetic. I knew his wife wouldn't understand. I pulled out my phone and called Nina. When Callie came to the table, I ordered for both of us.

Nina arrived in ten minutes. Breathless, she said, "Sorry it took so long. I had to drop Peanut off at the doggy daycare. He's too young to stay home alone. What's up?"

"I guess I know who my friends are." I told her what happened with Wolf.

When Callie brought our tea and delicious treats, I said, "Would you please ask Martha to join us for a few minutes?"

Callie looked from me to Nina and back. "Is something wrong? This is Shelley bone china. It's very popular. Would you rather drink out of a different pattern?"

The teal rims were laced with gold. Pears, grapes, and plums on a white background graced the middles of the teacups.

"They're lovely. I just wanted to talk to Martha."

"All right." Callie appeared dubious.

Martha arrived more quickly than I expected. "It's so kind of you to come in again. As you can see, business is slowly beginning to pick up."

I handed her the newspaper clipping.

She smiled. "Gee, this seems like a long time ago but it was only nine months! I was so grateful for coverage in the local newspaper. Where did you find this?"

"At Robert's house."

The smile faded, and she swallowed hard. Her voice sounded hollow and forced. "How nice of him to keep it."

"It was printed months before he moved here." I took a chance. "You knew him, didn't you?"

Martha wouldn't have looked more miserable if I had knocked over her china display. "When Callie told me about Hunter, I knew it was just a matter of time."

Martha sat down with us and spoke in a soft voice. "Remember how I told you that I went to stay with my great-aunt Antonella in Italy? My parents sent me there because my fiancé had broken off our engagement. I was devastated. That doesn't begin to cover it. I was a wreck. All of my plans, my dreams, the life I had envisioned, it was all over. In a split second. Just like that. Robert came from a well-to-do family and my parents were thrilled that I was marrying up. The wedding plans had to be canceled. The engagement gifts had to be returned. And all I could do was cry."

She stopped talking and sat there in her own little world, thinking.

"And then," I prompted.

"And two days later, Rosie disappeared. The police paid us a visit but, of course, I had been home with my parents. And I had never met Rosie. I was such a mess. That was why my parents shipped me off to my great-aunt. They thought I would recover from my broken heart in Italy."

"Did you keep in touch with Robert?"

She seemed surprised. "No! I never saw him again until the day he walked into The Parlour."

"Why didn't you tell anyone?" I asked.

She placed her palms on her cheeks. "I couldn't bear the whole ugly thing about Rosie resurfacing. It was such a nightmare. You can't imagine. Everyone was out looking for her. That poor girl. And the accusations against Robert. I thought that was over. It was so long ago. I've been so many places and done so many things. Well, who would ever expect it to rear its ugly head again? And then Robert died, and I thought, *That's the end. Finally, that's the end.*"

"You never told your husband." Nina didn't ask. It was an affirmative statement.

Martha shook her head. "No. I didn't want him to know I had been engaged before. Even my parents and my great-aunt advised against that. We buried it. That was what people did then. They moved on and put the horrible memories behind them."

"Do you think Robert killed Rosie?" I asked.

"I doubt it. He'd broken off *our* engagement. He had no reason to murder her."

"Who did?" asked Nina.

Martha's eyes jumped wide in surprise. "I haven't a clue. I never knew the girl."

She rose and forced a wan smile. "If you'll excuse me, I believe Callie needs a hand.

"I didn't see that coming." Nina dug in. "I love these pumpkin scones with the bourbon cream."

I sat back, sipped my Golden Monkey black tea, and spoke softly lest anyone overhear. "Could Martha have murdered Rosie? Did Robert write those little poems intending to torment Martha? Maybe that was why he saved her picture and moved here."

Nina swallowed and nodded. "But why did she murder Elise?"

Good question. "I might have guessed jealousy, but Elise was bragging to Martha about Alex being her new boyfriend."

I was a little bit disappointed when we walked home. Even though I had been correct, the relationship between Martha and Robert hadn't led anywhere. We didn't know more now than we had in the morning.

I tidied up the house and did some laundry, still thinking about Robert and Rosie. I was in the kitchen folding towels when Mars stopped by.

He opened the kitchen door and asked, "Who wants to go for a run?"

We smiled like proud parents when Daisy leaped to her feet. Her tail wagging, she followed Mars to her harness, waited impatiently while he put it on her, and then Daisy led the way out the kitchen door. She would miss him when he was gone again.

I watched the two of them jog down the street, noting that the streetlights would be on soon. I was sweeping the kitchen floor and thinking about Martha when the phone rang.

Alex sounded as though he was in a panic. "Sophie, is Kevin with you?"

"No. Has he run off again?"

"We can't find him anywhere."

"I can come help you look," I offered.

"I'd rather you stayed home. He's likely to go to your place."

I promised I would call if Kevin showed up.

Not five minutes later, I heard something at the door. I looked out the peephole but couldn't see anyone. It had to be Kevin.

I was opening the door when someone on the other side pushed it with force. A tall man in a gray sweatshirt with a hood slammed the door behind him. The light glinted off a knife in his hand.

CHAPTER THIRTY-THREE

Dear Natasha,

I always look forward to hearing your annual "in" color predictions. I base my wardrobe around them! What color should I be looking for next year?

—Always Stylish in Rust, Michigan

Dear Always Stylish,

There's no question about it. We fashionable types will be gravitating to rust red next year. It's as fabulous in clothes as it is on walls. And think how great it will look with all the gray accents we already have!

—Natasha

It was Martha's husband, Max! My heart pounded in my ears. Odd thoughts ran through my head as I backed up. Mars had been correct when he told me the Taser would not be helpful if it was in a drawer. Natasha was right about how tall he was. He must have followed Callie and Natasha,

and killed Elise. He was mad. Stark raving mad. I backed
into the kitchen, praying I might find something to use to
defend myself.

In the back of my house, something crashed.

"What's that?" he growled.

I had no idea. "Cat." *Please let it be Mars!*

Another noise from the back. But this time I was ready.
In the brief seconds that Max was distracted I grabbed a
bottle of wine, rushed at him and crashed it on his forehead.
The glass shattered and rained on the floor, falling into the
puddle of white wine. Blood ran down his face in streams.

I backed out of his reach and to the side, toward my kitchen
knives. He was still standing, if wobbling and a bit dazed. I
wondered if I had only succeeded in angering him.

And then, out of nowhere, I heard, "Aaaaragh!"

Kevin raced at Max from behind, gripping Bernie's
halberd. He lodged the spear end squarely in Max's right
buttock. "Kowabunga!"

Kevin ran to me. I pulled him close and backed toward
the kitchen door. We had to get out.

And then Max fell flat on his face into the shards of glass
and the little lake of wine. His blood tinged it red in spots.

"Is he unconscious?" asked Kevin.

"Stay right where you are." I edged toward Max and
kicked the knife away from his hand.

Of course, Kevin hadn't listened to me. He stood next
to me, gazing at the halberd handle that stuck up in the air.
He said slowly, "That's gotta hurt."

I grabbed the phone and dialed 911.

"Sophie, in the movies the bad guys always wake up."

He was right. I handed him the telephone and scurried
to a drawer where I kept extension cords.

Working fast in case Max came around, I pulled his
wrists together across his back and tied them tight.

Meanwhile, Kevin asked me my address. He repeated it
into the phone and said, "We got him out cold on the floor,
and he's a big sucker. Sophie, she wants to know if he's
breathing."

"Oh, yeah. But they better send an ambulance."

"He needs an ambulance 'cause I speared him."

About that time, Mars walked in with Daisy. "What happened here? I was only gone twenty minutes."

Was that all? It felt like an eternity.

Kevin handed me the phone. "She wants to talk to you."

This was one time I didn't mind staying on the phone until the officers arrived. Adrenaline still coursed through my veins. Mars was high-fiving with Kevin.

When Wong walked into my house, I handed the phone to Mars. "Call Alex and let him know Kevin is with us and safe. And keep an eye on him. He likes to wander."

"I don't think he's going anywhere. He just said *this is way better than TV.*"

"Is Bernie here?" asked Wong.

"No."

"Isn't that his antique weapon?"

I started to laugh. "I guess it is."

"Oh no," Mars groaned. "She's getting giddy."

I was a little. Now that it was over.

Kevin proudly proclaimed, "It was in the den. I saw it when I was here before."

"How did you get into the house?" I asked.

"I saw him hide after he knocked. Normal people don't do that. Then he pushed his way in. So I ran around to the sunroom door and broke a window. Sorry about that."

I hugged him. "I'm so glad you did."

Wong walked away, and I asked Kevin, "What were you doing here?"

"They were all arguing. My mom's parents said I would never see my dad again." Tears welled in his eyes.

"Oh, honey. They're upset because they lost their daughter. I'm sure they didn't mean that."

"I haven't seen him since he was arrested," Kevin said.

"I might be wrong, but I have a strong hunch you're going to see him very, very soon."

"Promise?"

I could hear people yelling Kevin's name outside. I

spied Wong and asked if she needed a statement from Kevin before he went home.

She sat down with him at the kitchen table while the EMTs discussed the best way of transporting Max without removing the halberd. Apparently, there was some fear that taking it out might spur bleeding and it was best done in a hospital.

When Wong was finished, I walked Kevin outside. Four worried grandparents descended upon him. Alex grabbed me in a big bear hug.

"I think they might release Rosey," I whispered. "I'll be very surprised if Max isn't the one who murdered Elise."

Alex gazed at Kevin. "Maybe the knowledge that he helped take down his mom's killer will give him some closure later in life."

Nina, Francie, Wanda, Natasha, and Harvey crowded around us. I didn't have time to go into all the details.

A car screeched to a halt on the street. Martha jumped out and ran to us. "Max. Is he all right? I got a call . . ."

"Sophie!" called Wong.

"Come with me, Martha," I said.

She pulled a shawl tight around her shoulders and walked with me. They had Max on a gurney, ready to load him into the ambulance.

"Max? Honey, can you hear me?"

For the first time, Max stirred. "Martha?" He slurred her name.

I was just glad he didn't say *Rosie*.

"Oh, Max, what have you done?"

"For you, Martha. For you." His words were faint and imprecise but the meaning was certainly clear.

They wheeled him away, and Martha turned to me. "I don't know what to say other than how very sorry I am." She tented her hands and held them over her nose and mouth as she walked out with her head bowed.

Martha followed the ambulance to the hospital. My friends poured into my house, Kevin left with his grandparents, and I got down on my knees to pick up the broken glass on my kitchen floor. Wanda revved up the steam mop to clean up the blood and wine. We hit the broken glass in the sunroom next, and Bernie taped a flattened cardboard box over the hole. With everyone pitching in, we were done faster than I could have imagined.

They peppered me with questions but all I wanted was a cup of tea.

Half an hour later, we all sat around the fire in my kitchen, while I sipped the strongest black tea I had and told them what a hero little Kevin was.

Natasha and Wanda were horrified and so grateful that Natasha had survived Max's attack on her.

Everyone was thrilled that he was off the streets, and we could go back to walking freely in our beloved community. And Bernie couldn't wait to tell his mom that the halberd had actually been used.

I slept better that night than I had in a long time. Things would finally start going back to normal. After breakfast, Nina, Francie, Daisy, Duke, Peanut, and I walked over to Robert's house to help with the endless packing so Velma could finally put the place on the market.

Nina and I tackled the high kitchen shelves so that Velma and Francie wouldn't have to climb ladders. Daisy and Duke stretched out in the hallway. Energetic little Peanut ran around them and tried to engage them in play by pulling on their ears and yipping at them.

"So let me understand this." Velma placed a toaster into a box. "Martha's husband, Max, was some kind of serial attacker?"

"First he went after Natasha but she got away from him, probably because Sophie arrived." Nina wrapped an empty sugar bowl in newspaper. "Then he tried following Callie but she had the luck to run into Sophie and Mars. It looks like Elise was his only victim."

"But why?" asked Francie.

I gazed down at her. "He didn't seem to like Callie and thought she wasn't a good employee. But that's hardly reason to attack her. And I don't think Natasha even knows him."

"Maybe he thought they were threats to Martha?" Velma speculated. "Maybe he thought Martha should have a TV show like Natasha?"

"What about me?" I asked. "Or Elise?"

"Maybe he's just a sicko who has an issue with women," said Nina. "He didn't go after any men, probably because he knew they could overpower him."

As Nina spoke, I wondered if it was Max who had been down by the river with Natasha. Maybe he went there to throw the knife in the water. He might have reported Natasha and me to throw suspicion on us instead. But I felt as though something was wrong with that scenario.

Nina chattered on about Max and how clever Kevin had been.

I stood on the counter and handed her items from the top shelf. With a start, I realized what was bothering me. *It was the wrong night!* Natasha had dumped Wanda's potion containers *before* Elise died. It still could have been Max who saw her at the river and reported her, but it couldn't have been Natasha who threw the knife in the water because she was there before Elise was murdered.

"Imagine how Martha must feel today. I don't think I would have the courage to show my face in town," said Francie.

Velma nodded, examining the backside of a platter. "At least there's *something* they're not trying to blame on poor old Robert."

I stopped working and stared down at the top of her perfectly styled hair. "I thought you had come to terms with that, Velma. Are you saying you don't believe Callie or Hunter?"

"I don't know what to think. All we know is what they said, and they could both be lying. And, I'd like to point out that just as I predicted, they now have Elise's killer but I don't see any cops nosing around here looking for Robert's murderer."

"But what about the Rosie notes?" Nina signaled me to hand her more items. "Don't they substantiate the fact that Robert killed Rosie?"

"Not if Hunter, Eddie, whoever he is, wrote them." Velma closed a drawer. "There's no concrete evidence."

They didn't know about Martha's story yet. Nina looked up at me, her eyebrows raised. When I didn't say anything, she nudged my ankle.

"Well I'm telling them if you're not!" Nina said.

In a way, I hated for Martha's story to get around town. She had enough troubles with Max. On the other hand, her story did back up what Hunter had told us, so it was only fair for Velma to know. "Go ahead," I said.

I shuffled over to the next cabinet and opened it while Nina relayed the sad story about Martha's broken engagement.

"But that doesn't prove anything, either!" Velma threw her hands in the air. "It makes me sad for Martha, but goodness, she wasn't there. She doesn't know any more than Wanda did. It could have been Hunter who killed Rosie. Or her own father. Or maybe Rosie had another boyfriend who was jealous."

Francie shrugged. "Velma, I'm not sure there will ever be enough proof for you."

"That day when Callie told us about Robert murdering Livy, I could hardly take it," Velma said. "The mere thought was just unbearable. But the next morning I realized that she lies. She makes up stories to entertain people. Who marries two thoroughly odious men and has to run away from them?"

"She didn't make up that scar," I noted.

"Who knows where she got that? It could have been in a car accident for all we know. Same with the picture. Maybe she worked for Robert. It doesn't mean anything more than that. I think she's had a hard life and she invents stories to make it more interesting. And then she went and got Hunter involved in her nonsense."

Francie regarded her friend with sadness. I gathered Francie didn't agree with Velma's take on things.

"I'm starving." Nina finished filling up a box. "How about we take a lunch break?"

"We could eat out on the patio in the back." Francie looked out the window in the back door. "It's such a nice day with the sun shining and that blue sky. Won't be long before it's too cold to eat outside."

I climbed down and peered into the garden. "Nina, if you bring us some lunch, I'll rake up the leaves. It's a mess back there."

"Would you, dear?" Velma gazed around. "I think I saw some of those leaf bags. Here they are!"

The four of us ventured outside. Daisy, Duke, and Peanut seemed happy to have a new place to sniff around. Francie and Velma settled at the table, and Nina left to buy lunch.

Francie turned her face up to the sun. "I never imagined cleaning out a house would take so long. You should have just marked prices on everything and had a garage sale right in the house. That way everyone would have had to cart their stuff off themselves."

I found a rake in a little storage corner and filled two bags quickly. The patio was small. I would be done in no time. I pulled the rake along the edge of the brick wall nearest the house. Something glinted in the sunlight. I peered closer and moved leaves aside until I saw it again.

CHAPTER THIRTY-FOUR

Dear Natasha,

I am brokenhearted because movers dropped a box and my collection of china was shattered. All I have left is shards! I don't have the heart to throw them away. Any suggestions?

—Sad in Broken Bow, Oklahoma

Dear Sad,

Make a mosaic! I've seen them on walls and floors. Depending on the location, it won't matter if all the pieces aren't flat. Or make mosaic stepping stones out of them with concrete. They'll be stunning!

—Natasha

I picked it up. It was glossy white on one side and bent at almost a forty-five-degree angle. The edges were rough where it had broken. I flipped it over and knew in an instant what it was and to whom it probably belonged. The gorgeous flowers and gold trim couldn't have been anything else.

"What have you got there?" Velma craned her neck to see.

"A piece of china." I was sorry I'd handled it. I hurried into the kitchen and found a plastic grocery bag. Not perfect, but it was better than nothing. I slid my hand into it like a glove.

I returned to the patio and showed the shard to Velma and Francie. "It's Schumann. I'm certain of it."

Francie sat up and peered at it. "I think you're right. Isn't this what Martha collects?"

"I'm not surprised," Velma said. "She has such exquisite taste. What a shame that a piece broke. I'd like to have this china pattern."

I wasn't quite ready to tell them what I was thinking. I left the shard on the table and raked more, watching for any other pieces. Sure enough, two of them turned up. Someone had dropped a Schumann soup bowl on the brick floor of the patio.

Before I let myself jump to conclusions, I ventured into the house and had a look at the breakfront in the dining room. It was loaded with crystal, china, and silver. Not particularly surprising for the owner of an antiques store. I opened the upper doors and searched for any sign of a Schumann plate or compote. Nothing. I looked inside the lower cabinets. Still nothing.

Yet someone had dropped a piece on the patio. From the looks of the shards, I thought it had happened recently. They didn't show much dirt.

I called Wolf.

"Hi. How are you feeling? I heard you had quite a night."

At least he was being friendly today. "I'm fine, thanks," I said.

"Where on earth did that little boy get a halberd? I had to look it up. They haven't been used in centuries, except for ceremonial stuff."

"A gift from Bernie's mother. I'm sure she never expected anyone would actually use it. How's Max doing?"

"He won't be sitting down for a while. He's still in the hospital."

"Has he confessed?" I asked.

"Denies everything," Wolf said. "He's clammed up and wants a lawyer."

"Wolf, I found some shards of china in Robert's backyard. Do you think they could be tested for botulism? Would there be remnants on them?"

"Outdoors? In the weather?" He sounded doubtful.

"Maybe. They tell me it's hard to kill. Why do you think they might have botulism on them?"

"Because they're the china pattern that Martha Carter collects, and I found them on Robert's patio."

"Are they rare?"

"Not particularly. A lot of people have a piece or two. But this looks to be a soup bowl. The sort of thing someone would have if she owned an entire set."

"Sophie . . ." From the sound of his voice, I could tell he thought I was being ridiculous. "The health department went through Robert's kitchen."

"I think Martha must have dropped it on her way out. Maybe something alarmed her or she slipped or was just nervous. But in the dark she didn't see all the pieces and then leaves blew over them."

"Yeah, all right." He let out a sigh.

"You'll do it?"

"Only because we're hitting walls on the source of the botulism. Not because I think we'll find anything."

"Thanks for your confidence."

"Just being honest. Don't get your hopes up."

He agreed to pick them up at Robert's house. When he arrived, I showed him where I found them.

Nina had returned and offered him a slice of pizza. "We have barbecued chicken and Chicago-style meat lovers!"

He selected a slice of the meat-lovers pizza but didn't sit down. "Thanks. Nice house."

"Want to buy it? It's going up for sale," said Velma.

"Probably not in my budget."

Velma looked at him with resignation. "Thank you for

coming out here to get those pieces of china. I'm overjoyed that someone is *finally* looking into the circumstances of Robert's death." Velma sucked in a deep breath. "I don't want to believe that he was an evil man. And I can't bear to imagine that my darling sister died at his hand. I've been thinking about it sitting out here where he probably sat and reflected on his life. Whatever the truth is about Robert, it's best to know. If he was the fiendish man they say, then I was the fool to be suckered in by him. But the truth always comes out in the end, doesn't it? It's time we knew."

Francie patted her friend's hand. "That's very brave of you."

Wolf thanked us for the pizza and promised to let us know the results as soon as he could.

After lunch, we tackled the breakfront. I handled everything very carefully because most of it was antique. I recognized the frosted appearance of Lalique in the shape of a lion and asked Nina, "Are you sure you have a grip on it?" before I let go.

"That was one of Livy's favorites," exclaimed Velma. "Maybe I should send it to auction. I bet it will bring in a lot of dough."

I reached up and pulled out a crystal sailing ship with three masts and rectangular sails. "This doesn't look like an antique, but the detail is incredible." I handed it to Nina carefully.

She set it on the dining table.

Velma admired it. "Hunter asked me about a sailing ship. A necklace or something. Robert must have had a thing for these old-timey sailing vessels."

The dining table filled quickly. I stopped emptying the breakfront to help the others wrap, pack, and label the boxes.

By midafternoon, everyone except Peanut was beat. Nina and I walked Velma and Francie home.

"I'm so bushed. I'm ordering takeout tonight. Francie, how about you?" asked Nina.

"I'm in. Is it just me or is it getting colder? Brrr. I'm not going far tonight."

"How about that rotisserie chicken?" I asked.

"The one with that comes with three sauces? I love that stuff. Not sure I want to know what's in them, but they're so good!"

"My house at six?" I asked.

"I'll order the chicken," said Nina.

We split up and went to our respective homes with our dogs. I walked into my kitchen and found Bernie and Mars lounging by the fire. "Hi, guys."

"Martha Carter dropped this off for you." Bernie pointed to a package wrapped in cellophane and tied with a golden bow.

I opened it with Mochie looking on, curious about the crackling cellophane. Inside was a perfect Bundt cake with a sugary drizzle over it. The card read *I will never be able to apologize sufficiently. Yours truly, Martha Carter.*

Mars grabbed a knife and aimed it at the cake.

I seized his arm. "No!"

"You don't want to share? You can't eat that whole thing."

"I think Martha is the one who poisoned Robert."

Mars wrapped it up and flung it into the trash can.

"What are you doing?" I screeched.

"Sophie, you're the one who said it's not safe to eat." Mars shook his head.

I dug it out of the trash, wrapped it in a clean plastic bag, and placed it in a closet out of reach of Daisy and Mochie. "Maybe Wolf should have it tested for botulism."

I sat by the warm fire and told them about Martha's engagement to Robert and about the dish shards that I had found. "Wolf is having them checked right now."

Mars sputtered, "That makes no sense. I never even met the woman until last night. Why would she poison me with botulism? And how?"

Bernie seemed thoughtful. "You think she killed Robert because he called off their engagement so many years ago? That doesn't seem likely."

"Maybe she killed Rosie and Robert knew that," I suggested.

"Not to belabor the question, but then how and why was I subject to that stuff?" Mars asked. "I've never been to Robert's house. Didn't hang out with him. I didn't know these people."

Bernie sat up. "The Laughing Hound. Martha and Max were there for dinner the night before you got sick."

"It's not like I had dinner with them."

"You ate in the bar that night," Bernie said. "Martha could have easily slipped something into your food."

"What? Why? She didn't know me."

I saw where Bernie was going with his thoughts. "She didn't care who you were. She needed someone to get sick at The Laughing Hound so the health department would move on and get off *her* back."

"Ugh! That's the lowest of the low," Mars said.

Bernie scowled. "What a couple. He was running around attacking women while she was poisoning men!"

At five thirty, Mars stretched and whistled for Daisy. "Soph, want to come along for a walk?"

The last thing in the world I wanted to do at that moment was go out into the cold. But Daisy nudged me with her nose and had the nerve to bark at me. "Okay, okay. You win."

I slid on a warm jacket while Mars helped Daisy with her harness. Lucky Bernie still napped, or pretended to, in the chair by the fire with his feet up on a hassock.

We stepped out into the chill. "How can the temperature change so fast?" I asked. "We ate lunch outside today."

"'Tis the season. I heard there was a cold front moving in." Mars zipped his jacket and steered us toward Bernie's house.

"It's nice walking leisurely again and not worrying about Max jumping out at us."

"Do you think Bernie is right about Martha slipping something into my food?" Mars asked.

"It's actually the first theory that made sense. And as you have pointed out, that's the only time you two were in the same place."

"So why do you think Robert's last word was *Rosie*?"

"I'm not sure we'll ever know. Maybe because of those threatening notes he received? Maybe Velma has been right all along. He was afraid of the person who wrote those notes and thought he'd been poisoned because of Rosie."

"That would point a finger at that Hunter guy, wouldn't it?" asked Mars.

"It would. I can't quite reconcile that with Martha poisoning Robert."

"Maybe Hunter sent the notes to torment Robert, and Martha killed him out of some deep-seated resentment?"

"You mean there might not have been a connection?"

"Rosie must have been the connection. But maybe both of them wanted him dead," Mars said.

"Hunter got lucky because Martha beat him to it?" I asked.

"Imagine being such a heinous person that two people wanted to kill you!"

We rounded the block and started back.

When we passed the entry to the alley where Natasha's garage was located, Daisy pulled toward the garage.

"What's that sound?" asked Mars.

I couldn't help giggling. "There are chickens in your garage. Harvey's truck broke down, so he and Wanda hid them in the garage."

"This I gotta see."

We walked to the door that led to Natasha's workshop. Mars twisted the handle and opened the door. "Look at this," he griped. "I had that alarm system installed for nothing. She doesn't even lock the doors, much less use the alarm.

He opened the door that led to the garage, and we stepped into chaos. Chickens and feathers were everywhere. Eggs had been laid on the velvet settee. Chicken feed was strewn around the concrete floor. The car doors were open and the chickens appeared to have adopted the car as their hen house.

Mars's mouth dropped open. "Natasha will have a heart attack if she sees this."

I shouldn't have giggled. But after all her criticisms of me, after all her pretentious superiority, I had to laugh. In fact, I couldn't stop, and Mars joined in.

The two of us were tearing up from laughing when we heard something that definitely wasn't a chicken.

CHAPTER THIRTY-FIVE

Dear Natasha,

My sister and I have a fancy dinner riding on this bet. I think Spode's Stafford Flowers is the most expensive china pattern available today. My sister says it's Raynaud Duchess by Raynaud. Who's right?

—The Younger Sister in Sisters, Oregon

Dear The Younger Sister,

Better go Dutch. You're both wrong. At this moment it appears that Flora Danica by Royal Copenhagen takes the title of the most expensive pattern.

—Natasha

It was a whimper.

My thoughts flew to Kevin. Had he run away yet again? "Kevin? Kevin, are you in here?"

I walked to the other side of the car.

A person sat on the floor with her knees drawn up. Her head was bowed to her knees and hair flowed over her face.

"Who is that?" whispered Mars.

I knew it wasn't Kevin. "Hello? Excuse me. Ma'am?" She didn't respond.

Mars and I weren't laughing anymore.

"I'll call the police." Mars pulled his cell phone out of his pocket.

"No police." The voice was muffled. The head lifted but there was so much hair I still couldn't see her face.

I edged closer, leaning to the side, hoping to recognize her. I saw the nose first. The long straight nose. "Martha?"

She turned her head in my direction. Hair still flew around her features but I could tell it was definitely her.

"Martha! What happened?" I crouched beside her and pushed her hair out of her face.

Her lips quivered when she said, "Rosie."

I looked back at Mars. "Well, help me!"

He took one arm, and I took the other. We assisted her to her feet. Behind her head, Mars mouthed, "She tried to kill me."

There was that. But she needed our help. "Let's take her home and see what's going on, okay?"

Mars's eyes grew wide. "Uh, Soph, we really should call Wolf."

"We will, as soon as we get home."

"No," she moaned. Her head hung forward and she walked as though she had no strength left.

The entire way home, Mars tried to convince me to leave her in the garage. It was cold out. The chickens had feathers to keep them warm, but I wasn't about to abandon Martha there.

We walked in the front door, and it looked like a party was going on. Nina waltzed up to us with drinks but stopped cold at the sight of Martha.

The chatter ebbed and everyone grew quiet as they recognized Martha.

Bernie took over for me and helped her to a seat by the fire. Francie brushed Martha's hair out of her face.

"What's going on?" I asked.

"You're always cooking for everyone else and you had such a fright last night that we wanted to do something nice for you," Wanda said.

I sniffed the air. "Rotisserie chicken with the three sauces?"

Nina whispered, "What happened to Martha?"

"We found her hiding in Natasha's garage. I think she's having some kind of breakdown."

Wanda opened the cabinets in my kitchen. "I don't know how you girls manage without decent medicinals," she said. "Chamomile tea will have to do. It will have you back on your feet in no time, dear." She filled the kettle and set it on the stove.

I hadn't noticed Callie or Hunter. Callie made her way over to Martha and knelt on the floor by her. "Martha, what happened? You look a mess."

"She'll feel better when she drinks some tea." Wanda poured boiling water into a mug.

Callie took the tea to her and urged her to drink.

People whispered in the background as we all watched.

Callie wrapped an arm around Martha and squeezed. "Are you feeling any better, honey? You wanna tell us what happened?"

And Martha began to talk. "Rosie."

Her gaze drifted and stopped on Hunter/Eddie. "I never knew your sister but in the back of my mind I always suspected that the truth would come out one day."

Hunter drew closer and pulled up a chair. "Do you know what happened to her?"

"I was there."

Martha took a deep breath. "I am ashamed to admit that I went a little nuts when Robert broke off our engagement. Nothing too bad compared with what some people do today, I guess, but I stalked Robert. I couldn't sleep or eat. I couldn't believe it was happening to me. I had picked out my china pattern! To be honest, every time I see it I get a little sick to my stomach. It's the one pattern I won't buy. My world had ended. I couldn't believe that he dumped me for another girl."

Martha kneaded a tissue in her fingers. "I followed Robert to a lovers' leap kind of place. It was high on a cliff overlooking a wild river. I imagine it might have been romantic under other circumstances but to me that day, it was isolated and eerie. I kept just inside the tree line and watched him when he met Rosie."

"Did he know you were there?" asked Francie.

"I have always wondered about that. He didn't act like it. I had never seen Rosie before. She was very sweet. A little younger than me, I thought. Very pretty, and she looked so innocent."

The muscles in Hunter's jaw jerked.

"You can imagine how it felt to watch my fiancé with another woman. He was toying with her. Laughing and teasing her closer to the edge. The jealousy that had consumed me started to turn into concern. I could see what he was doing, but she appeared oblivious, as though she was enthralled with him."

Martha took a deep breath. "I edged closer and closer. I tried to save her." Martha closed her eyes. "Dear heaven, I tried my best. To this day I can feel the warmth of her hand brushing against mine, trying to get a grip. My other hand grasped wildly toward her blouse." She swallowed hard and opened her eyes again. "I watched her tumble, hitting rocks on the way down, until she reached the river. It closed in over her and the current must have carried her away." A little twinge shook her shoulder.

Hunter winced and his head bent forward. Callie rested her hand on his shoulder.

"I was holding her necklace. A chain with a sailing ship hanging from it."

Hunter's head snapped up. That must have rung true to him.

"Robert had given it to me," Martha continued, "and I

had taken it off my neck and returned it to him when he broke up with me. And now I held that stupid thing. It was all that remained of Rosie, a ship on a broken chain. I looked into the cold and calculating eyes of a man who was a stranger to me. I feared I was next and tried to run. He caught me and told me he loved me. That we would be together always. That nothing would ever come between us again."

"You must have been terrified!" said Wanda.

"You're lucky to be alive." Callie shook her head. "We both are."

"I thought I would follow Rosie over that cliff. I played along with Robert to save myself. I pretended all was right again between us. And then I drove home and told my parents. You can imagine their horror. I heard them talking about it through the night. They didn't know what to do. Who would? In the morning, the police came to our house because Rosie was missing. My parents, bless them, lied for me. They said I had been at home with them."

Hunter buried his head in his hands. "You could have spared us so much grief!"

"I'm so sorry. Robert's family had already brought in their lawyers, and it was abundantly clear that their goal was to build a case against me."

Hunter nodded. "I remember those guys. They made Robert clam up. You were the missing link all along. They could have prosecuted him. You were an eyewitness."

She sat up straighter and wiped the skin under her eyes. "Wouldn't have done any good. I had gotten away from Robert that night, but his lawyers intended to see me in prison. Rumors moved fast, and people began to hear that I had killed Rosie. It was horrible. As soon as my parents were able to borrow enough money, I was on my way to Italy. For almost forty years I thought I had escaped. I thought it was over. That it was behind me. My parents moved to New Jersey, and I never went back. It was never spoken of again. And then, two months ago, Robert Johnson walked into my tearoom and my life turned into a nightmare."

Velma rose. "Anyone else want some Scotch? Nina, where does Sophie keep that stash?" She steadied herself as she walked. I knew it had to be hard for her to hear this. She was probably thinking that Martha could say anything she wanted now that Robert was dead. Maybe so.

Velma poured drinks for herself, Harvey, and Nina. When she sat down, Martha continued.

"Robert told me he had never stopped loving me. That he had searched for me his whole life and now we could finally be together."

I gasped. "He saw the story in the newspaper about The Parlour and recognized you! Velma, did Robert take a copy of the local newspaper?"

She nodded. "My sister did."

Martha pushed back her hair. As stunning as she was with it up, she now appeared bedraggled and haggard. Almost witchy. "Robert's alleged love for me only made me fear for my husband. I knew Robert had it in him to murder because I had seen him do it. I love my husband. In spite of his idiotic attempt to harm you, Sophie, he's really a decent and noble man."

I had my doubts about that. What kind of guy ran around attacking women? It sure wasn't decent and noble of him to kill Elise.

"Every day," Martha said, "it seemed like matters became worse with Robert. I tried placating him by bringing him food and trying to be a friend. But I was very wary. One day I was in his house, and I saw little verses he had written. Terrible ones about the past and the fact that Rosie was dead. They were designed to evoke guilt. And I realized that he was planning to blame me for Rosie's death. The torture would begin all over again."

Hunter groaned. "Oh no." His whole body sagged.

"But why would Robert do that?" asked Nina.

"I don't know. To convince me to leave my husband? To blackmail me? All I knew was that I was dealing with a demented man. One evil enough to kill an innocent girl who got in his way."

"So you brought him something laced with botulism?" I guessed.

She nodded. "I opened a jar of potatoes. Oddly enough they were a gift from someone who canned them herself. I knew instantly that they were bad. The lid was warped and there was a film on the top. Any sane person would have thrown them out. But a time bomb hung over me, and it was ticking faster and faster with each passing day. I was living the life of my dreams until Robert walked back into my world. And I saw my opportunity."

Martha sat quietly for a moment. "I still have nightmares of Rosie falling. They all end the same way. All that is left of her is that crazy ship necklace. Not a day has gone by that I haven't thought of her. It's hard to explain. I didn't know her, but that terrible last moment of her life bonded me to her. In a peculiar way, I felt like Rosie was with me. Like I was doing it not just to save Max and me, but in revenge for Rosie. So when I saw the tainted potatoes, well, Robert had a strong fondness for vichyssoise." Martha shrugged. "It was that simple."

"How could you think you would get away with something like that?" Velma's tone was tinged with contained outrage.

Martha responded softly. "Robert murdered Rosie and got away with it. I didn't think it would be that difficult."

She gazed around at us. "I knew Robert had admirers, but I never expected to run into one! I was picking up the soup bowl from Robert when Elise arrived at the back door. I couldn't let her see me. I hid until she was in Robert's living room, and then I sneaked out the back way and tripped. My beautiful bowl crashed. I was sure she heard me, and I left in a hurry."

"Is that why Max murdered Elise? You were afraid she saw you?" I asked.

"Max didn't kill Elise."

CHAPTER THIRTY-SIX

Dear Sophie,

I appreciate my son and daughter-in-law enormously. They are very good to me, and I realize that they're busy. But some idiot told my daughter-in-law that she could microwave the water for my tea. Please set her straight?

—Grateful Old Dad in Strain, Missouri

Dear Grateful Old Dad,

Every tea drinker knows that microwaved tea is horrible. Hardly drinkable in my opinion. I'm told it's because the microwave doesn't heat the water evenly. I think there's probably more to it than that, but your daughter-in-law should stick to boiling water for tea in a kettle.

—Sophie

I was afraid to hear what Martha was going to say next. After that strange withdrawal, Martha had turned rather calm. Maybe there *had* been poison in the cake Mars threw out. Martha scared me a little bit by shifting from being hopeless to almost prim again. I excused myself and phoned Wolf from my office.

He answered my call saying, "You were right. I was just going to let you know the shards turned up botulism spores and Martha's fingerprints. We're looking for her now."

"You don't need to go far. She's here at my house spilling her guts. But, Wolf, I think there might be something wrong with her. I found her in Natasha's garage kind of zoned out. I think the pressure might have been too much for her."

"I'll be right over."

When I returned to the kitchen, Martha was saying, "Max had nothing to do with Elise's death. I don't think they ever met. Elise attacked *me*."

Was Martha trying to protect Max?

"Under other circumstances, I would have gone to the police about it immediately. But I didn't dare bring myself to their attention. Elise thought I was Callie."

"Me?" cried Callie. "I don't understand. Are you saying that Elise meant to kill *me*? I didn't even know the woman."

"Apparently so. She said, 'I've been looking for you, Callie.' And when I turned around, she lunged at me. I could see the light glinting off the blade of her knife. We wrestled, and I told her"—she shook her head incredulously—"'I'm not Callie. I'm not Callie.'"

Martha stared off to the side. "For a split second, Elise paused. And then she said, 'You! I saw you in his backyard trying to get away unseen. You're the woman who murdered Rosie so you could be with Robert. The woman Robert loved. The one he'd been looking for. He didn't want *me* anymore because he finally found you.' She drove the knife into me with a quick jab right at the level of my waist. It hit my metallic belt buckle, slipped, and the knife was deflected back at her. It all happened so fast. I was trying to grab it to protect myself, and it just flipped toward her. I guess she was putting her whole body into the force behind it. When it stabbed her, I jumped back, and Elise fell to the ground. The knife was still in my hand. I expected her to get up but

she moaned terribly. She had enough strength to turn over.
I was afraid she would attack me again, so I took off. I just
wanted to get away from her. I was distressed when I heard
she died. It didn't have to happen. I'll always wonder if she
would have lived if I had done something differently. But
I didn't hurt her. That was totally self-defense. If she hadn't
hit my belt buckle, I would be the dead one today."

"Then you murdered Rosie, not Robert!" said Hunter.

Martha slowly shook her head. "No. Elise had that wrong.
Maybe that's what Robert told her."

Callie eyed her friend with a doubtful expression. "Martha, you've been a good friend to me, but there was no
reason for Elise to seek me out, let alone kill me."

Francie spoke up. "Not so fast, Callie. Didn't Sophie and
Mars find you running from someone on the street?"

"But that was Max."

Martha was indignant. "Max would never have chased you."

"There *is* one person who would have liked to see you
dead, Callie," said Francie.

I was shocked. "Francie!"

"How quickly you forget." Francie shook her forefinger
at Callie. "The woman who was present when Robert murdered his wife, Livy, would have reason to shut you up."

"And Robert was having an affair with Elise! Of course.
Elise was the woman you saw at Robert's house, Callie. She
was his accomplice in Livy's murder. Elise would have gone
to prison along with him if you turned them in. You didn't
know who *she* was, but Robert probably told her who *you*
were."

"I knew it all along!" Velma declared.

I tried to hide my amusement at Velma's proclamation.

It took a moment for everything to register. "Martha, it
was *you* who threw the knife in the river, then. Was it you
who saw Natasha a few nights before?"

"I was so irritated. I needed to get rid of everything that
was botulism-tainted. The container in which I had transported it, and the shards of the bowl that I dropped. I couldn't

pitch them in a trash bin. And there you were, Natasha, exactly where I had planned to toss them. As it turned out, it was a good thing I still had them."

Mars glared at her. "What did you do? Rinse them and dump some of it on my food at The Laughing Hound?"

Martha *tsk*ed at him. "It was just the dregs. I knew it wouldn't hurt anyone. But it would move all the attention away from The Parlour."

"Yes, thank you for that, Martha." Bernie controlled his anger but I could see him seething underneath.

Wanda stroked Natasha's arm. "Baby doll, what were you doing wandering around down by the river at night by yourself?"

Natasha's eyes met mine. I planned to play dumb.

"I couldn't sleep because Mars left me."

Oho! Cleverly played.

Wolf tapped on the kitchen door and opened it. Two uniformed officers were with him.

"Martha Carter? I have a warrant for your arrest." He recited her Miranda rights, and one of the officers hand-cuffed her.

As she walked out the door, Martha turned back. "Open The Parlour tomorrow morning, Callie. I might be a little late."

When the door closed, Francie said, "That woman has slipped over the edge. It's like she doesn't understand what's happening."

"Do you think we can believe anything she said?" asked Mars.

"It's sort of hard not to." Nina peered into her empty glass. "Her version answered too many of the things we didn't understand. Is anyone else starved?"

Everyone crowded in. Some sat at the banquette. Mars and Bernie brought in chairs from other rooms.

"We could eat in the dining room," I suggested. But no one moved.

We chowed down on those luscious savory, slightly salty, smoky chickens and the three sauces. Nina had bought huge quantities of home fries, fried platanos, black beans, and Caesar salad. White wine and apple cider bottles were passed around.

Mars glanced at Bernie. "Weren't you bringing dessert?"

"Indeed!" Bernie bounded to his feet and pulled a box from the cold oven. The logo of Big Daddy's bakery was on the side. Bernie opened the top. "Sophie's favorite, Apple Harvest Cupcakes with Salted Caramel Frosting."

Those cupcakes were tied with Krispy Kreme doughnuts in my affections.

I jumped up, gave Bernie a big smooch on the cheek, and picked out a cupcake.

Francie and Velma were the first to head home. Bernie and Mars walked with them on the pretense of giving Daisy, Duke, and Peanut some exercise.

Wanda, Harvey, and Natasha were next. As they walked out the door, I pulled Wanda back for a moment. She had been so helpful and kind to Martha. If she had truly spent the night with Robert, wouldn't she have called someone for help when he was so ill? "Wanda, if you didn't spend the night with Robert, where were you your first night here?"

Wanda smiled at me. "I couldn't sleep knowing my baby had been attacked. At the first light of day, I made my bed, found some gloves, and pulled weeds in Natasha's garden for a couple of hours. When she still wasn't up, I took a nice long stroll around Old Town. It sure is a charming place. I'm not surprised that you girls like living here."

I felt a bit foolish for having jumped to conclusions. "One more thing. How it is possible that Natasha doesn't know about the chickens yet? She must wonder what Harvey did with them."

"I made up a story about her car being in the shop and offered to let her use my car temporarily. And she never once even thought to ask where the chickens went! I guess my Natasha was meant to be a star, not a country girl. She's been thinking a lot about Mars, though. I don't want you two girls fighting over him, you hear me?"

"Yes, ma'am." I closed the door behind her, thinking that Natasha might have a tough time getting Mars back.

When I returned to the kitchen, Nina was eating a cupcake, Hunter/Eddie was stoking the fire, but Callie appeared uncomfortable.

Callie toyed with a napkin. "Sophie, is Alex expensive? Do you know what he charges?"

Nina's eyebrows lifted. "Oh? Do you need a lawyer?"

"I don't know."

Eddie, whom I still thought of as Hunter, swung around and studied her. "Maybe I can help pay for him, Callie. Are you in trouble?" He slid into the banquette next to her.

"Hunter, you're too sweet." Callie pecked him smack on the lips. "I don't know if I'm in trouble. If I keep my mouth shut, it might just go away."

I saw a sparkle in Nina's eyes. "You're among friends. Why don't you tell us? Maybe we can help you?"

Ohhhh. Bad Nina!

"You understand, I'm not saying this actually happened, but supposing someone entered someone else's house through an unlocked door at night. I'm afraid that's some kind of crime, but it's not breaking and entering because the door was unlocked."

"And did this person happen to take something from that house?" asked Nina.

"Absolutely not. And what she went there for was hers anyway."

I exchanged a glance with Nina. What was Callie talking about?

"So this totally hypothetical person walked into an unlocked house to take something that belonged to her? You mean the owner of the house stole something of hers?" I asked.

"Not quite, but close. I'm not sure the owner of the house even knew she had it. She never would have missed it. I'm certain of that."

Breaking and entering? What had she done? "I gather you weren't caught?"

Callie's mouth twisted to the side. "The hypothetical person may have slammed a pillow on the other person's head."

"Oh the horror of it all. Not a pillow!" Nina quipped. "What a vicious burglar."

"Are you talking about Natasha?" I asked.

"This is strictly hypothetical," protested Hunter.

"You were Natasha's intruder?" I couldn't help chuckling a little bit. "And you hit her with a pillow?"

"What did Natasha take from you?" Nina was smiling.

"I'm not saying this happened, but she might have bought a sideboard with something of mine in it."

"The rock! It was the rock Robert used to kill Livy!" Finally, it was making sense. "It was you who broke into Natasha's house looking for the sideboard. But it wasn't there."

"How do you know that?" asked Callie.

"Because it was in Natasha's detached garage near the alley. So that's what you were looking for!"

Nina frowned at Callie. "You must have hit her with more than a pillow. I saw some of her bruises."

Callie threw her hands up. "I don't know how that happened. The pillow was soft as could be."

"Callie's telling the truth," I said. "I picked up the pillow. It was in the upstairs hallway. Natasha passed out and must have gotten bruised when she fell."

Nina slapped her thigh. "That's the funniest story I've ever heard. Natasha acted like someone tried to kill her—with a pillow!"

"Then that was you I saw in The Parlour the night of the auction," I said. "You went to retrieve the rock."

"I have a key for The Parlour. I had every right to be there."

"Did you find the rock?"

"I did! The movers must have wondered what was shifting around inside the sideboard."

I sat back and studied the two of them. "Callie, the day of the auction, you were late and so coy about it when Velma asked if you were out on a date with Hunter the night before. What was that about?"

"Obviously, I didn't handle that as well as I hoped," Callie said. "I overslept because I was out half the night sneaking into Natasha's house. I couldn't say I had a date with Hunter because I was afraid someone might ask him about it, and I would be caught in a lie."

Nina looked at me. "So Callie was Natasha's attacker, and Elise was the one who chased Callie the night she ran into you and Mars. So Max wasn't running around attacking women."

"Except for me," I said.

Hunter frowned. "I think it's best that we keep this amongst ourselves. You're right, Callie, it might go away on its own."

He seemed glum while Nina and I were amused. I thought I knew why.

"You have a little problem of your own, don't you?"

"Oh, Hunter!" Callie cried. "Maybe we can help?"

He shook his head.

"A typical man," said Nina. "He'll keep it inside, and it will fester until he's reduced to a quivering mess like Martha."

"Allow me to take a stab." I thought back to our conversation at the grocery store. "You wrote those awful poems and slipped them to Robert."

Nina gazed at me. "I thought Robert wrote them intending to torture Martha."

I stared at Hunter. "They were meant to torture, all right. The poems, the paper rose, and all the rose items were intended to make sure Robert, in his comfortable life, did not forget what he did to Rosie. That must be why Robert said *Rosie* to me when he was dying. Those poems were threats, and he knew it. Martha simply misinterpreted the situation and thought they were meant for her."

Hunter neither admitted nor denied the veracity of my guess. But I knew he would always feel guilty. It was his horrible, guilt-inducing reminders about Rosie that finally prompted Martha to take action against Robert. Or maybe he was glad they helped lead to Robert's death. Maybe he felt it was some kind of closure and that in a small way, he had finally brought punishment to the man who killed his sister.

CHAPTER THIRTY-SEVEN

Dear Sophie,

My daughter and I are planning a tea party bridal shower for her best friend. My daughter is thoroughly modern and into blacks and grays. Her friend loves pastels and is using pinks and roses as her wedding colors. Are we under any obligation to use the wedding colors for our party?

—Worried Mom in Weddington, Arkansas

Dear Worried Mom,

You are not under any obligations. But it's the friend's day and you are having the party for her. Why not use her favored pastels to make her happy? Your daughter can use grays when she marries.

—Sophie

My home was blissfully quiet in the morning. Daisy stretched out beside me, and Mochie slept with his head on my arm. I rose and padded down the stairs. I looked out the window when I poured water into the kettle. Life went on in Old Town as if nothing had ever happened.

After breakfast, I dressed in a long-sleeved white turtleneck, stretchy jeans, and a not-too-puffy blue zip-up vest. With Daisy wearing her harness, I set off to do some shopping.

Mars jogged up beside me wearing running attire and breathing heavily. "That was some wild dinner last night."

"Think Martha will be okay?" I asked.

"She's going to do time, for sure. Maybe not much, though. Imagine being the prosecutor. If Martha takes the stand and tells that story about trying to save Rosie, there won't be a dry eye in the jury. On the other hand, if she doesn't testify on her own behalf, do you think a jury will buy that she intentionally used the tainted potatoes to murder Robert?"

"You think a jury would find it hard to believe that anyone would intentionally murder with botulism poisoning? They'll think it was an accident?" As I considered his point, I added, "It might hit close to home for some of them. No one wants to make people sick, but haven't we all wondered if some food item was still good or not?"

"I bet they plea bargain," said Mars.

"Where are you off to?" I asked.

"Right now I'm running. But I'm leaving tonight and probably won't be back for a couple of weeks. Think you can manage without me?"

"I'll try."

"Daisy, want to run down by the river?" Mars asked.

Daisy wagged her tail, and I handed over her leash. The two of them jogged away.

I stopped in one of my favorite stores and bought a gift for Kevin. The saleswoman asked if she should wrap it for a wedding.

I eyed the pastel papers. "What have you got that would be right for a ten-year-old boy?"

"You're in the wrong store, honey."

"I don't think so."

"We have this silvery gray that's very popular."

Maybe for a wedding gift. "How about that nice blue?"

When I left with my package, I heard her say, "I don't know why I bothered ringing that up. It will be returned for sure!"

I hoofed it over to Alex's office, glad that it wasn't far because my purchase weighed a ton.

I pushed the door open and found Kevin there with a large group of people. "Just who I'm looking for!"

I set down the package and Kevin raced over to me for a big hug.

A man who resembled Kevin looked on with pride. "Are you Sophie? I'm Kevin's dad, Rosey."

I reached out my hand but he grabbed me in a bear hug. "Thank you. This has been a difficult time for Kevin."

He introduced me to both sets of Kevin's grandparents.

Kevin tugged at my vest. "Guess what my dad said I can do!"

"Umm, are you getting a puppy?"

A look of wonder crossed Kevin's face. "Dad?"

"There's a strong possibility that we'll be doing that."

Kevin grinned and high-fived me. "It's something else!"

"I give up."

"I'm going to baking camp this summer!"

"That's great. I'm excited for you. I brought you something." I pointed to the package on the floor.

Kevin kneeled on the floor and ripped into it. "A mixer! Just like yours except it's the cobalt blue one." Kevin jumped up and hugged me again. "I'm going to miss you, Sophie."

"When you come back for a visit, be sure to come see me, okay?"

His father groaned. "Nothing personal. This is a pretty place but I don't believe I'll be crossing the border into Virginia for a while."

I could understand that.

Two days later, the whole gang met at The Laughing Hound's grand reopening. It didn't appear that anyone in Old Town was worried about botulism, because everyone turned out. I mingled with a wineglass in my hand.

Nina rushed up to me. "Look! Bernie's serving warm pimento dip!"

"I've always said everyone has some domestic diva in them. Even you, Nina."

I spied Callie with Hunter and Natasha. "What's going to happen with The Parlour?"

"You wouldn't believe it. When news got out about Martha murdering Robert to avenge Rosie's death, people packed the place! Who'd have expected that? We've been so busy I can hardly keep up."

"I think she should buy it from Martha," said Hunter.

"I don't have the money for that." Callie shook her head.

"And I keep telling you that I could finance it."

"I keep telling *you* that I'm not taking your money! Besides, I don't know if I could do it without Martha. She brought a certain elegance to the place."

Natasha gasped. "I could be your Martha. I could buy The Parlour, and you could work for me!"

Callie smiled graciously but when Natasha chattered on about painting it gray and replacing the tables with Lucite and reupholstering the sofas in black, Callie leaned over and whispered in my ear, "There aren't enough pillows in the world . . ."

Velma wandered up to join us.

Natasha grabbed her arm. "Is it true that you're going to keep the antiques store open?"

"I had mixed feelings about it. But people have short memories. I think they'll shop there if I change the name, don't you?"

"How would you like to buy back some pieces I bought from Robert?" asked Natasha.

"I knew it!" I shouldn't have blurted it quite that way.

"You hate antiques. Why did you buy them in the first place?"

Natasha's gaze wandered but apparently she wasn't finding a suitable way to get out of a truthful answer. With a heavy sigh, she said, "I wanted him to like me. I kept going into his store to chat and wound up buying things."

"You couldn't just buy a vase?"

"I might have sort of told him that I was planning to redecorate the house with antiques when Mars left. Don't you roll your eyes at me, Sophie. You have bigger problems attracting men than I do!"

At that moment, Alex showed up and kissed me on the cheek. "Looks like a great turnout!"

I couldn't help grinning at Natasha. "How's Kevin?"

"He missed a little school, but with the help of a tutor, they think he can catch up. He's a bright little guy."

"I guess his dad is happy to have this behind him."

Nina joined us. "Alex, you knew Elise better than any of us. Why do you think she said *Rosie*?"

"Her husband, Rosey, wants to think she was calling for him. That in her last moment, she cried out for the one person she thought she could count on. Now that I know about Elise's dark side, I think she couldn't remember Martha's name, but she knew that Martha was involved with Rosie. She probably wanted to pin blame on Martha, but *Rosie* was the best she could do as she died."

"Any word on Martha and Max?" asked Nina.

"Max is out of the hospital. You know, in a weird way, love was at the root of a lot this."

"Love?" Was he serious?

"Sure. Rosie's brother tracked down Robert out of love for his sister. Robert moved here because he still loved Martha. Martha loved her husband, Max, and didn't want him to find out about her previous engagement or that she was involved with Rosie's murder."

"Martha acted so odd when I mentioned that she worked long hours. She denied it right away, as if she didn't want Max to know."

Alex chuckled. "Turns out she was running around town at night trying to dump the dishes that were tainted by botulism. She was afraid to wash them in her sink in case it was inspected and remnants clung to the pipes. Apparently, she was slipping crushed sleeping pills into her husband's dinner every night so he wouldn't know she was gone."

"Then why did Max come after me? If he wasn't attacking women, why did he pick on me?"

Bernie overheard us as he swapped my wine for a glass of champagne. "Because he loved Martha. She finally told him about Robert. They were afraid you would sort it all out. You, my dear friend, were the one who was putting the pieces together."

"How do you know that?" asked Alex.

"Rumors, my man. I hear a lot of rumors here. Besides, it's not too hard to figure out. I'd have done the same thing for Sophie." He clinked his champagne glass to mine.

<hr />

Nina and I walked home with Hunter and Callie. I wasn't quite sure why, since Callie lived in the other direction. We were almost at our block when Nina made a phone call.

When we reached her house, the door opened and little Peanut bounded out to us. Hunter picked him up, and Peanut rewarded him with puppy kisses. He laughed and said, "Thanks, Nina."

"You're adopting Peanut?"

"I spent a long time searching for Robert, Sophie. It didn't bring Rosie back but I did everything I could for her. It's time I lived my life now." He flashed a fond glance at Callie, who was petting Peanut.

"I thought you couldn't have dogs until you bought a place."

"The ink is drying on the contract. The house is empty, so I'm renting it for a month until the sale closes."

"Robert's house?" I asked.

"No, I'm getting a fixer-upper." He glanced at Callie. "But I think it will do just fine for two people and a pup."

Callie and Hunter walked away with Peanut, and Nina went home to pay the dog sitter.

I breathed the night air, relieved that no one was lurking in the shadows anymore. I unlocked my front door, latched Daisy's leash on her collar, and strolled with her under the streetlamps.

Suddenly, we heard a scream. A bloodcurdling scream of total hysteria. And then the word *Mom* echoed through the entire neighborhood.

"Daisy," I said, "I believe Natasha finally found those chickens."

RECIPES

Cucumber Sandwiches

½ cucumber
salt
good-quality soft white bread
unsalted butter (or mayonnaise)

Peel the cucumber and slice as thin as possible. Sprinkle with a pinch of salt and allow to drain in a colander for about 20 minutes. Butter the bread. Pat the cucumber slices dry. Layer them on the bread, overlapping them. Top with another slice of buttered bread. Cut off the crusts. Cut the sandwiches into thin bite-sized rectangles, or dainty triangles.

Lemon Tarts

PASTRY

1¾ cups flour plus extra for rolling out
7 tablespoons cold butter
½ cup powdered sugar
1 cold egg

Cut the butter into 7 pieces. In a food processor whir together the flour and the butter until the butter disappears. Add the powdered sugar. Pulse to combine. Add the egg and whir until it starts to form a ball. Shape into a ball, wrap in wax paper, and refrigerate for ½ hour. Preheat the oven to 350 degrees. Roll out the dough and cut into 3- to 4-inch circles. Tuck the circles into the wells of a cupcake pan and bake 12–15 minutes until baked and light golden.

FILLING

6 tablespoons butter, room temperature
1 cup sugar
4 eggs
½ cup lemon juice
⅛ teaspoon salt
1 teaspoon lemon zest (optional)

Cream the butter with the sugar in a stand mixer. Beat in each egg. Add the lemon juice, salt, and lemon zest (if using) and beat. In a heavy-bottomed saucepan, cook over low heat until it begins to bubble, roughly 10 minutes. Pour into baked shells and refrigerate until firm.

Bacon Cheddar Cheese Scones

2 cups flour plus extra for kneading
1 tablespoon baking powder
½ teaspoon salt
4 tablespoons cold unsalted butter
1 cup shredded sharp cheddar cheese
1 egg
½ cup heavy cream
1 tablespoon mustard
1 cup (about 5 slices) crumbled cooked bacon

Preheat the oven to 400 degrees. Cover a baking sheet with parchment paper.

Place the pastry blade into a food processor and add the flour, baking powder, and salt. Pulse twice. Cut the butter into cubes. Add to the flour, along with the cheese, and pulse until combined and the butter is barely visible anymore.

In a large bowl, whisk together the egg, cream, and mustard. Turn out the flour mixture on top of it and mix gently with a large serving spoon two or three times. Add the bacon and mix until large clumps begin to take shape.

Sprinkle flour on a cutting board and dust your hands with flour. Turn the dough onto the cutting board and knead 8–10 times, adding just a sprinkle of flour if necessary. Pat the dough into a 9-inch cake pan. Turn it out onto the parchment paper and cut the round into 8 equal pieces with a very sharp knife. It's best to press the knife into the dough instead of dragging it through the dough. Slide a knife or thin spatula under each slice and pull away from the center slightly to separate them. (At this point they can be frozen up to one month and baked when needed.) Bake 20–22 minutes. Serve plain or with Maple Bourbon Butter.

MAPLE BOURBON BUTTER

> 4 tablespoons (½ stick) unsalted butter
> 1 teaspoon maple syrup
> 1 teaspoon bourbon (plain, not flavored)

Bring the butter to room temperature so it is soft. Place the butter, maple syrup, and bourbon in a mini food processor and combine. Place in a mold or shape by hand and refrigerate. (Note: this can also be done in a bowl with a fork, but I find I get better results with a food processor.)

Pumpkin Scones

Author's note: Thanks to the pumpkin, these scones will not be as dry as most scones. Serve them plain, with Bourbon Cream, or top with one or both of the following sugar drizzles.

> 2 cups flour plus extra for kneading
> ¼ cup pecans
> ⅓ cup dark brown sugar
> 1 tablespoon baking powder
> ½ teaspoon salt
> 1 teaspoon cinnamon
> ½ teaspoon cloves
> ½ teaspoon ginger
> ¼ teaspoon nutmeg
> 6 tablespoons cold unsalted butter
> 1 egg
> ½ cup heavy cream
> ½ cup pumpkin

Preheat the oven to 400 degrees. Cover a baking sheet with parchment paper.

Place the cutting blade into a food processor and add the flour, pecans, brown sugar, baking powder, salt, cinnamon, cloves, ginger, and nutmeg. Process until the pecans are fine. Cut the butter into tablespoons, and then into 24 small cubes. Add to the flour and pulse until combined and the butter is barely visible anymore.

In a large bowl, whisk together the egg, cream, and pumpkin. Turn out the flour mixture on top of it and mix gently with a large serving spoon until large clumps begin to take shape.

Sprinkle flour on a cutting board and flour your hands. Turn the dough onto the cutting board and knead 10–12 times, adding just a sprinkle of flour if necessary. Pat the dough into a 9-inch cake pan. Turn it out onto the parchment paper and cut the round into 8 equal pieces with a very sharp knife. It's best to press the knife into the dough instead of dragging it through the dough. Slide a knife or thin spatula under each slice and pull away from the center slightly to separate them. (At this point they can be frozen up to one month and baked when needed.) Bake 12–15 minutes.

PUMPKIN SCONE SUGAR DRIZZLE (OPTIONAL)

1 cup powdered sugar
2 tablespoons milk or cream

Whisk to combine, adding milk gradually until it's smooth and of just-past-spreading consistency. Spread over the tops of the cooled scones.

PUMPKIN SCONE SPICED SUGAR DRIZZLE (OPTIONAL)

1 cup powdered sugar
¼ teaspoon cinnamon
⅛ teaspoon nutmeg

pinch of cloves
¼ teaspoon vanilla
3–4 teaspoons milk or cream

Whisk the dry ingredients to combine. Slowly add the vanilla and part of the milk, and mix, adding milk until it reaches drizzle consistency. Use mini whisk, fork, or squeeze bottle to drizzle over the scones.

BOURBON CREAM

1 cup heavy cream
⅓ cup powdered sugar
¼ teaspoon vanilla
1 tablespoon bourbon

Whip the cream until it begins to take shape. Add the powdered sugar, the vanilla, and the bourbon and beat until it holds a soft peak.

Caramel Appletinis

2 ounces apple vodka
1 ounce butterscotch schnapps
garnish with an apple slice

Mix the vodka with the schnapps in a martini glass. Cut a notch into the inner side of an apple slice and place on the rim of the glass.

Apple Crostata

PASTRY

 1 cup flour plus extra for rolling out
 1 tablespoon sugar
 pinch kosher salt
 7 tablespoons cold butter
 1 tablespoon vodka
 1 tablespoon ice cold water
 1 egg beaten
 2 teaspoons sugar

Place flour, sugar, and salt in a food processor. Pulse to combine. Cut the butter into 12 pieces. Add to food processor. Pulse, pulse, pulse until butter is tiny. Add vodka and ice water and pulse until the dough begins to cling together but stop before it becomes a ball. Wrap in plastic wrap and refrigerate for one hour.

FILLING

 3 apples
 2 tablespoons crushed honey graham crackers
 2 tablespoons brown sugar (or more if you
     have a sweet tooth)
 1 teaspoon apple pie spice
 1 teaspoon lemon juice

Peel and slice the apples. Preheat the oven to 425 degrees. Toss the apples, graham cracker crumbs, brown sugar, apple pie spice, and lemon juice in a bowl.

Dust your work surface with flour. Roll the dough into a circle about 9 inches in diameter. It's okay if it's not a perfect circle. *Move to parchment paper at this point.* Spoon the apple mixture into the middle and spread a bit toward the edges, leaving the outer 1½ inches or so empty. Fold the edge up over the filling, turning and folding until complete. Brush with egg wash and sprinkle with remaining 2 teaspoons of sugar. Bake 20–25 minutes or until golden.

Serve warm with vanilla ice cream or whipped cream.

Warm Pimento Cheese Dip

1 container pimento cheese
1 box of your favorite crackers

Spoon the pimento cheese into a microwave-safe bowl. Microwave 20–30 seconds until creamy. Serve with crackers.

Thick Pork Chops
with Bourbon Cider Cream Sauce

2 tablespoons high temperature oil like
  sunflower (not olive oil!)
2 two-inch-thick pork chops with rib
salt and pepper
1 cup apple cider or apple juice
1½ tablespoons packed light brown sugar
1 tablespoon prepared mustard
1 tablespoon bourbon
¼ cup heavy cream

Wash the pork chops and dry with paper towels. Salt and pepper both sides. Let them rest on the kitchen counter. Heat a heavy pan on medium high for about three to four minutes. Meanwhile, line a lipped baking tray with foil and slide it into the oven. Preheat the oven to 425 degrees. Add the oil to the pan on the stove. Give it a minute to heat up and then add the pork chops. Brown on each side for 4 minutes. Move the browned chops to the hot baking pan and roast in oven. Pour off all but 1 tablespoon of the liquid in the pan. Pour in the apple juice and scrape up any bits sticking to the pan (deglaze). Add the brown sugar, mustard, and bourbon. Bring to a simmer, whisking as needed to blend. Check the internal temperature of the meat after 8 minutes. You're shooting for 140–145 degrees. When it reaches the correct temperature, remove from the pan and let stand for 5–10 minutes. Just before serving, remove the pan with the sauce from the heat, stir in the cream, and pour over the pork chops to serve.

(makes 2, double recipe for 4)

KEEP READING FOR A PREVIEW
OF KRISTA DAVIS'S NEXT
CLAWS & PAWS MYSTERY . . .

Mission Impawsible

COMING SOON FROM
BERKLEY PRIME CRIME!

The greatest love is a mother's; then a dog's;
then a sweetheart's.

—POLISH PROVERB

By six o'clock on Thursday afternoon, one Gustav Vogel had failed to check into his room at the Sugar Maple Inn. Ordinarily, this would not be a matter of concern or great consequence. But it wasn't an ordinary day. It was the first day of the Animal Attraction matchmaking event in Wagtail. All our other guests had arrived and were already participating.

We were always booked in the summer, and this particular week had filled up especially fast. Gustav had a mere three hours to go before he forfeited his reservation, and we could give his room to someone else.

It was my turn to take over the Live, Love, Bark table. I left the mayhem at the reception desk as people poured through the door, hoping we still had rooms available. Until nine o'clock arrived, we had to turn them away. I stepped out onto the front porch that spanned the main building of the Sugar Maple Inn and observed the crowd that had collected on the plaza.

Maybe there truly was someone for everyone. People of every shape, size, and possible description milled about, alike only in the fact that a dog or cat accompanied almost every one of them. Yet all these people hadn't found compatible human mates. Why was it so much harder to find the right person than it was to find the right pet?

I was no exception. My dog, Trixie, left my side to scamper down the stairs and join the fun. The little Jack Russell terrier I had rescued at a gas station had blossomed and become my constant companion.

My calico cat, Twinkletoes, had chosen me as her person. I would have readily adopted her, but as cats do, she was the one who made the decision that we belonged together. She observed the commotion from the safety of the front porch.

Trixie and Twinkletoes were my nearly perfect darlings. Granted, they did get into trouble now and then, but for the most part they behaved very well.

My love life, however, was a miserable mess. Nonexistent, really. Maybe I shouldn't have balked at the notion of being matched to a guy this weekend. My grandmother, whom I called Oma—German for *Grandma*—hadn't pussyfooted around. She had come right out and told me this was my chance to meet a man. I was a little bit sad that she encouraged me, because she had hoped I would end up with Holmes Richardson, a friend from my childhood. No one else had ever stolen my heart quite like Holmes, and I wasn't sure I was ready to give up on him yet. It was complicated, though, because he lived in Chicago and was engaged to be married. It wasn't in my nature to chase a man who was engaged to someone else, so like a fool I waited for his relationship to implode on its own. Sometimes I wondered if it was time for me to give up on him.

The daily Yappy Hour parade had ended. I spied Oma at a table with Macon Stotts and walked toward them.

Oma and her best friend, Rose, had come up with the Animal Attraction matchmaking idea after hearing about a famous matchmaking week in Ireland. They had hired Macon Stotts, a Southerner who claimed to be matchmaker to the stars, to arrange the various events and help match people up. I assumed he meant Hollywood stars, but if the tabloids were any indication, I doubted that they really needed matchmaking help.

Animal Attraction was a somewhat literal name because the people attending were bringing their dogs and cats with them to help with the matchmaking. The benefits, according to Oma and Rose, were that the animals would break the ice, making it easier for their people to meet, and the human participants would know up front that they all shared a love of animals. Their pets would help them connect.

"Still no sign of Gustav?" asked Oma. She hated that she spoke with a German accent in spite of the fact that she had lived in the United States since before my father was born, over fifty years. Most people found her accent charming, but I was so used to it that I didn't notice it much anymore.

"Not yet."

She glanced at her watch. "There is still time. You are here to relieve me?"

"Just tell me what to do."

Oma held up a slip of paper. "Macon has set up a Live, Love, Bark app and a Live, Love, Mew app. This contains the address and password."

I took it and frowned. Wagtail was notorious for its poor Internet connection. Only one carrier worked at all, and it was iffy at best.

"If they have trouble," said Oma, placing her hand on a stack of papers, "here are forms they can fill out instead. Make sure they know there will be other matchmaking events. This is only one option. When they bring them back, they go into this box. Macon will pick them up and make the matches."

Macon jumped to his feet. "My word! These people are clueless." He swept by me, reminding me of a penguin. His black hair was combed back and gleamed with some kind of gel. He was short for a man, broad through the middle, and waddled when he walked rapidly. In a slightly nasal Southern accent, he cried out, "Dahlin', put-chore puppy down!"

I couldn't help smiling when he dragged out *down* into two syllables, *day-own.*

The stunning young woman with skin the rich color of honey appeared surprised. A fluffy little dog rode in her shoulder bag, his face peering out like a tiny white Wookie.

"Put him down, sweetheart. He can't do his job matchin' you up if he's confined to a bag."

"On the ground?" Her brow furrowed. "He'll get dirty paws."

"Anybody with a fancy bag like that must surely have booties." Macon held out his hands, palms up.

He'd nailed it. She produced tiny blue dog booties and slid them onto the feet of her dog with Macon's help. Once he was placed on the concrete plaza, the dog wasted no time at all mingling with the others.

"They'll bite him!" she said with a desperate look at Macon. "He's so tiny. That big black dog will think he's a snack."

The other dogs did seem very interested in him, but not because of his size. Even my Trixie wanted to know what those funny things were on his feet.

"I have to rescue him. Look what they're doing!"

Macon placed a hand on her arm. "Honey, that's just what polite dogs do. Sniffin' is how they shake hands. Don't you ever let him play with other dogs?"

A group of young men distracted Macon. He raised his hand, pointed at one of them, and waddled away, shouting, "Young fella, your dog is tryin' to introduce you to that pretty girl with the tuxedo cat."

The man standing beside me uttered dryly, "Is that Macon Stotts? I thought that old fraud was dead."

FROM *NEW YORK TIMES* BESTSELLING AUTHOR
KRISTA DAVIS

The Diva Frosts a Cupcake

A Domestic Diva Mystery

Sophie Winston and her BFF, Nina Reid Norwood, share a sweet spot for animals. So Sophie is delighted to help when Nina cooks up Cupcakes and Pupcakes—a fund-raising event for animal shelters. All the local bakeries will be selling treats, with the profits going to pups and kitties in need. But Old Town is in for a whole batch of trouble when a cupcake war erupts between two bakeries—and the employee of one of the bakeries is found dead. Now Sophie and Nina have to sift through the clues and discover who isn't as sweet as they seem...

**"Reader alert: Tasty descriptions may
spark intense cupcake cravings."**
—*The Washington Post*

kristadavis.com
facebook.com/KristaDavisAuthor
penguin.com

M1630T0115

FROM *NEW YORK TIMES* BESTSELLING AUTHOR
KRISTA DAVIS

The Diva Wraps It Up

A Domestic Diva Mystery

The holidays are domestic diva Sophie Winston's favorite
time of year. But this season, there seem to be more mishaps
than mistletoe.

Sophie arrives at the annual holiday cookie swap with
high spirits and thirteen dozen chocolate-drizzled ginger-
snaps. But when an argument erupts and a murder ensues,
it becomes clear that the recent string of events is anything
but accidental. Now Sophie has to make a list of suspects and
check it twice—before the killer strikes again.

"Loaded with atmosphere and charm."
—*Library Journal*

kristadavis.com
facebook.com/KristaDavisAuthor
penguin.com